SB

Shojo Beat

The Cain Saga

forgotten juliet

Earl Cain Series 1

Story & Art by Kaori Yuki

Read Kaori Yuki's entire
Earl Cain Series

Series 1:
The Cain Saga: Forgotten Juliet

Series 2:
The Cain Saga: The Sound of a Boy Hatching

Series 3:
The Cain Saga: Kafka

Series 4:
The Cain Saga: The Seal of the Red Ram, Volumes 1 & 2

Series 5:
Godchild, Volumes 1–8

Welcome to *Forgotten Juliet*, the first volume of *The Cain Saga* and, in the timeline of Cain's life, the first installment in the *Earl Cain Series*. A prequel to *Godchild*, which is actually *Earl Cain Series* 5 (all eight volumes of it — are you still with us?), *The Cain Saga* chronicles the early adventures of Cain and the rest of the characters involved in the Hargreaves legacy. Whether you are already familiar with Kaori Yuki's work in *Godchild* or not, I think you'll find the haunting tome of *Forgotten Juliet* an excellent addition to the *Earl Cain Series* canon. You can start here and work up to *Godchild*, or read them at the same time!

Enjoy,
Joel Enos
Editor
Earl Cain Series

Contents

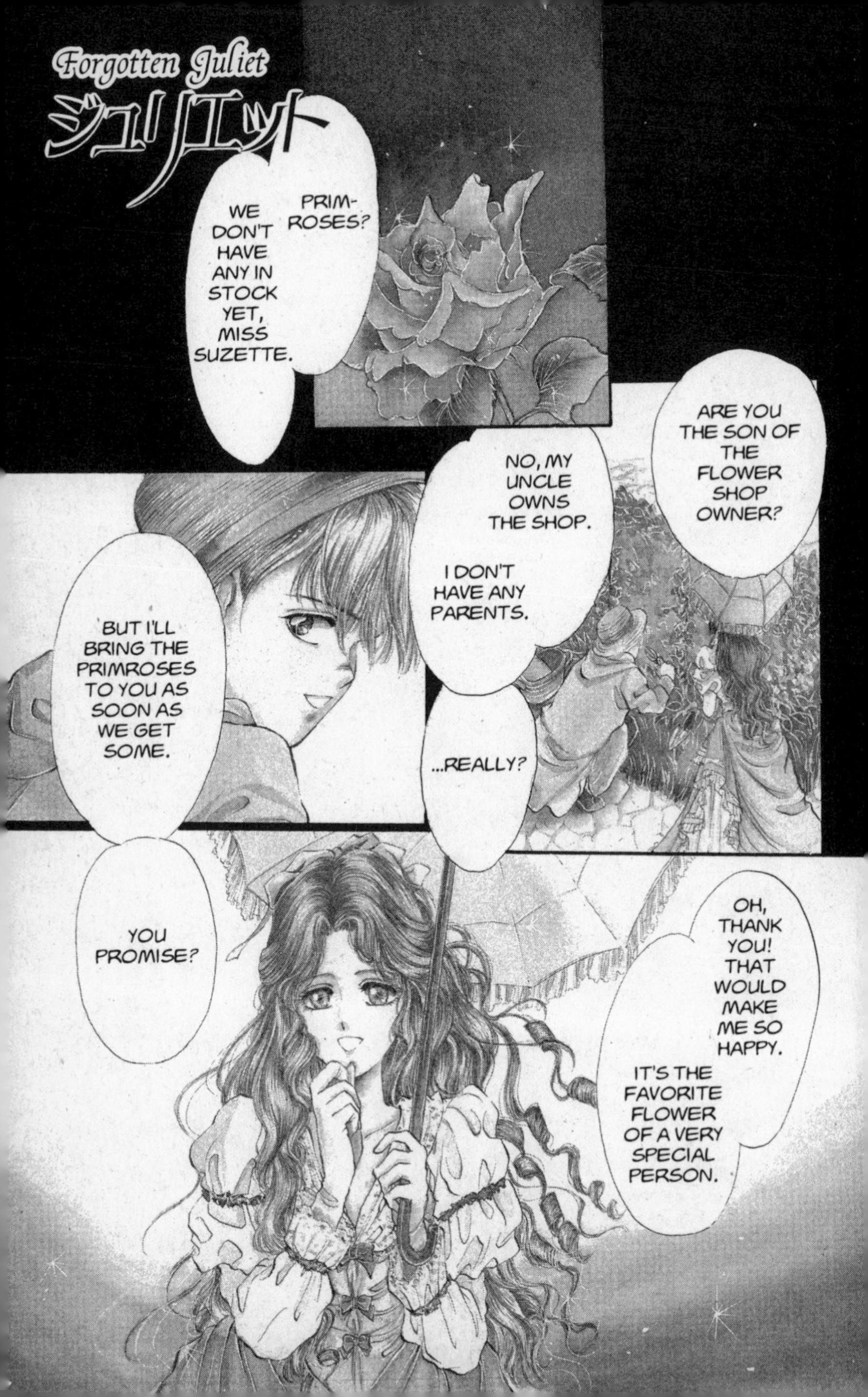
Forgotten Juliet
ジュリエット
PRIM-ROSES?
WE DON'T HAVE ANY IN STOCK YET, MISS SUZETTE.
ARE YOU THE SON OF THE FLOWER SHOP OWNER?
NO, MY UNCLE OWNS THE SHOP.
I DON'T HAVE ANY PARENTS.
...REALLY?
BUT I'LL BRING THE PRIMROSES TO YOU AS SOON AS WE GET SOME.
OH, THANK YOU! THAT WOULD MAKE ME SO HAPPY.
IT'S THE FAVORITE FLOWER OF A VERY SPECIAL PERSON.
YOU PROMISE?

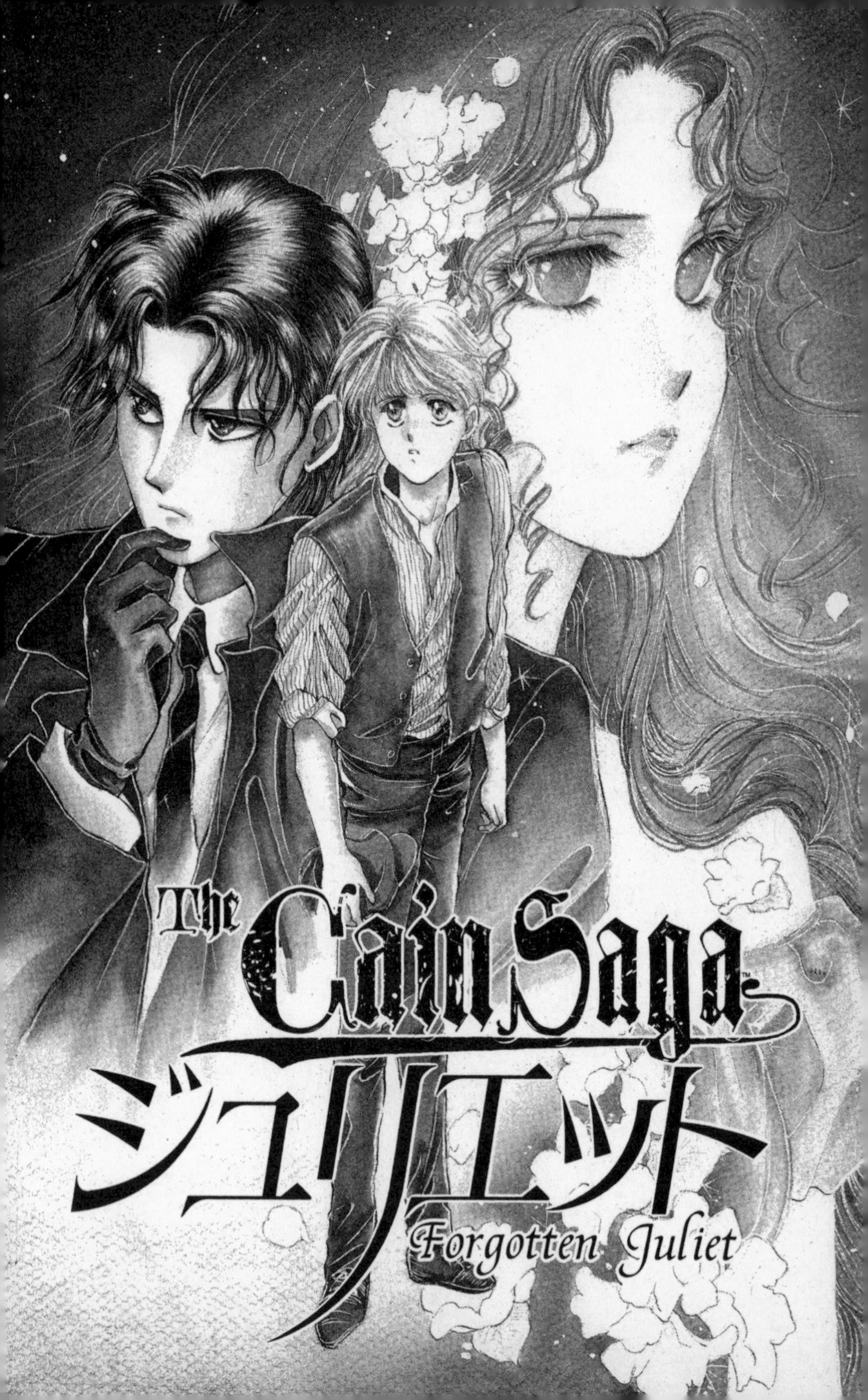
The Cain Saga™
ジュリエット
Forgotten Juliet

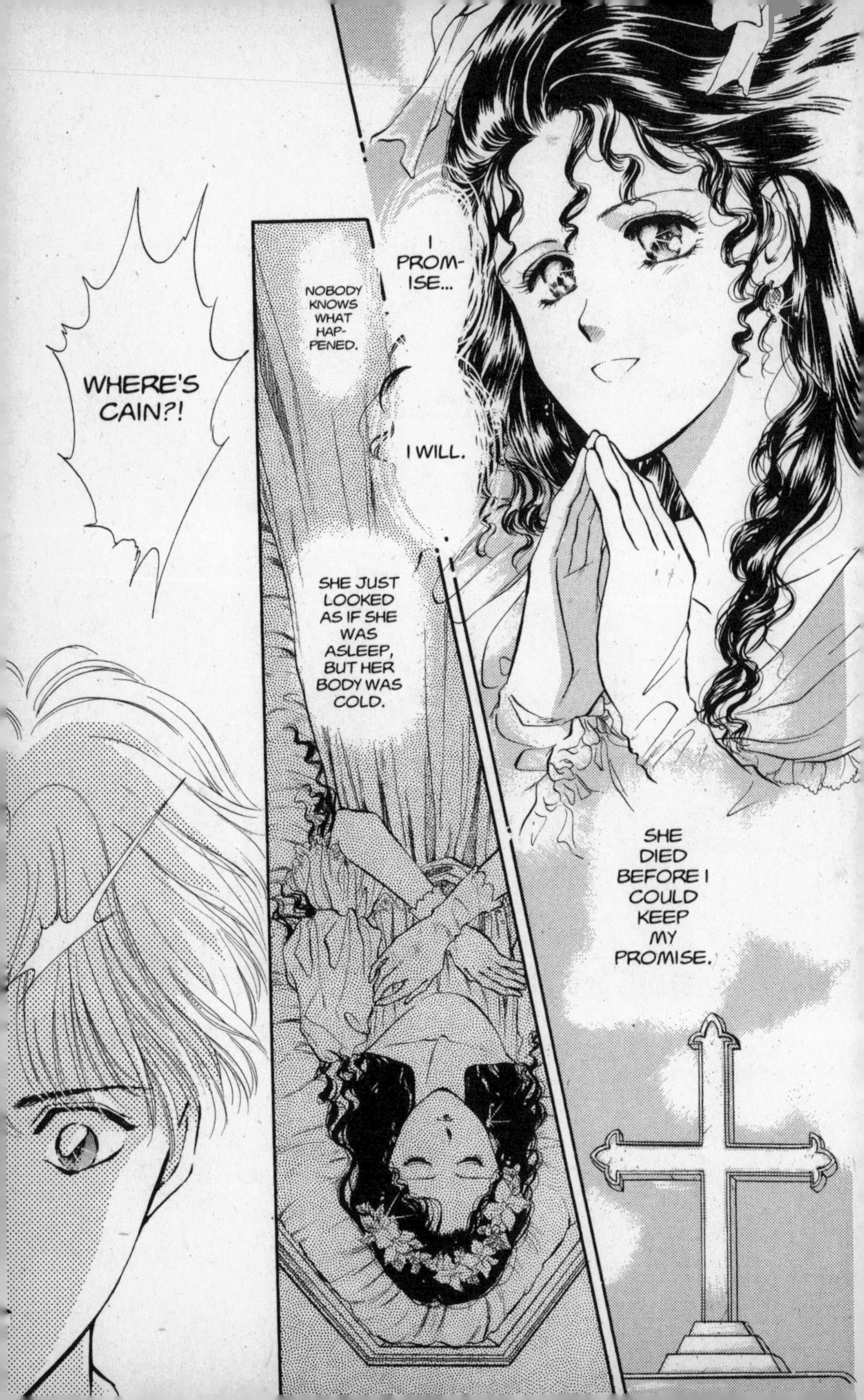
I PROM-ISE...
I WILL.
SHE DIED BEFORE I COULD KEEP MY PROMISE.
NOBODY KNOWS WHAT HAP-PENED.
SHE JUST LOOKED AS IF SHE WAS ASLEEP, BUT HER BODY WAS COLD.
WHERE'S CAIN?!

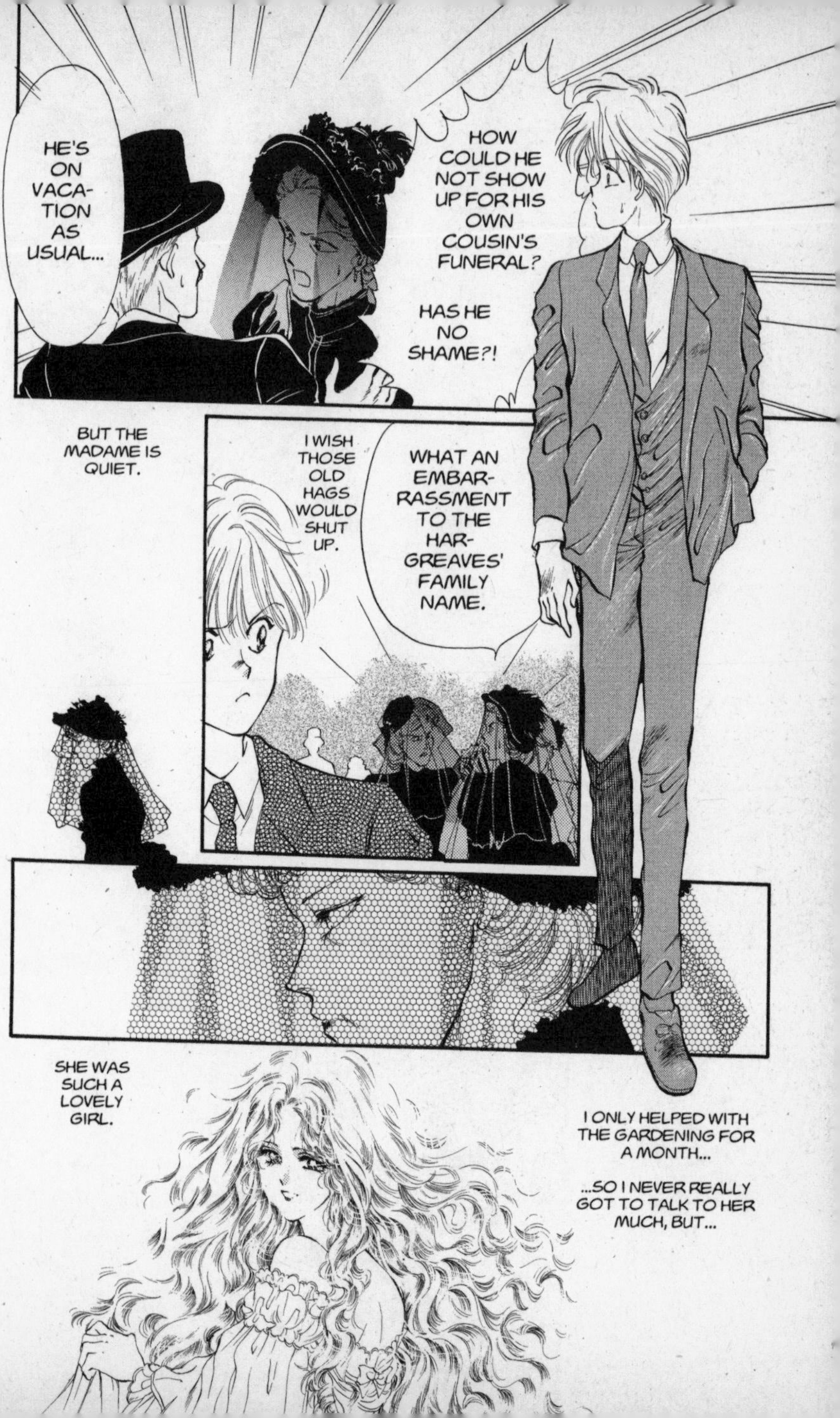
HOW COULD HE NOT SHOW UP FOR HIS OWN COUSIN'S FUNERAL?
HAS HE NO SHAME?!
HE'S ON VACATION AS USUAL...
WHAT AN EMBARRASSMENT TO THE HARGREAVES' FAMILY NAME.
I WISH THOSE OLD HAGS WOULD SHUT UP.
BUT THE MADAME IS QUIET.
I ONLY HELPED WITH THE GARDENING FOR A MONTH...
...SO I NEVER REALLY GOT TO TALK TO HER MUCH, BUT...
SHE WAS SUCH A LOVELY GIRL.

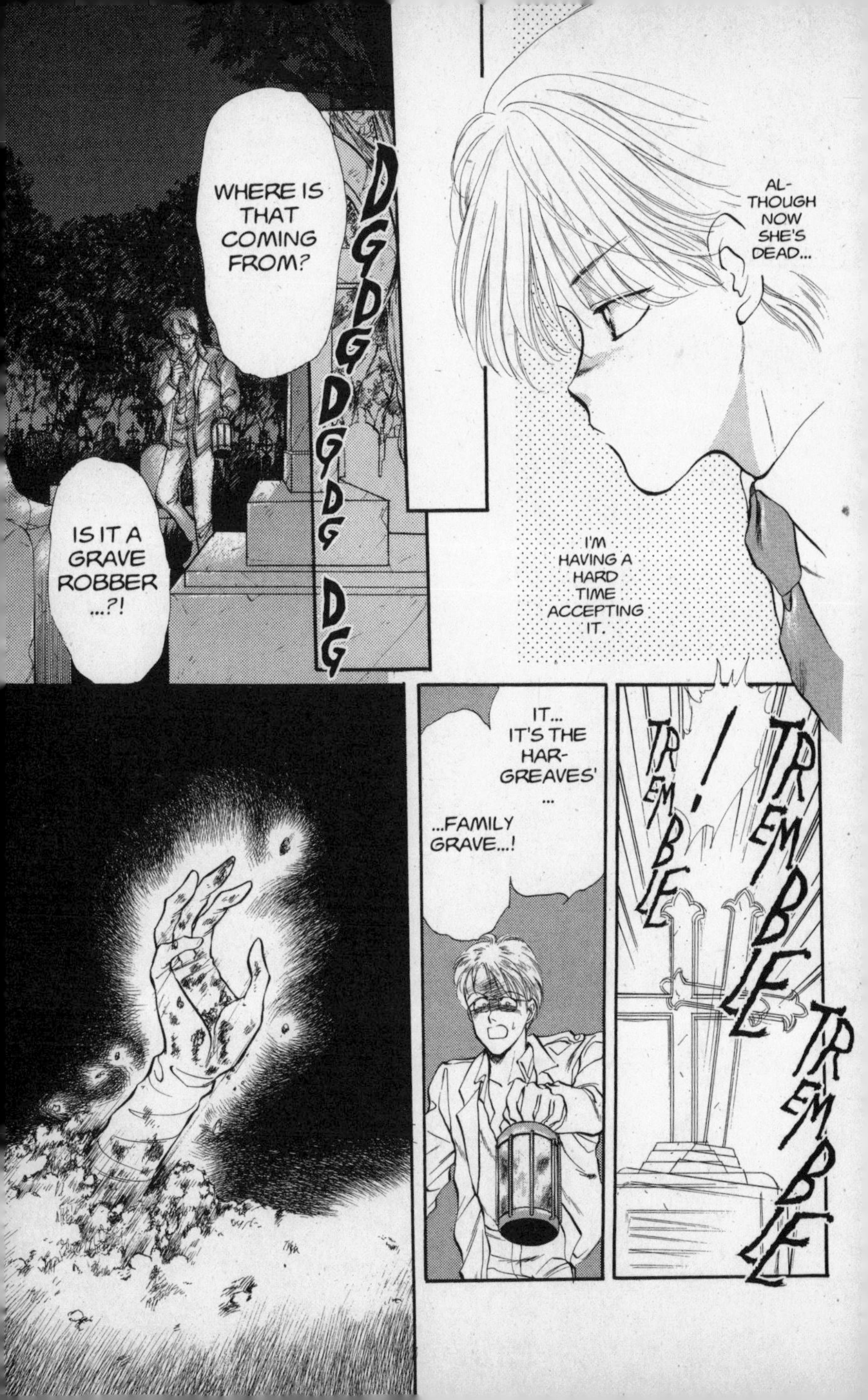
AL-THOUGH NOW SHE'S DEAD...
I'M HAVING A HARD TIME ACCEPTING IT.
WHERE IS THAT COMING FROM?
DGDGDG DGDGDG DG
IS IT A GRAVE ROBBER ...?!
TREMBLE TREMBLE TREMBLE
!
IT... IT'S THE HAR-GREAVES' ...
...FAMILY GRAVE...!

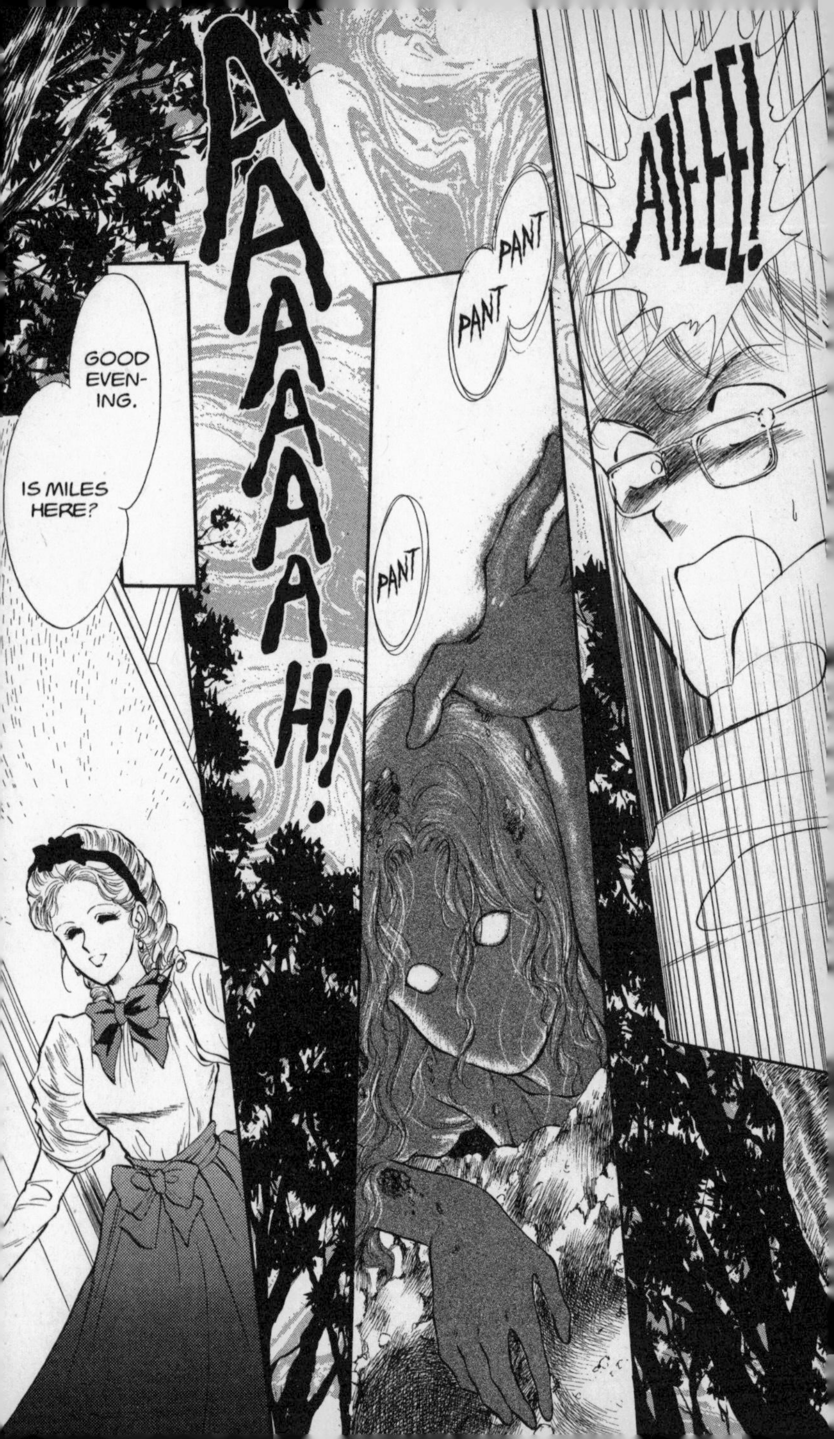
AIEEE!
PANT PANT
PANT
AAAAAAH!
GOOD EVEN-ING.
IS MILES HERE?

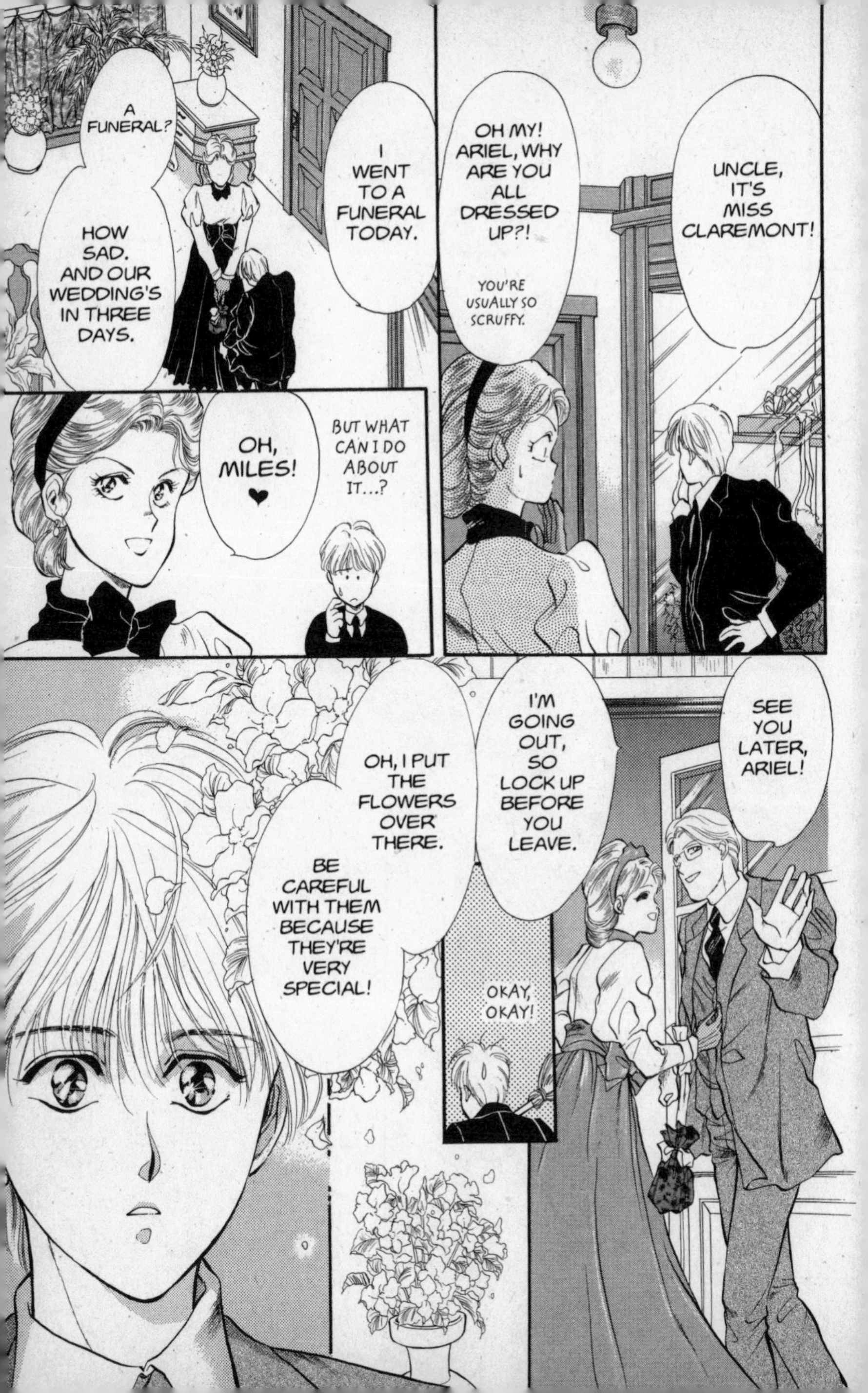
UNCLE, IT'S MISS CLAREMONT!
OH MY! ARIEL, WHY ARE YOU ALL DRESSED UP?!
YOU'RE USUALLY SO SCRUFFY.
I WENT TO A FUNERAL TODAY.
A FUNERAL?
HOW SAD. AND OUR WEDDING'S IN THREE DAYS.
OH, MILES! ❤
BUT WHAT CAN I DO ABOUT IT...?
SEE YOU LATER, ARIEL!
I'M GOING OUT, SO LOCK UP BEFORE YOU LEAVE.
OKAY, OKAY!
OH, I PUT THE FLOWERS OVER THERE.
BE CAREFUL WITH THEM BECAUSE THEY'RE VERY SPECIAL!

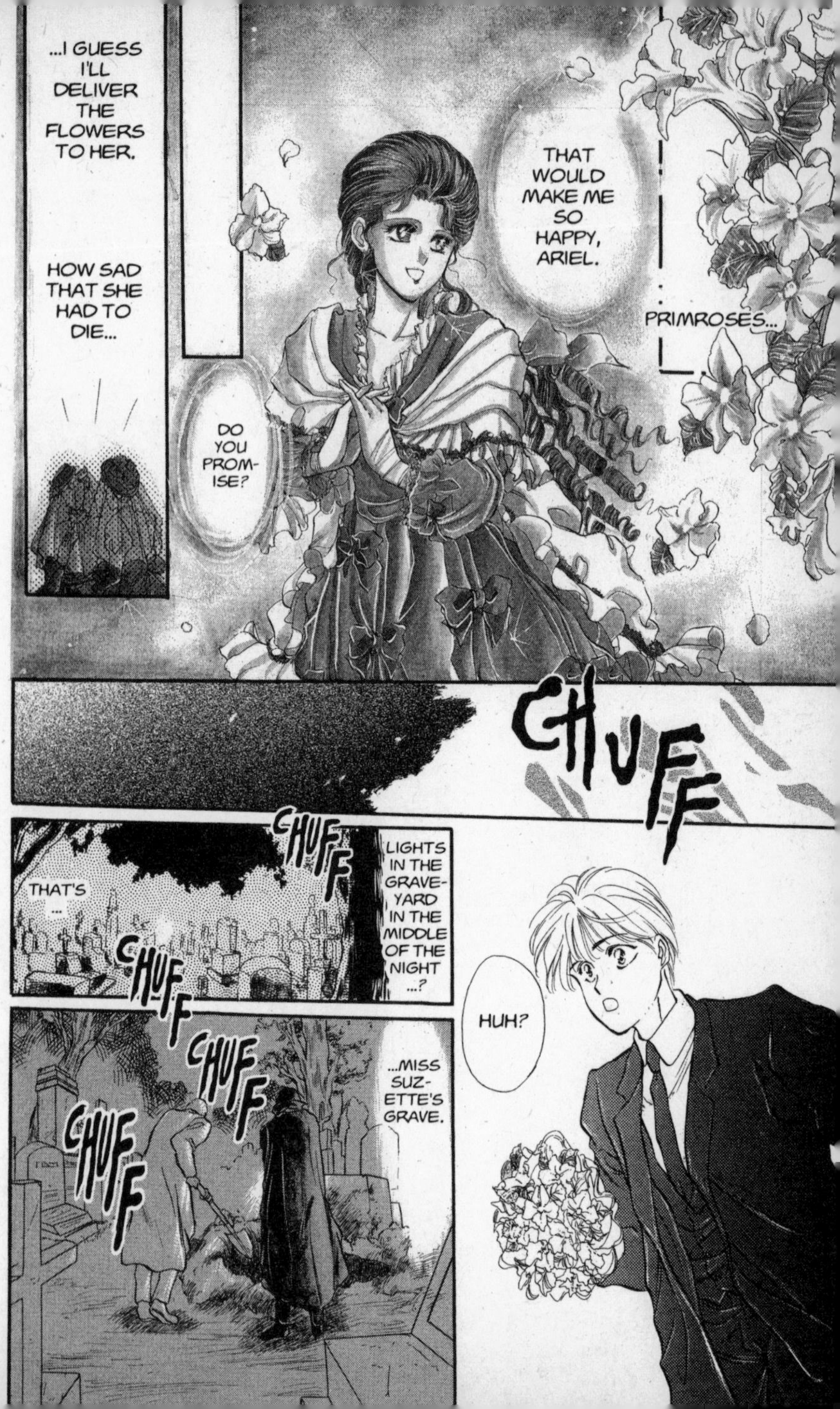
PRIMROSES...
THAT WOULD MAKE ME SO HAPPY, ARIEL.
DO YOU PROMISE?
...I GUESS I'LL DELIVER THE FLOWERS TO HER.
HOW SAD THAT SHE HAD TO DIE...
CHUFF
HUH?
CHUFF
LIGHTS IN THE GRAVE-YARD IN THE MIDDLE OF THE NIGHT ...?
THAT'S ...
CHUFF
CHUFF
...MISS SUZ-ETTE'S GRAVE.
CHUFF

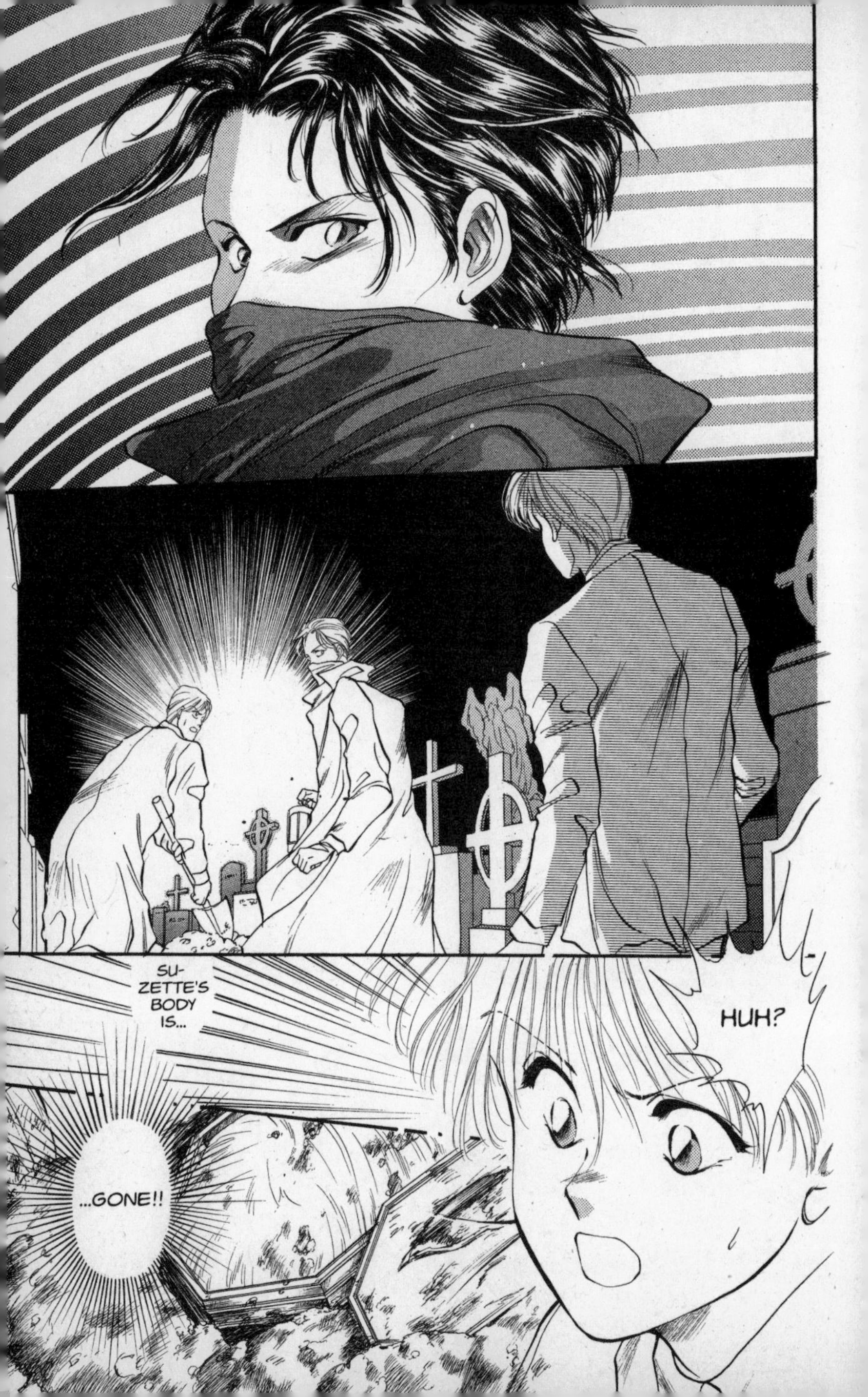
HUH?
SU-ZETTE'S BODY IS...
...GONE!!

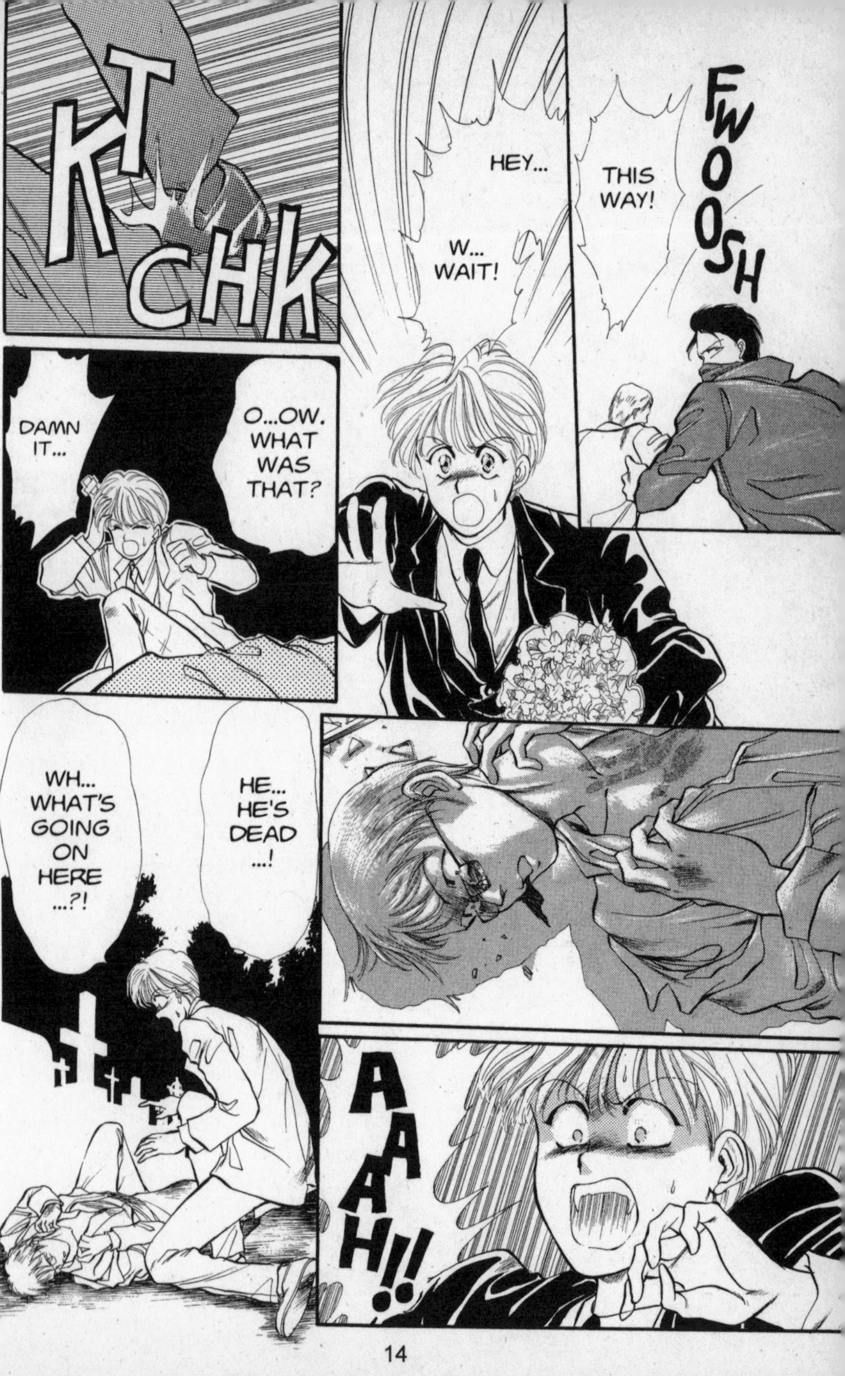
THIS WAY!
FWOOSH
HEY...
W... WAIT!
KT CHK
O...OW. WHAT WAS THAT?
DAMN IT...
AAAAH!!
HE... HE'S DEAD ...!
WH... WHAT'S GOING ON HERE ...?!

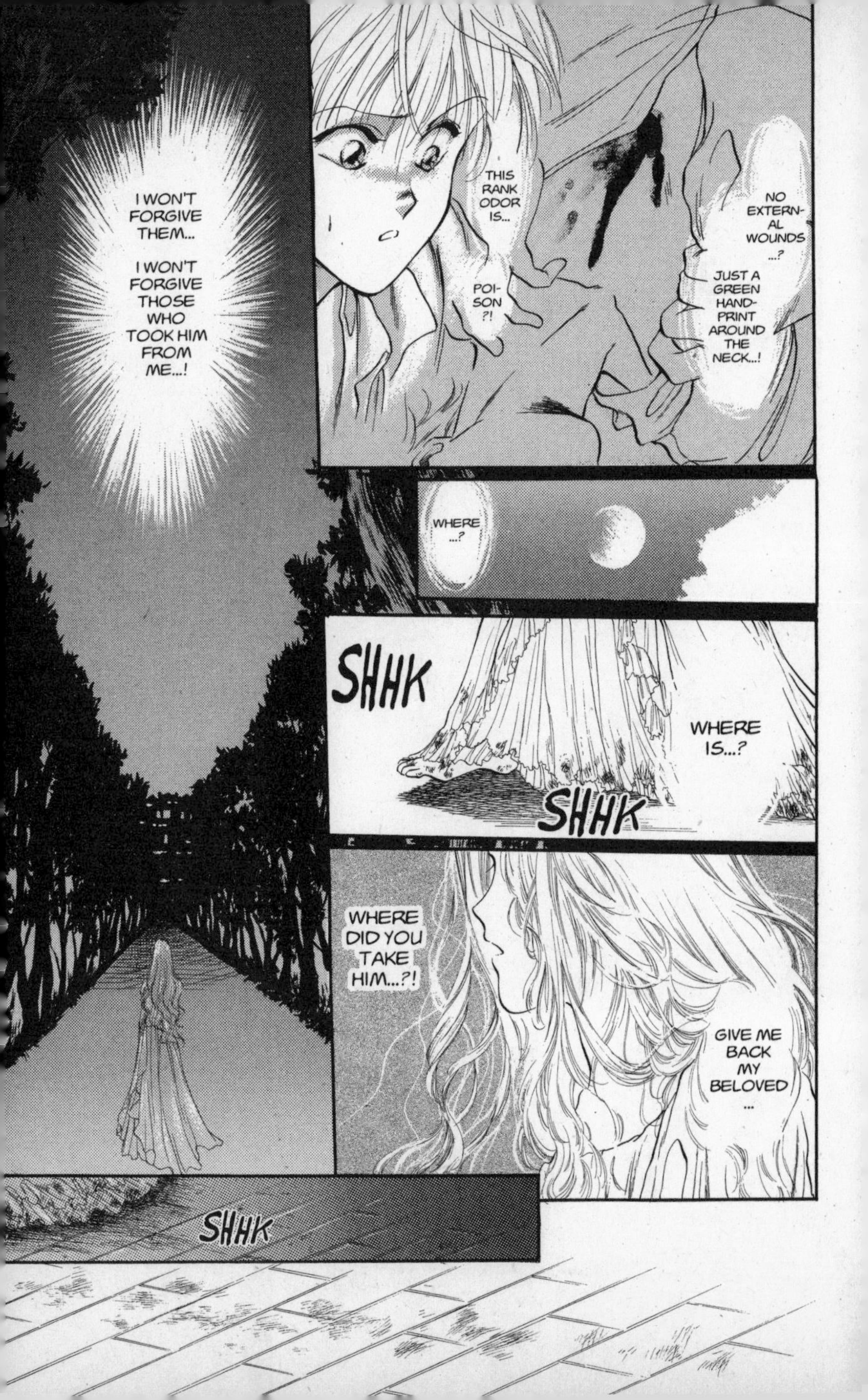
NO EXTERNAL WOUNDS...?
JUST A GREEN HANDPRINT AROUND THE NECK...!
THIS RANK ODOR IS...
POISON?!
WHERE...?
WHERE IS...?
SHHK
SHHK
GIVE ME BACK MY BELOVED...
WHERE DID YOU TAKE HIM...?!
I WON'T FORGIVE THEM...
I WON'T FORGIVE THOSE WHO TOOK HIM FROM ME...!
SHHK

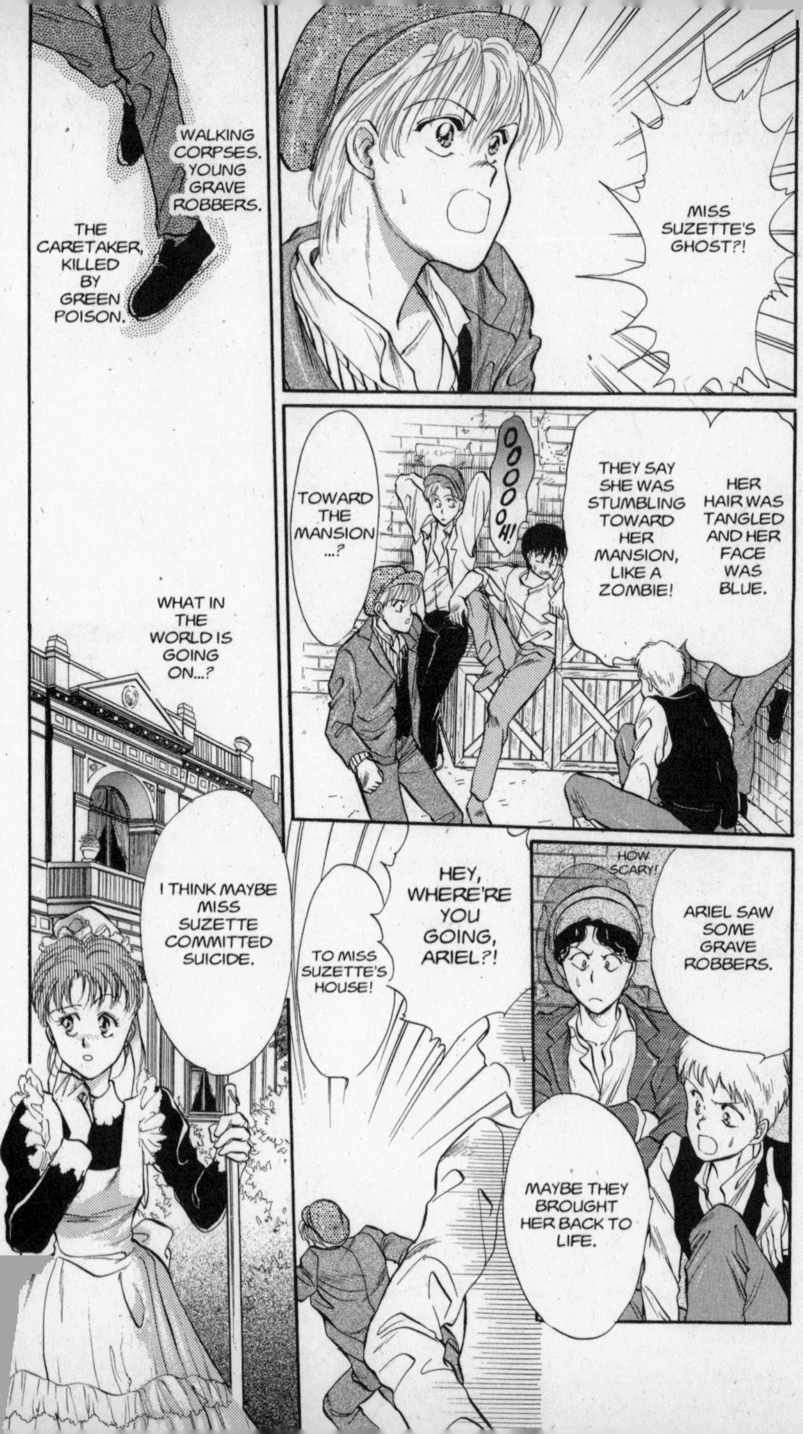
MISS SUZETTE'S GHOST?!
HER HAIR WAS TANGLED AND HER FACE WAS BLUE.
THEY SAY SHE WAS STUMBLING TOWARD HER MANSION, LIKE A ZOMBIE!
OOOOOOH!
TOWARD THE MANSION ...?
HOW SCARY!
ARIEL SAW SOME GRAVE ROBBERS.
MAYBE THEY BROUGHT HER BACK TO LIFE.
HEY, WHERE'RE YOU GOING, ARIEL?!
TO MISS SUZETTE'S HOUSE!
WALKING CORPSES. YOUNG GRAVE ROBBERS.
THE CARETAKER, KILLED BY GREEN POISON.
WHAT IN THE WORLD IS GOING ON...?
I THINK MAYBE MISS SUZETTE COMMITTED SUICIDE.

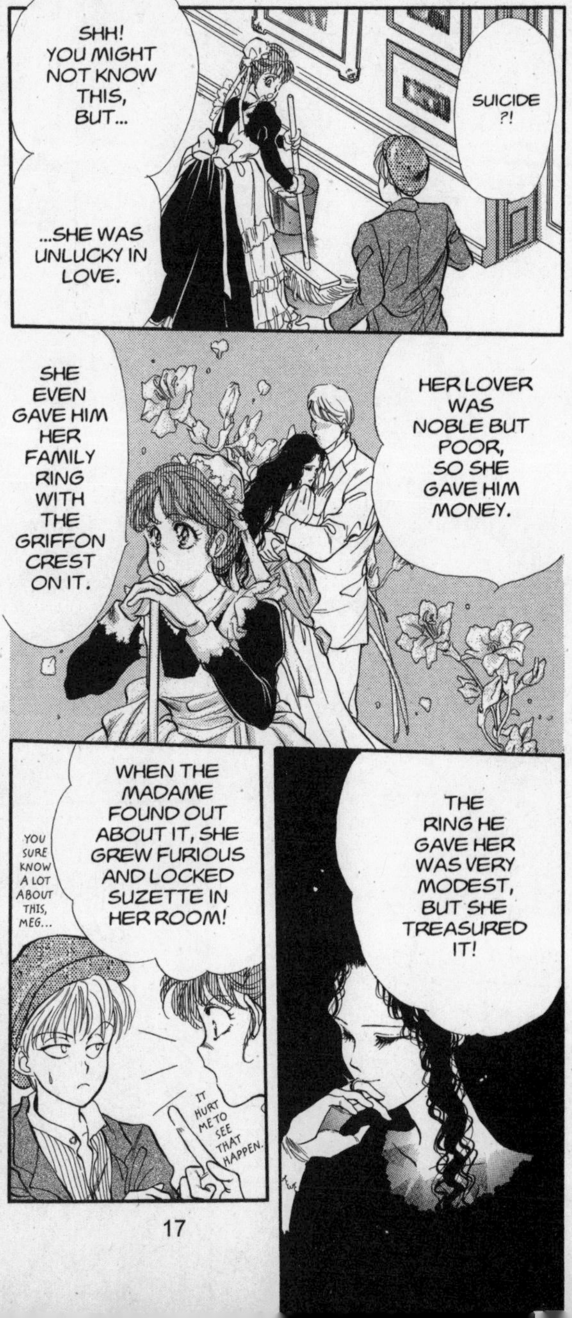
SUICIDE?!
SHH! YOU MIGHT NOT KNOW THIS, BUT...
...SHE WAS UNLUCKY IN LOVE.
HER LOVER WAS NOBLE BUT POOR, SO SHE GAVE HIM MONEY.
SHE EVEN GAVE HIM HER FAMILY RING WITH THE GRIFFON CREST ON IT.
THE RING HE GAVE HER WAS VERY MODEST, BUT SHE TREASURED IT!
WHEN THE MADAME FOUND OUT ABOUT IT, SHE GREW FURIOUS AND LOCKED SUZETTE IN HER ROOM!
YOU SURE KNOW A LOT ABOUT THIS, MEG...
IT HURT ME TO SEE THAT HAPPEN.

WILD TALK

HELLO, EVERYONE! I'M EXCITED ABOUT THIS FIRST VOLUME OF THE NEW SERIES. OH... IT'S BEEN FIVE YEARS SINCE I BEGAN... WHAT A LONG, LONG ROAD IT'S BEEN! I MYSELF AM AMAZED THAT I DIDN'T GIVE UP ALONG THE WAY. I'M GRATEFUL TO ALL THE MYSTERY FANS OUT THERE! I'VE ALWAYS LOVED MYSTERIES AND OLD BRITISH MOVIES, SO I'VE BEEN WRITING ABOUT WHAT INTERESTS ME. I'VE ALWAYS DREAMED OF WRITING SOMETHING IN THIS SPACE, BUT NOW THAT I FINALLY HAVE THE OPPORTUNITY, I'M STUMPED. ANYWAY, PLEASE STICK WITH ME FOR AT LEAST A LITTLE WHILE...

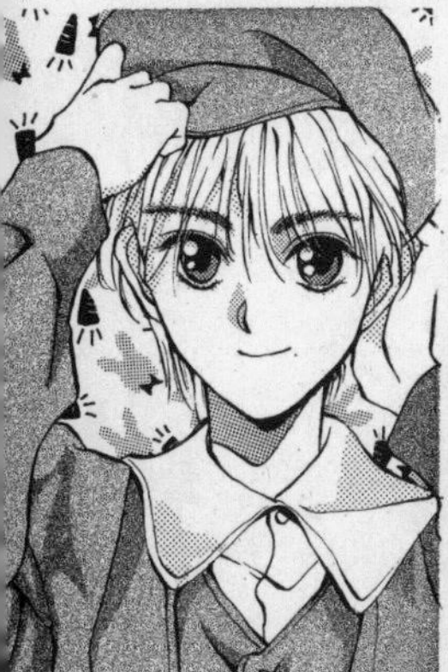

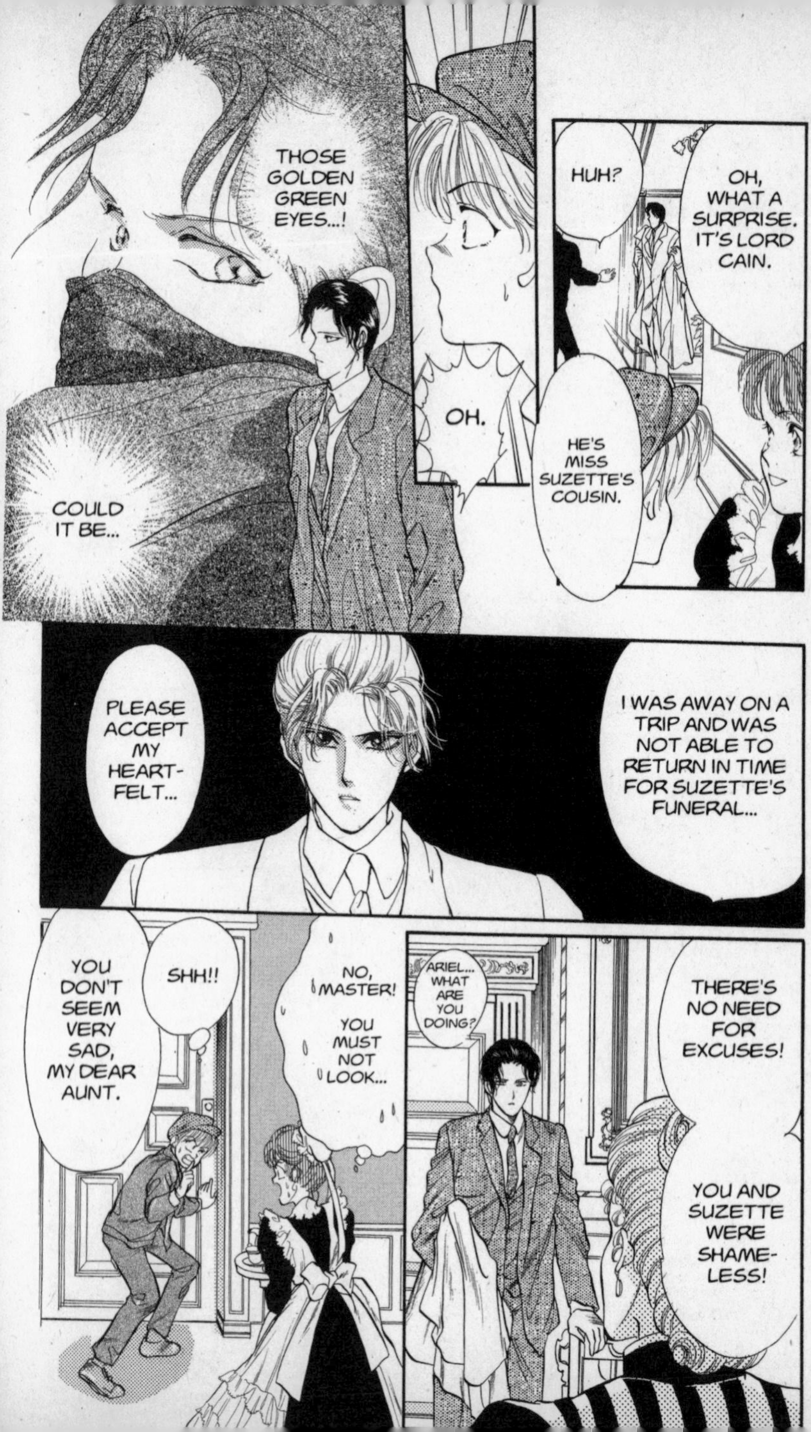
OH, WHAT A SURPRISE. IT'S LORD CAIN.
HUH?
HE'S MISS SUZETTE'S COUSIN.
OH.
THOSE GOLDEN GREEN EYES...!
COULD IT BE...
I WAS AWAY ON A TRIP AND WAS NOT ABLE TO RETURN IN TIME FOR SUZETTE'S FUNERAL...
PLEASE ACCEPT MY HEART-FELT...
THERE'S NO NEED FOR EXCUSES!
YOU AND SUZETTE WERE SHAME-LESS!
ARIEL... WHAT ARE YOU DOING?
NO, MASTER!
YOU MUST NOT LOOK...
SHH!!
YOU DON'T SEEM VERY SAD, MY DEAR AUNT.

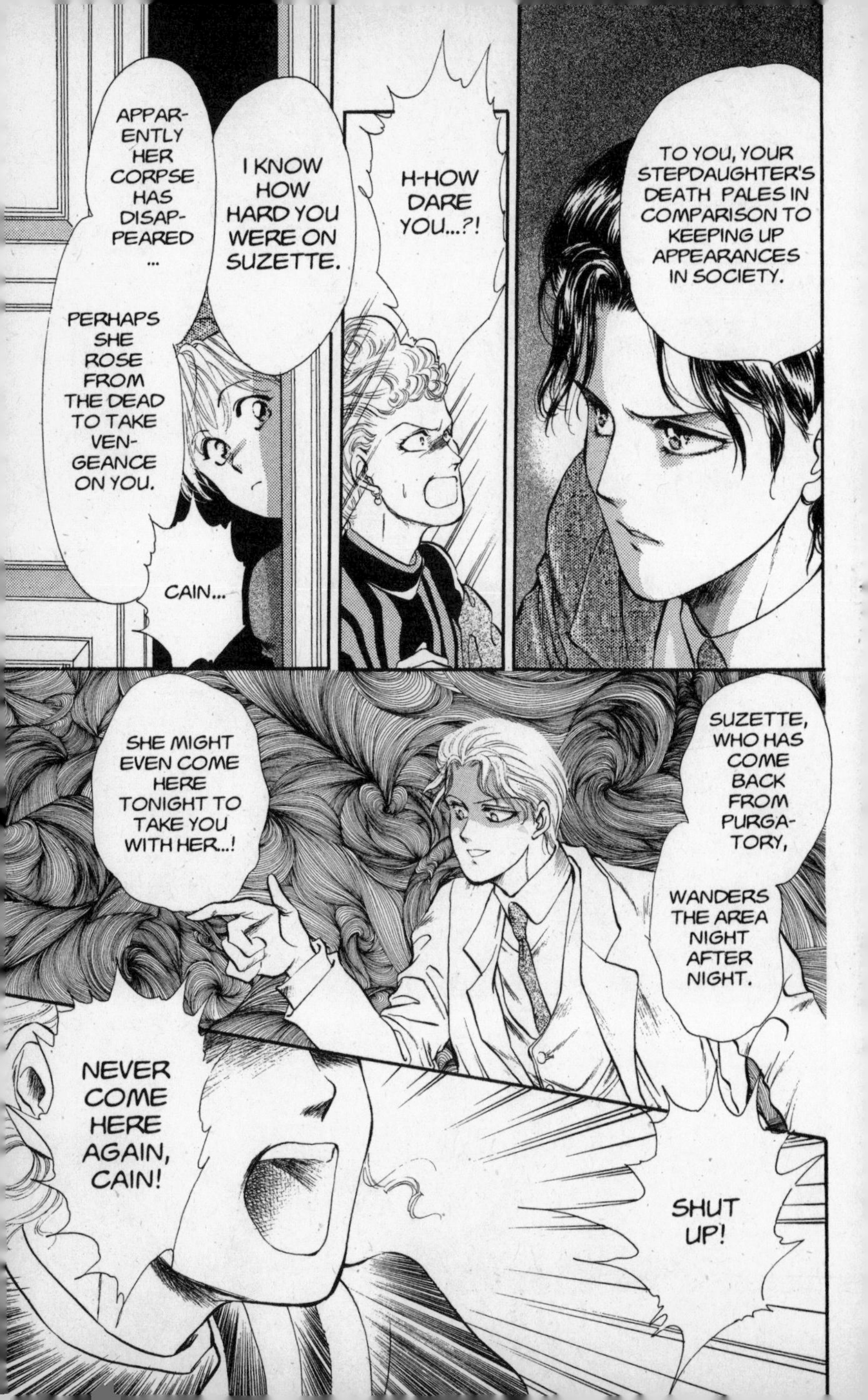
TO YOU, YOUR STEPDAUGHTER'S DEATH PALES IN COMPARISON TO KEEPING UP APPEARANCES IN SOCIETY.
H-HOW DARE YOU...?!
I KNOW HOW HARD YOU WERE ON SUZETTE.
APPAR-ENTLY HER CORPSE HAS DISAP-PEARED ...
PERHAPS SHE ROSE FROM THE DEAD TO TAKE VEN-GEANCE ON YOU.
CAIN...
SUZETTE, WHO HAS COME BACK FROM PURGA-TORY,
WANDERS THE AREA NIGHT AFTER NIGHT.
SHE MIGHT EVEN COME HERE TONIGHT TO TAKE YOU WITH HER...!
SHUT UP!
NEVER COME HERE AGAIN, CAIN!

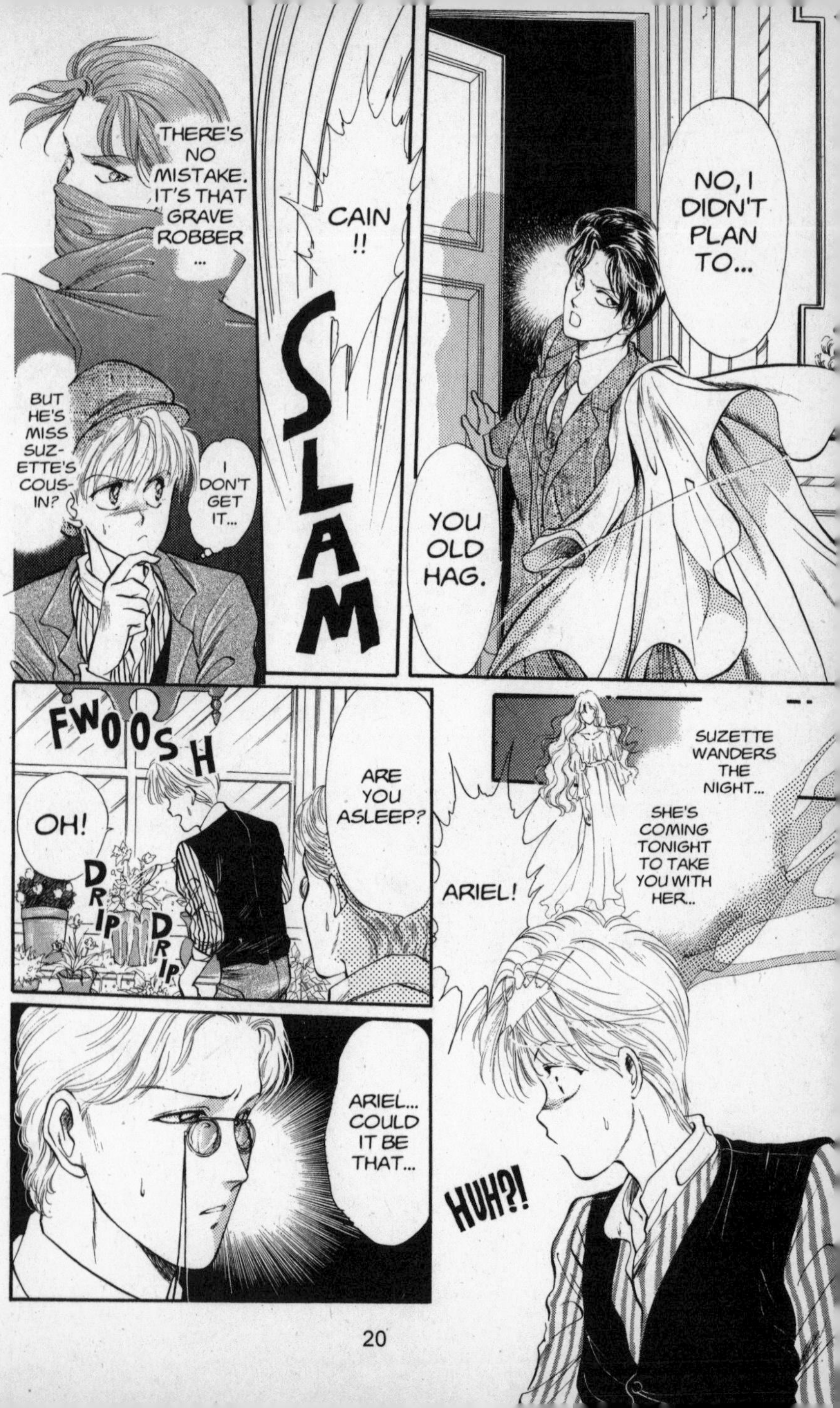
NO, I DIDN'T PLAN TO...
YOU OLD HAG.
CAIN !!
SLAM
THERE'S NO MISTAKE. IT'S THAT GRAVE ROBBER ...
BUT HE'S MISS SUZETTE'S COUSIN?
I DON'T GET IT...
SUZETTE WANDERS THE NIGHT...
SHE'S COMING TONIGHT TO TAKE YOU WITH HER..
ARIEL!
HUH?!
ARE YOU ASLEEP?
FWOOSH
OH!
DRIP DRIP DRIP
ARIEL... COULD IT BE THAT...

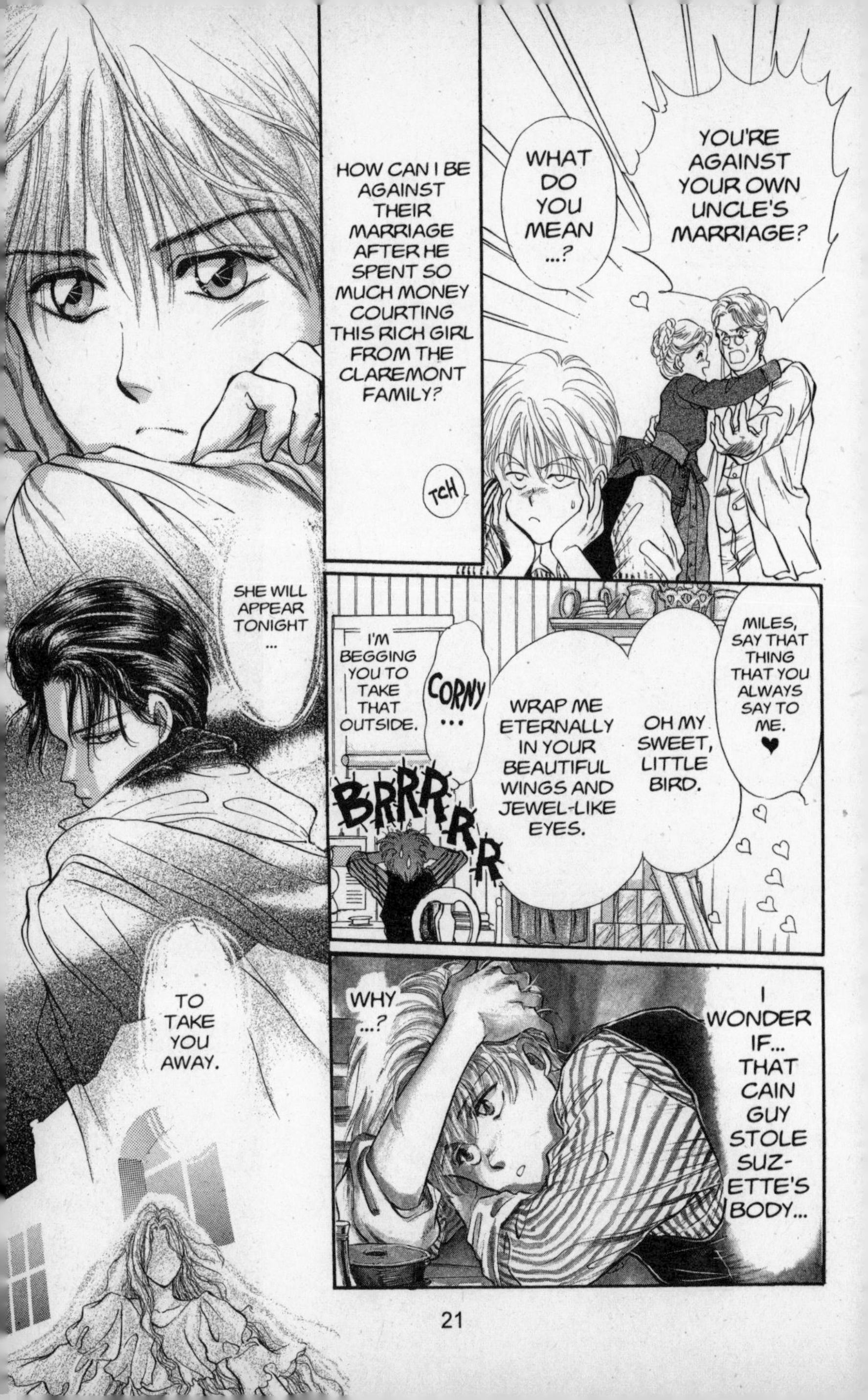
YOU'RE AGAINST YOUR OWN UNCLE'S MARRIAGE?
WHAT DO YOU MEAN ...?
HOW CAN I BE AGAINST THEIR MARRIAGE AFTER HE SPENT SO MUCH MONEY COURTING THIS RICH GIRL FROM THE CLAREMONT FAMILY?
TCH
MILES, SAY THAT THING THAT YOU ALWAYS SAY TO ME. ♥
OH MY SWEET, LITTLE BIRD.
WRAP ME ETERNALLY IN YOUR BEAUTIFUL WINGS AND JEWEL-LIKE EYES.
CORNY ...
I'M BEGGING YOU TO TAKE THAT OUTSIDE.
BRRRRRR
I WONDER IF... THAT CAIN GUY STOLE SUZETTE'S BODY...
WHY ...?
SHE WILL APPEAR TONIGHT ...
TO TAKE YOU AWAY.

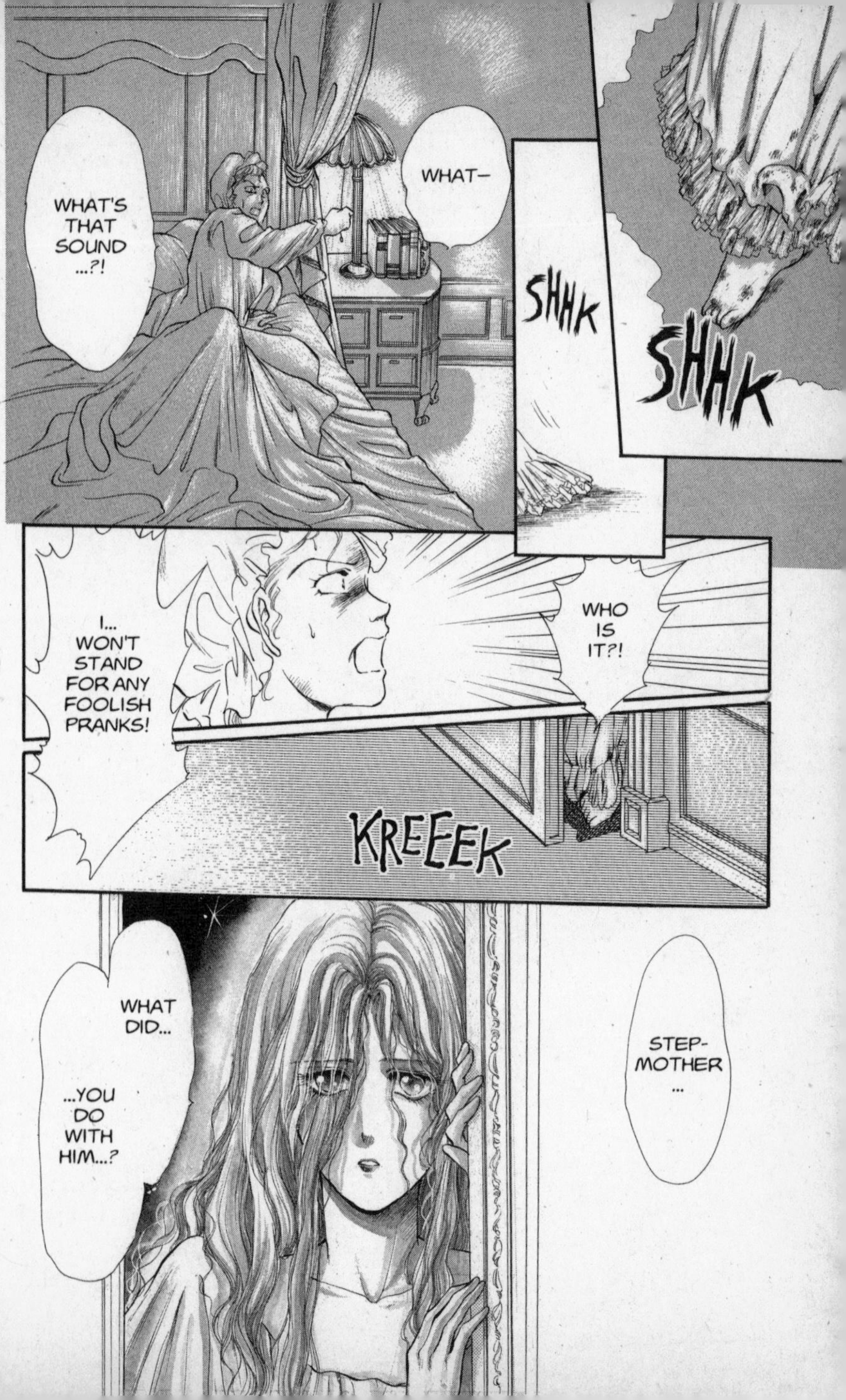
SHHK
SHHK
WHAT—
WHAT'S THAT SOUND ...?!
WHO IS IT?!
I... WON'T STAND FOR ANY FOOLISH PRANKS!
KREEEK
STEP-MOTHER ...
WHAT DID...
...YOU DO WITH HIM...?

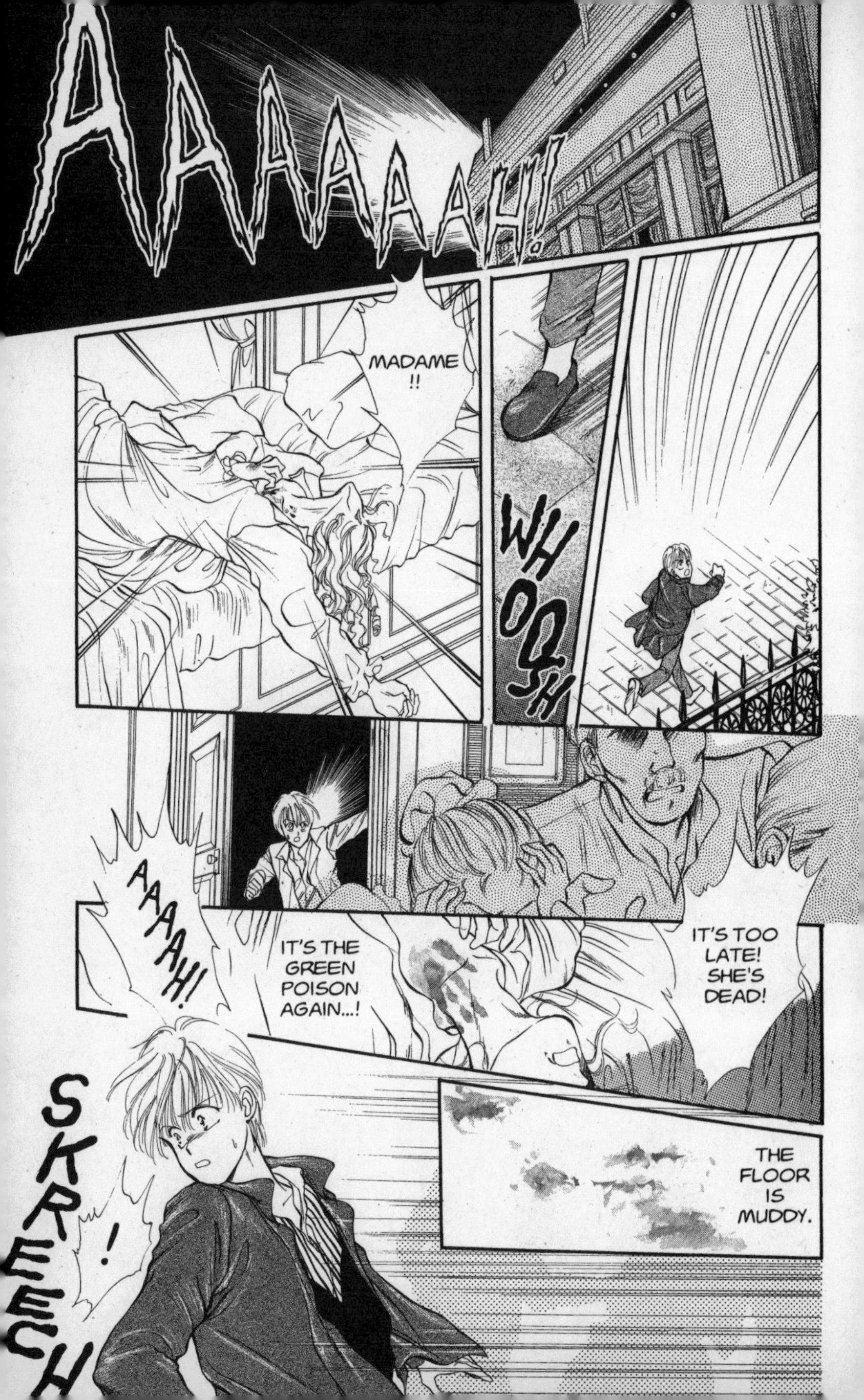
AAAAAH!!
WHOOOSH
MADAME !!
IT'S TOO LATE! SHE'S DEAD!
IT'S THE GREEN POISON AGAIN...!
AAAAAH!
THE FLOOR IS MUDDY.
SKREECH!

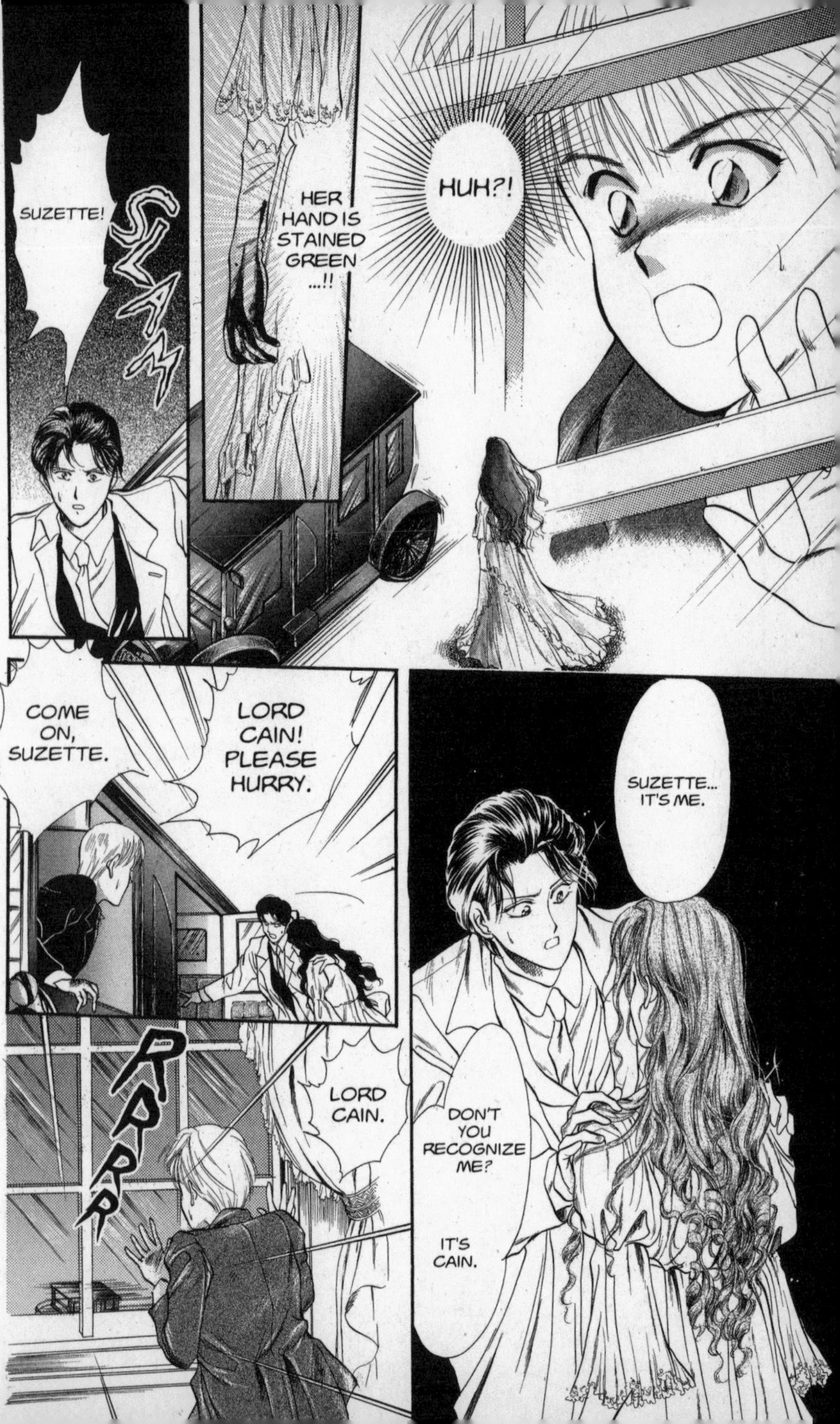
HUH?!
HER HAND IS STAINED GREEN ...!!
SLAM
SUZETTE!
SUZETTE... IT'S ME.
DON'T YOU RECOGNIZE ME?
IT'S CAIN.
LORD CAIN! PLEASE HURRY.
COME ON, SUZETTE.
LORD CAIN.
RRRRR

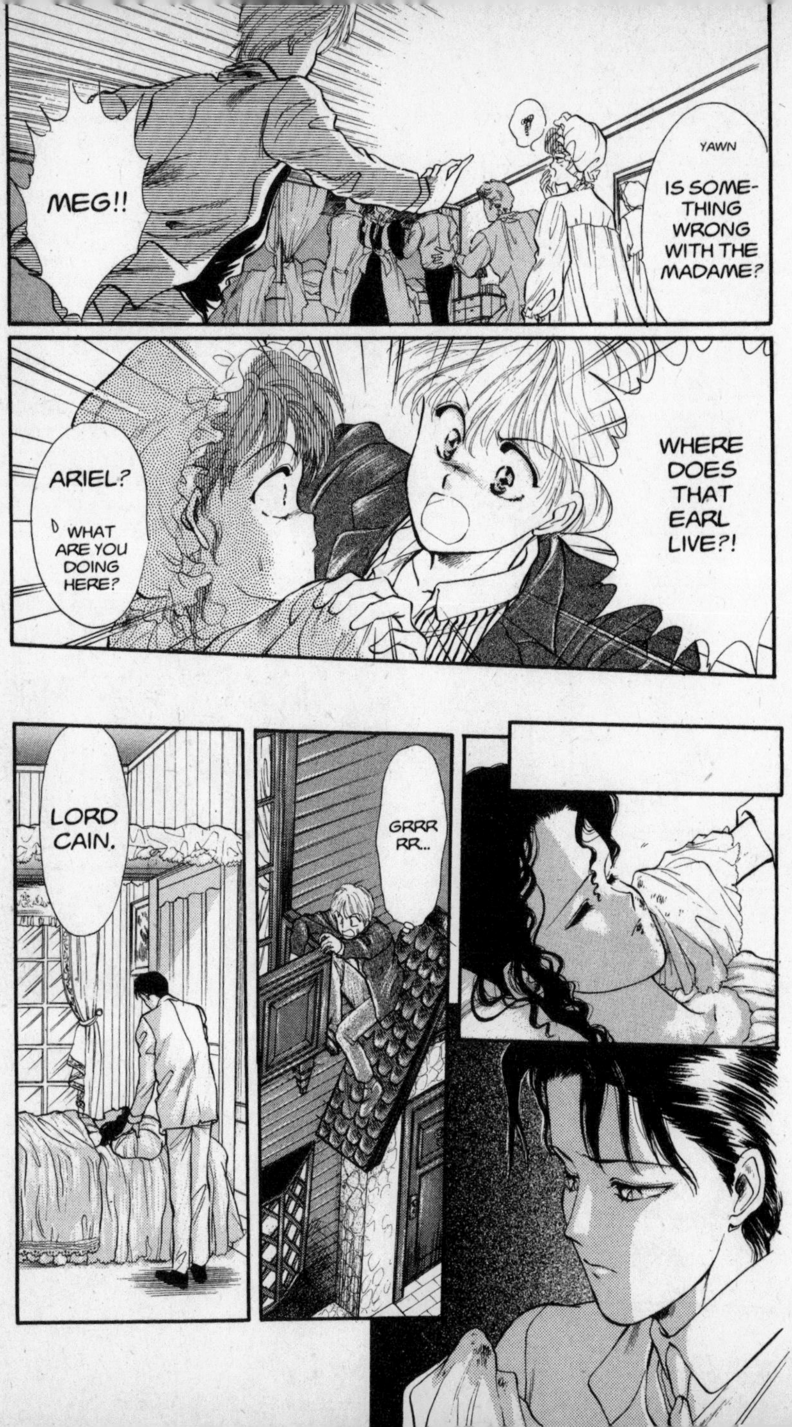
?
YAWN
IS SOMETHING WRONG WITH THE MADAME?
MEG!!
WHERE DOES THAT EARL LIVE?!
ARIEL?
WHAT ARE YOU DOING HERE?
GRRR RR...
LORD CAIN.

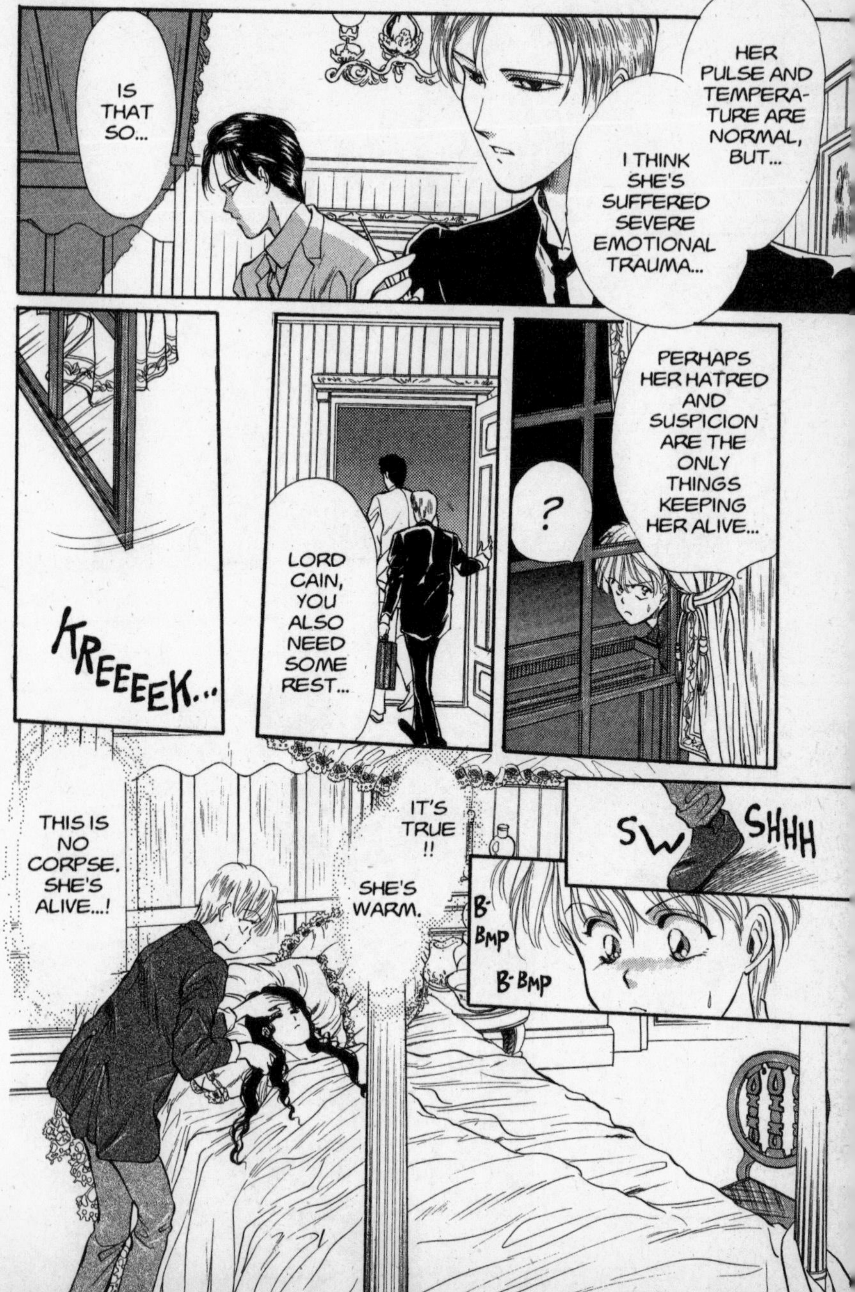
HER PULSE AND TEMPERA-TURE ARE NORMAL, BUT...
I THINK SHE'S SUFFERED SEVERE EMOTIONAL TRAUMA...
IS THAT SO...
PERHAPS HER HATRED AND SUSPICION ARE THE ONLY THINGS KEEPING HER ALIVE...
?
LORD CAIN, YOU ALSO NEED SOME REST...
KREEEEK...
SW SHHH
B-BMP
B-BMP
IT'S TRUE!!
SHE'S WARM.
THIS IS NO CORPSE. SHE'S ALIVE...!

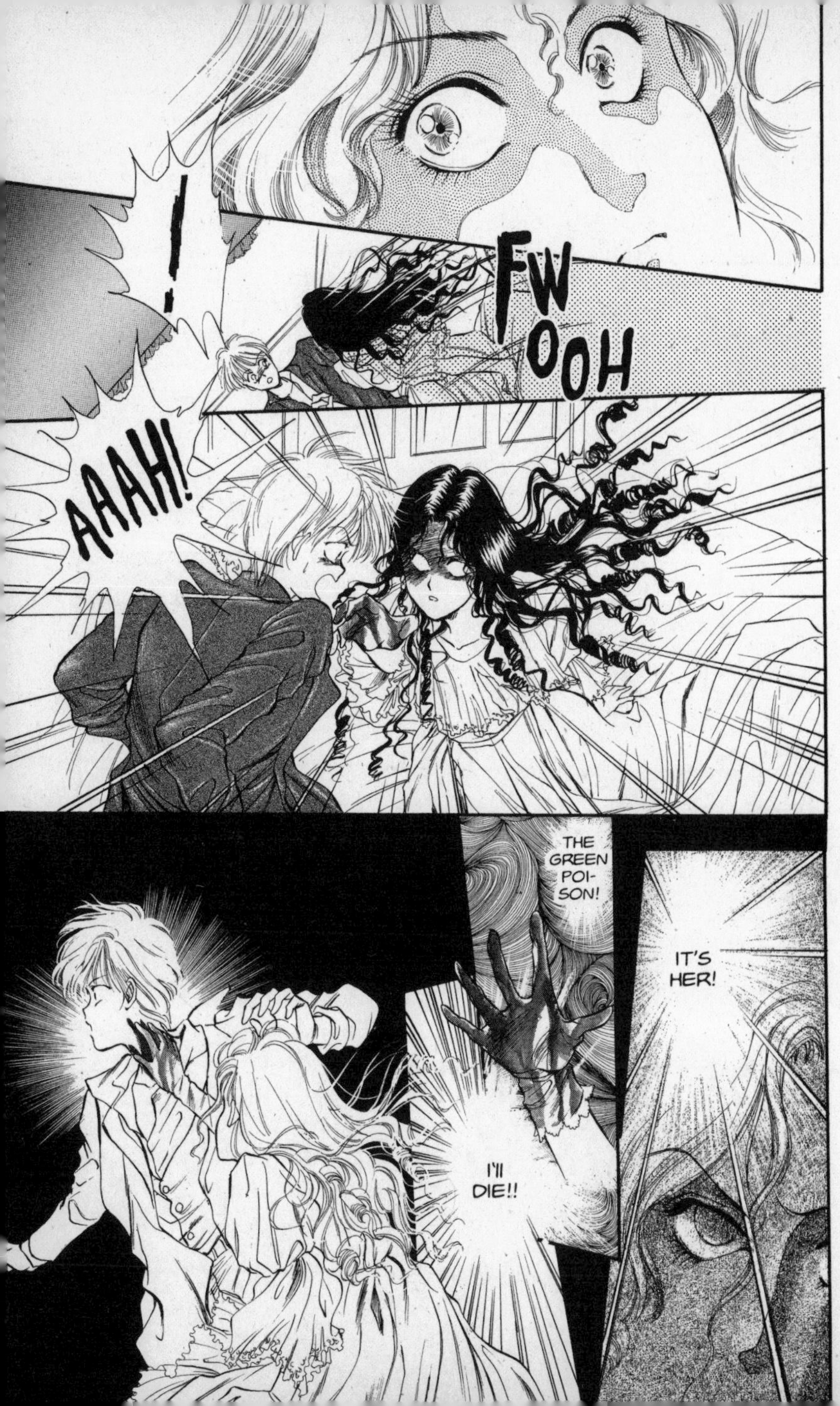
FWOOH
!
AAAH!
IT'S HER!
THE GREEN POI-SON!
I'LL DIE!!

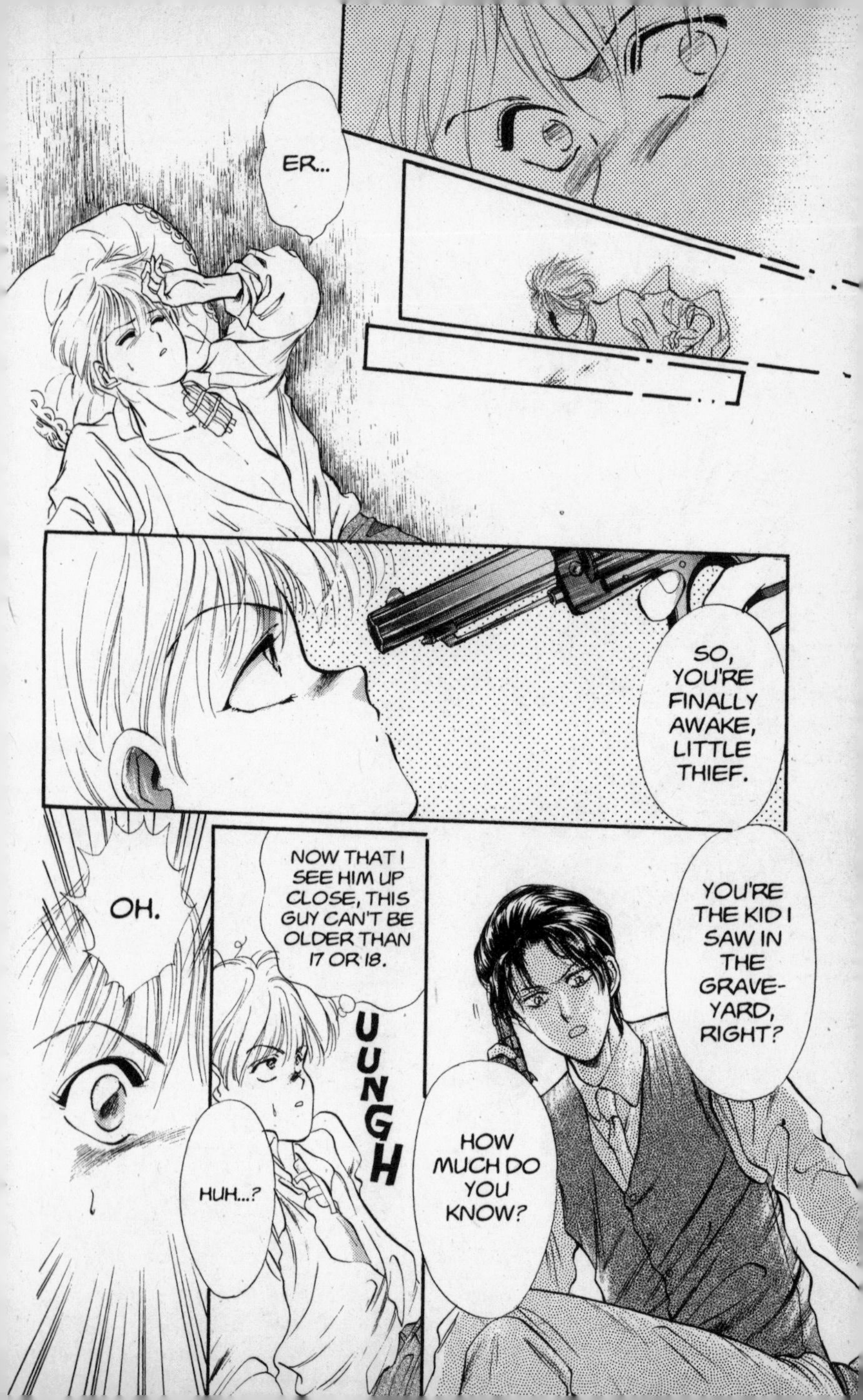
ER...
SO, YOU'RE FINALLY AWAKE, LITTLE THIEF.
YOU'RE THE KID I SAW IN THE GRAVEYARD, RIGHT?
HOW MUCH DO YOU KNOW?
NOW THAT I SEE HIM UP CLOSE, THIS GUY CAN'T BE OLDER THAN 17 OR 18.
UUNGH
HUH...?
OH.

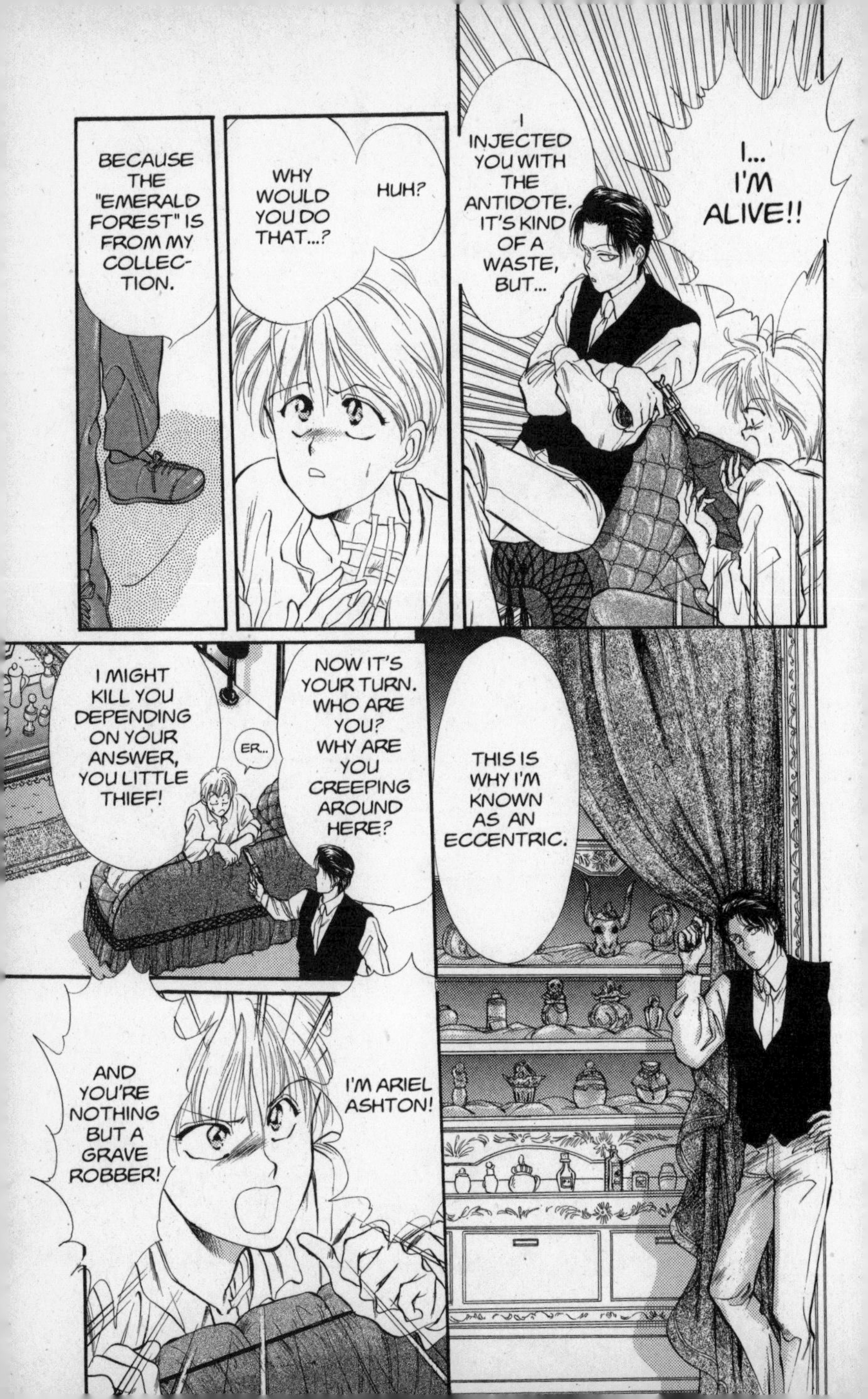
I... I'M ALIVE!!
I INJECTED YOU WITH THE ANTIDOTE. IT'S KIND OF A WASTE, BUT...
HUH?
WHY WOULD YOU DO THAT...?
BECAUSE THE "EMERALD FOREST" IS FROM MY COLLECTION.
THIS IS WHY I'M KNOWN AS AN ECCENTRIC.
NOW IT'S YOUR TURN. WHO ARE YOU? WHY ARE YOU CREEPING AROUND HERE?
ER...
I MIGHT KILL YOU DEPENDING ON YOUR ANSWER, YOU LITTLE THIEF!
I'M ARIEL ASHTON!
AND YOU'RE NOTHING BUT A GRAVE ROBBER!

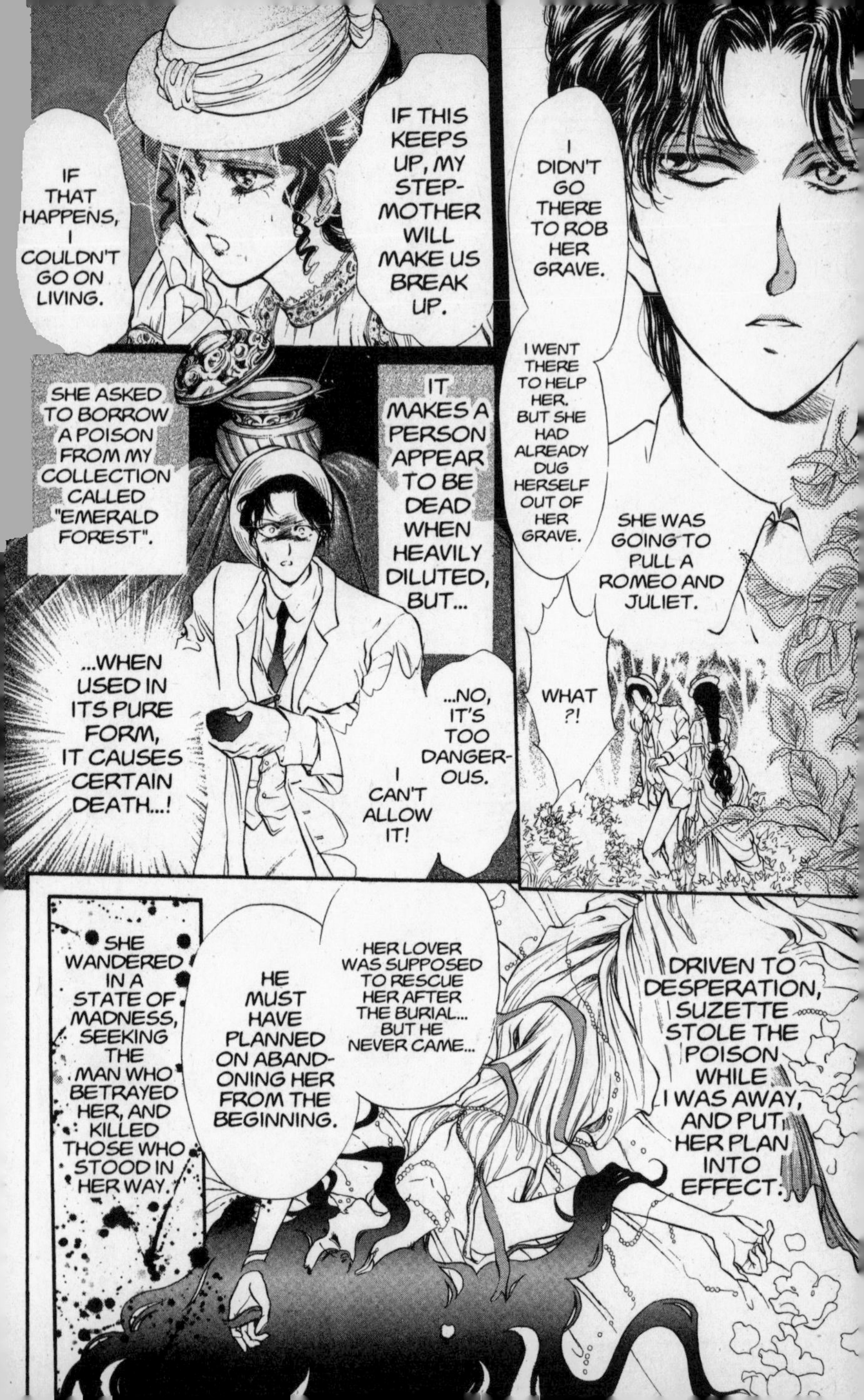

I DIDN'T GO THERE TO ROB HER GRAVE.
I WENT THERE TO HELP HER. BUT SHE HAD ALREADY DUG HERSELF OUT OF HER GRAVE.
SHE WAS GOING TO PULL A ROMEO AND JULIET.
WHAT ?!
IF THIS KEEPS UP, MY STEP-MOTHER WILL MAKE US BREAK UP.
IF THAT HAPPENS, I COULDN'T GO ON LIVING.
SHE ASKED TO BORROW A POISON FROM MY COLLECTION CALLED "EMERALD FOREST".
IT MAKES A PERSON APPEAR TO BE DEAD WHEN HEAVILY DILUTED, BUT...
...WHEN USED IN ITS PURE FORM, IT CAUSES CERTAIN DEATH...!
...NO, IT'S TOO DANGER-OUS.
I CAN'T ALLOW IT!
DRIVEN TO DESPERATION, SUZETTE STOLE THE POISON WHILE I WAS AWAY, AND PUT HER PLAN INTO EFFECT.
HER LOVER WAS SUPPOSED TO RESCUE HER AFTER THE BURIAL... BUT HE NEVER CAME...
HE MUST HAVE PLANNED ON ABAND-ONING HER FROM THE BEGINNING.
SHE WANDERED IN A STATE OF MADNESS, SEEKING THE MAN WHO BETRAYED HER, AND KILLED THOSE WHO STOOD IN HER WAY.

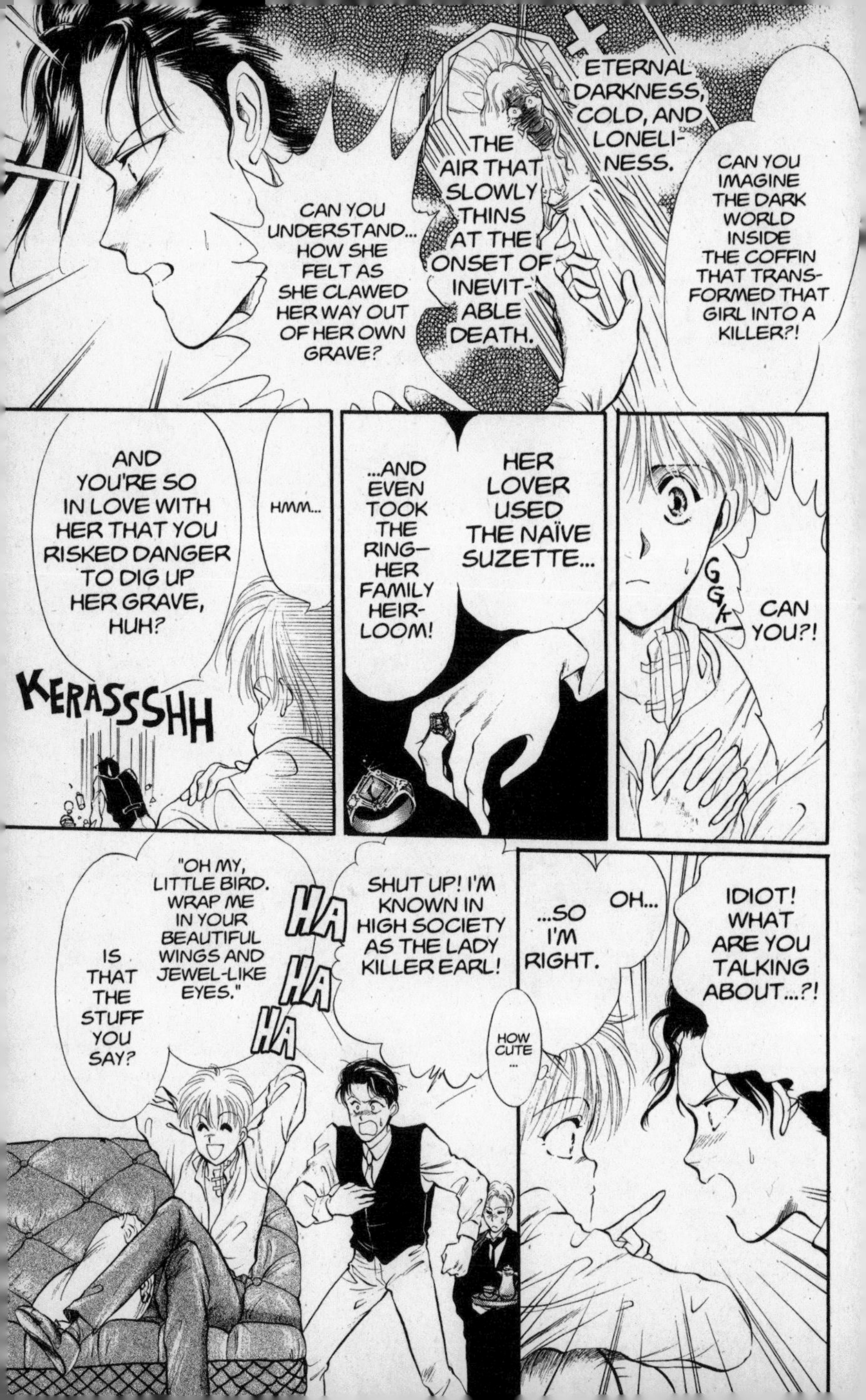
CAN YOU IMAGINE THE DARK WORLD INSIDE THE COFFIN THAT TRANSFORMED THAT GIRL INTO A KILLER?!
ETERNAL DARKNESS, COLD, AND LONELINESS.
THE AIR THAT SLOWLY THINS AT THE ONSET OF INEVITABLE DEATH.
CAN YOU UNDERSTAND... HOW SHE FELT AS SHE CLAWED HER WAY OUT OF HER OWN GRAVE?
GGK
CAN YOU?!
HER LOVER USED THE NAÏVE SUZETTE...
...AND EVEN TOOK THE RING— HER FAMILY HEIRLOOM!
HMM...
AND YOU'RE SO IN LOVE WITH HER THAT YOU RISKED DANGER TO DIG UP HER GRAVE, HUH?
KERASSSHH
IDIOT! WHAT ARE YOU TALKING ABOUT...?!
OH...
...SO I'M RIGHT.
HOW CUTE...
SHUT UP! I'M KNOWN IN HIGH SOCIETY AS THE LADY KILLER EARL!
HA HA HA
"OH MY, LITTLE BIRD. WRAP ME IN YOUR BEAUTIFUL WINGS AND JEWEL-LIKE EYES."
IS THAT THE STUFF YOU SAY?

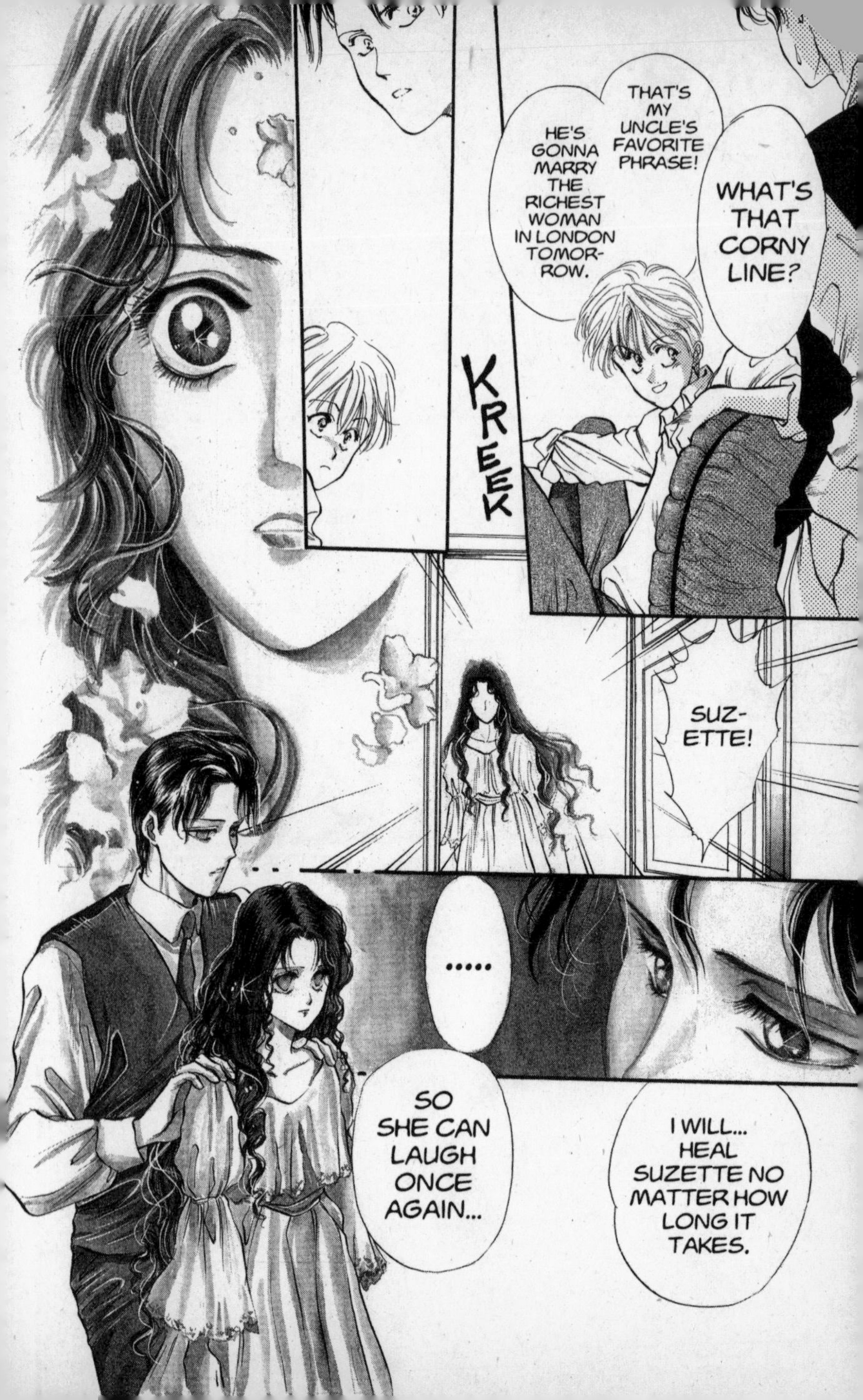
HE'S GONNA MARRY THE RICHEST WOMAN IN LONDON TOMORROW.
WHAT'S THAT CORNY LINE?
THAT'S MY UNCLE'S FAVORITE PHRASE!
KREEK
SUZ-ETTE!
.....
I WILL... HEAL SUZETTE NO MATTER HOW LONG IT TAKES.
SO SHE CAN LAUGH ONCE AGAIN...

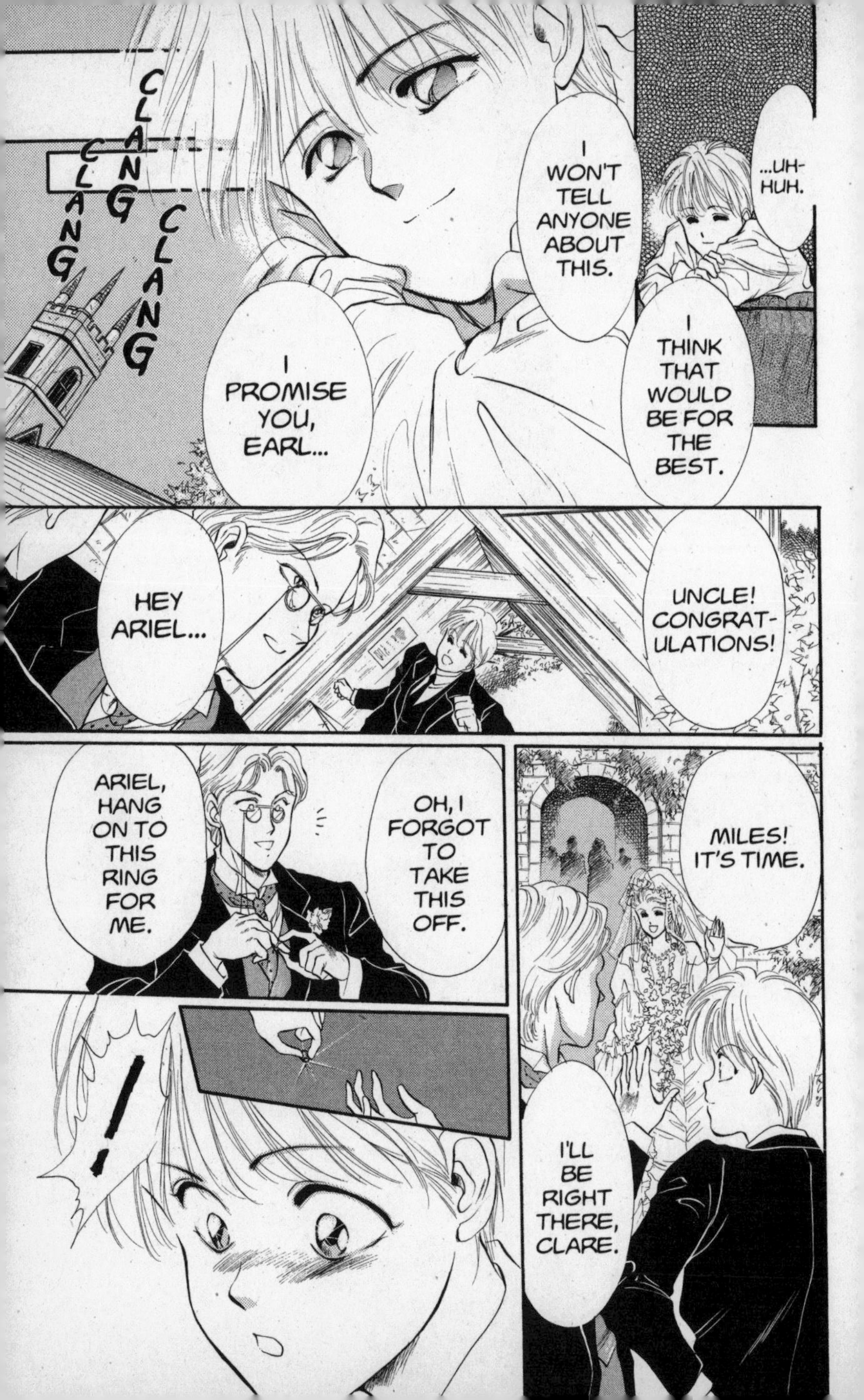
...UH-HUH.
I WON'T TELL ANYONE ABOUT THIS.
I THINK THAT WOULD BE FOR THE BEST.
I PROMISE YOU, EARL...
CLANG CLANG CLANG CLANG
UNCLE! CONGRAT-ULATIONS!
HEY ARIEL...
MILES! IT'S TIME.
I'LL BE RIGHT THERE, CLARE.
OH, I FORGOT TO TAKE THIS OFF.
ARIEL, HANG ON TO THIS RING FOR ME.
!

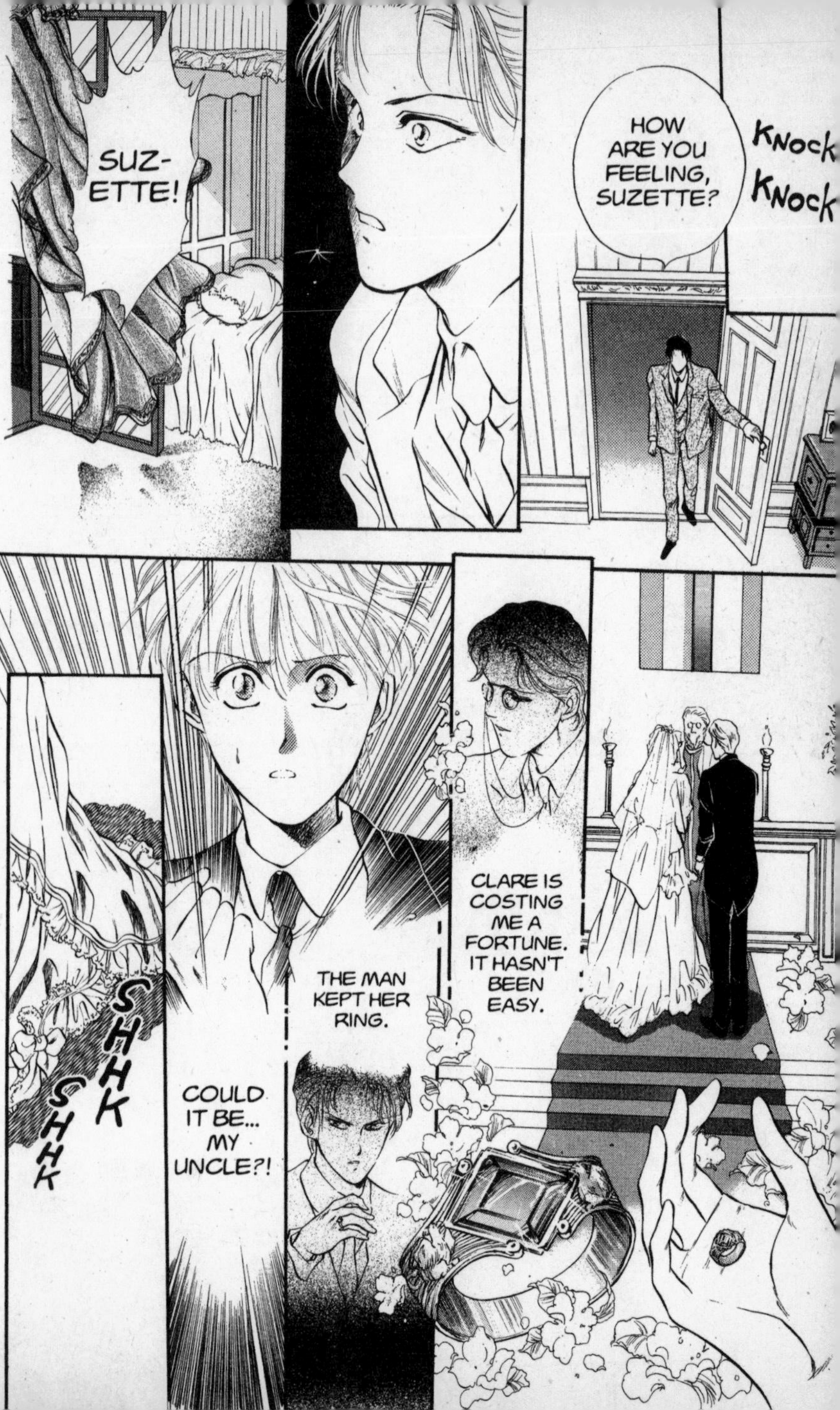
KNOCK KNOCK
HOW ARE YOU FEELING, SUZETTE?
SUZ-ETTE!
CLARE IS COSTING ME A FORTUNE. IT HASN'T BEEN EASY.
THE MAN KEPT HER RING.
COULD IT BE... MY UNCLE?!
SHHK SHHK

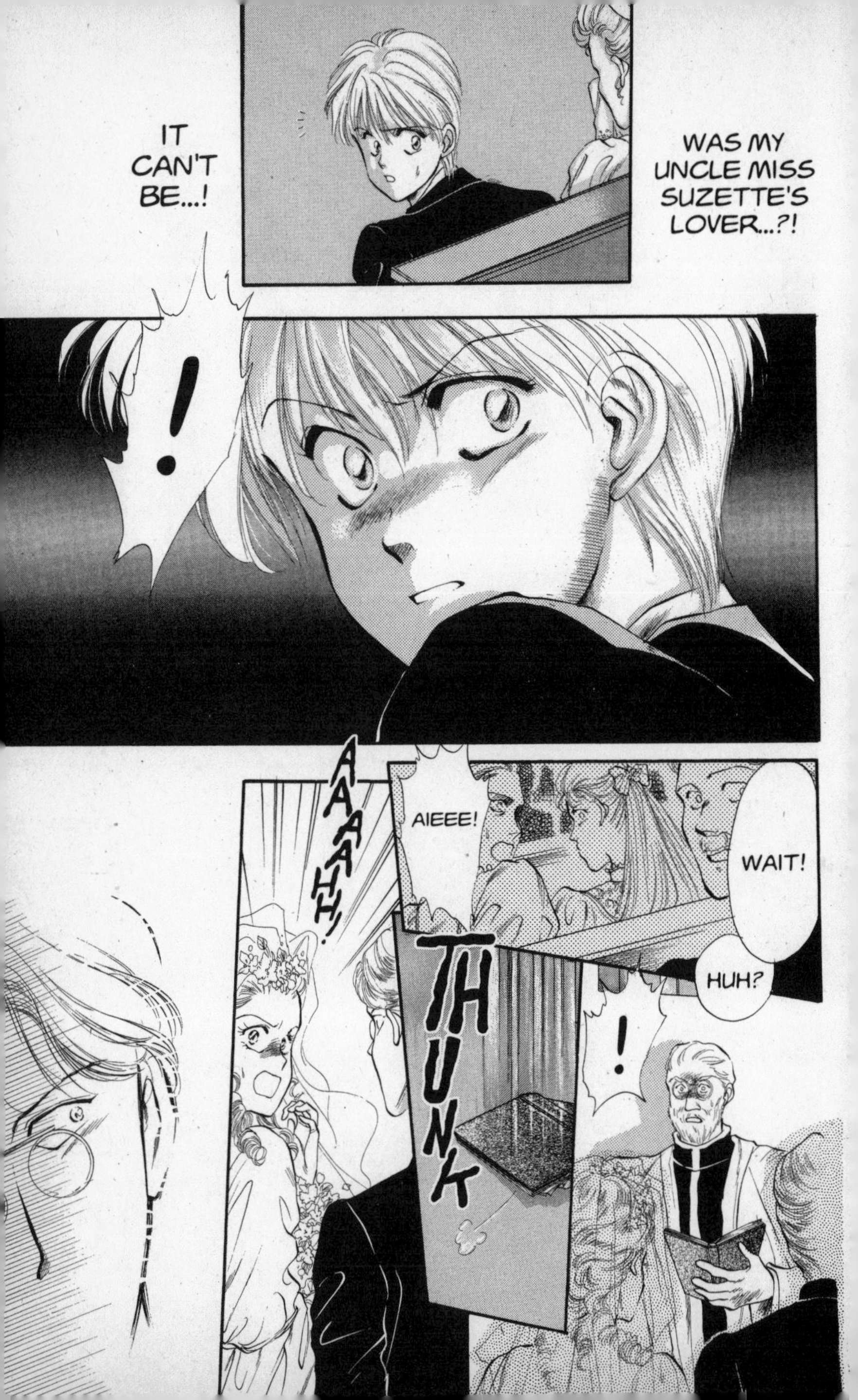
WAS MY UNCLE MISS SUZETTE'S LOVER...?!
IT CAN'T BE...!
!
WAIT!
HUH?
AIEEE!
AAAAAHH!
THUNK
!

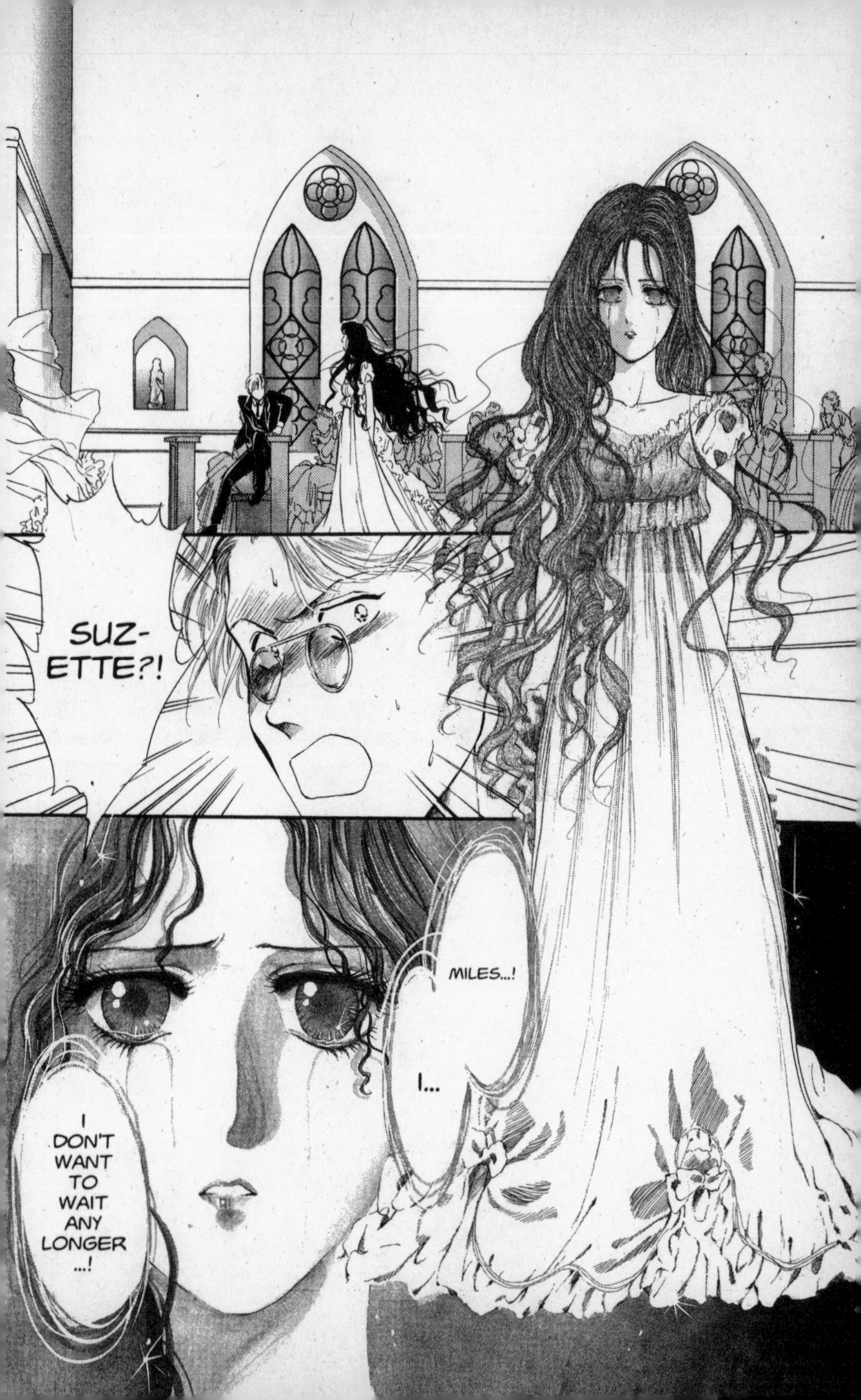
SUZ-ETTE?!
MILES...!
I...
I DON'T WANT TO WAIT ANY LONGER...!

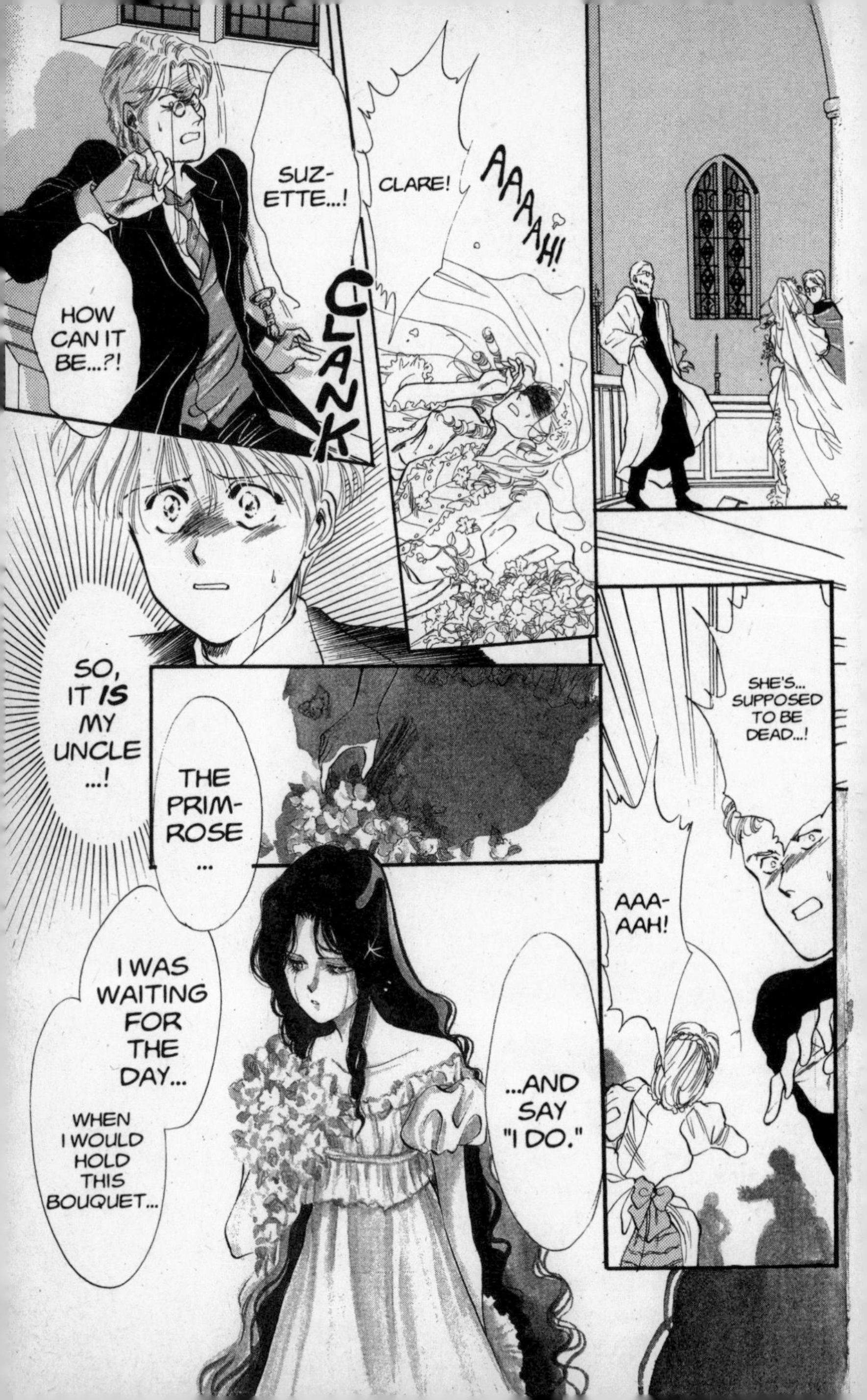
AAAAAH!
CLARE!
SUZ-ETTE...!
CLANK
HOW CAN IT BE...?!
SHE'S... SUPPOSED TO BE DEAD...!
AAA-AAH!
SO, IT *IS* MY UNCLE...!
THE PRIM-ROSE...
...AND SAY "I DO."
I WAS WAITING FOR THE DAY...
WHEN I WOULD HOLD THIS BOUQUET...

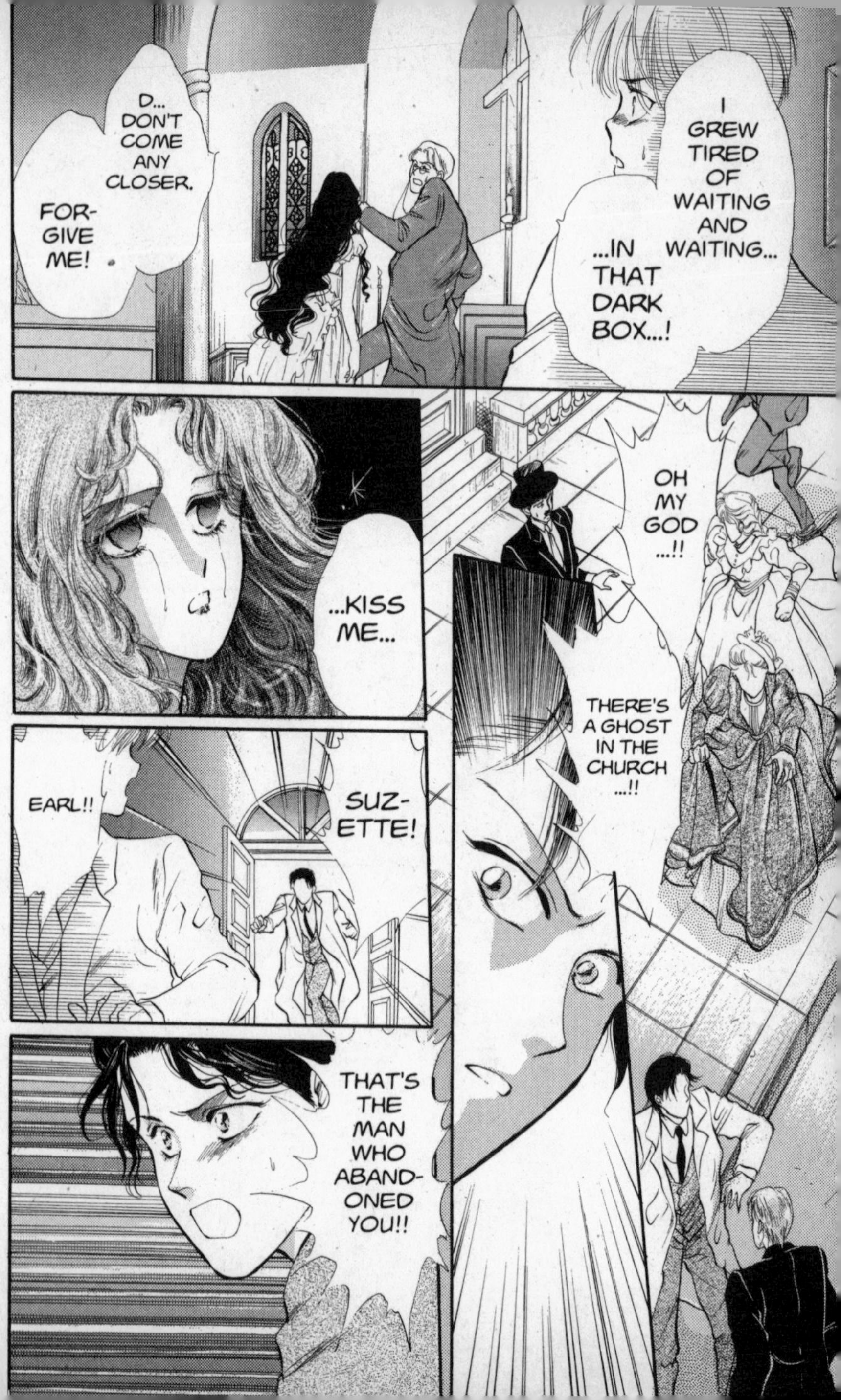
I GREW TIRED OF WAITING AND WAITING...
...IN THAT DARK BOX...!
D... DON'T COME ANY CLOSER.
FOR-GIVE ME!
OH MY GOD ...!!
THERE'S A GHOST IN THE CHURCH ...!!
...KISS ME...
SUZ-ETTE!
EARL!!
THAT'S THE MAN WHO ABAND-ONED YOU!!

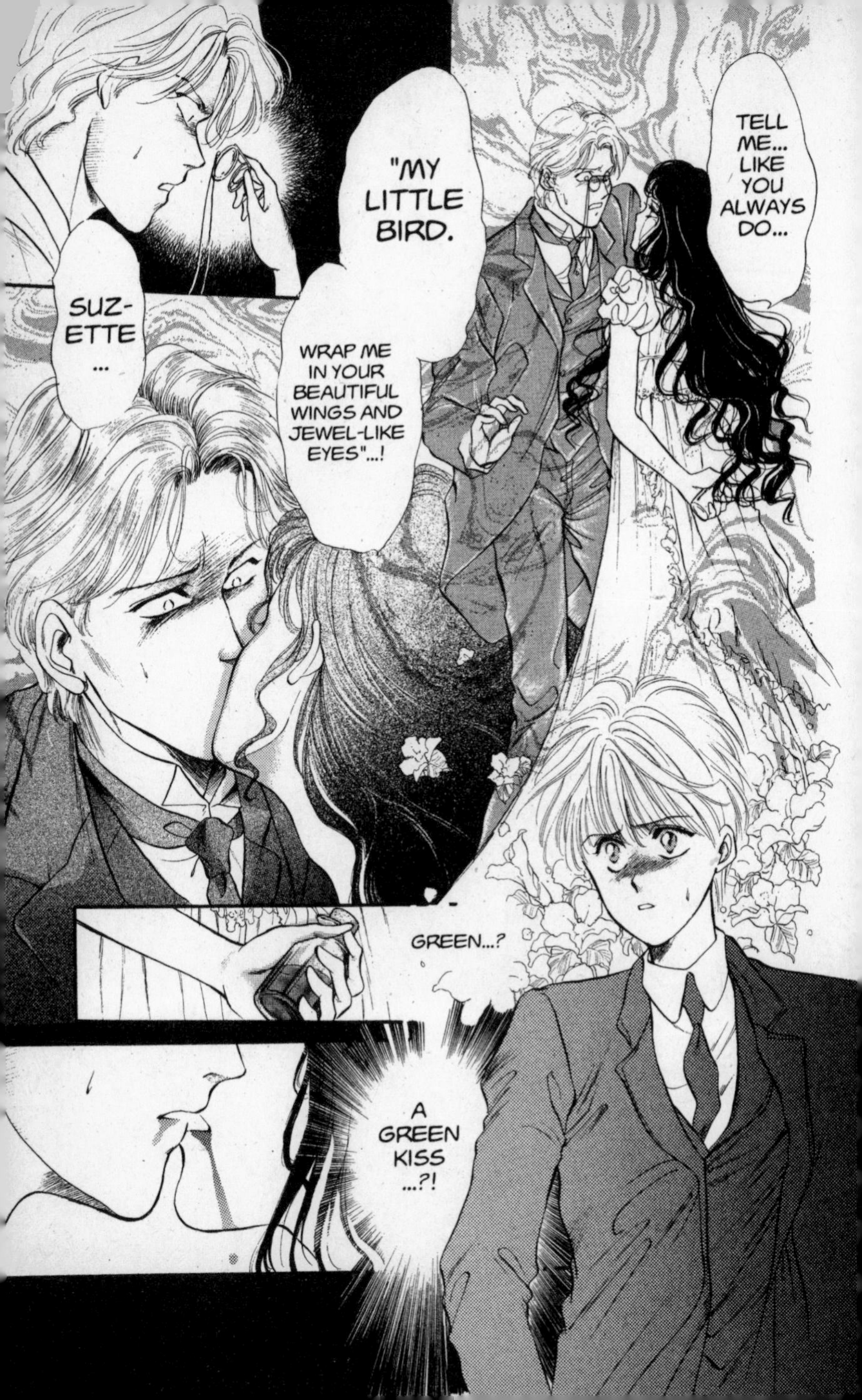
TELL ME... LIKE YOU ALWAYS DO...
"MY LITTLE BIRD.
WRAP ME IN YOUR BEAUTIFUL WINGS AND JEWEL-LIKE EYES"...!
SUZ-ETTE ...
GREEN...?
A GREEN KISS ...?!

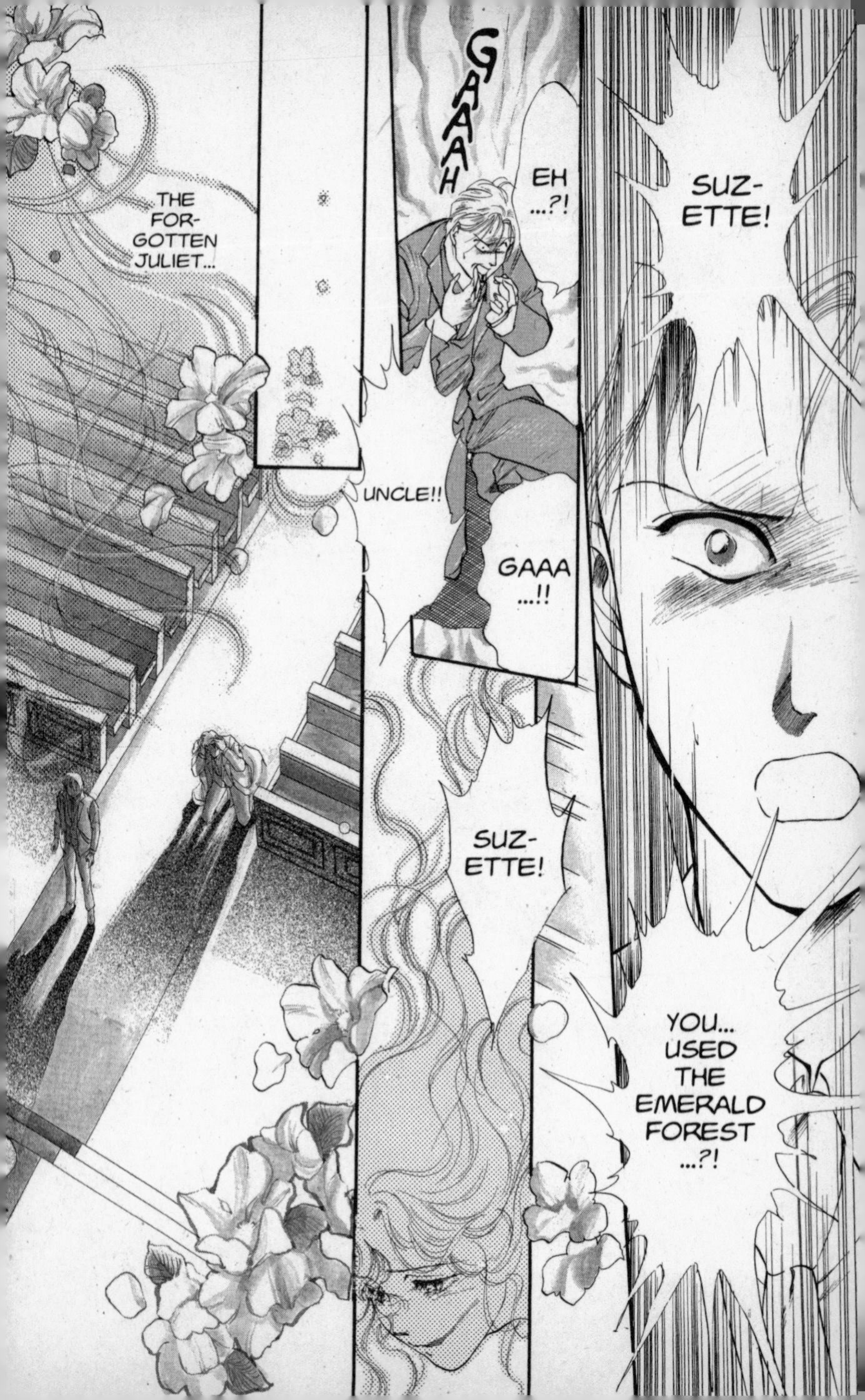
SUZ-
ETTE!
YOU...
USED
THE
EMERALD
FOREST
...?!
EH
...?!
GRAAAH
GAAA
...!!
UNCLE!!
SUZ-
ETTE!
THE
FOR-
GOTTEN
JULIET...

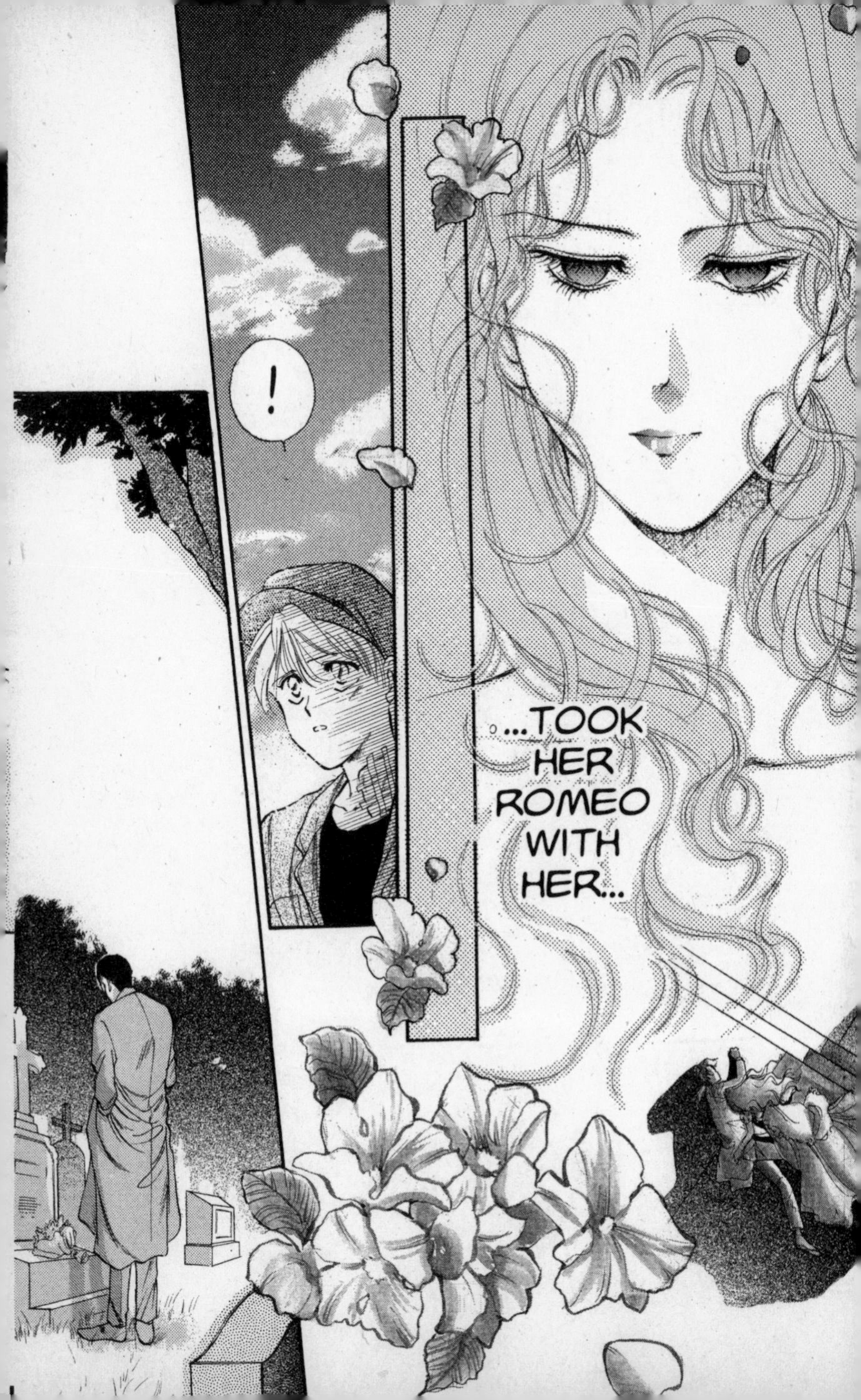
!
...TOOK HER ROMEO WITH HER...

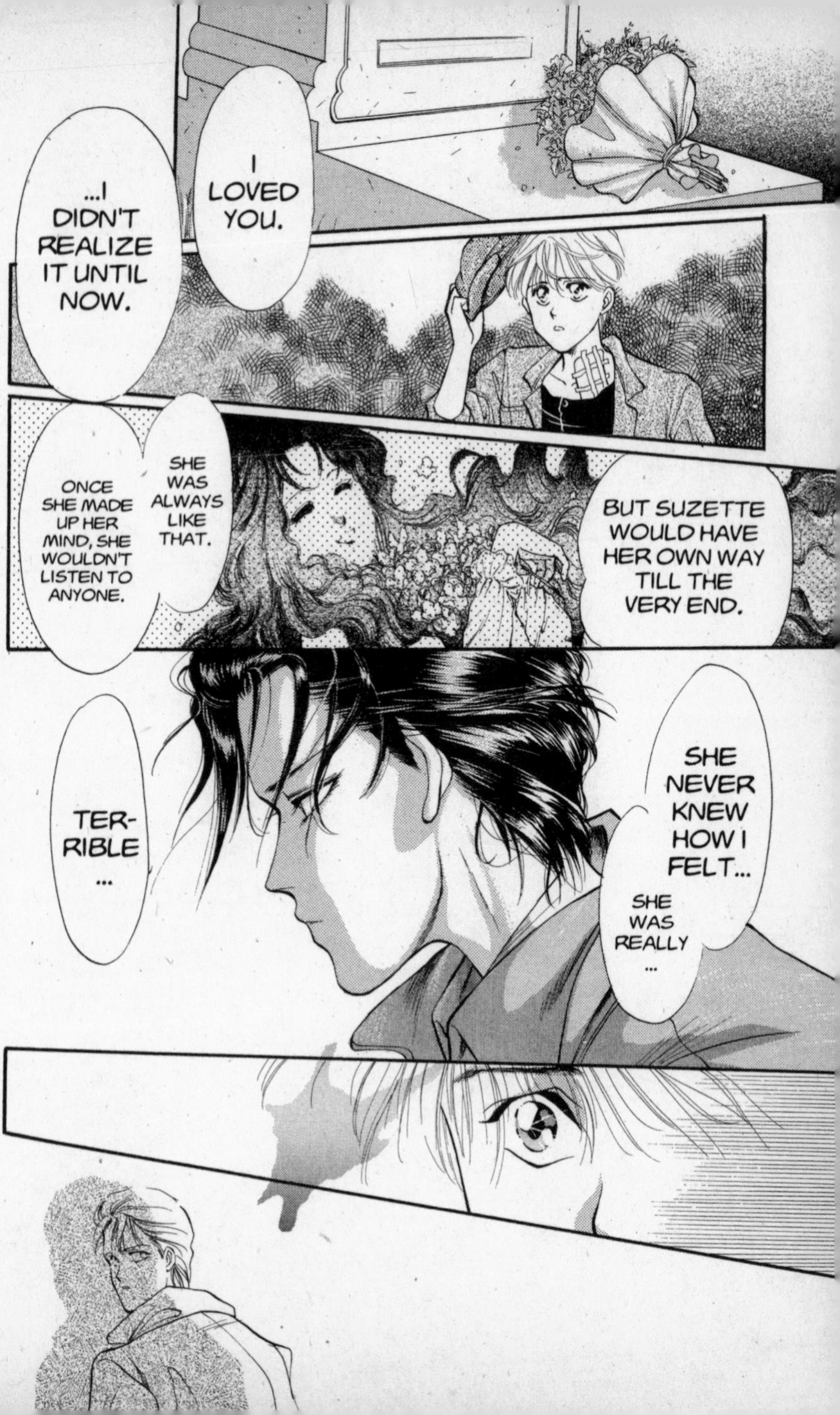
I LOVED YOU.
...I DIDN'T REALIZE IT UNTIL NOW.
BUT SUZETTE WOULD HAVE HER OWN WAY TILL THE VERY END.
SHE WAS ALWAYS LIKE THAT.
ONCE SHE MADE UP HER MIND, SHE WOULDN'T LISTEN TO ANYONE.
SHE NEVER KNEW HOW I FELT...
SHE WAS REALLY ...
TER-RIBLE ...

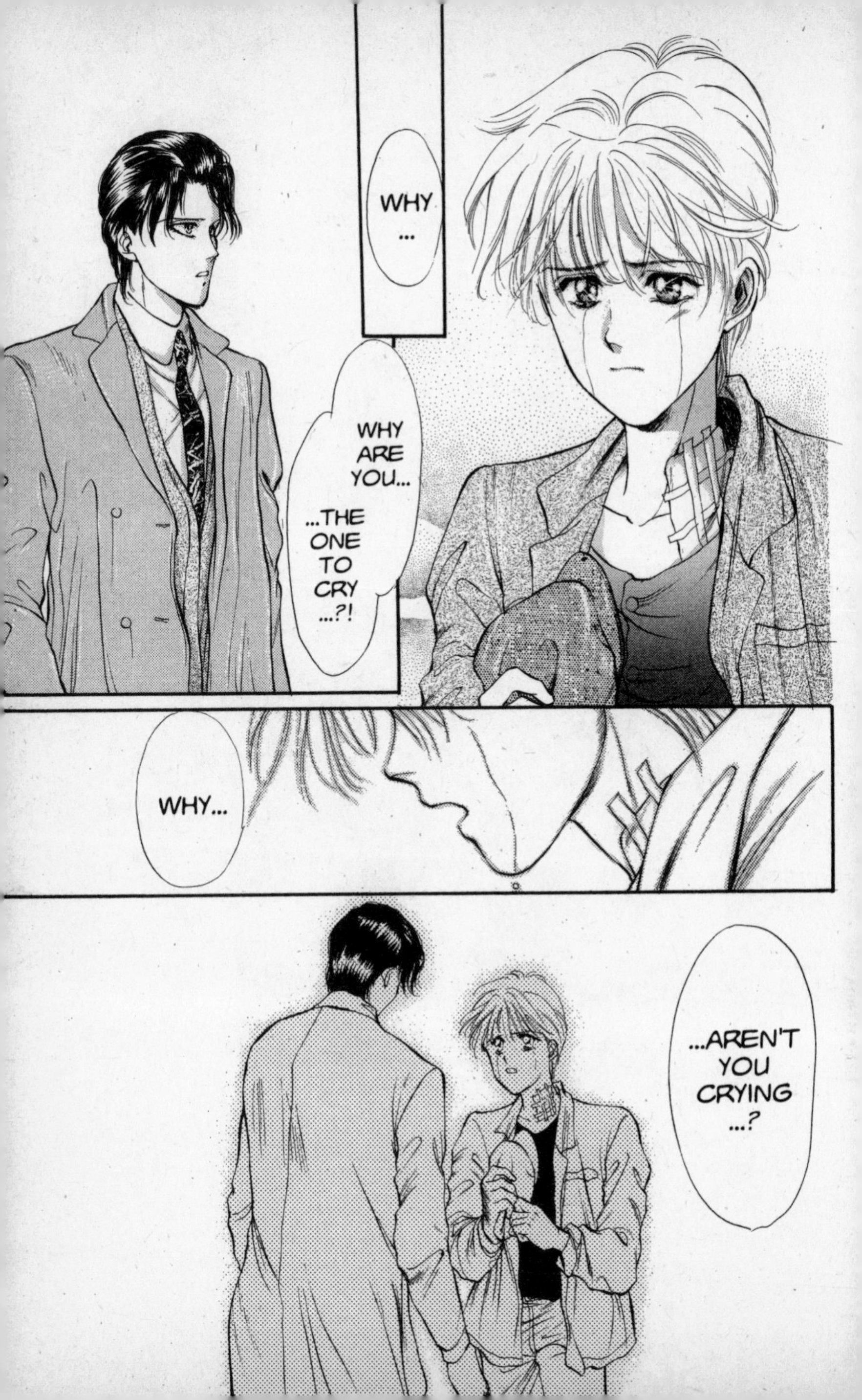
WHY ...
WHY ARE YOU... ...THE ONE TO CRY ...?!
WHY...
...AREN'T YOU CRYING ...?

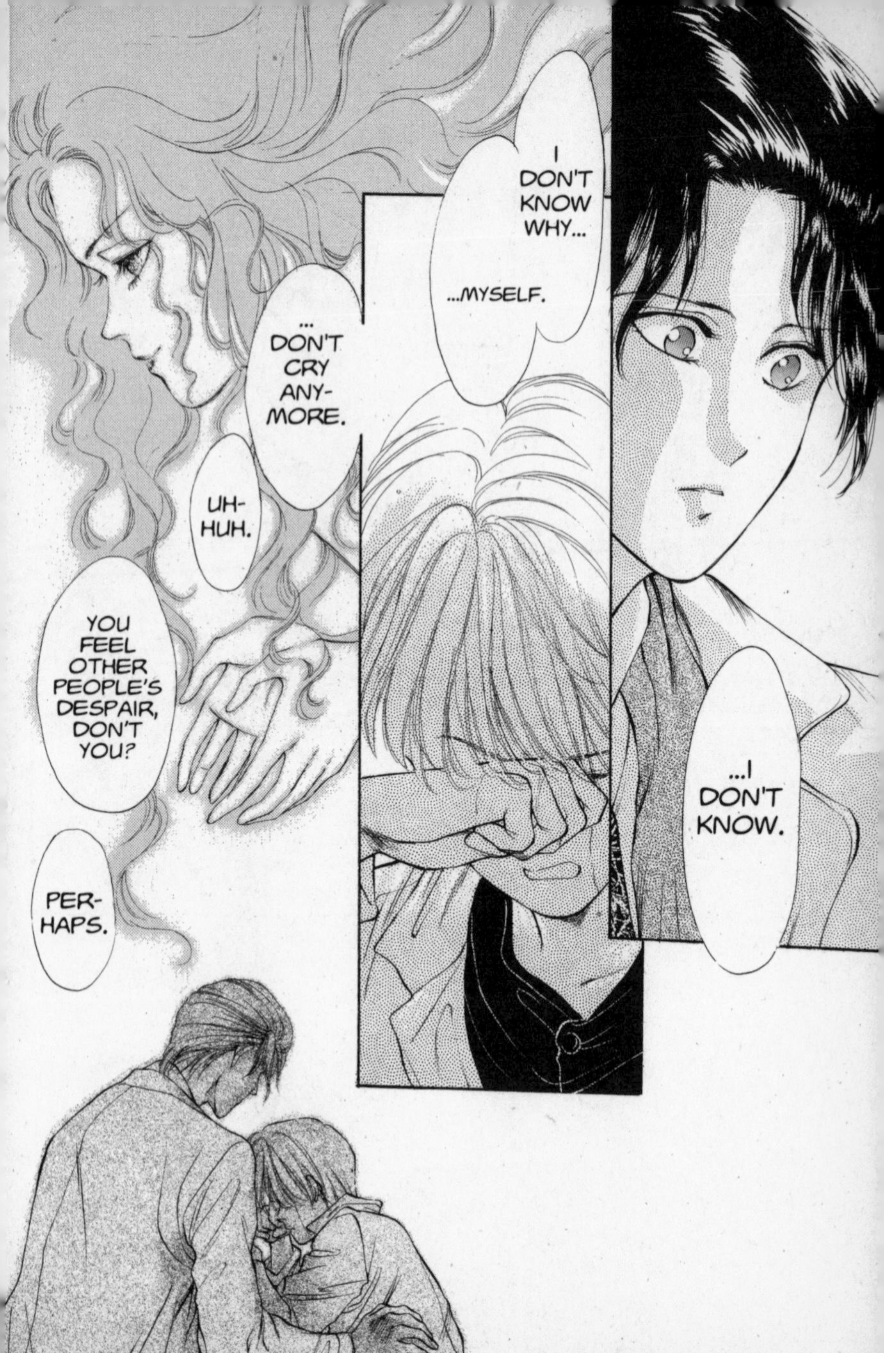
I DON'T KNOW WHY...
...MYSELF.
...I DON'T KNOW.
... DON'T CRY ANY-MORE.
UH-HUH.
YOU FEEL OTHER PEOPLE'S DESPAIR, DON'T YOU?
PER-HAPS.

Forgotten Juliet/The End

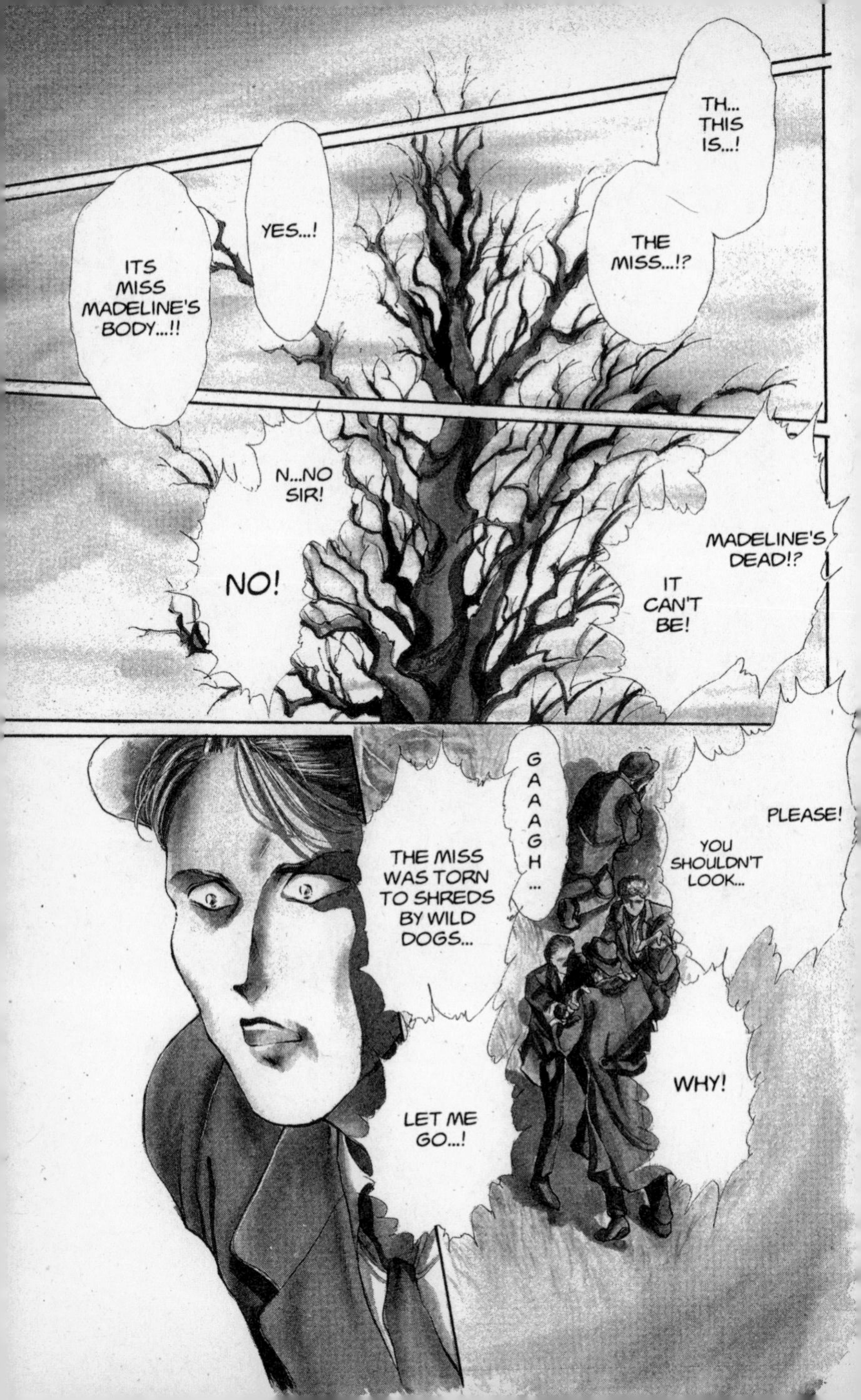
TH... THIS IS...!
THE MISS...!?
YES...!
ITS MISS MADELINE'S BODY...!!
MADELINE'S DEAD!?
IT CAN'T BE!
N...NO SIR!
NO!
PLEASE!
YOU SHOULDN'T LOOK...
GAAAGH...
THE MISS WAS TORN TO SHREDS BY WILD DOGS...
WHY!
LET ME GO...!

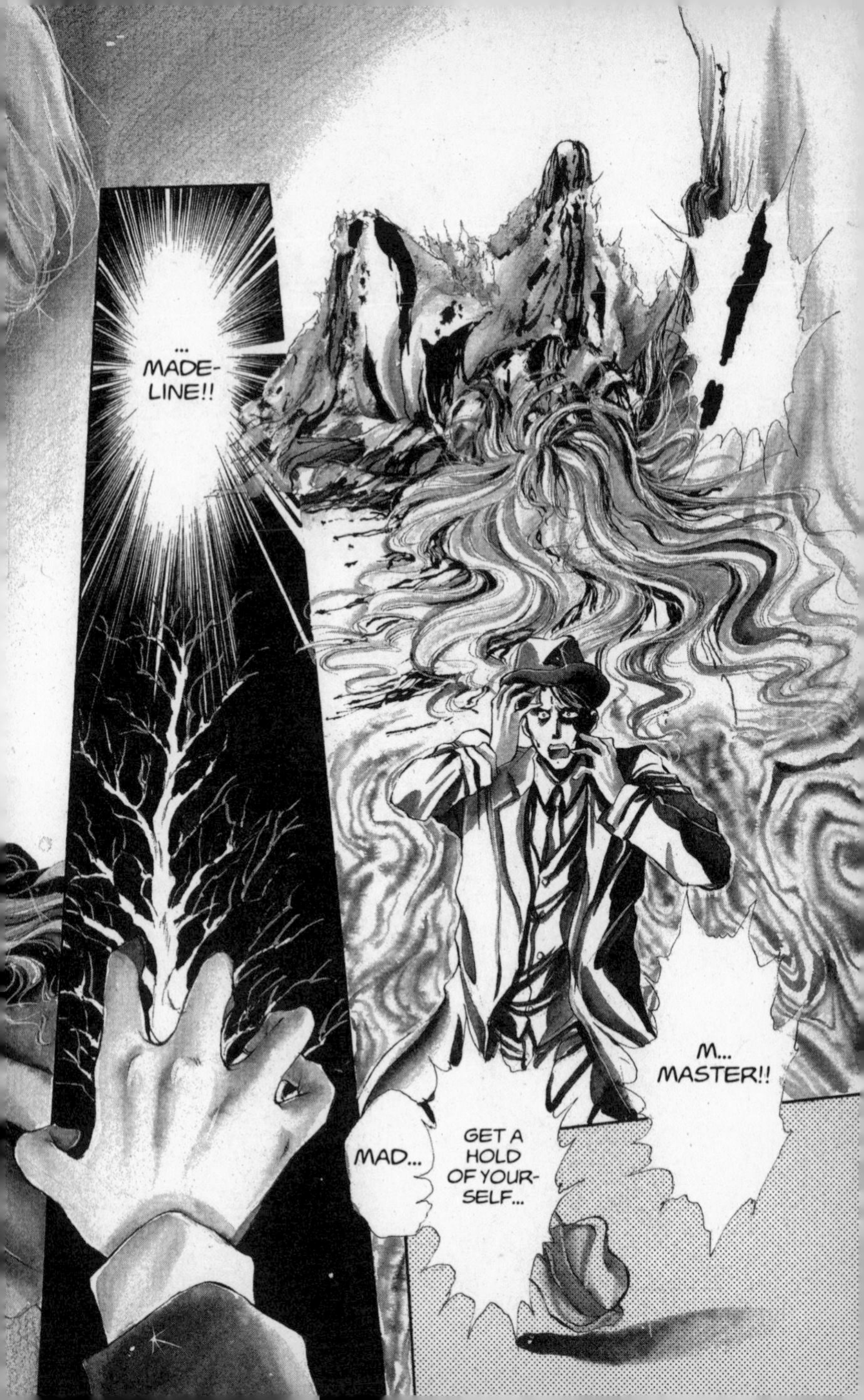
M... MASTER!!
GET A HOLD OF YOURSELF...
MAD...
... MADELINE!!

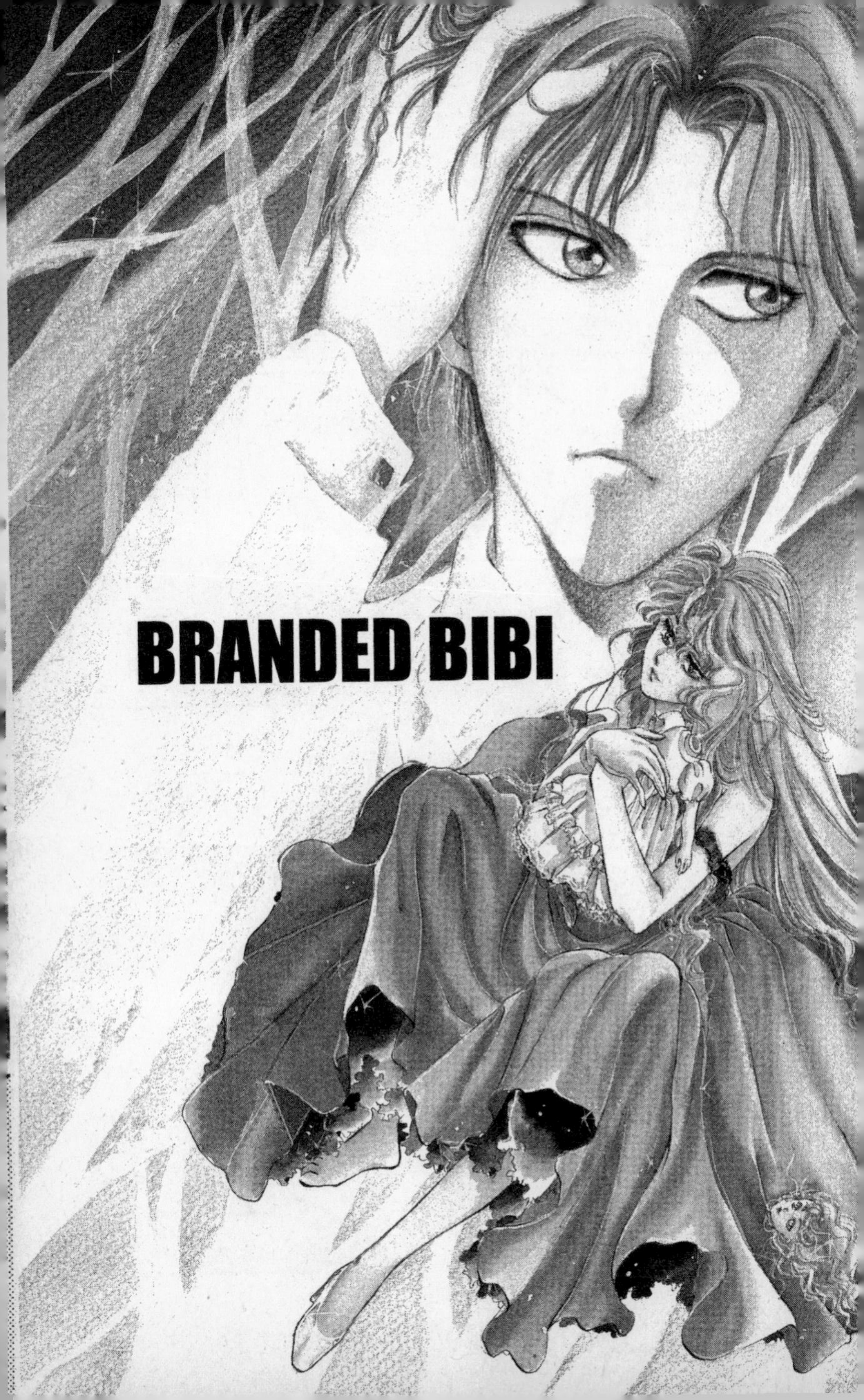
BRANDED BIBI

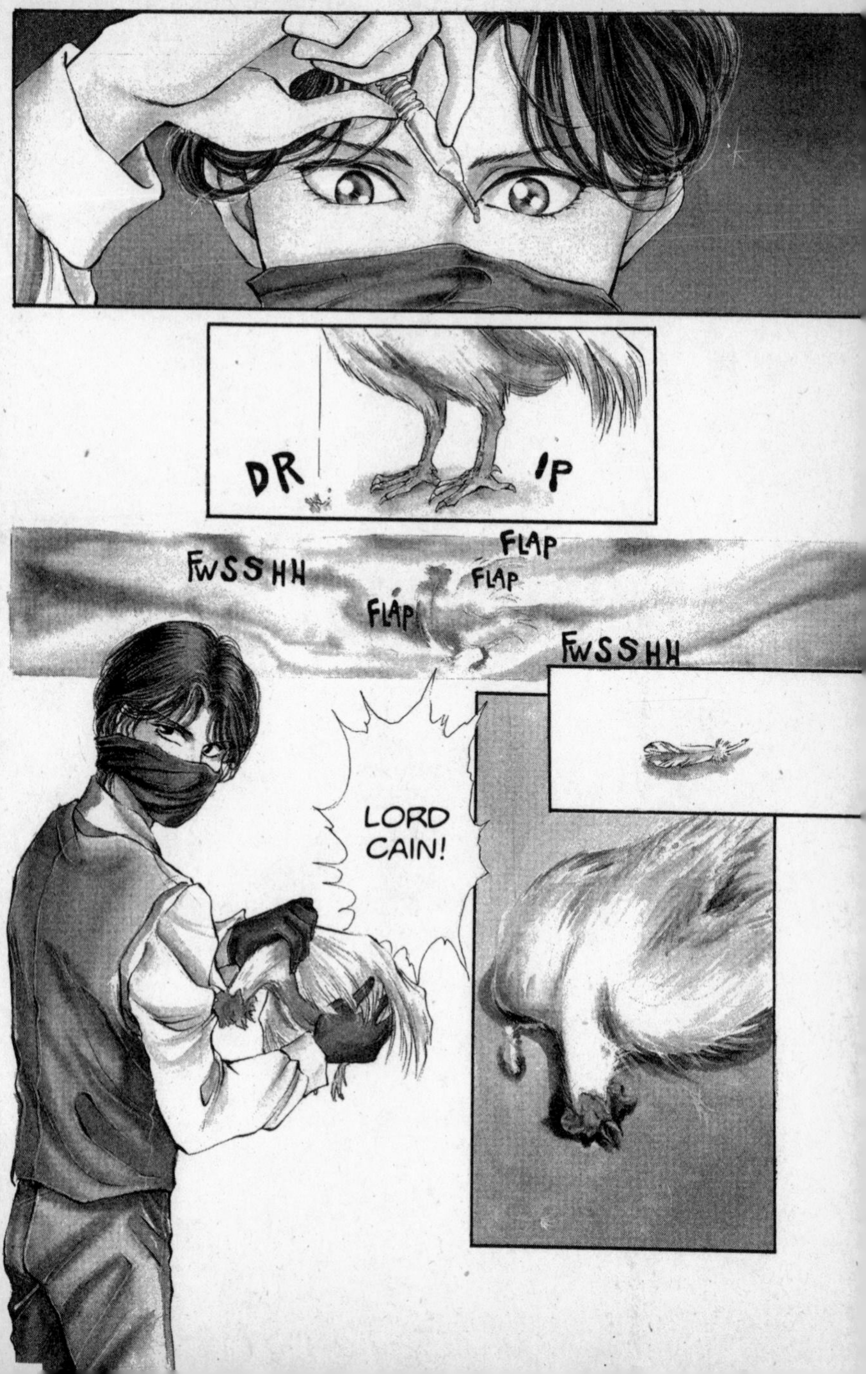
DR IP
FLAP
FLAP
FLAP
FWSSHH
FWSSHH
LORD CAIN!

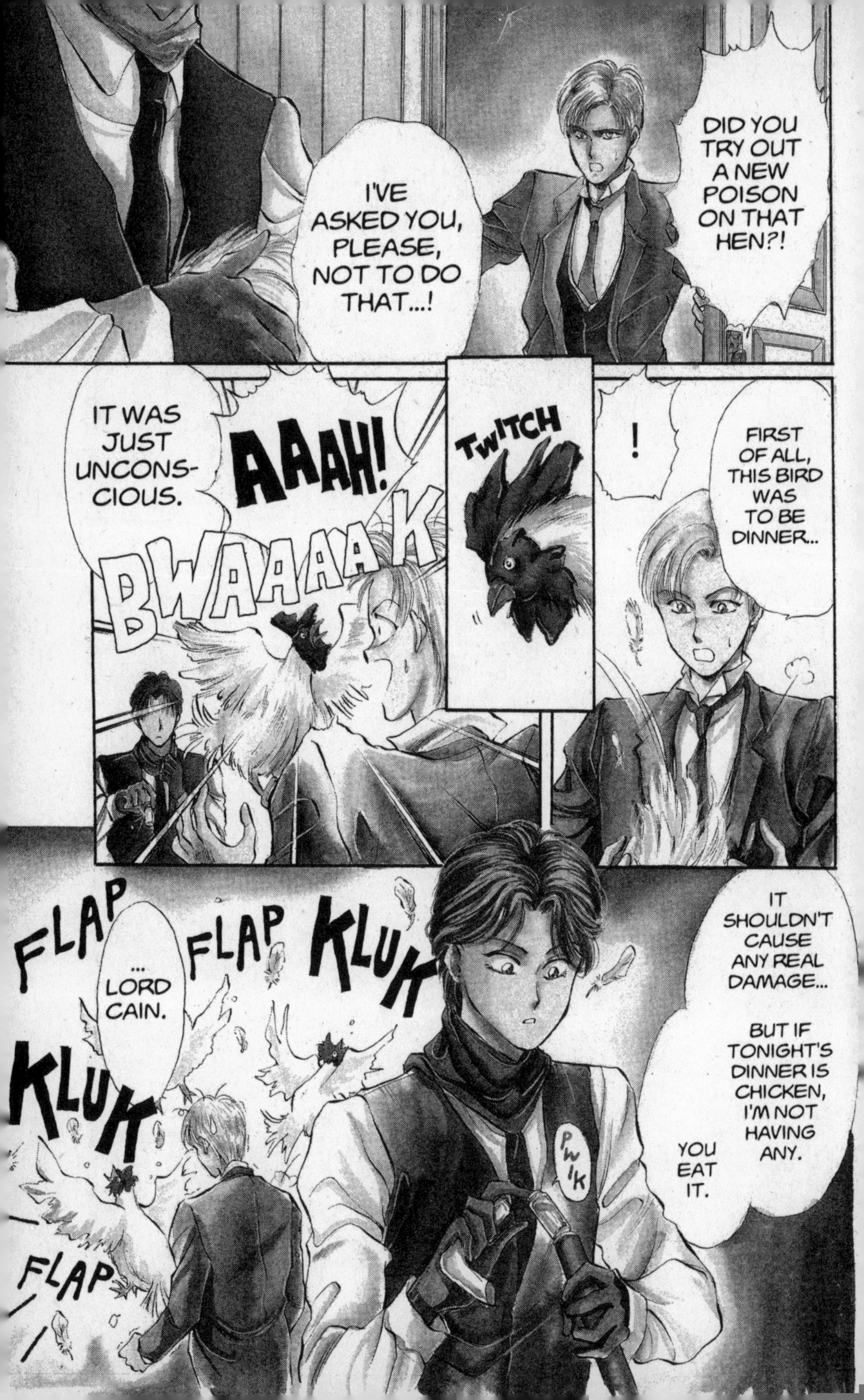
DID YOU TRY OUT A NEW POISON ON THAT HEN?!
I'VE ASKED YOU, PLEASE, NOT TO DO THAT...!
FIRST OF ALL, THIS BIRD WAS TO BE DINNER...
!
TWITCH
AAAH!
IT WAS JUST UNCONSCIOUS.
BWAAAAAK
IT SHOULDN'T CAUSE ANY REAL DAMAGE...
BUT IF TONIGHT'S DINNER IS CHICKEN, I'M NOT HAVING ANY.
YOU EAT IT.
PWIK
KLUK
FLAP
... LORD CAIN.
FLAP
KLUK
FLAP

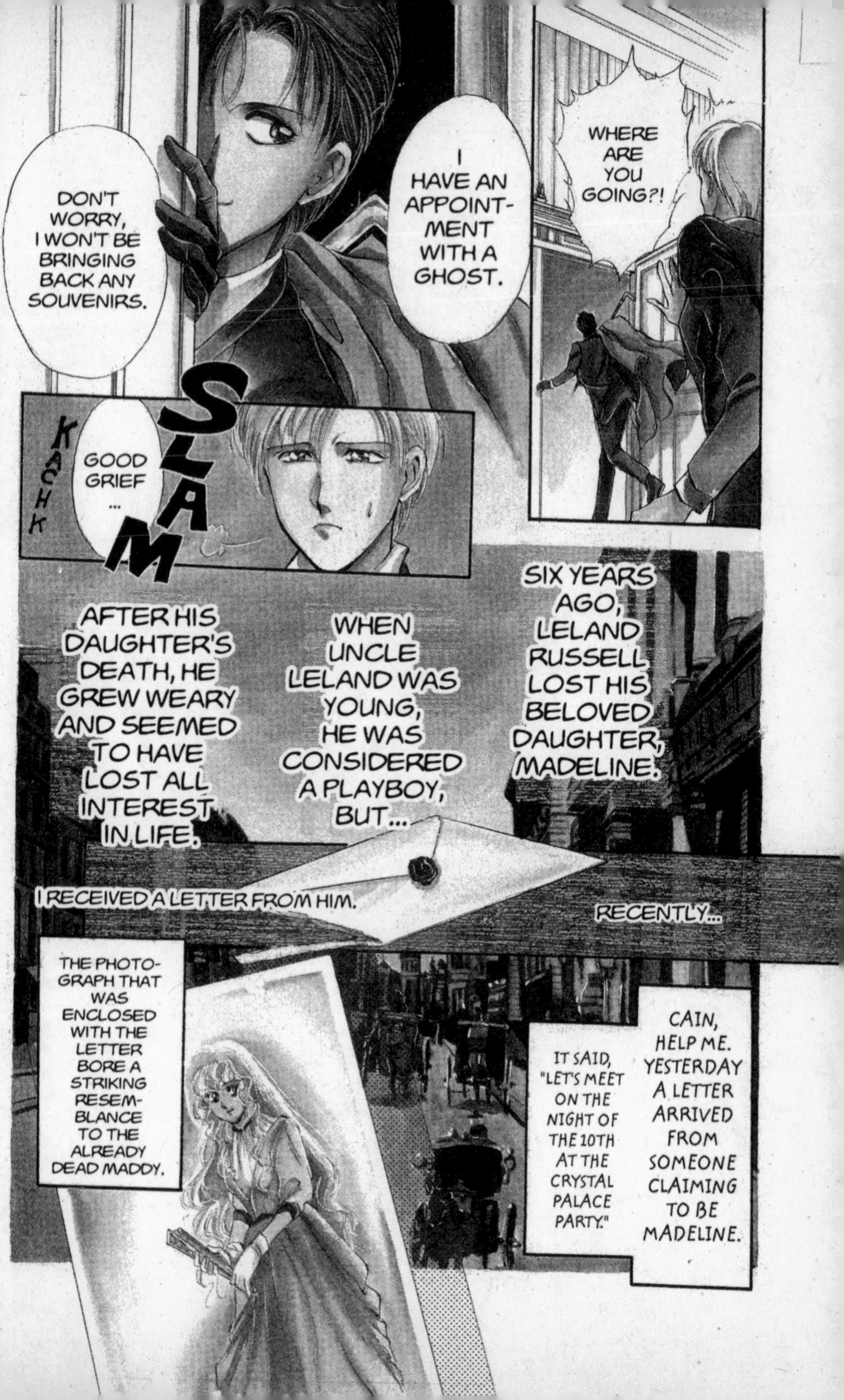
WHERE ARE YOU GOING?!
I HAVE AN APPOINTMENT WITH A GHOST.
DON'T WORRY, I WON'T BE BRINGING BACK ANY SOUVENIRS.
SLAM
GOOD GRIEF ...
KACHK
SIX YEARS AGO, LELAND RUSSELL LOST HIS BELOVED DAUGHTER, MADELINE.
WHEN UNCLE LELAND WAS YOUNG, HE WAS CONSIDERED A PLAYBOY, BUT...
AFTER HIS DAUGHTER'S DEATH, HE GREW WEARY AND SEEMED TO HAVE LOST ALL INTEREST IN LIFE.
RECENTLY...
I RECEIVED A LETTER FROM HIM.
CAIN, HELP ME. YESTERDAY A LETTER ARRIVED FROM SOMEONE CLAIMING TO BE MADELINE.
IT SAID, "LET'S MEET ON THE NIGHT OF THE 10TH AT THE CRYSTAL PALACE PARTY."
THE PHOTOGRAPH THAT WAS ENCLOSED WITH THE LETTER BORE A STRIKING RESEMBLANCE TO THE ALREADY DEAD MADDY.

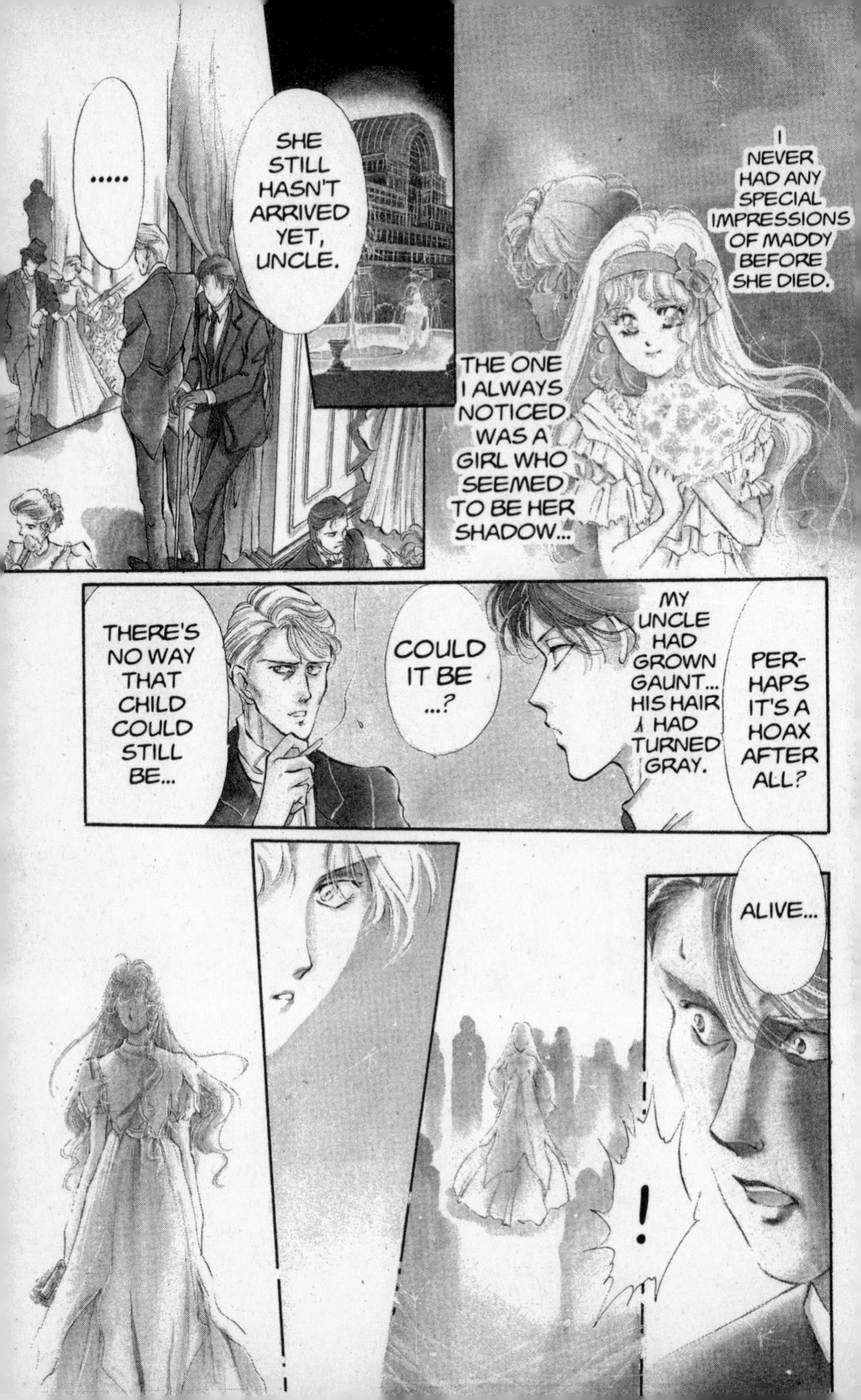
I NEVER HAD ANY SPECIAL IMPRESSIONS OF MADDY BEFORE SHE DIED.
THE ONE I ALWAYS NOTICED WAS A GIRL WHO SEEMED TO BE HER SHADOW...
SHE STILL HASN'T ARRIVED YET, UNCLE.
.....
PER-HAPS IT'S A HOAX AFTER ALL?
MY UNCLE HAD GROWN GAUNT... HIS HAIR HAD TURNED GRAY.
COULD IT BE ...?
THERE'S NO WAY THAT CHILD COULD STILL BE...
ALIVE...
!

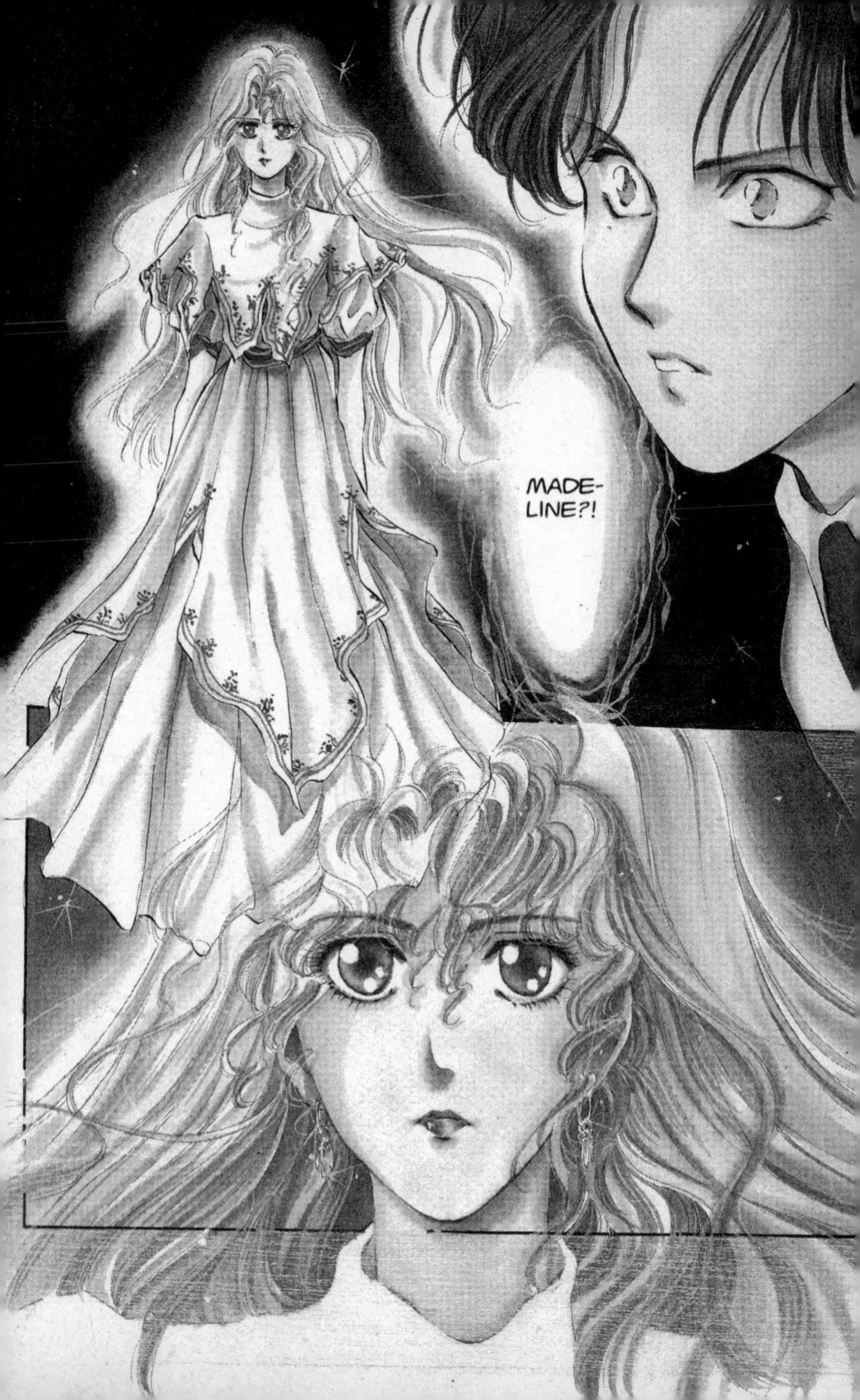
MADE-
LINE?!

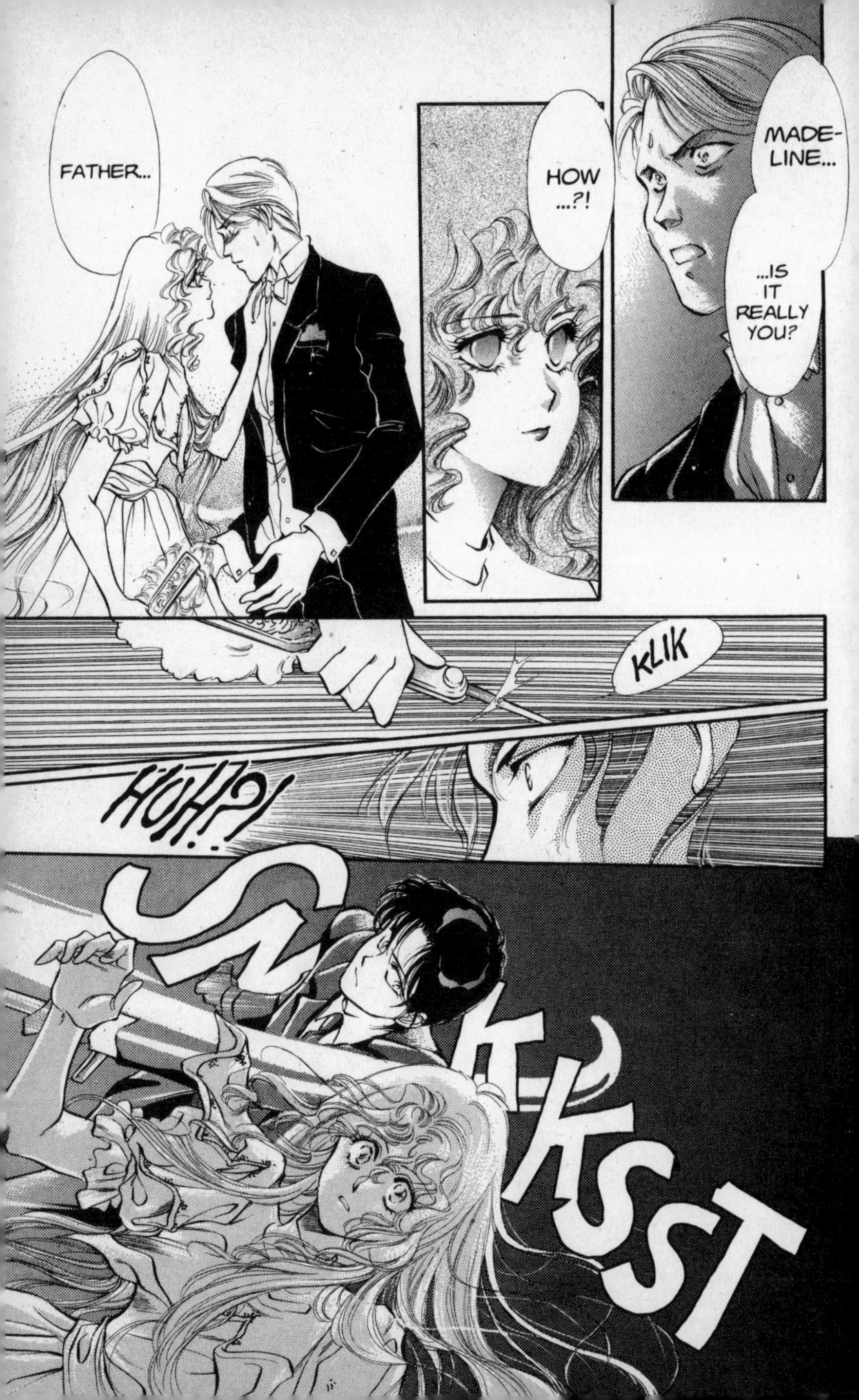
MADE-LINE...
...IS IT REALLY YOU?
HOW ...?!
FATHER...
KLIK
HUH?!..
SNK-KSST

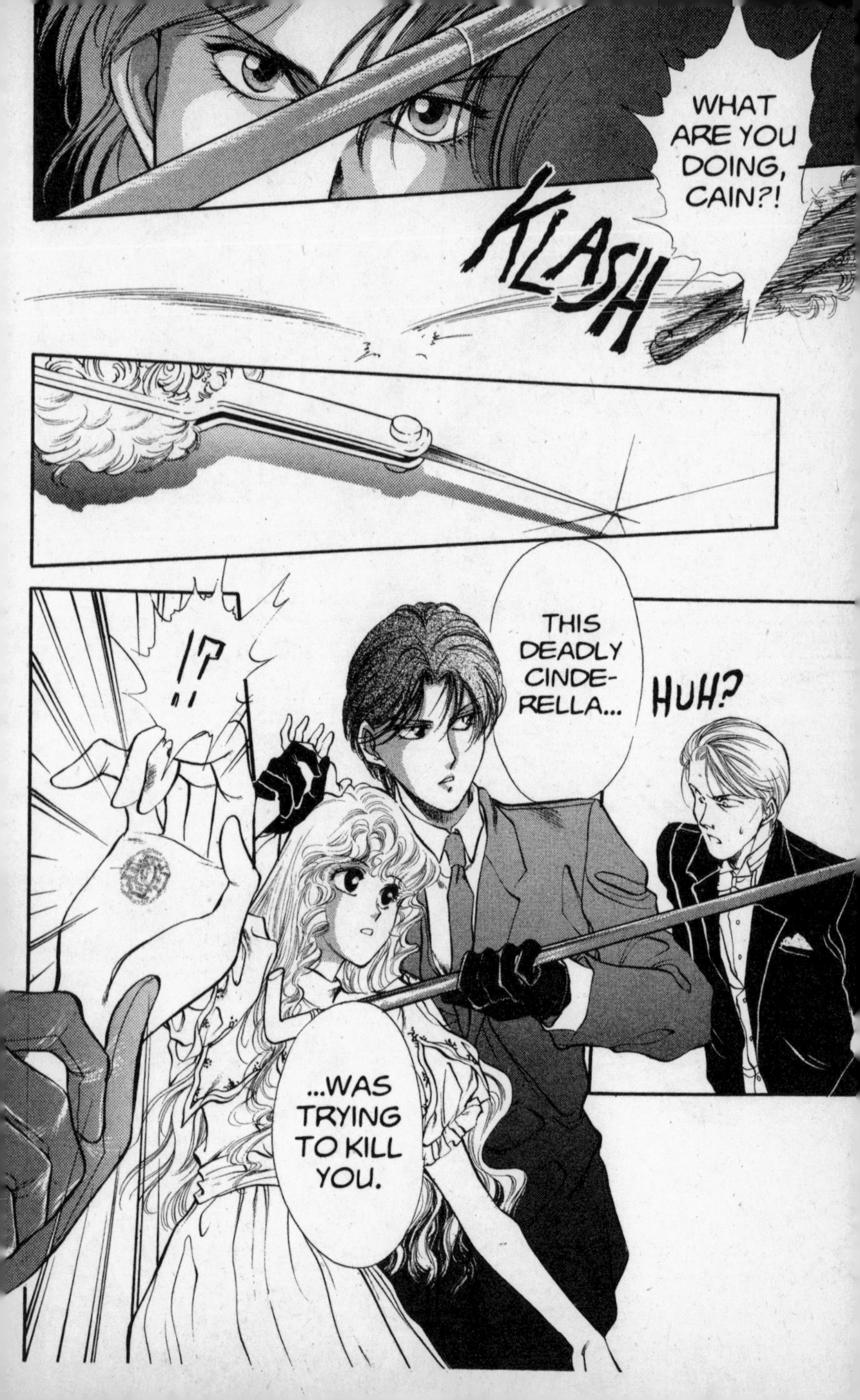
WHAT ARE YOU DOING, CAIN?!
KLASH
HUH?
THIS DEADLY CINDE-RELLA...
!?
...WAS TRYING TO KILL YOU.

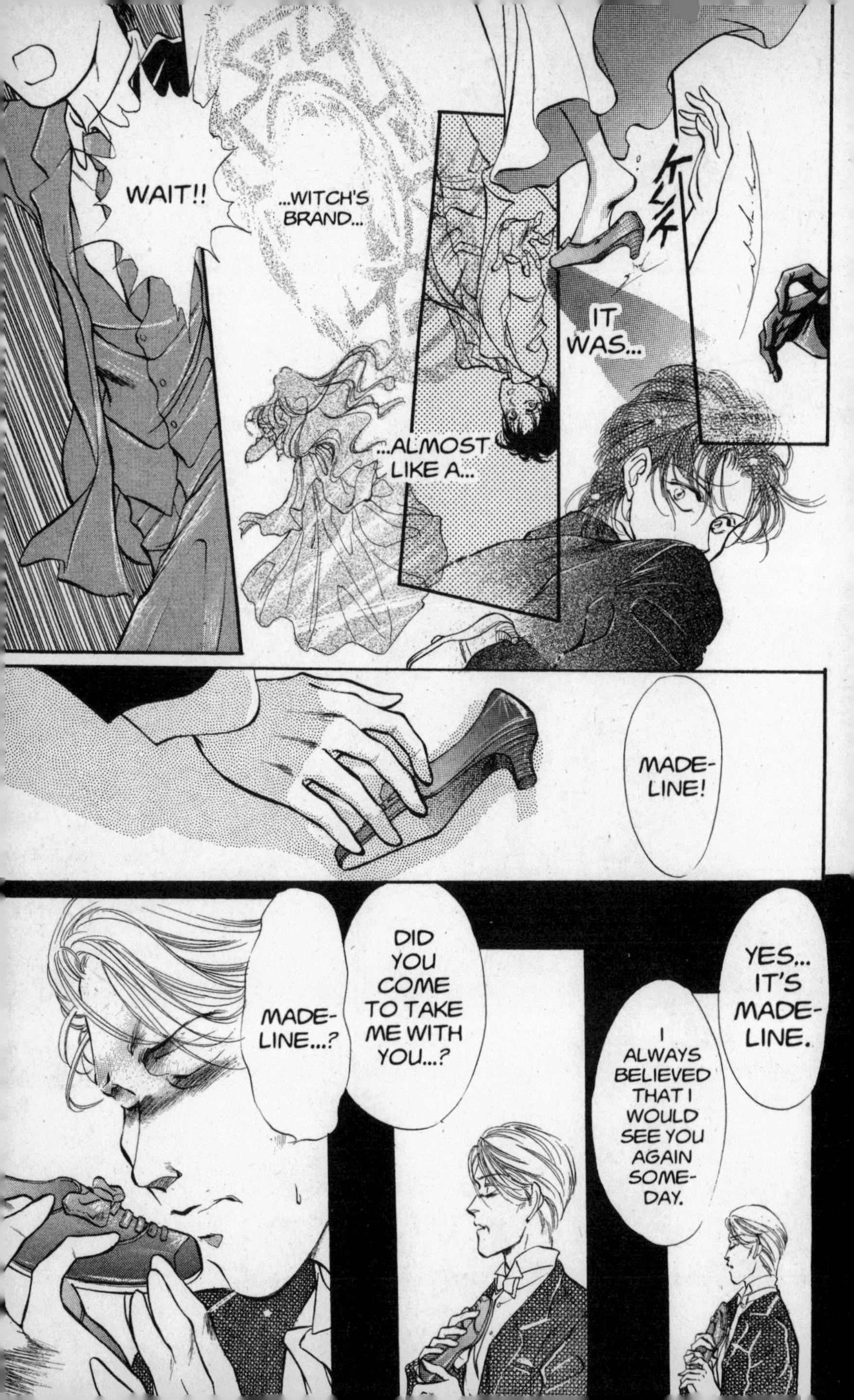
KLIK
IT WAS...
...ALMOST LIKE A...
...WITCH'S BRAND...
WAIT!!
MADE-LINE!
YES... IT'S MADE-LINE.
I ALWAYS BELIEVED THAT I WOULD SEE YOU AGAIN SOME-DAY.
DID YOU COME TO TAKE ME WITH YOU...?
MADE-LINE...?

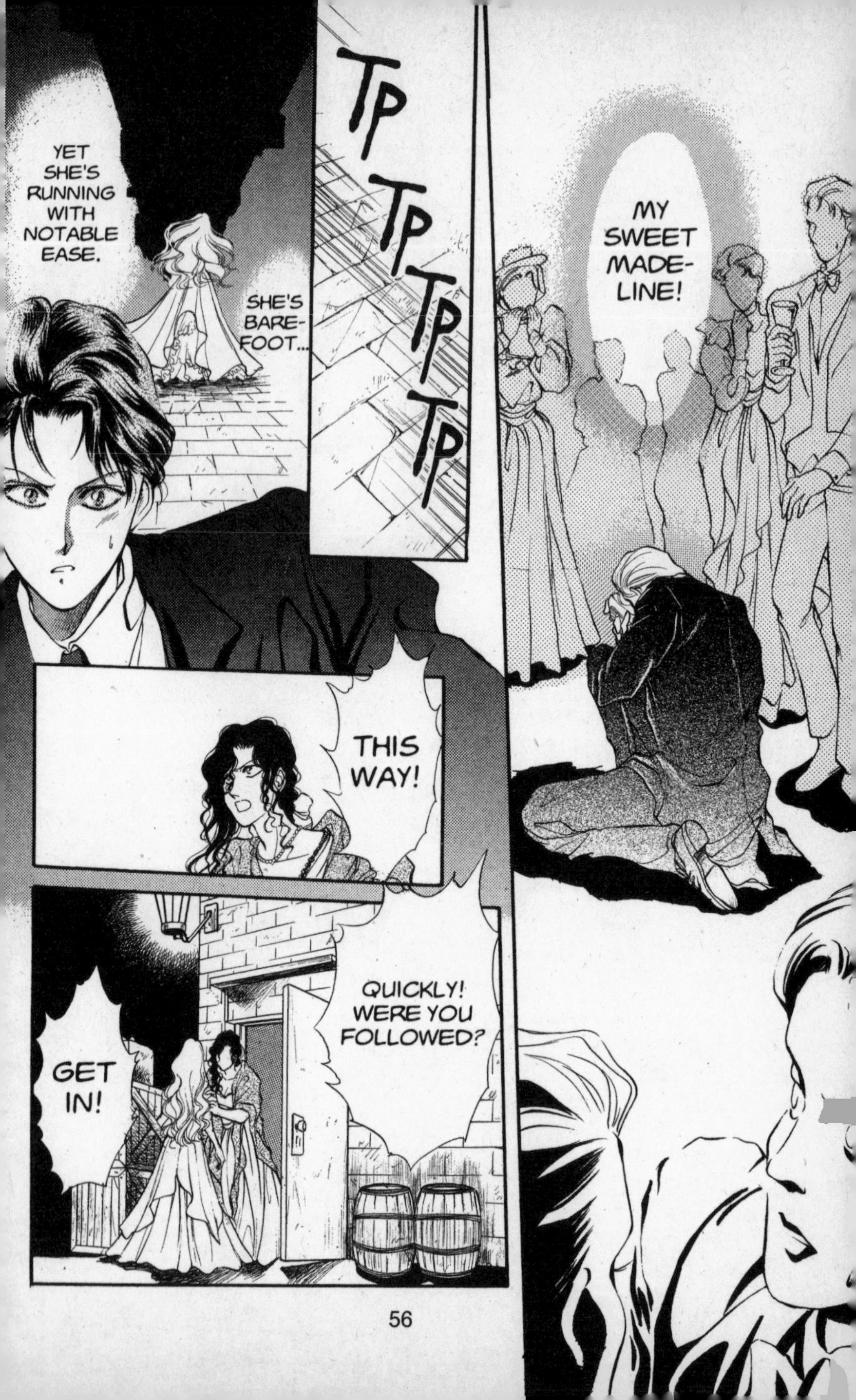
MY SWEET MADE-LINE!
TP TP TP TP TP
YET SHE'S RUNNING WITH NOTABLE EASE.
SHE'S BARE-FOOT...
THIS WAY!
QUICKLY! WERE YOU FOLLOWED?
GET IN!

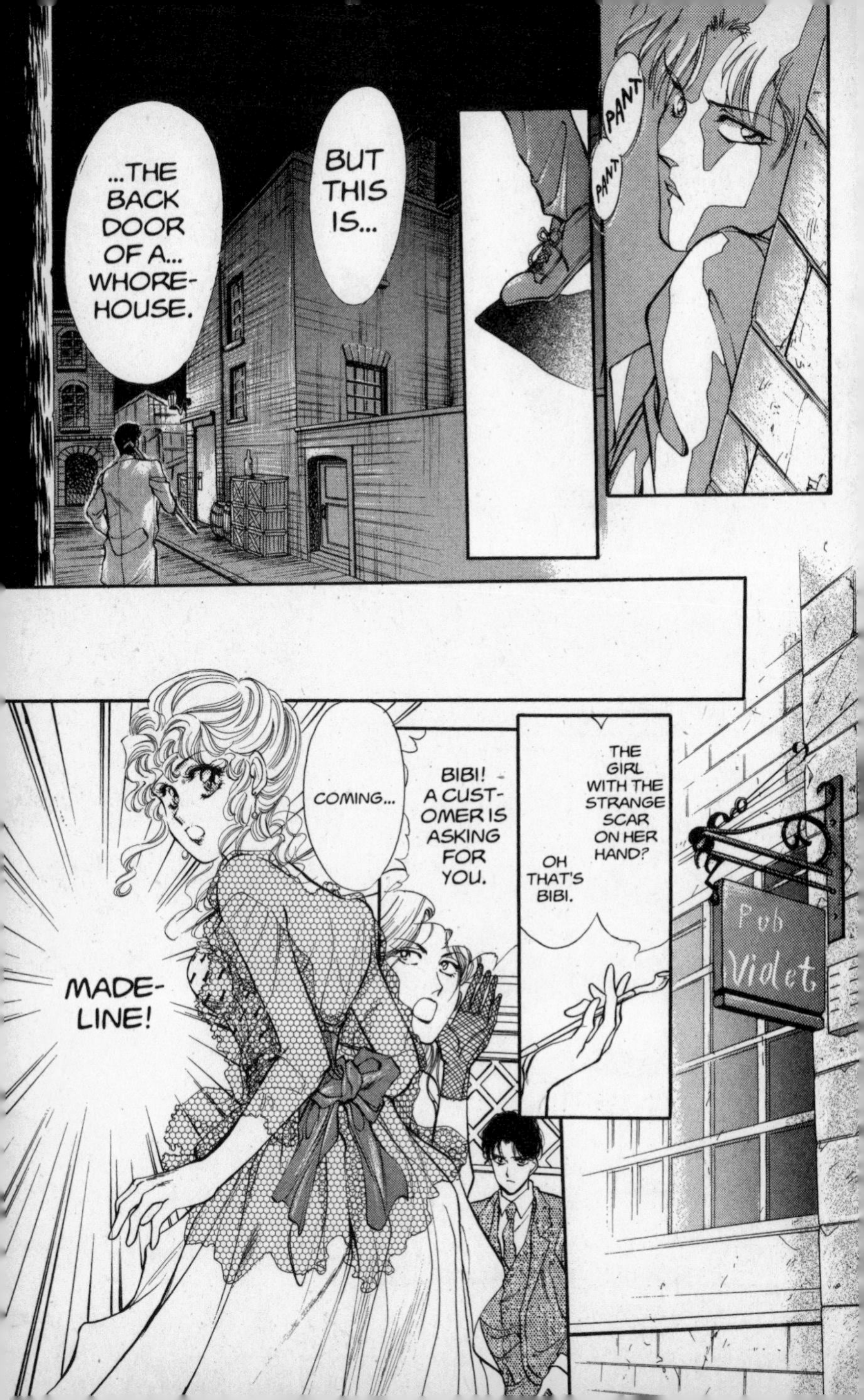
PANT
PANT
BUT THIS IS...
...THE BACK DOOR OF A... WHORE-HOUSE.
Pub Violet
THE GIRL WITH THE STRANGE SCAR ON HER HAND?
OH THAT'S BIBI.
BIBI! A CUST-OMER IS ASKING FOR YOU.
COMING...
MADE-LINE!

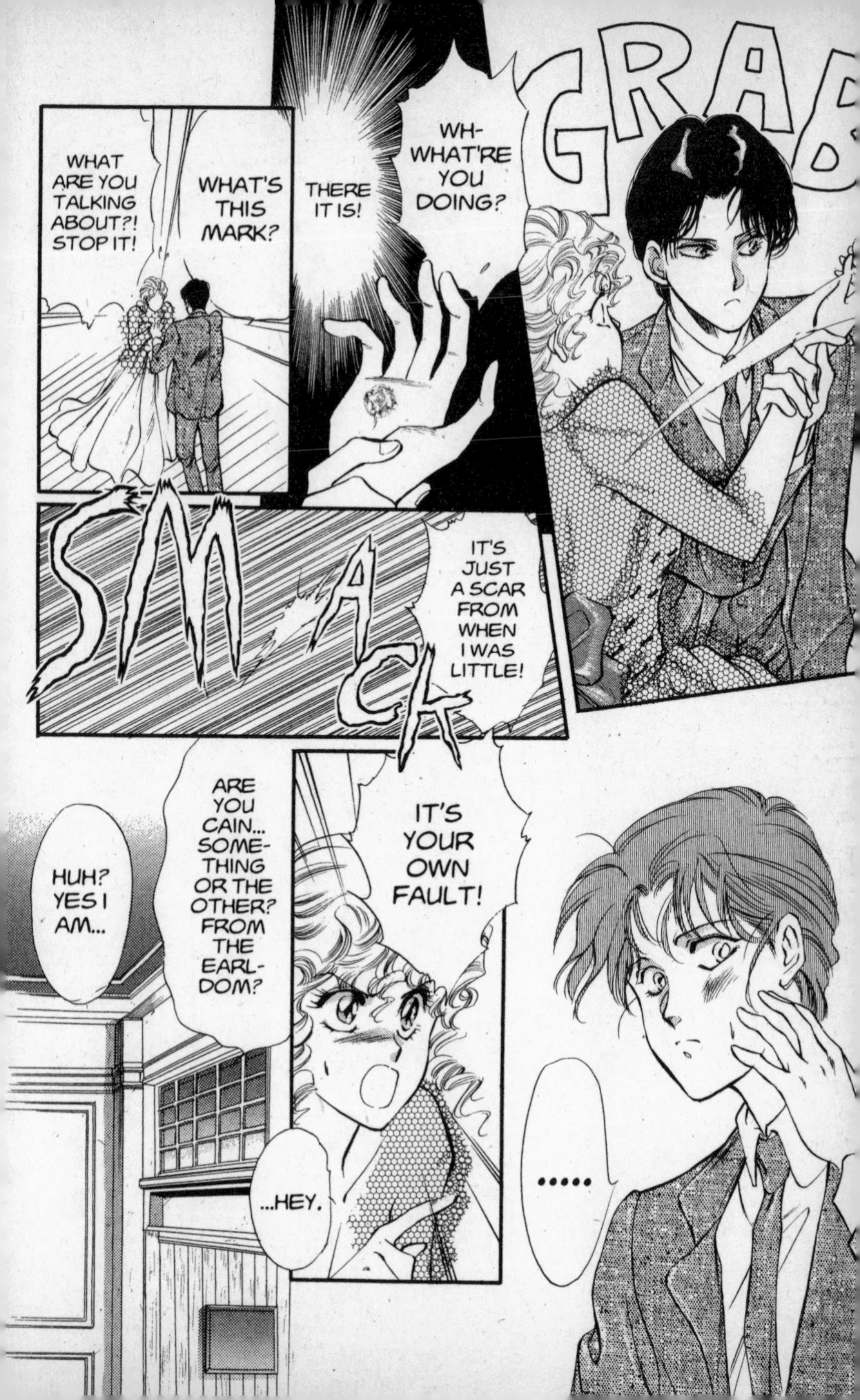
GRAB
WH- WHAT'RE YOU DOING?
THERE IT IS!
WHAT'S THIS MARK?
WHAT ARE YOU TALKING ABOUT?! STOP IT!
IT'S JUST A SCAR FROM WHEN I WAS LITTLE!
SMACK
.....
IT'S YOUR OWN FAULT!
...HEY.
ARE YOU CAIN... SOMETHING OR THE OTHER? FROM THE EARLDOM?
HUH? YES I AM...

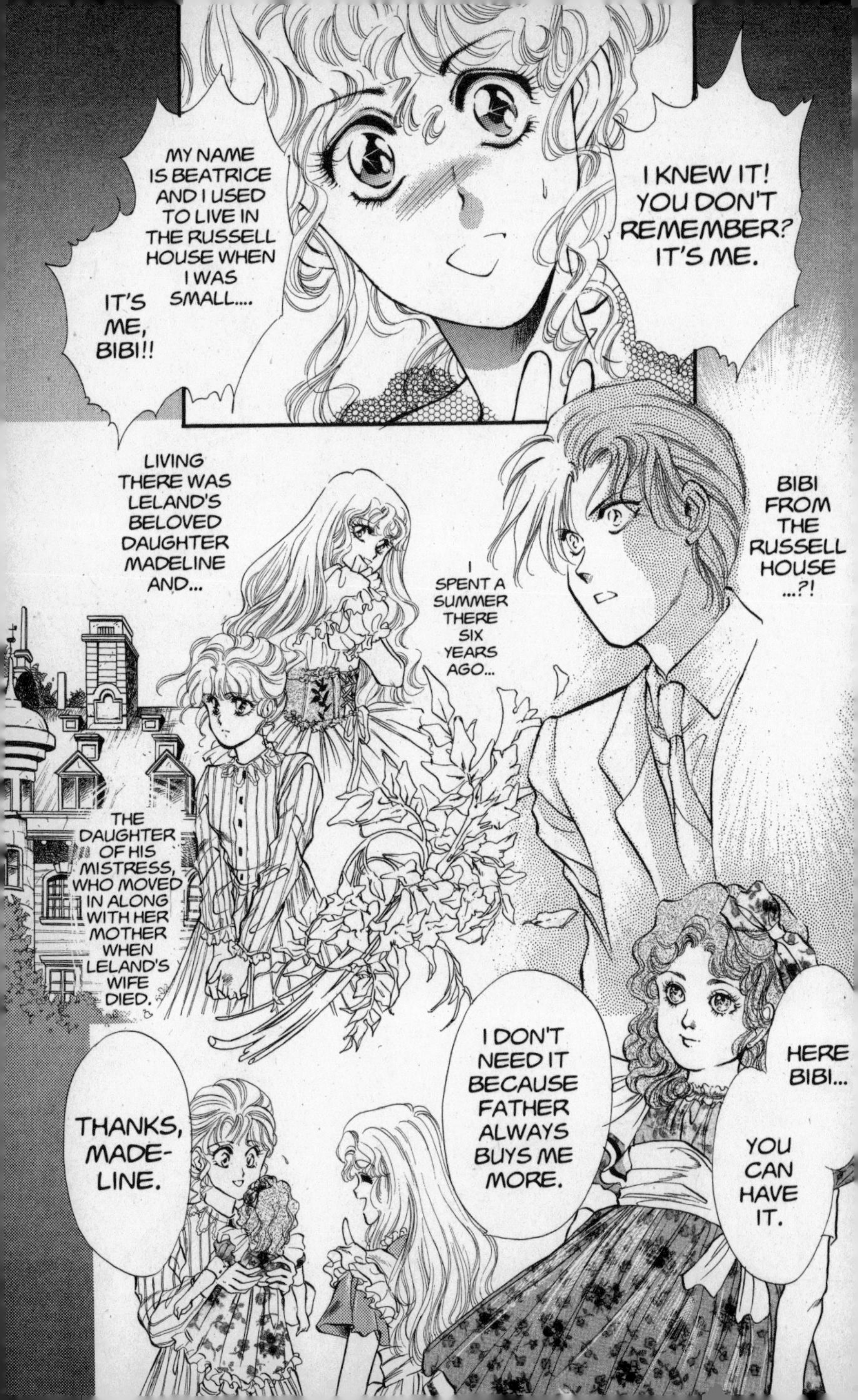
I KNEW IT! YOU DON'T REMEMBER? IT'S ME.
MY NAME IS BEATRICE AND I USED TO LIVE IN THE RUSSELL HOUSE WHEN I WAS SMALL....
IT'S ME, BIBI!!
BIBI FROM THE RUSSELL HOUSE ...?!
I SPENT A SUMMER THERE SIX YEARS AGO...
LIVING THERE WAS LELAND'S BELOVED DAUGHTER MADELINE AND...
THE DAUGHTER OF HIS MISTRESS, WHO MOVED IN ALONG WITH HER MOTHER WHEN LELAND'S WIFE DIED.
HERE BIBI...
YOU CAN HAVE IT.
I DON'T NEED IT BECAUSE FATHER ALWAYS BUYS ME MORE.
THANKS, MADE-LINE.

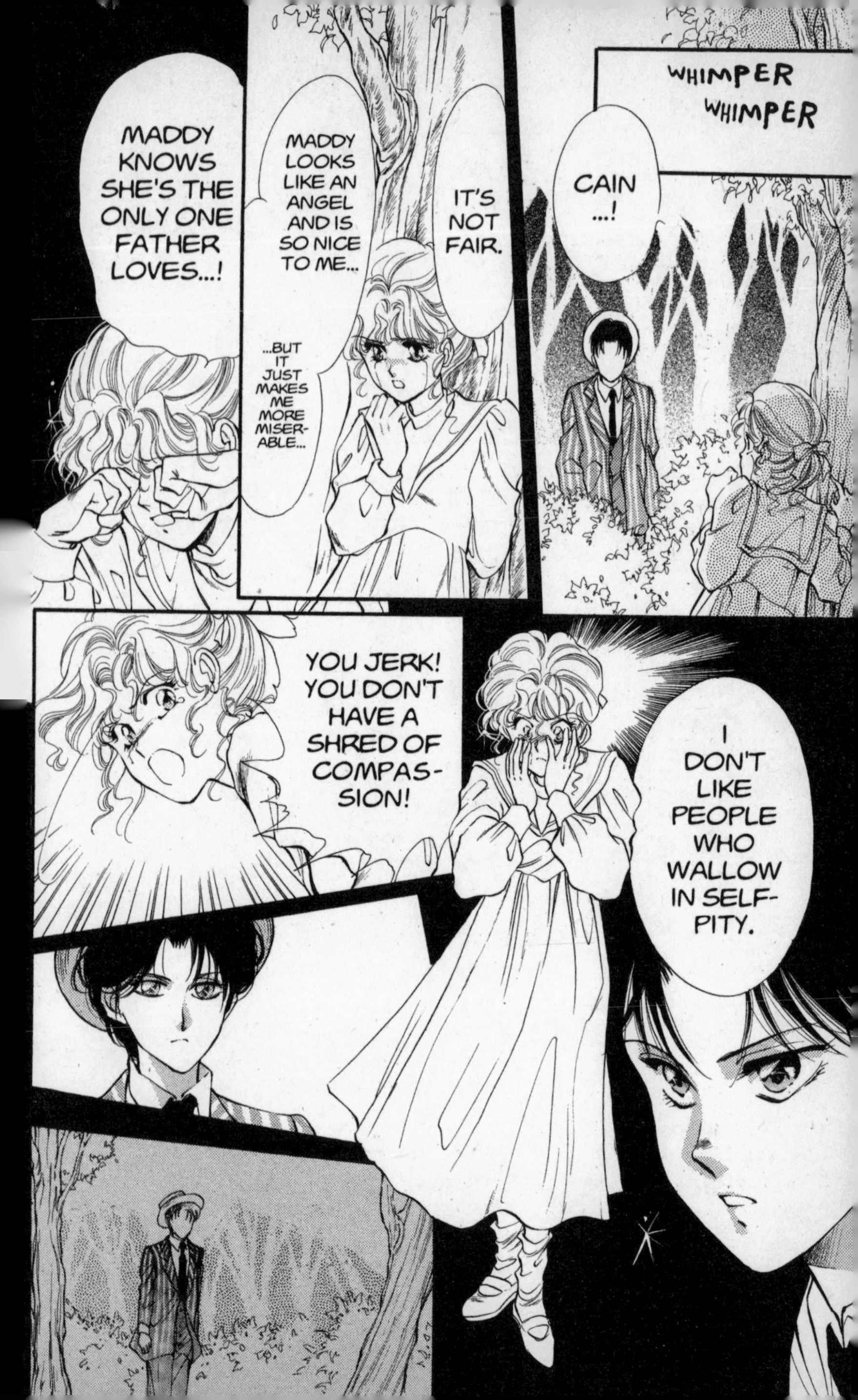
WHIMPER WHIMPER
CAIN ...!
IT'S NOT FAIR.
MADDY LOOKS LIKE AN ANGEL AND IS SO NICE TO ME...
...BUT IT JUST MAKES ME MORE MISERABLE...
MADDY KNOWS SHE'S THE ONLY ONE FATHER LOVES...!
I DON'T LIKE PEOPLE WHO WALLOW IN SELF-PITY.
YOU JERK! YOU DON'T HAVE A SHRED OF COMPASSION!

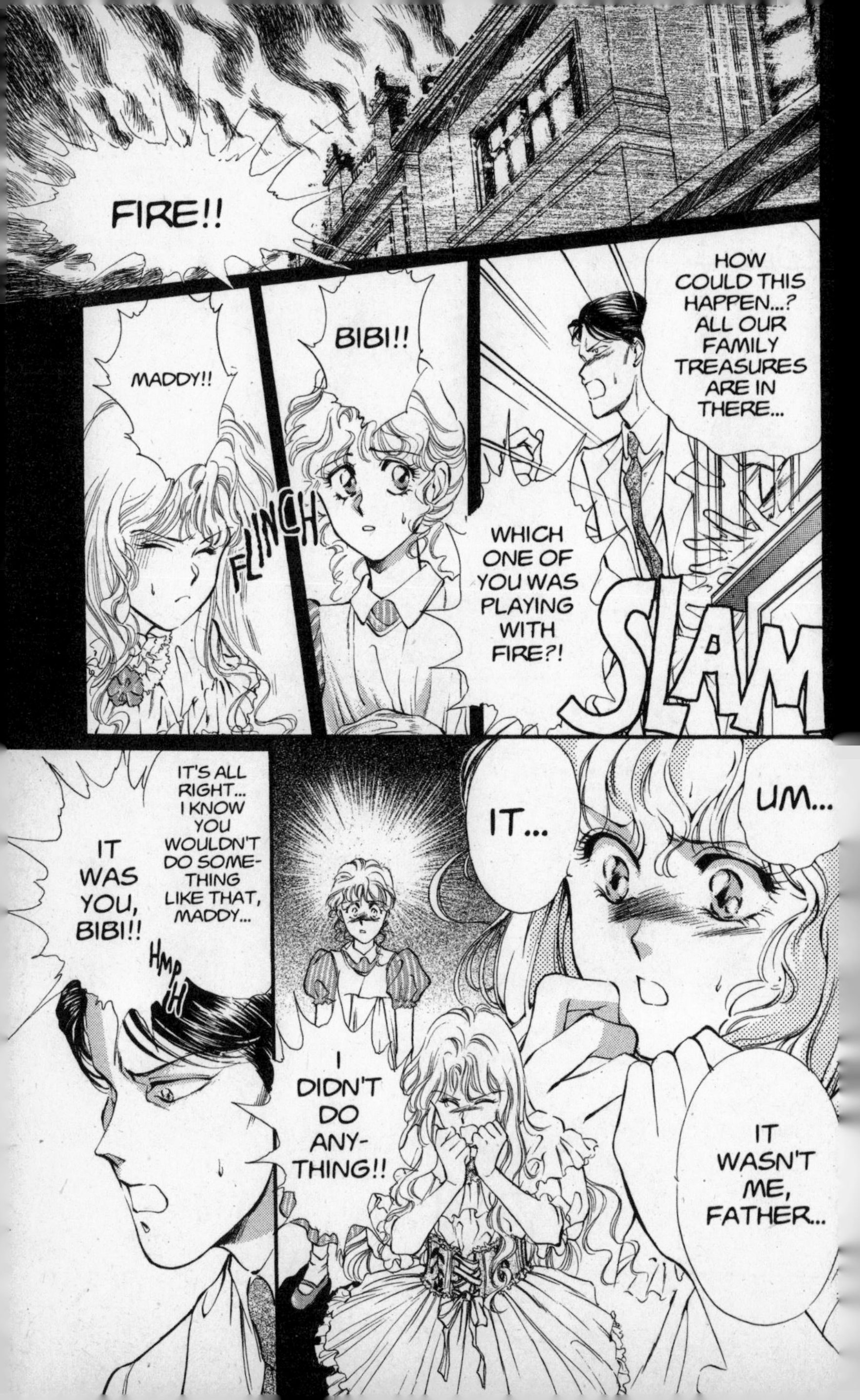
FIRE!!
HOW COULD THIS HAPPEN...? ALL OUR FAMILY TREASURES ARE IN THERE...
WHICH ONE OF YOU WAS PLAYING WITH FIRE?!
SLAM
BIBI!!
FLINCH
MADDY!!
UM...
IT...
IT WASN'T ME, FATHER...
I DIDN'T DO ANY-THING!!
IT'S ALL RIGHT... I KNOW YOU WOULDN'T DO SOME-THING LIKE THAT, MADDY...
IT WAS YOU, BIBI!!
HMPH

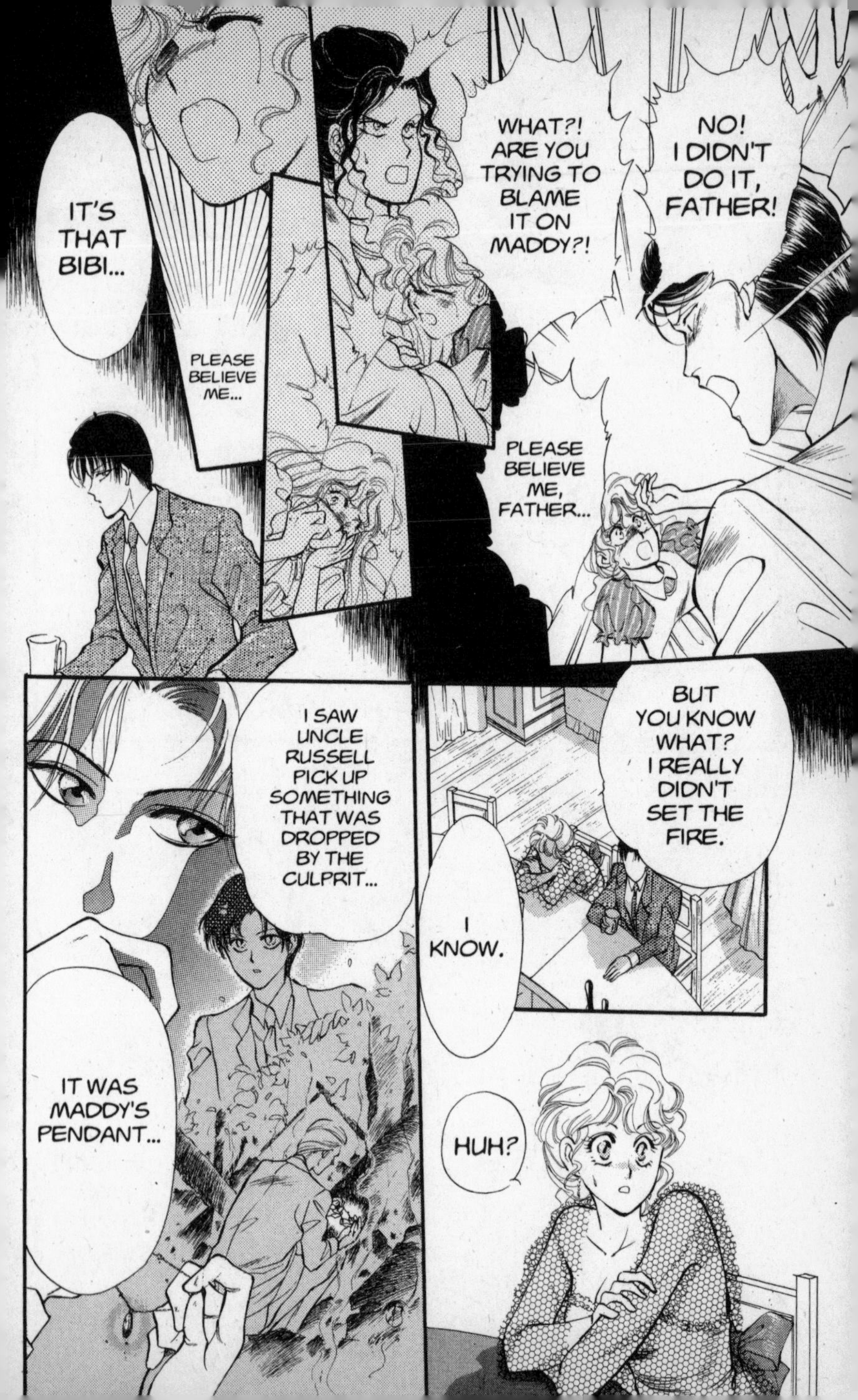
NO! I DIDN'T DO IT, FATHER!
WHAT?! ARE YOU TRYING TO BLAME IT ON MADDY?!
PLEASE BELIEVE ME, FATHER...
IT'S THAT BIBI...
PLEASE BELIEVE ME...
BUT YOU KNOW WHAT? I REALLY DIDN'T SET THE FIRE.
I KNOW.
HUH?
I SAW UNCLE RUSSELL PICK UP SOMETHING THAT WAS DROPPED BY THE CULPRIT...
IT WAS MADDY'S PENDANT...

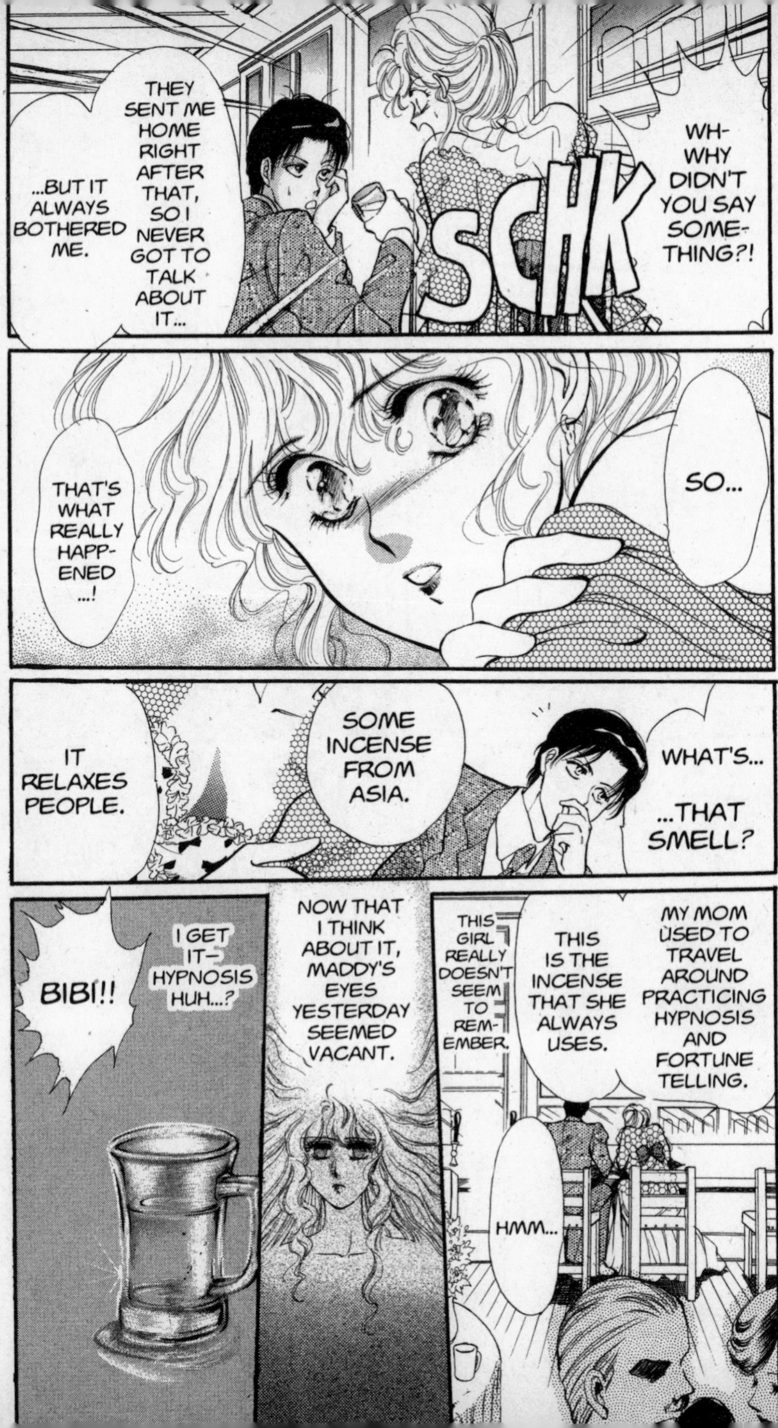
WH- WHY DIDN'T YOU SAY SOME-THING?!
SCHK
THEY SENT ME HOME RIGHT AFTER THAT, SO I NEVER GOT TO TALK ABOUT IT...
...BUT IT ALWAYS BOTHERED ME.
SO...
THAT'S WHAT REALLY HAPP-ENED ...!
WHAT'S...
...THAT SMELL?
SOME INCENSE FROM ASIA.
IT RELAXES PEOPLE.
MY MOM USED TO TRAVEL AROUND PRACTICING HYPNOSIS AND FORTUNE TELLING.
THIS IS THE INCENSE THAT SHE ALWAYS USES.
THIS GIRL REALLY DOESN'T SEEM TO REM-EMBER.
HMM...
NOW THAT I THINK ABOUT IT, MADDY'S EYES YESTERDAY SEEMED VACANT.
I GET IT— HYPNOSIS HUH...?
BIBI!!

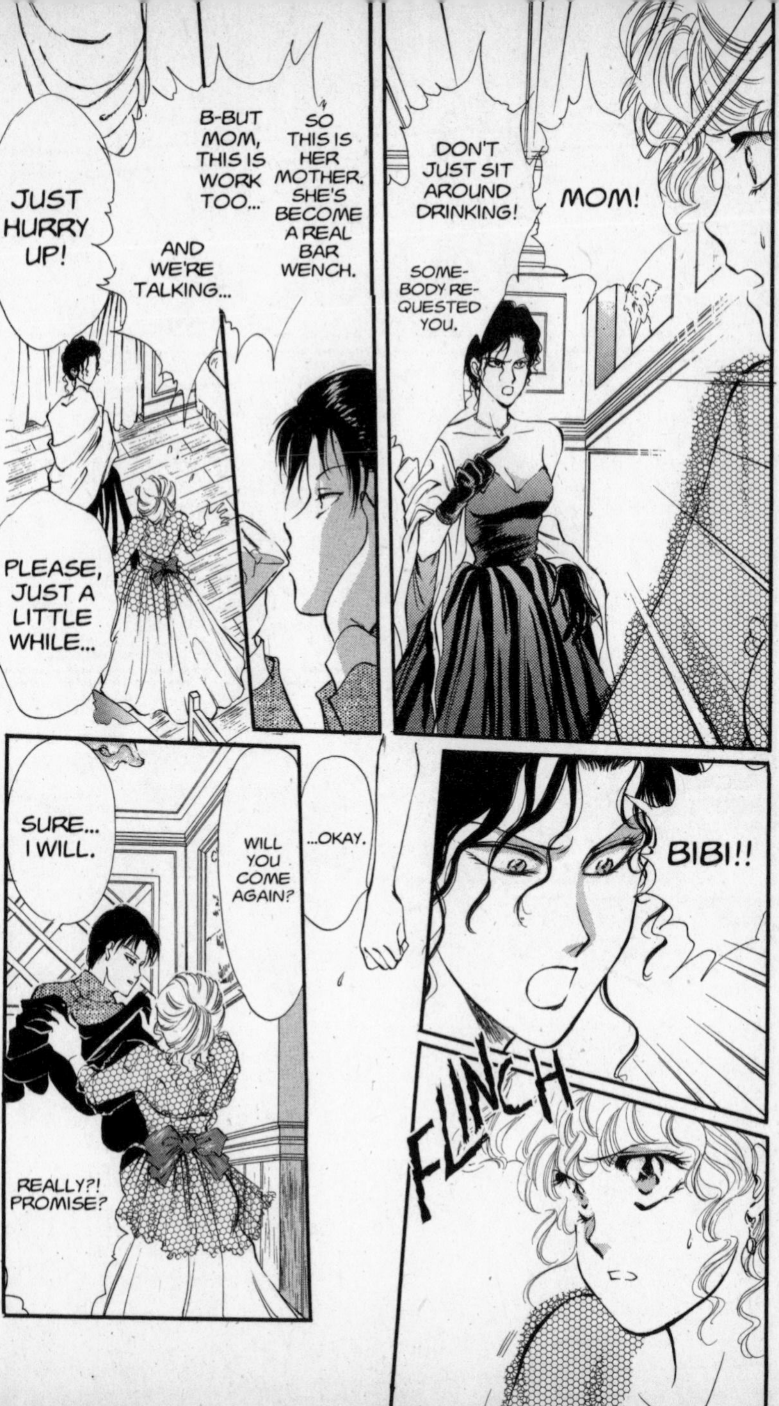
MOM!
DON'T JUST SIT AROUND DRINKING!
SOME-BODY RE-QUESTED YOU.
SO THIS IS HER MOTHER. SHE'S BECOME A REAL BAR WENCH.
B-BUT MOM, THIS IS WORK TOO...
AND WE'RE TALKING...
JUST HURRY UP!
PLEASE, JUST A LITTLE WHILE...
BIBI!!
FLINCH
...OKAY.
WILL YOU COME AGAIN?
SURE... I WILL.
REALLY?! PROMISE?

WILD TALK

THIS IS CAIN'S SECOND STORY. ACTUALLY THERE WAS ONE STORY BEFORE THIS, IN WHICH CAIN AND ARIEL FROM THE FIRST STORY END UP LIVING WITH EACH OTHER. THIS EPISODE INTRODUCES THE YOUNG BUTLER, RIFF. WHY IS HE CALLED RIFF? IS IT BECAUSE THE MAID'S NAME WAS MAGENTA? YOU DON'T GET IT? CAIN IS NOT FRANKENFURTER, BUT...HARGREAVES IS THE MARRIED NAME OF ALICE LIDDELL, THE MODEL FOR ALICE IN "ALICE IN WONDERLAND." IS ALL OF THIS A LITTLE FAR-FETCHED? WELL THEN, I'LL SEE YOU AGAIN IN ABOUT FOUR MORE PAGES.

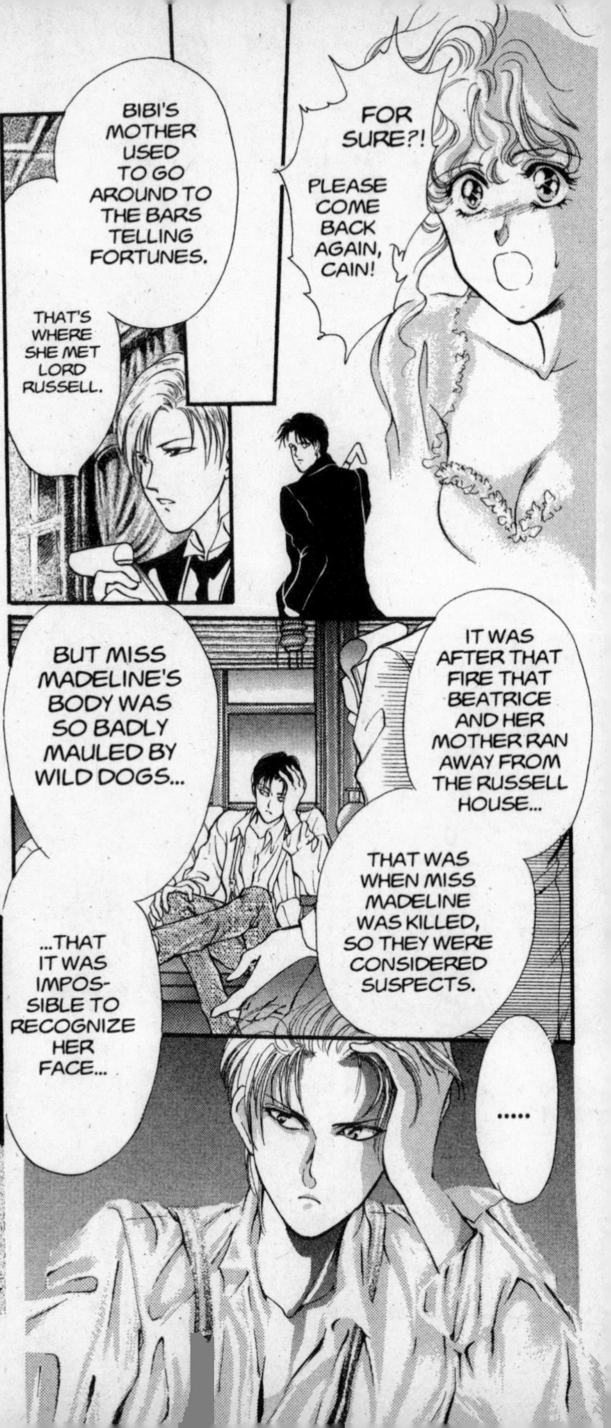
FOR SURE?!
PLEASE COME BACK AGAIN, CAIN!
BIBI'S MOTHER USED TO GO AROUND TO THE BARS TELLING FORTUNES.
THAT'S WHERE SHE MET LORD RUSSELL.
IT WAS AFTER THAT FIRE THAT BEATRICE AND HER MOTHER RAN AWAY FROM THE RUSSELL HOUSE...
THAT WAS WHEN MISS MADELINE WAS KILLED, SO THEY WERE CONSIDERED SUSPECTS.
BUT MISS MADELINE'S BODY WAS SO BADLY MAULED BY WILD DOGS...
...THAT IT WAS IMPOSSIBLE TO RECOGNIZE HER FACE...
.....

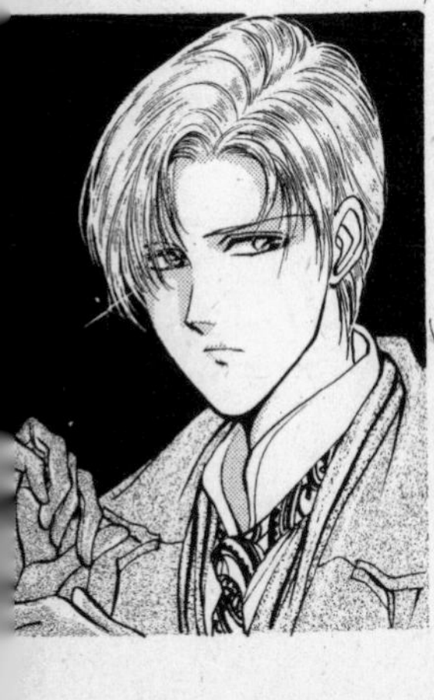

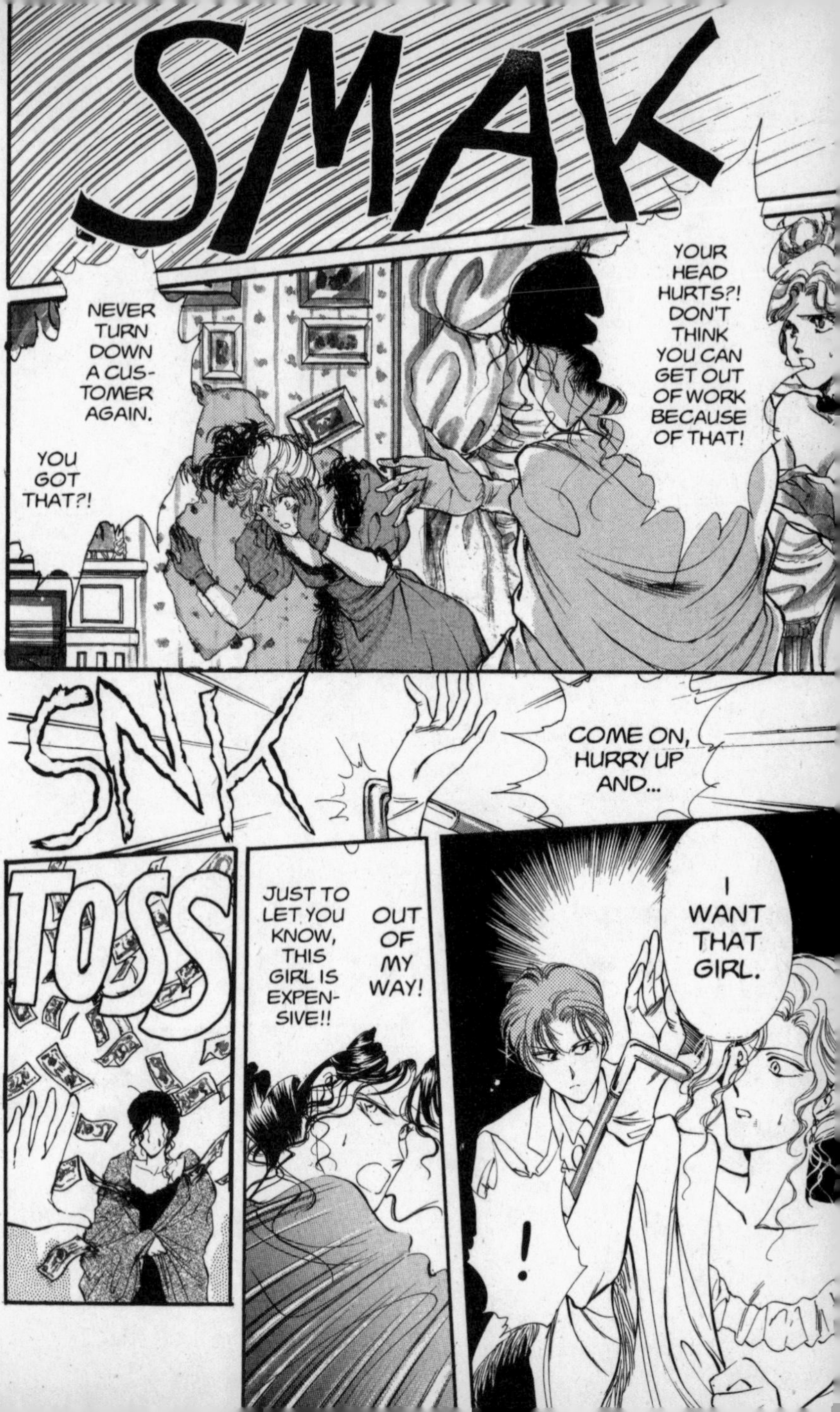
SMAK
YOUR HEAD HURTS?! DON'T THINK YOU CAN GET OUT OF WORK BECAUSE OF THAT!
NEVER TURN DOWN A CUS-TOMER AGAIN.
YOU GOT THAT?!
COME ON, HURRY UP AND...
SNK
I WANT THAT GIRL.
!
OUT OF MY WAY!
JUST TO LET YOU KNOW, THIS GIRL IS EXPEN-SIVE!!
TOSS

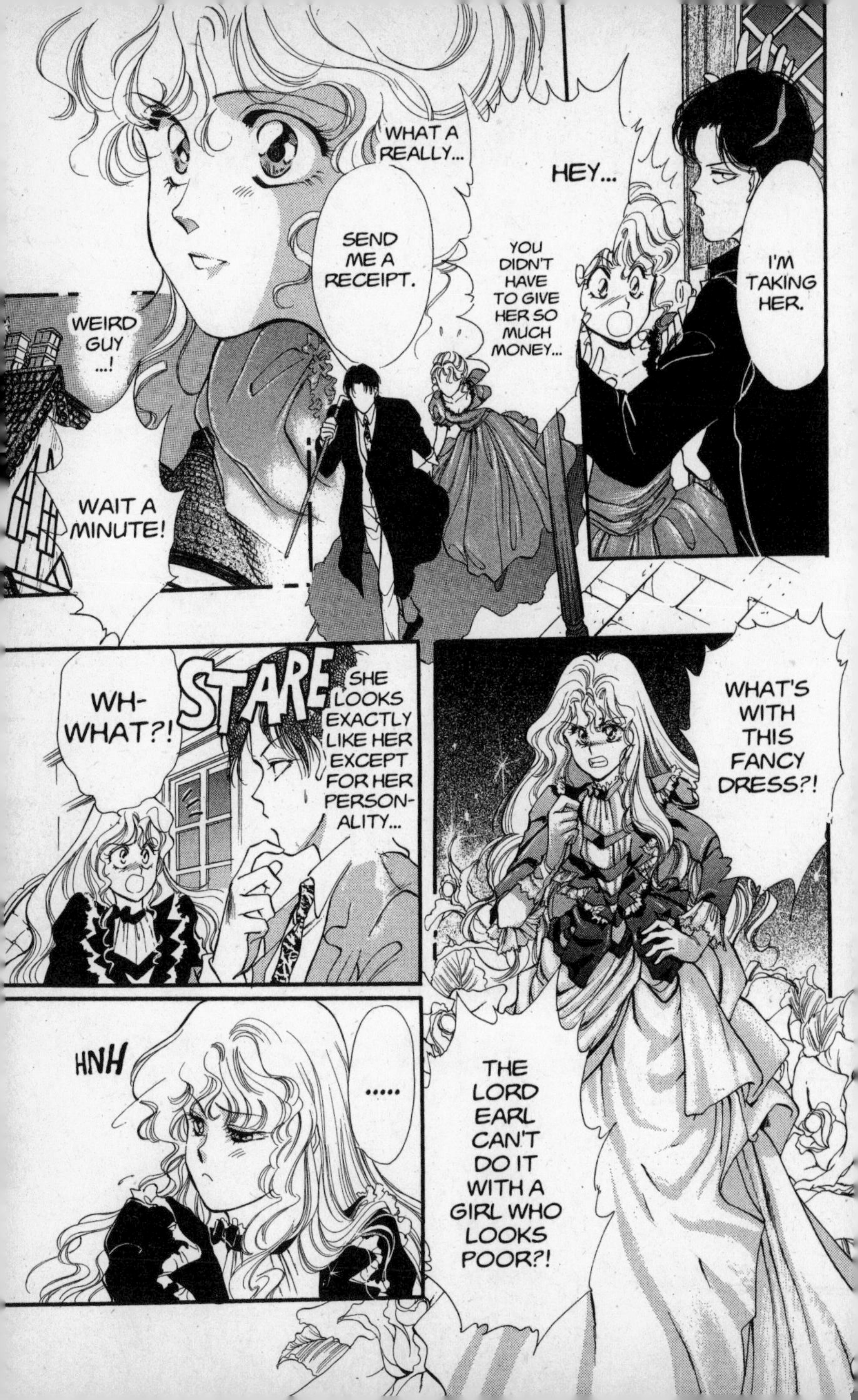
HEY...
I'M TAKING HER.
YOU DIDN'T HAVE TO GIVE HER SO MUCH MONEY...
SEND ME A RECEIPT.
WHAT A REALLY...
WEIRD GUY ...!
WAIT A MINUTE!
WHAT'S WITH THIS FANCY DRESS?!
STARE
SHE LOOKS EXACTLY LIKE HER EXCEPT FOR HER PERSON-ALITY...
WH-WHAT?!
THE LORD EARL CAN'T DO IT WITH A GIRL WHO LOOKS POOR?!
......
HNH

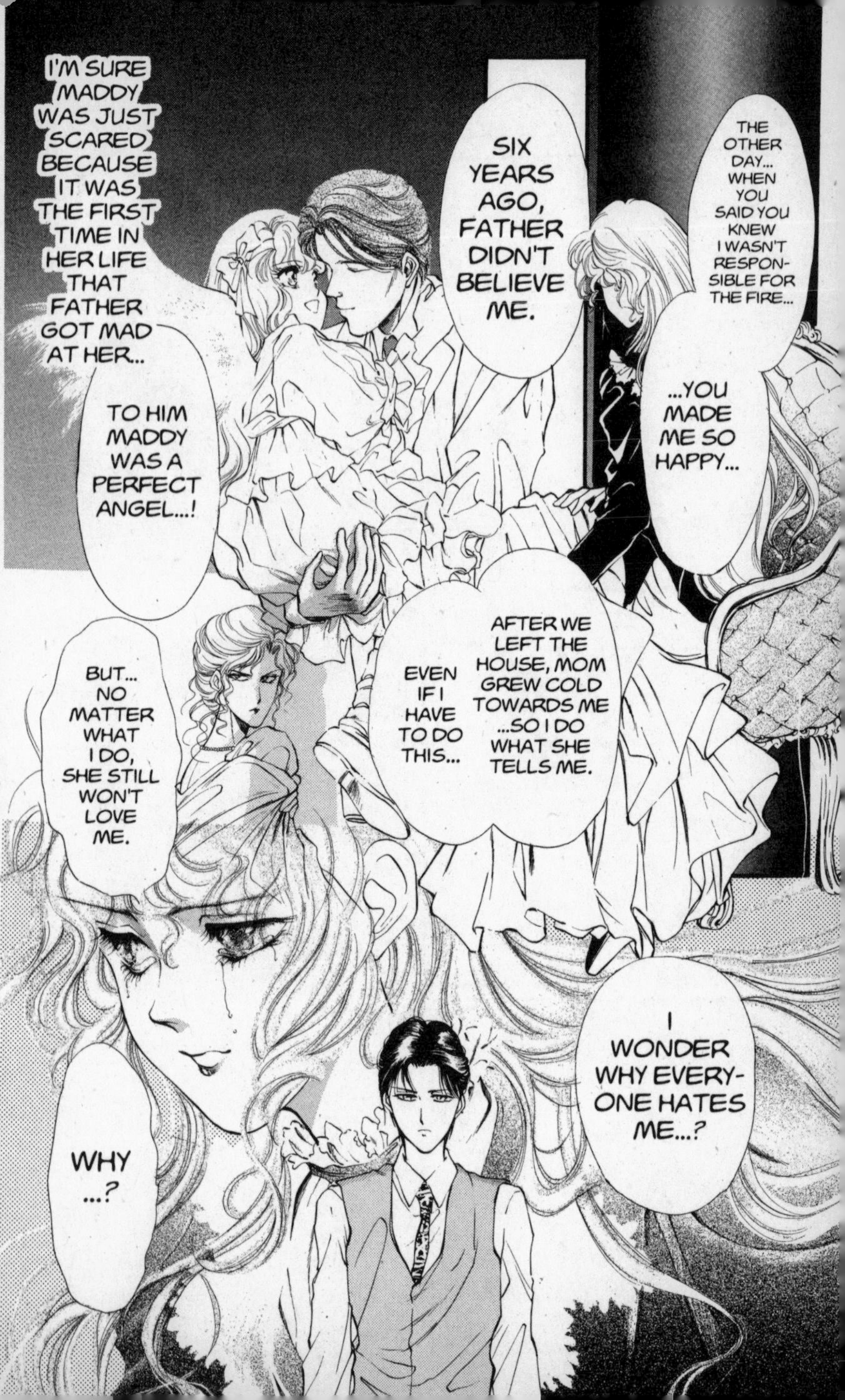
THE OTHER DAY... WHEN YOU SAID YOU KNEW I WASN'T RESPONSIBLE FOR THE FIRE...
...YOU MADE ME SO HAPPY...
SIX YEARS AGO, FATHER DIDN'T BELIEVE ME.
I'M SURE MADDY WAS JUST SCARED BECAUSE IT WAS THE FIRST TIME IN HER LIFE THAT FATHER GOT MAD AT HER...
TO HIM MADDY WAS A PERFECT ANGEL...!
AFTER WE LEFT THE HOUSE, MOM GREW COLD TOWARDS ME ...SO I DO WHAT SHE TELLS ME.
EVEN IF I HAVE TO DO THIS...
BUT... NO MATTER WHAT I DO, SHE STILL WON'T LOVE ME.
I WONDER WHY EVERYONE HATES ME...?
WHY ...?

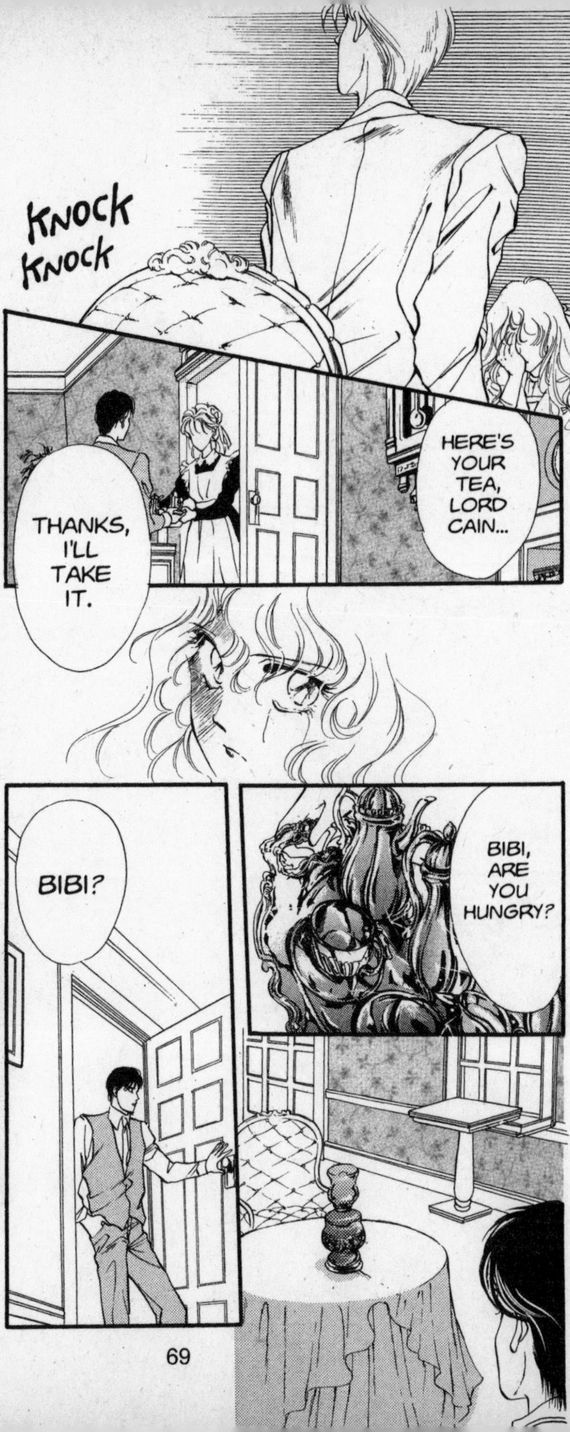
KNOCK
KNOCK
HERE'S YOUR TEA, LORD CAIN...
THANKS, I'LL TAKE IT.
BIBI, ARE YOU HUNGRY?
BIBI?

WILD TALK

WHEN I LOOK AT THIS NOW, IT REMINDS ME OF "TWIN PEAKS." I USED TO WATCH THAT EVERYDAY. WHEN IT WAS CHECKED OUT AT THE VIDEO STORE, I COULDN'T SLEEP AT NIGHT. EVEN THE NAMES MADDY AND LELAND ARE FROM THAT SHOW. BIBI'S MOM IS ALMOST LIKE BLACKY. WELL, MAYBE NOT. AND, OF COURSE, MR. COOPER. I REALLY LIKED AUDREY. SHELLY'S REALLY PRETTY, TOO. BUT DONNA WAS REALLY CUTE IN THE BEGINNING. JAMES REALLY TURNED OUT TO BE TERRIBLE IN THE END, TOO. THE "LAURA PALMER MURDER" EPISODES WERE THE BEST. WHAT WAS WITH THE WINDHAM EARL? OH...AND HOW ABOUT THAT CURSED LAST EPISODE THAT WAS IMPOSSIBLE TO UNDERSTAND...? MY FELLOW FANS, PLEASE WRITE!! THANKS FOR THE CAIN FAN CLUB.

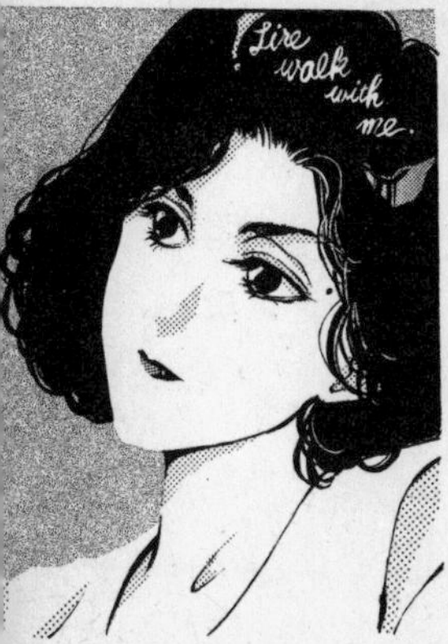
Fire walk with me.

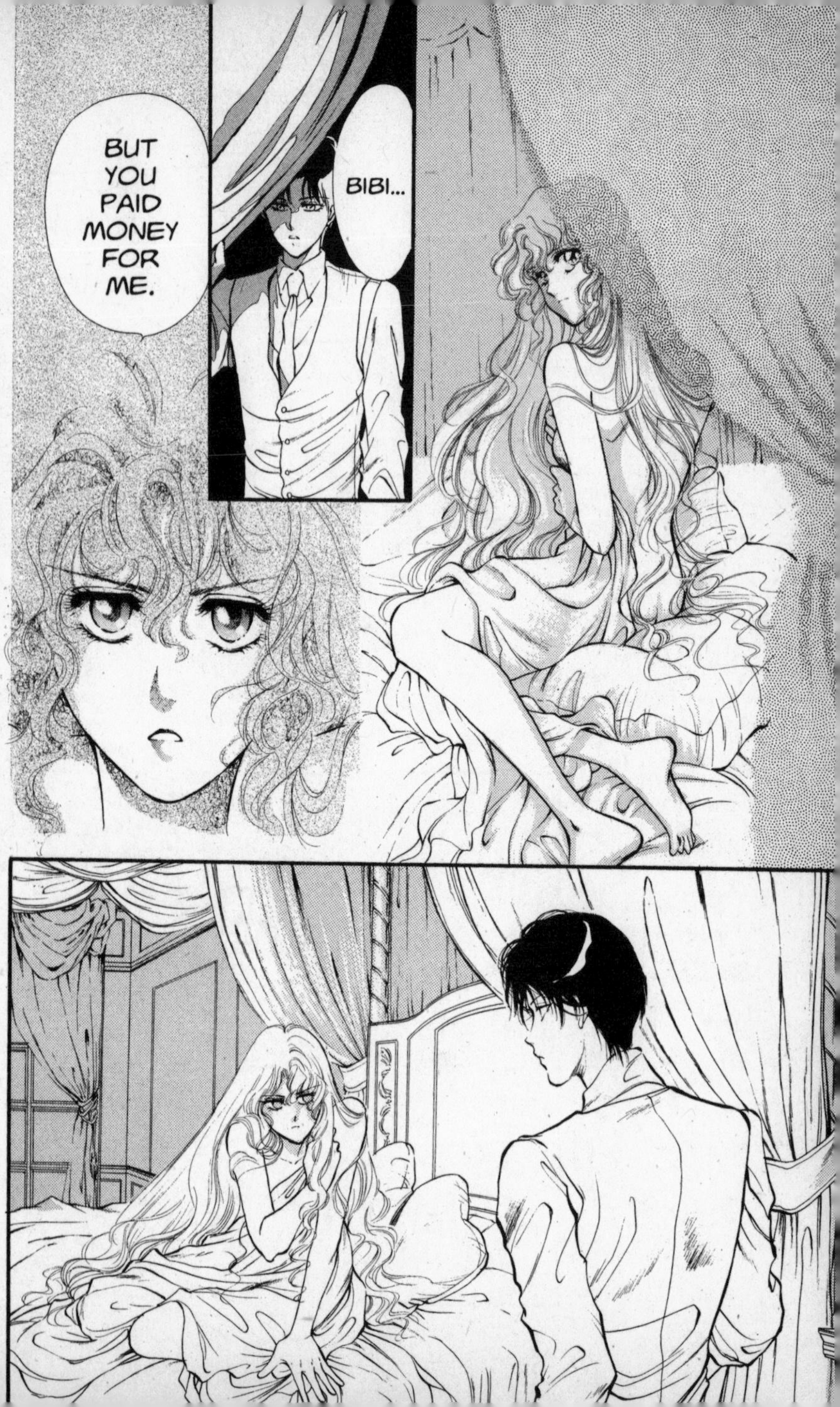
BIBI...
BUT YOU PAID MONEY FOR ME.

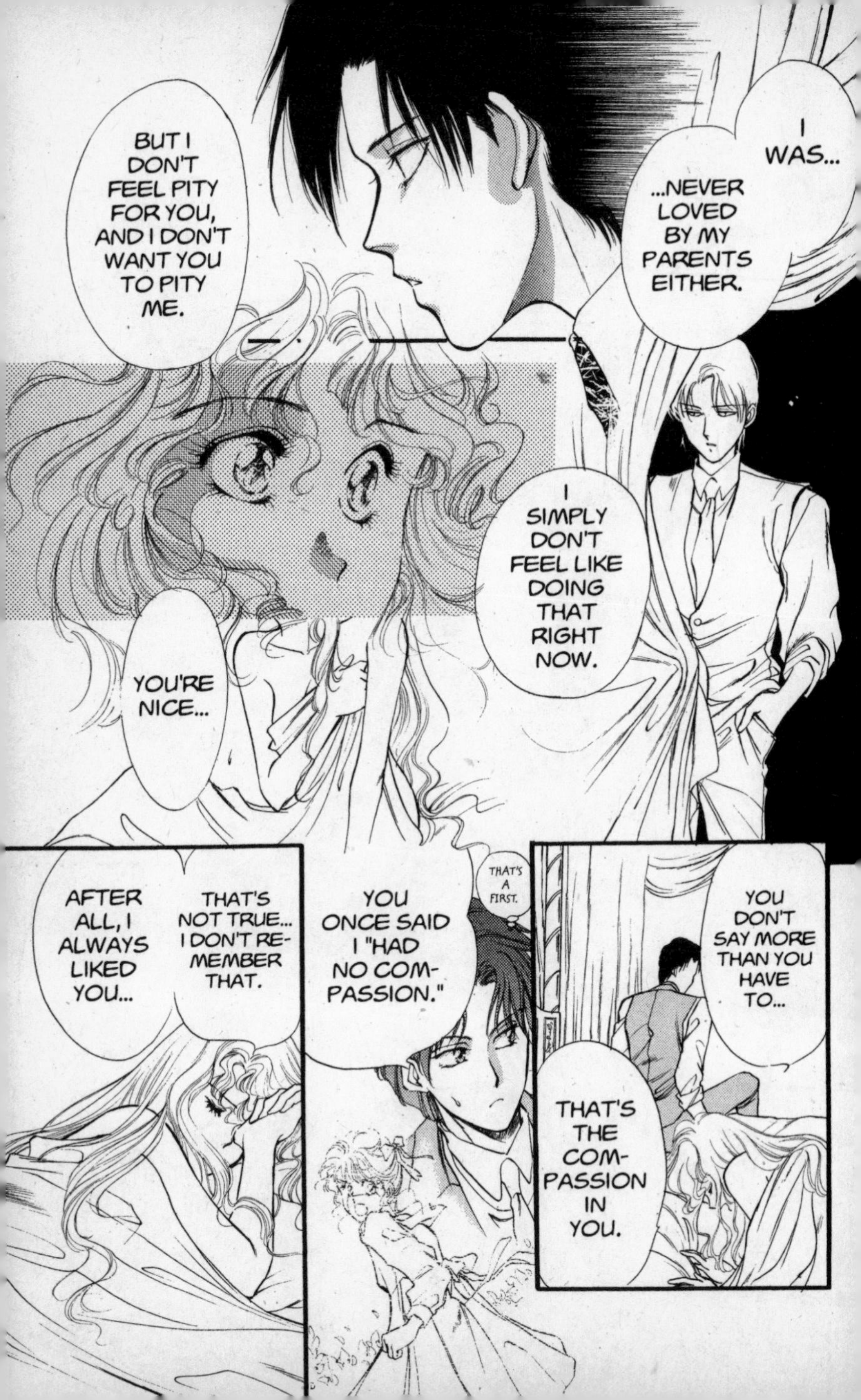
I WAS...
...NEVER LOVED BY MY PARENTS EITHER.
BUT I DON'T FEEL PITY FOR YOU, AND I DON'T WANT YOU TO PITY ME.
I SIMPLY DON'T FEEL LIKE DOING THAT RIGHT NOW.
YOU'RE NICE...
YOU DON'T SAY MORE THAN YOU HAVE TO...
THAT'S THE COMPASSION IN YOU.
THAT'S A FIRST.
YOU ONCE SAID I "HAD NO COMPASSION."
THAT'S NOT TRUE... I DON'T REMEMBER THAT.
AFTER ALL, I ALWAYS LIKED YOU...

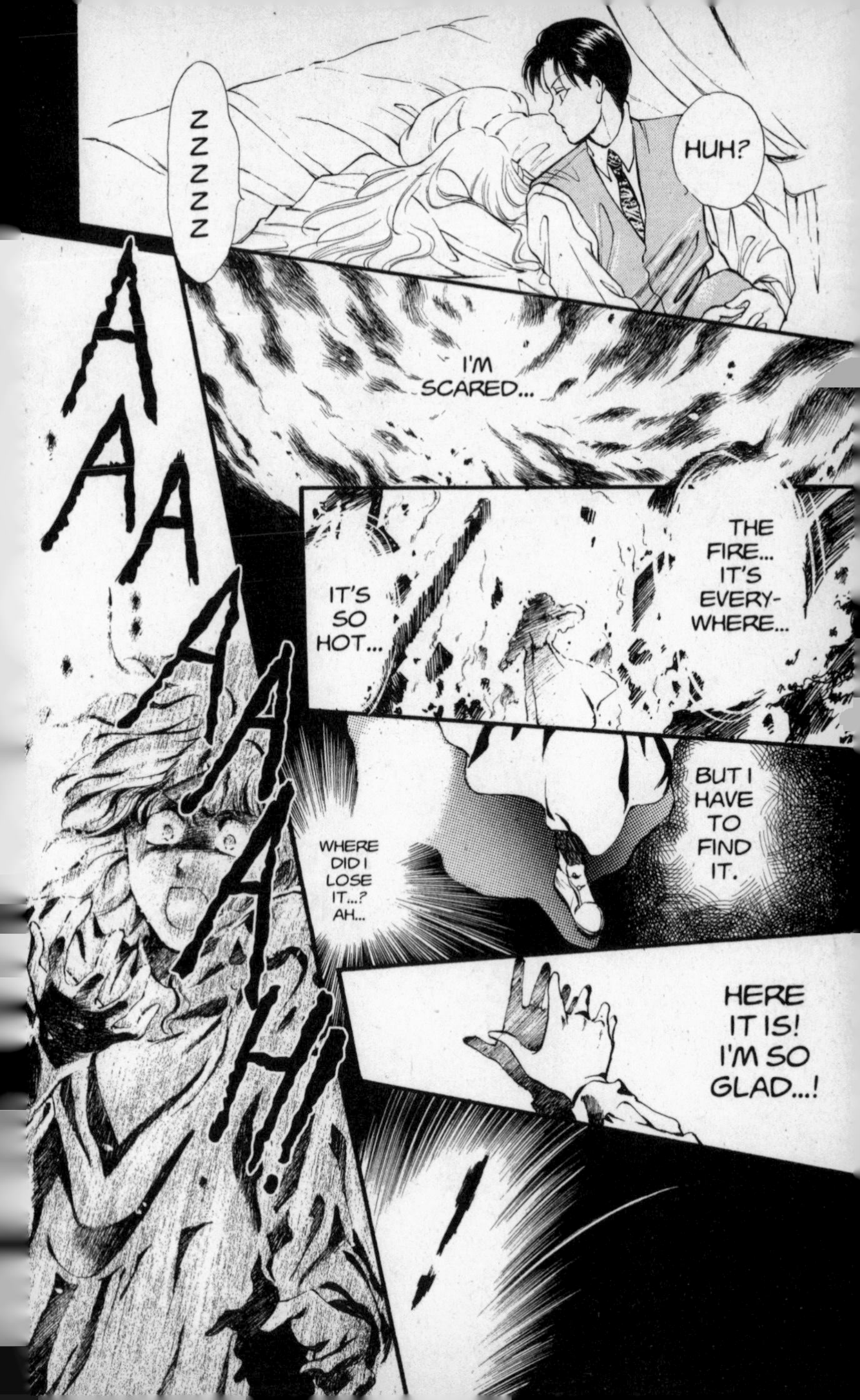
HUH?
ZZZZZ
I'M SCARED...
THE FIRE... IT'S EVERY-WHERE...
IT'S SO HOT...
BUT I HAVE TO FIND IT.
WHERE DID I LOSE IT...? AH...
HERE IT IS! I'M SO GLAD...!
AAAAAAH!!

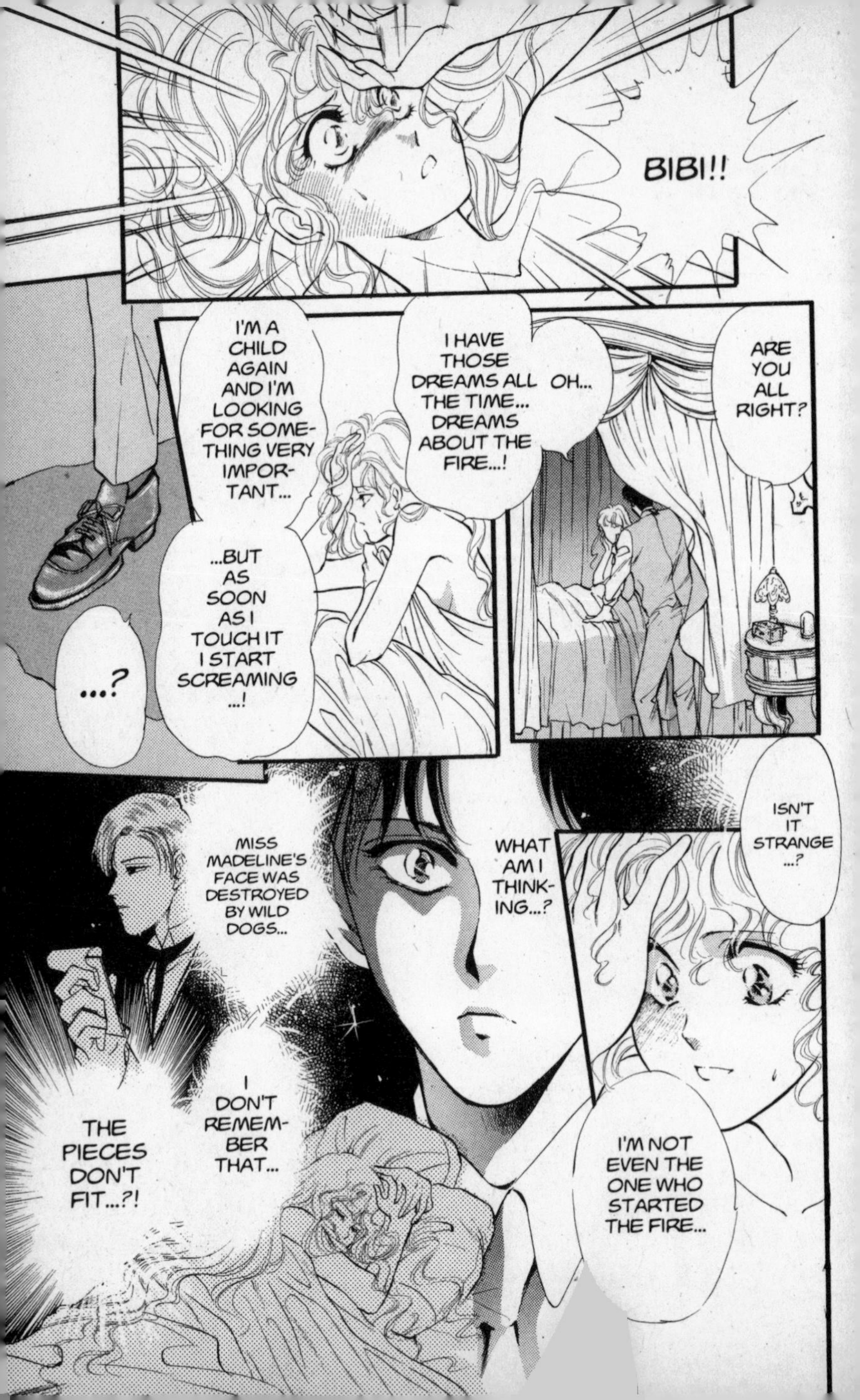
BIBI!!
ARE YOU ALL RIGHT?
OH...
I HAVE THOSE DREAMS ALL THE TIME... DREAMS ABOUT THE FIRE...!
I'M A CHILD AGAIN AND I'M LOOKING FOR SOME-THING VERY IMPOR-TANT...
...BUT AS SOON AS I TOUCH IT I START SCREAMING ...!
...?
ISN'T IT STRANGE ...?
I'M NOT EVEN THE ONE WHO STARTED THE FIRE...
WHAT AM I THINK-ING...?
MISS MADELINE'S FACE WAS DESTROYED BY WILD DOGS...
I DON'T REMEM-BER THAT...
THE PIECES DON'T FIT...?!

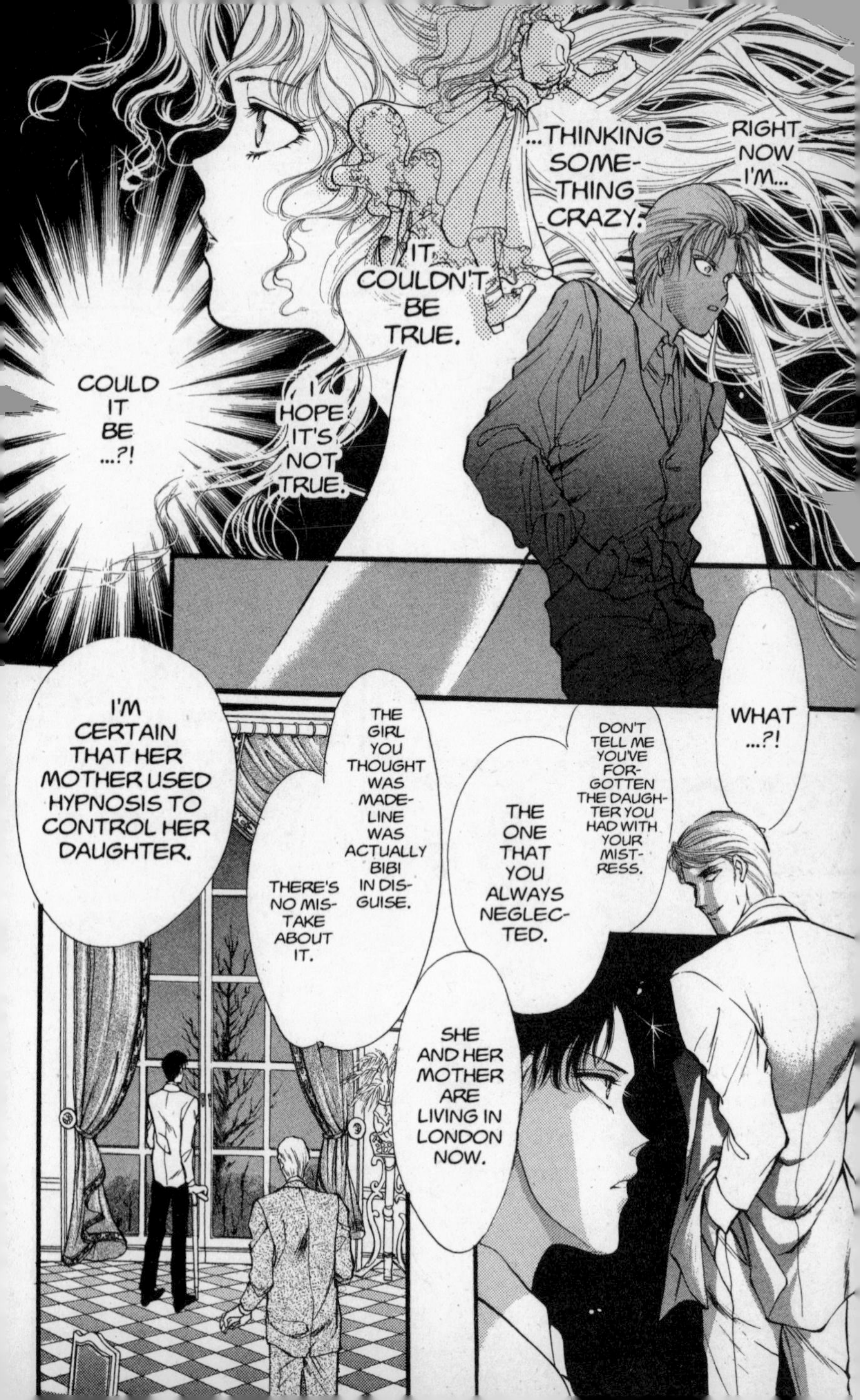
RIGHT NOW I'M...
...THINKING SOMETHING CRAZY.
IT COULDN'T BE TRUE.
I HOPE IT'S NOT TRUE.
COULD IT BE ...?!
WHAT ...?!
DON'T TELL ME YOU'VE FORGOTTEN THE DAUGHTER YOU HAD WITH YOUR MISTRESS.
THE ONE THAT YOU ALWAYS NEGLECTED.
THE GIRL YOU THOUGHT WAS MADELINE WAS ACTUALLY BIBI IN DISGUISE.
THERE'S NO MISTAKE ABOUT IT.
I'M CERTAIN THAT HER MOTHER USED HYPNOSIS TO CONTROL HER DAUGHTER.
SHE AND HER MOTHER ARE LIVING IN LONDON NOW.

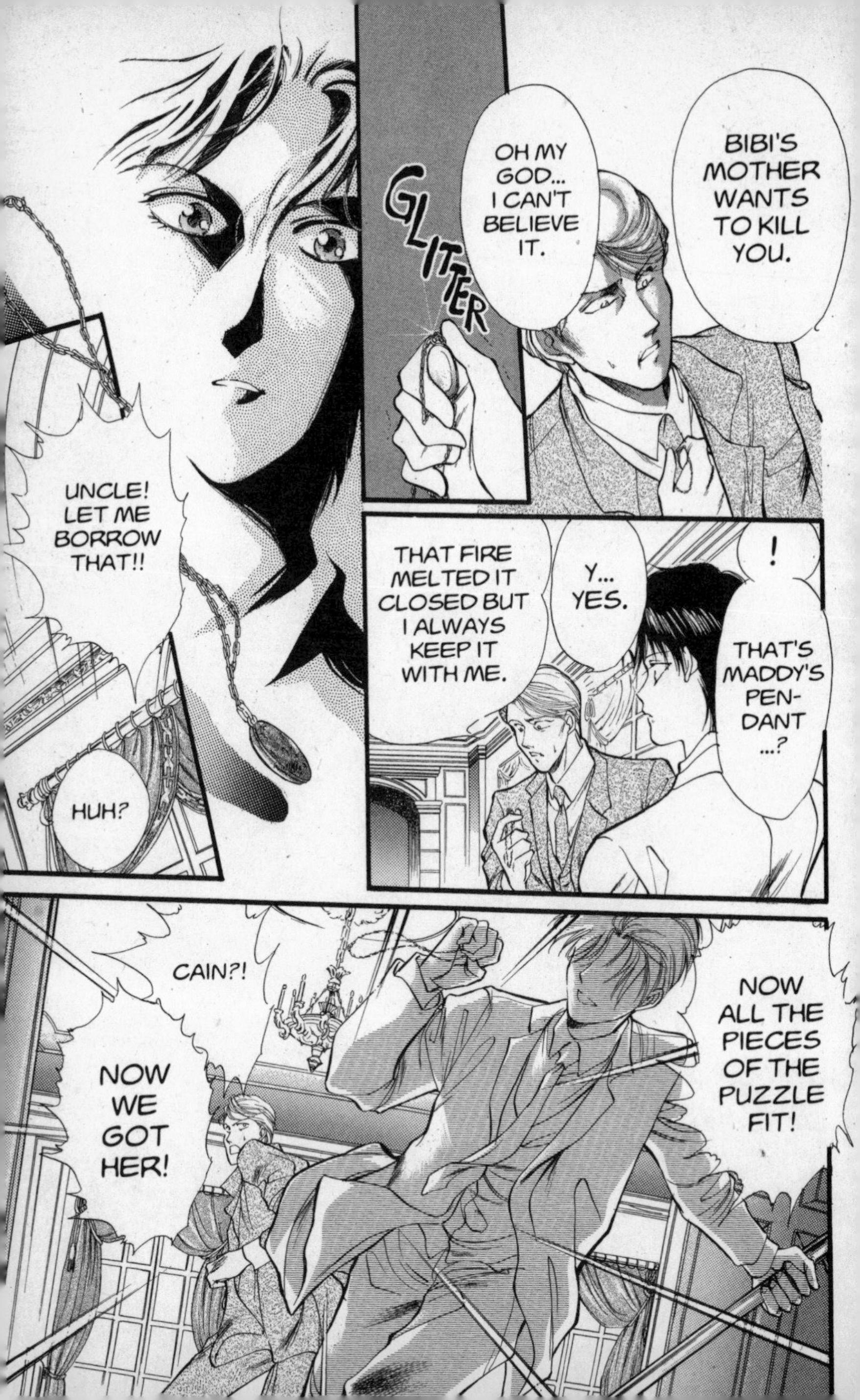
BIBI'S MOTHER WANTS TO KILL YOU.
OH MY GOD... I CAN'T BELIEVE IT.
GLITTER
!
THAT'S MADDY'S PEN-DANT ...?
Y... YES.
THAT FIRE MELTED IT CLOSED BUT I ALWAYS KEEP IT WITH ME.
UNCLE! LET ME BORROW THAT!!
HUH?
NOW ALL THE PIECES OF THE PUZZLE FIT!
CAIN?!
NOW WE GOT HER!

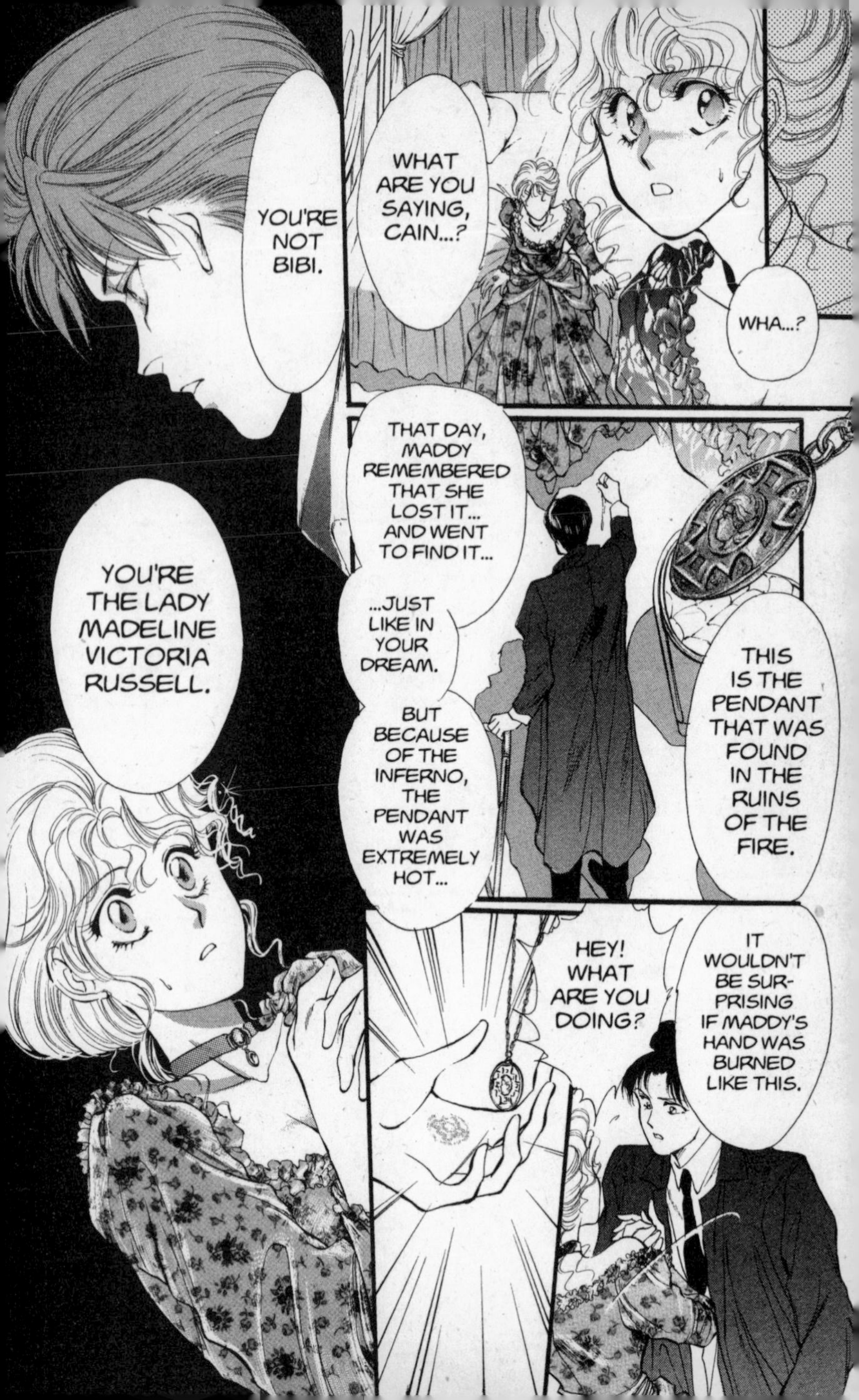
YOU'RE NOT BIBI.
WHA...?
WHAT ARE YOU SAYING, CAIN...?
YOU'RE THE LADY MADELINE VICTORIA RUSSELL.
THIS IS THE PENDANT THAT WAS FOUND IN THE RUINS OF THE FIRE.
THAT DAY, MADDY REMEMBERED THAT SHE LOST IT... AND WENT TO FIND IT...
...JUST LIKE IN YOUR DREAM.
BUT BECAUSE OF THE INFERNO, THE PENDANT WAS EXTREMELY HOT...
IT WOULDN'T BE SUR-PRISING IF MADDY'S HAND WAS BURNED LIKE THIS.
HEY! WHAT ARE YOU DOING?

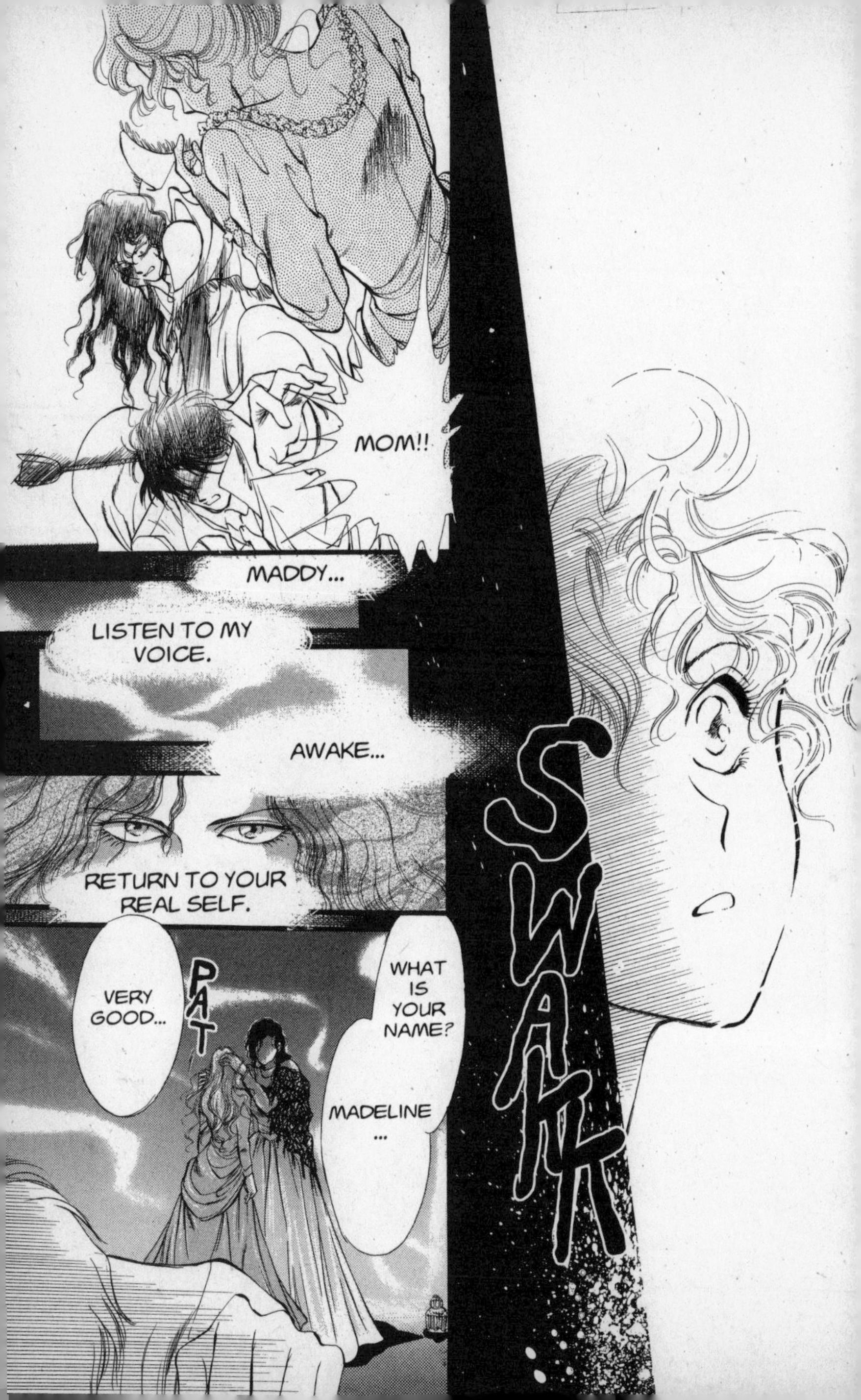
SWAK
MOM!!
MADDY...
LISTEN TO MY VOICE.
AWAKE...
RETURN TO YOUR REAL SELF.
WHAT IS YOUR NAME?
MADELINE ...
PAT
VERY GOOD...

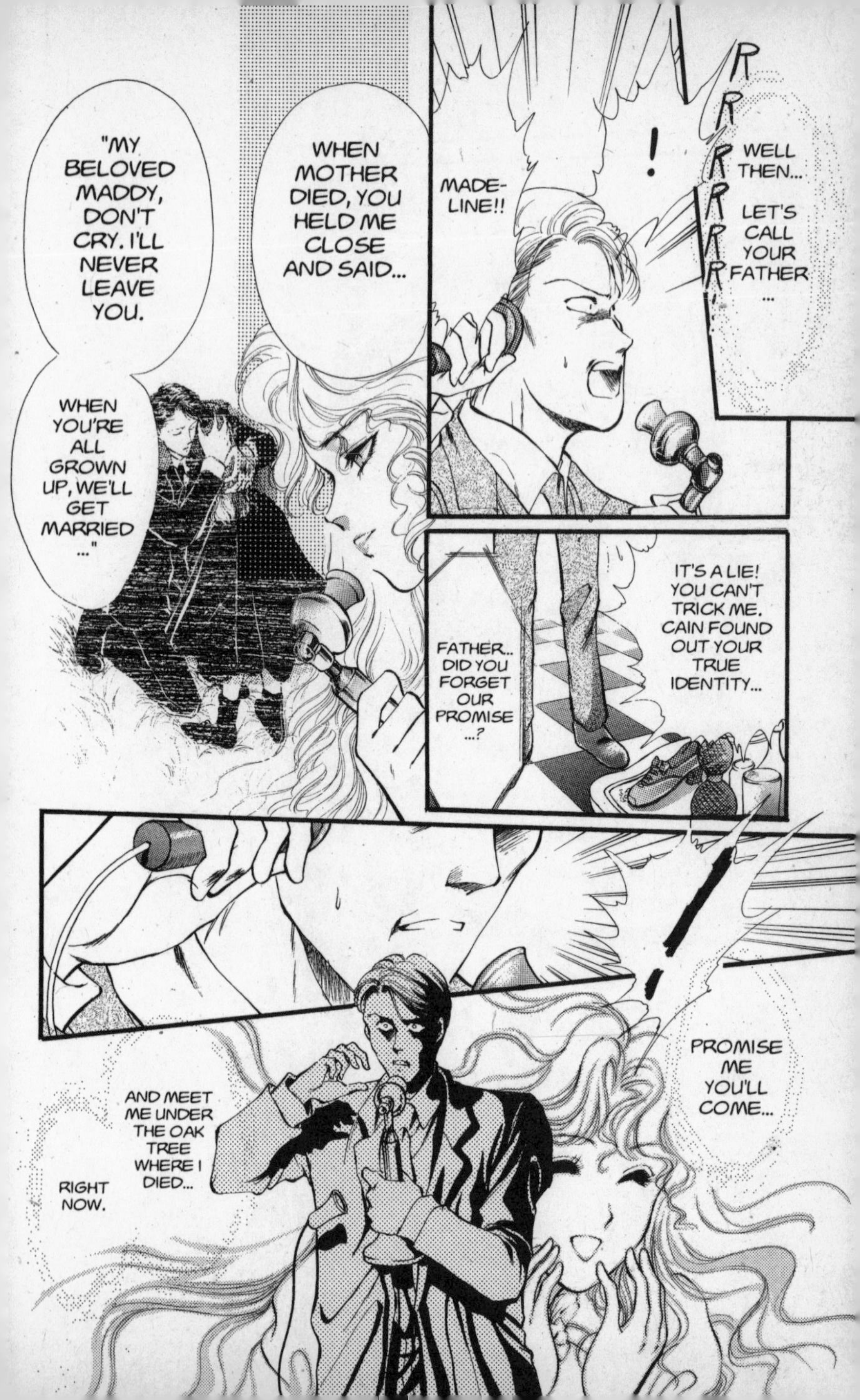
RRRRRR
WELL THEN...
LET'S CALL YOUR FATHER...
!
MADE-LINE!!
IT'S A LIE! YOU CAN'T TRICK ME. CAIN FOUND OUT YOUR TRUE IDENTITY...
FATHER.. DID YOU FORGET OUR PROMISE...?
WHEN MOTHER DIED, YOU HELD ME CLOSE AND SAID...
"MY BELOVED MADDY, DON'T CRY. I'LL NEVER LEAVE YOU.
WHEN YOU'RE ALL GROWN UP, WE'LL GET MARRIED..."
!
PROMISE ME YOU'LL COME...
AND MEET ME UNDER THE OAK TREE WHERE I DIED...
RIGHT NOW.

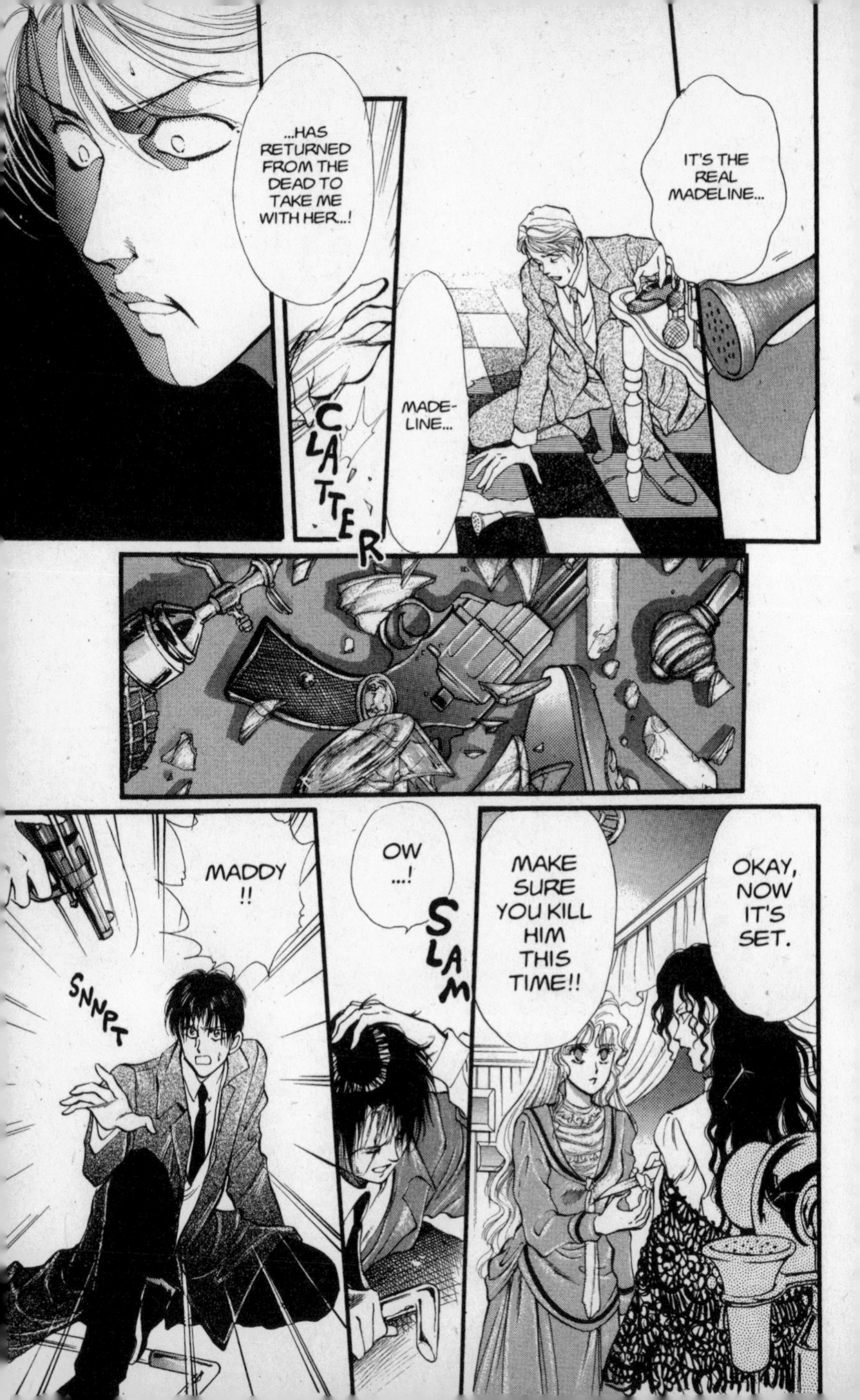
IT'S THE REAL MADELINE...
MADE-LINE...
CLATTER
...HAS RETURNED FROM THE DEAD TO TAKE ME WITH HER...!
OKAY, NOW IT'S SET.
MAKE SURE YOU KILL HIM THIS TIME!!
SLAM
OW ...!
MADDY !!
SNNPT

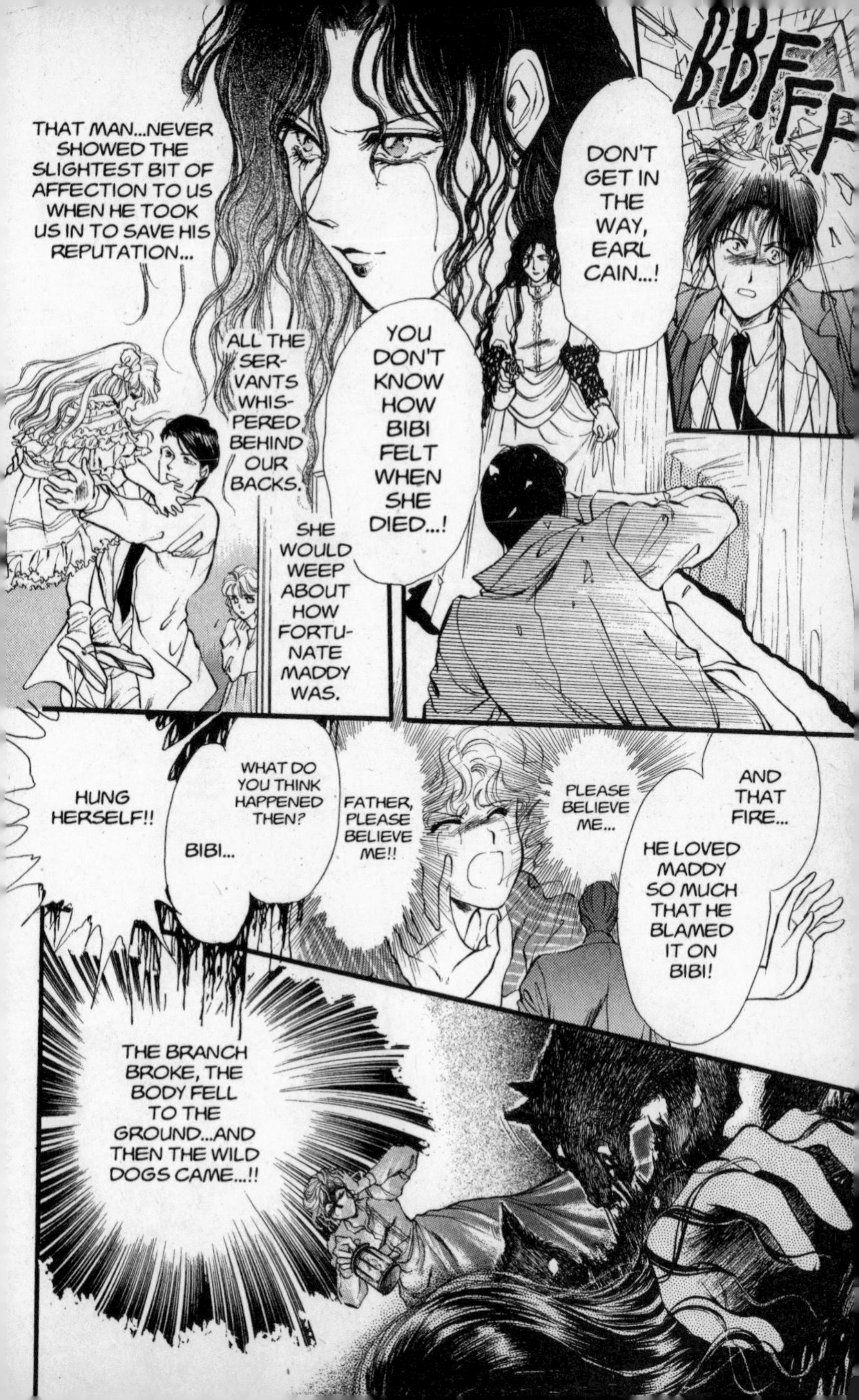
BBFFF
DON'T GET IN THE WAY, EARL CAIN...!
THAT MAN...NEVER SHOWED THE SLIGHTEST BIT OF AFFECTION TO US WHEN HE TOOK US IN TO SAVE HIS REPUTATION...
YOU DON'T KNOW HOW BIBI FELT WHEN SHE DIED...!
ALL THE SER-VANTS WHIS-PERED BEHIND OUR BACKS.
SHE WOULD WEEP ABOUT HOW FORTU-NATE MADDY WAS.
AND THAT FIRE...
HE LOVED MADDY SO MUCH THAT HE BLAMED IT ON BIBI!
PLEASE BELIEVE ME...
FATHER, PLEASE BELIEVE ME!!
WHAT DO YOU THINK HAPPENED THEN?
BIBI...
HUNG HERSELF!!
THE BRANCH BROKE, THE BODY FELL TO THE GROUND...AND THEN THE WILD DOGS CAME...!!

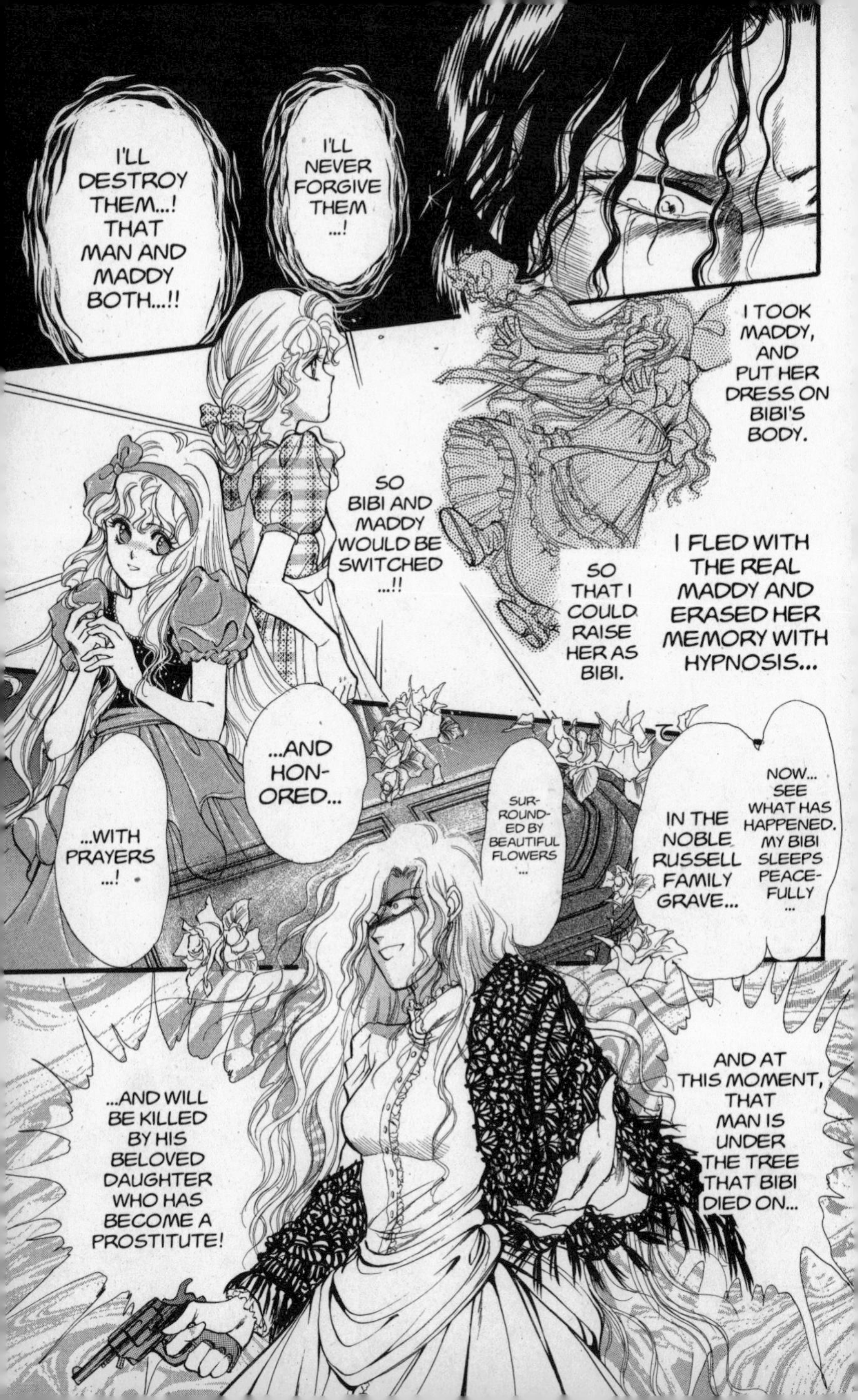
I'LL NEVER FORGIVE THEM ...!
I'LL DESTROY THEM...! THAT MAN AND MADDY BOTH...!!
I TOOK MADDY, AND PUT HER DRESS ON BIBI'S BODY.
I FLED WITH THE REAL MADDY AND ERASED HER MEMORY WITH HYPNOSIS...
SO THAT I COULD RAISE HER AS BIBI.
SO BIBI AND MADDY WOULD BE SWITCHED ...!!
NOW... SEE WHAT HAS HAPPENED. MY BIBI SLEEPS PEACE-FULLY ...
IN THE NOBLE RUSSELL FAMILY GRAVE...
SUR-ROUND-ED BY BEAUTIFUL FLOWERS ...
...AND HON-ORED...
...WITH PRAYERS ...!
AND AT THIS MOMENT, THAT MAN IS UNDER THE TREE THAT BIBI DIED ON...
...AND WILL BE KILLED BY HIS BELOVED DAUGHTER WHO HAS BECOME A PROSTITUTE!

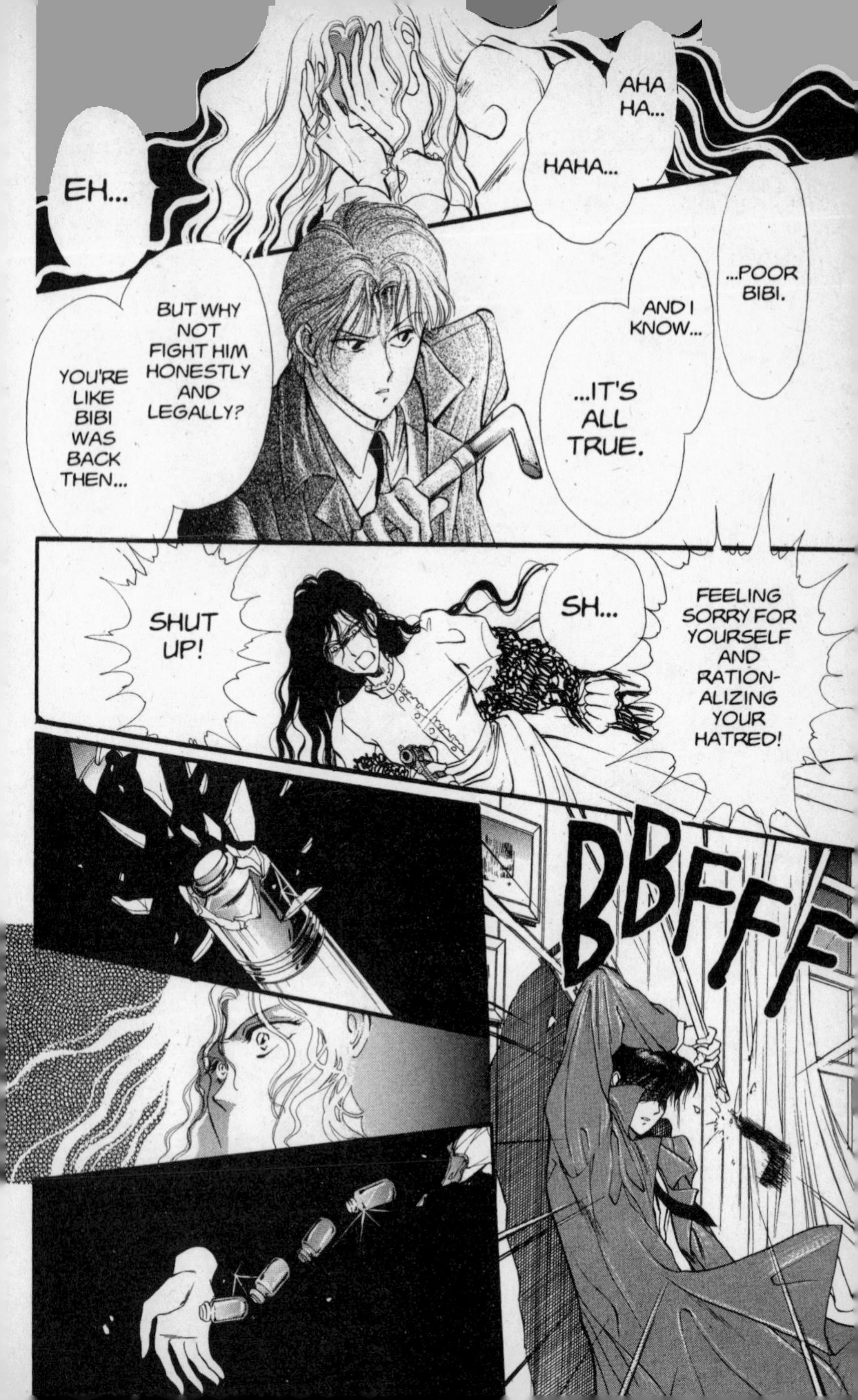
AHA HA...
HAHA...
EH...
...POOR BIBI.
AND I KNOW...
...IT'S ALL TRUE.
BUT WHY NOT FIGHT HIM HONESTLY AND LEGALLY?
YOU'RE LIKE BIBI WAS BACK THEN...
FEELING SORRY FOR YOURSELF AND RATION-ALIZING YOUR HATRED!
SH...
SHUT UP!
BBFFF

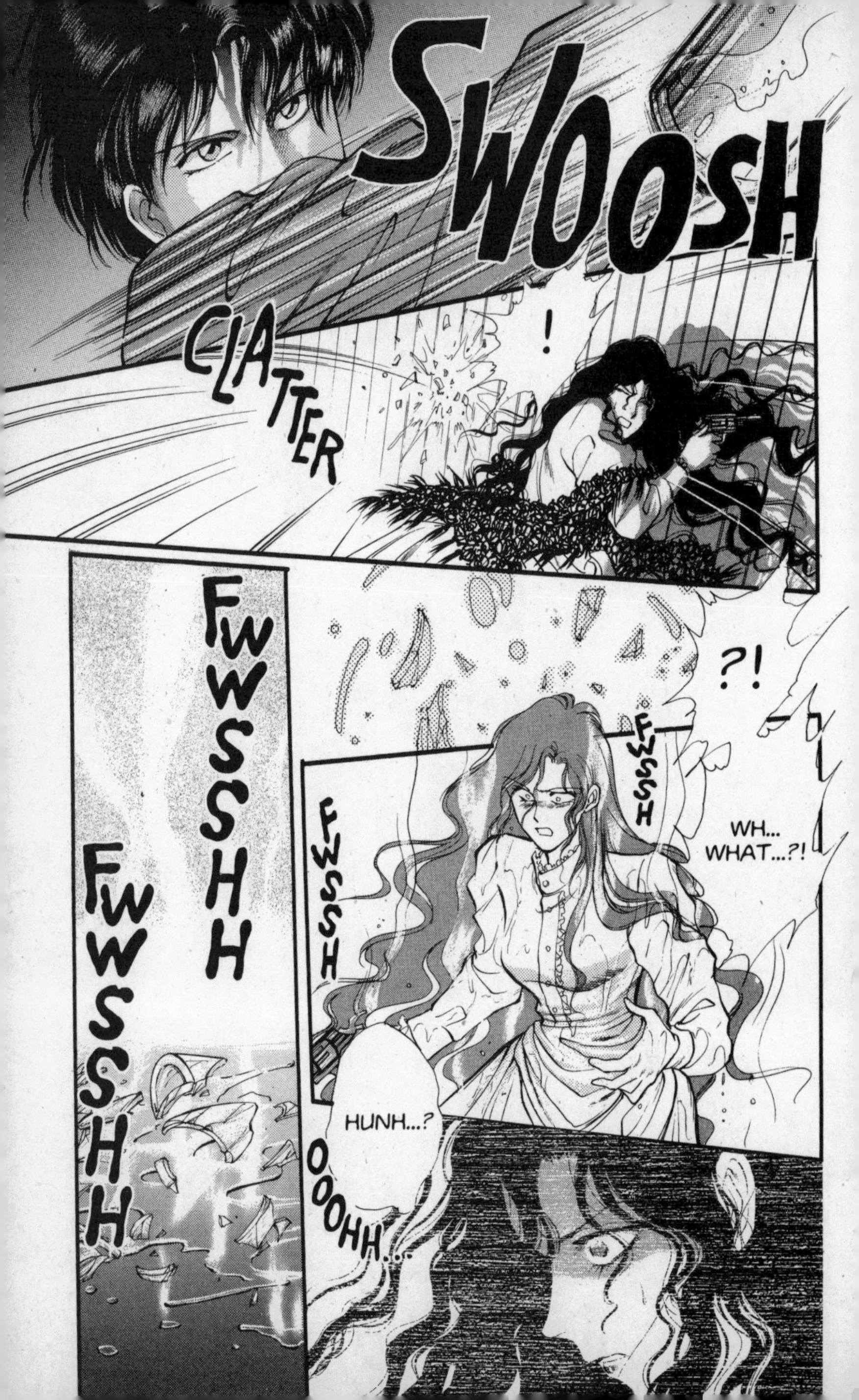
SWOOSH
CLATTER
!
?!
FWSSH
WH... WHAT...?!
FWSSH
HUNH...?
OOOHH...
FWWSSHH
FWWSSHH

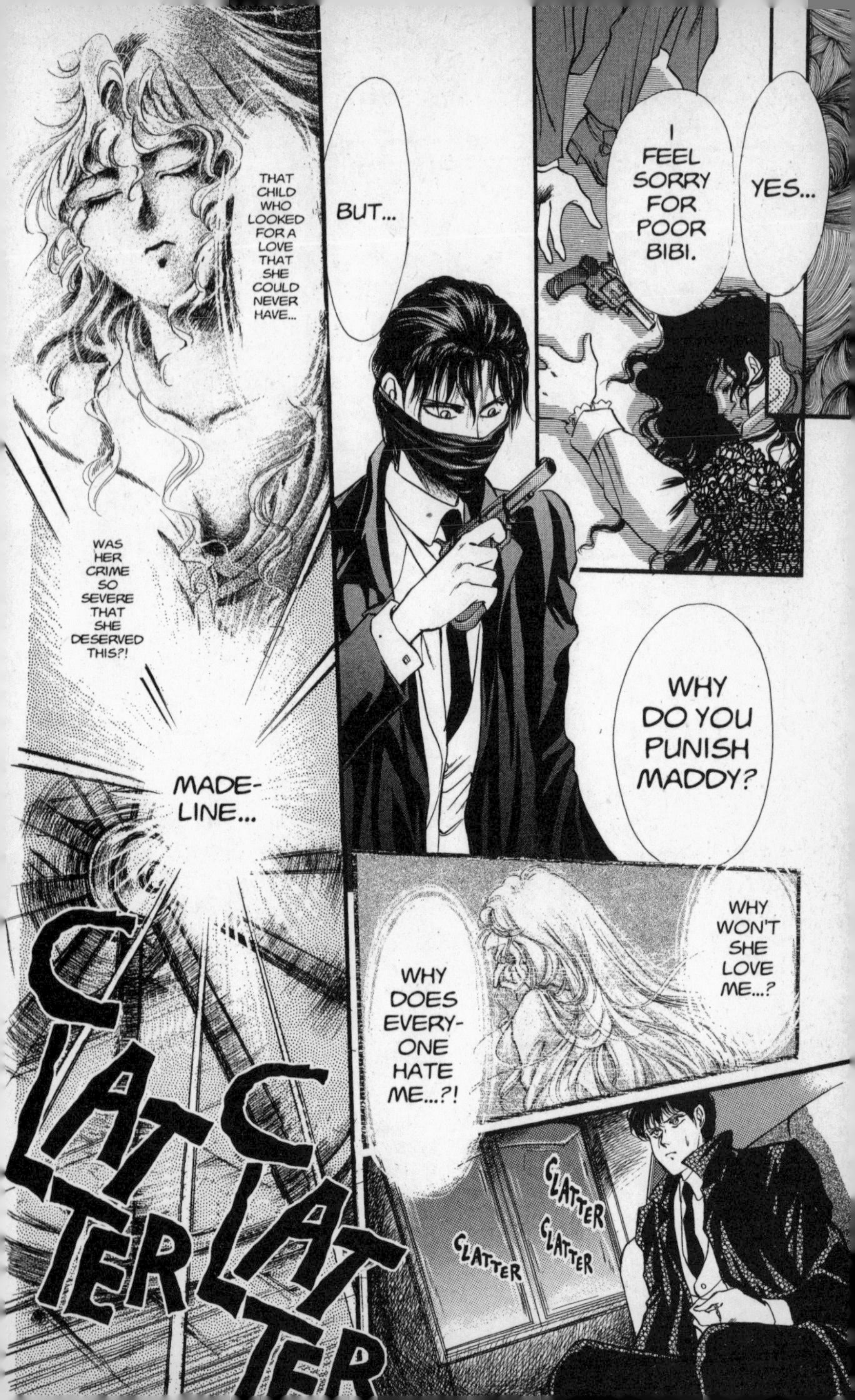
YES...
I FEEL SORRY FOR POOR BIBI.
BUT...
WHY DO YOU PUNISH MADDY?
WHY WON'T SHE LOVE ME...?
WHY DOES EVERY-ONE HATE ME...?!
CLATTER
CLATTER
CLATTER
CLATTER
THAT CHILD WHO LOOKED FOR A LOVE THAT SHE COULD NEVER HAVE...
WAS HER CRIME SO SEVERE THAT SHE DESERVED THIS?!
MADE-LINE...
CLATTER CLATTER

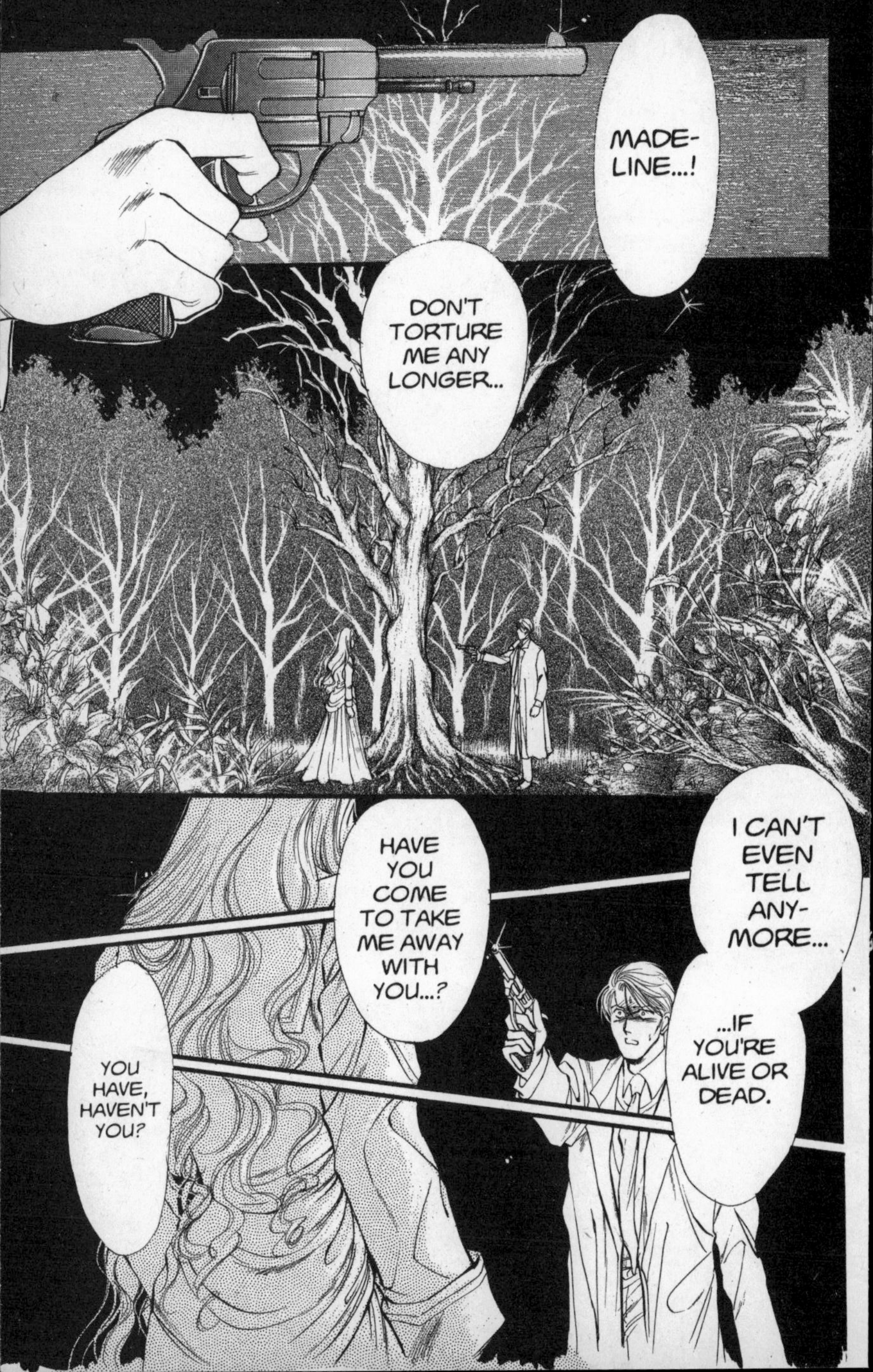
MADE-LINE...!
DON'T TORTURE ME ANY LONGER...
I CAN'T EVEN TELL ANY-MORE...
...IF YOU'RE ALIVE OR DEAD.
HAVE YOU COME TO TAKE ME AWAY WITH YOU...?
YOU HAVE, HAVEN'T YOU?

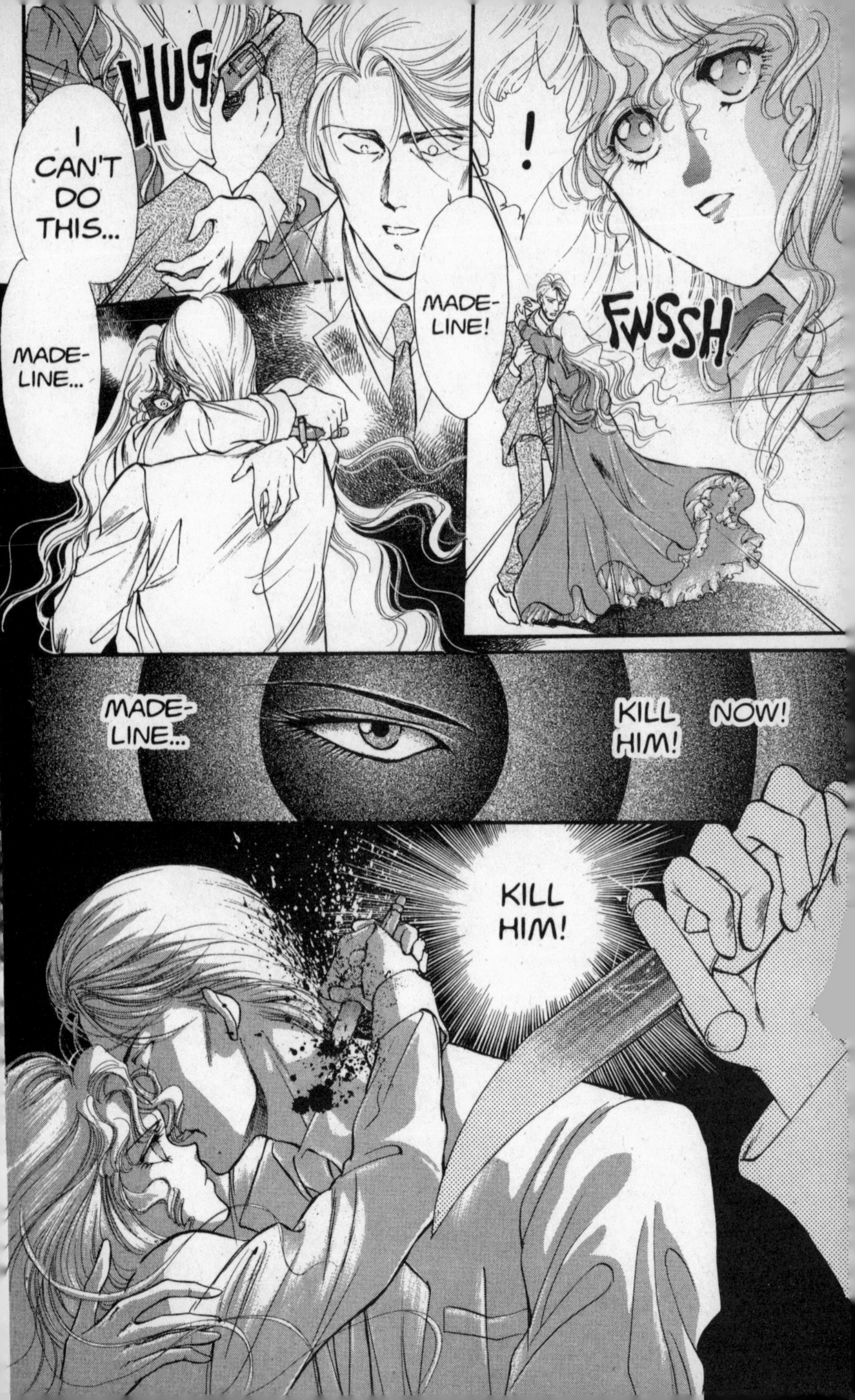

!
FWSSH
HUG
I CAN'T DO THIS...
MADE-LINE!
MADE-LINE...
NOW!
KILL HIM!
MADE-LINE...
KILL HIM!

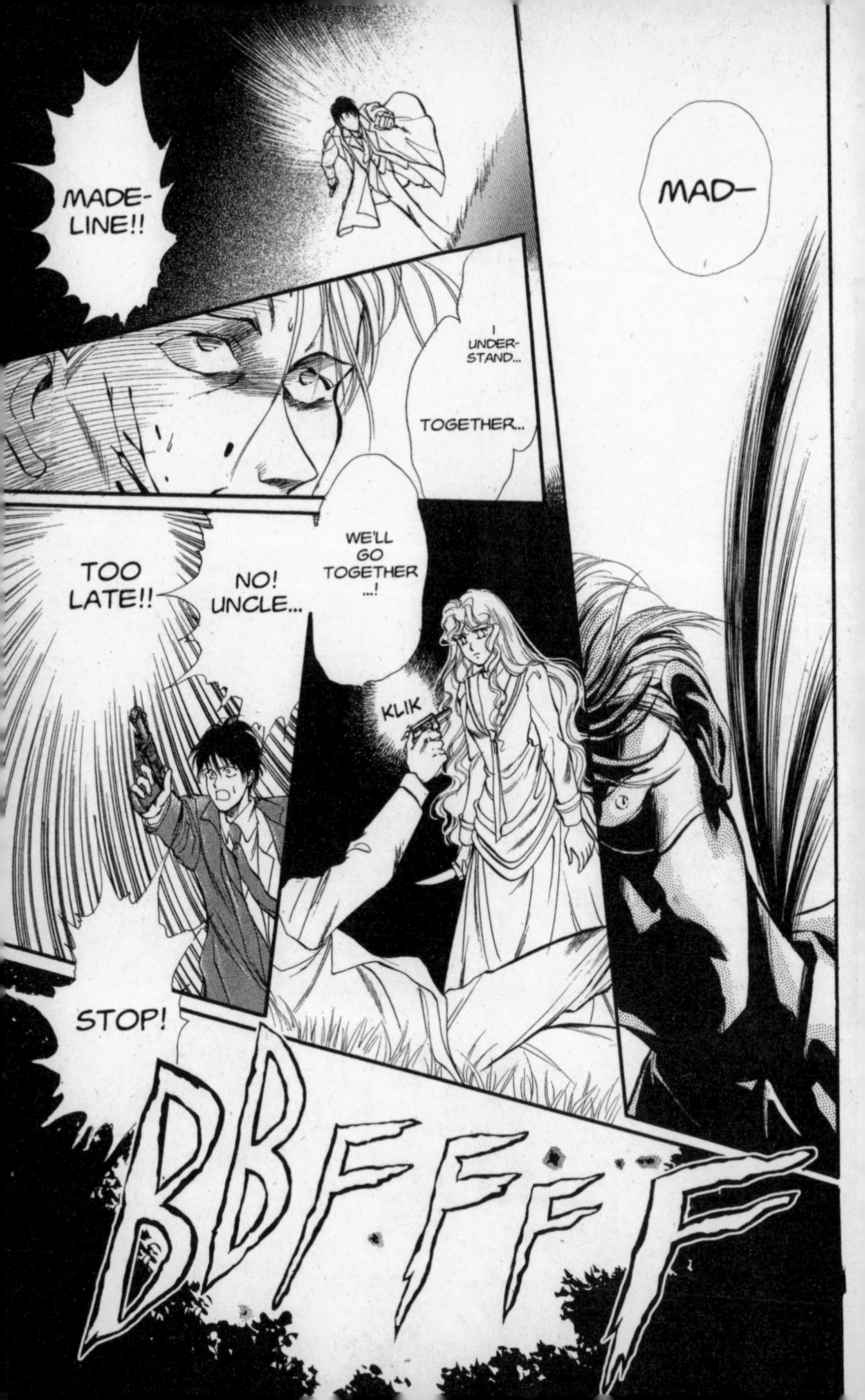
MAD—
MADE-LINE!!
I UNDERSTAND...
TOGETHER..
WE'LL GO TOGETHER ...!
KLIK
NO! UNCLE...
TOO LATE!!
STOP!
BBFFFF

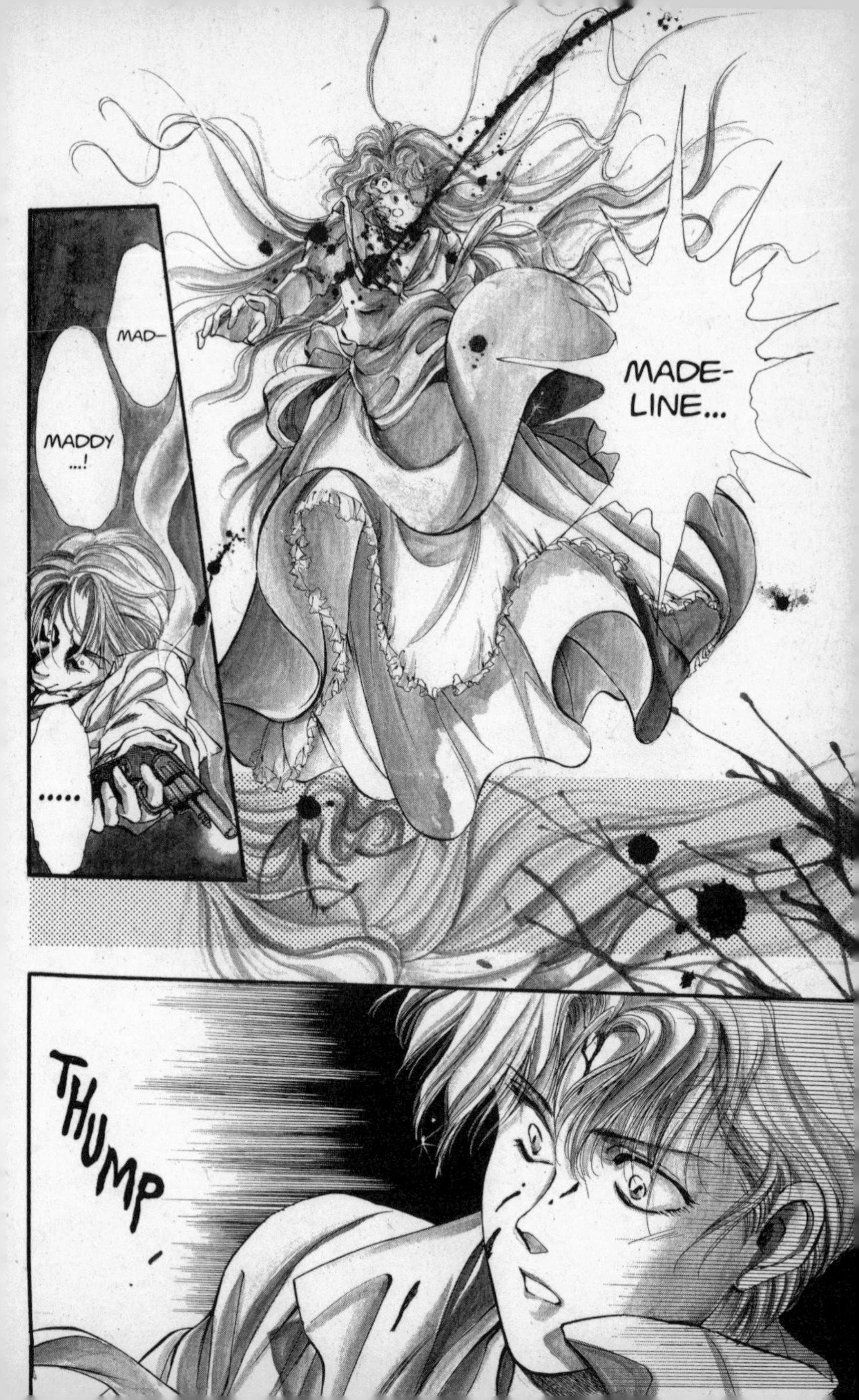
MADE-
LINE...
MAD-
MADDY
...!
.....
THUMP

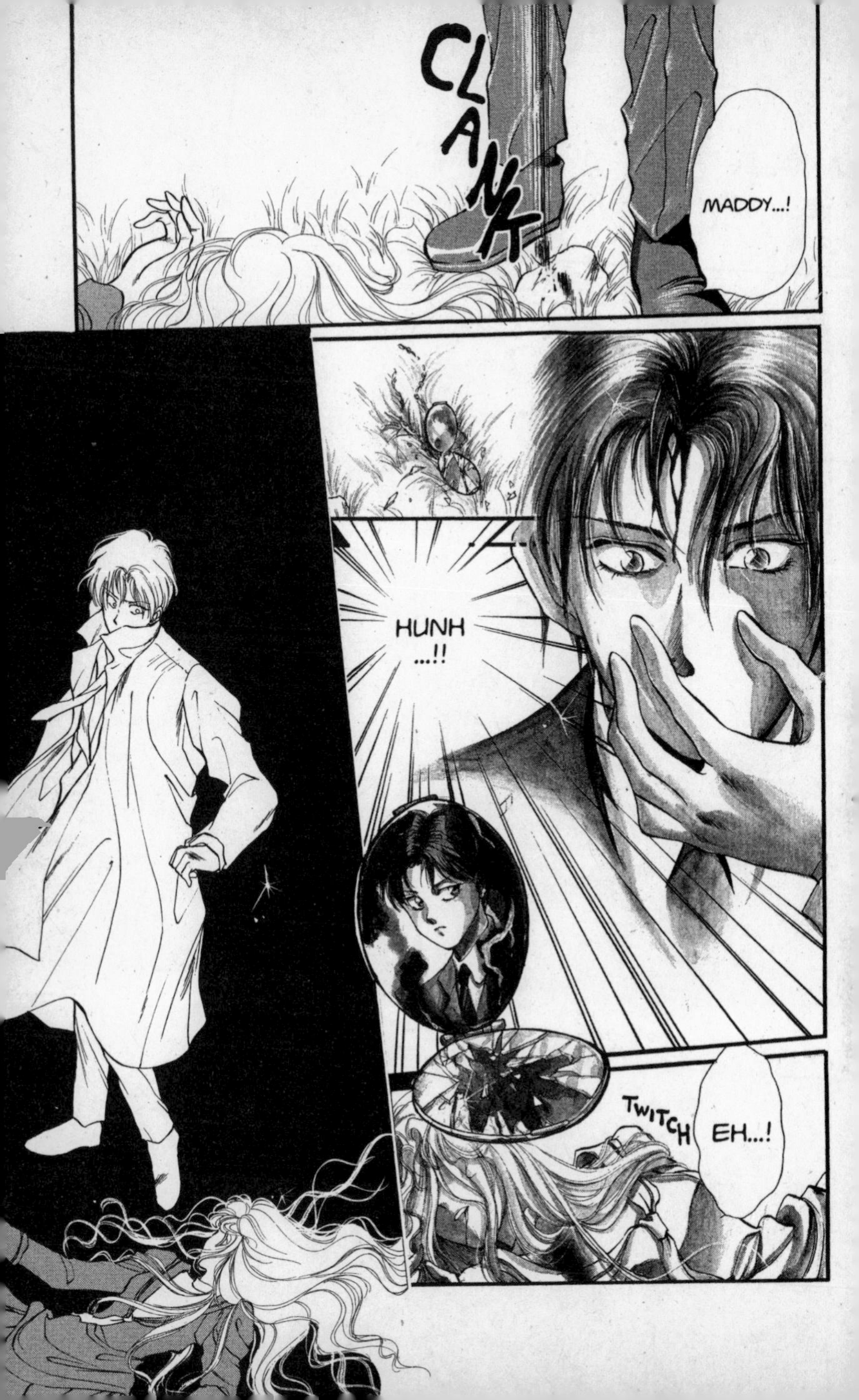
MADDY...!
CLANK
HUNH ...!!
EH...!
TWITCH

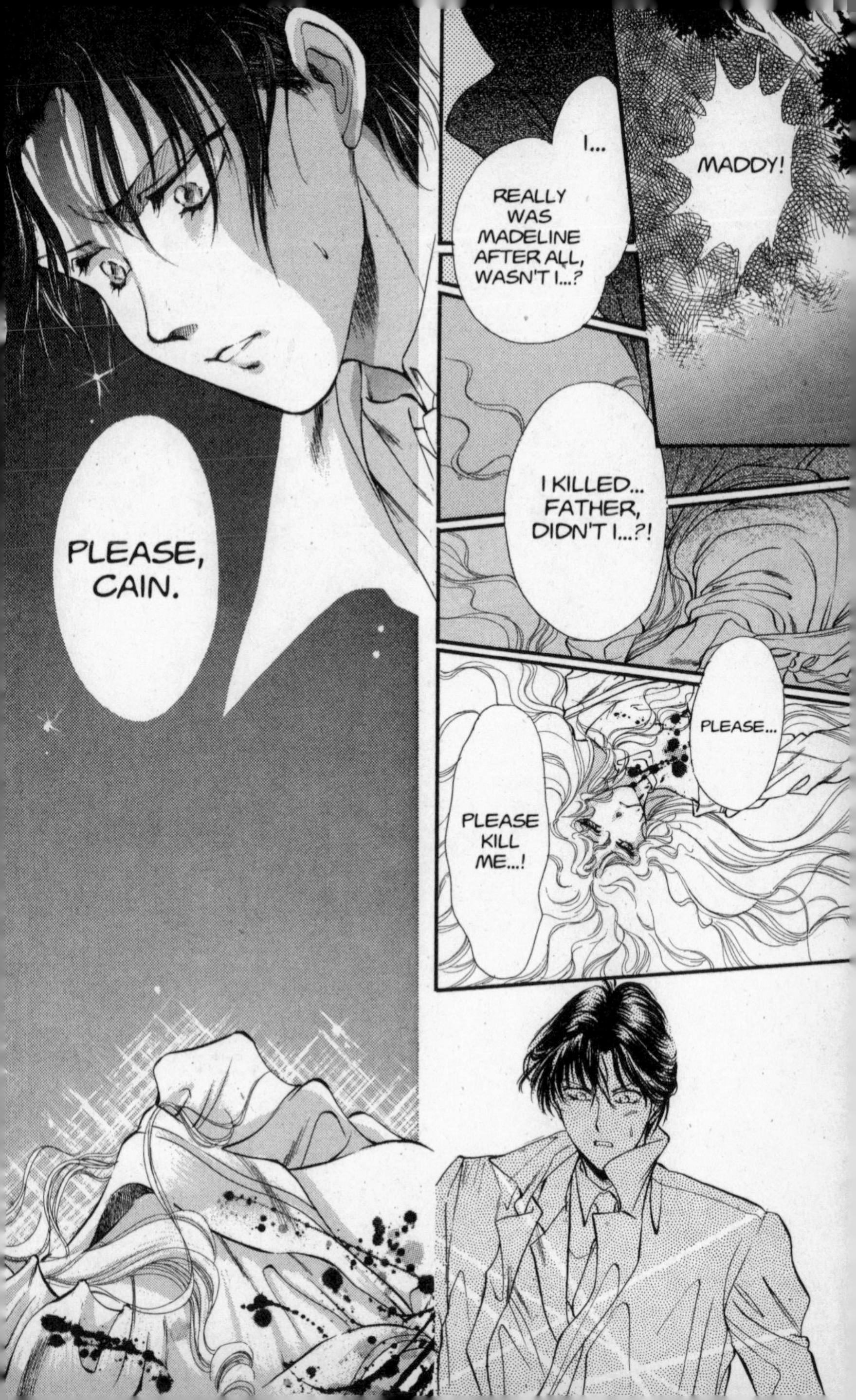
MADDY!
I... REALLY WAS MADELINE AFTER ALL, WASN'T I...?
I KILLED... FATHER, DIDN'T I...?!
PLEASE...
PLEASE KILL ME...!
PLEASE, CAIN.

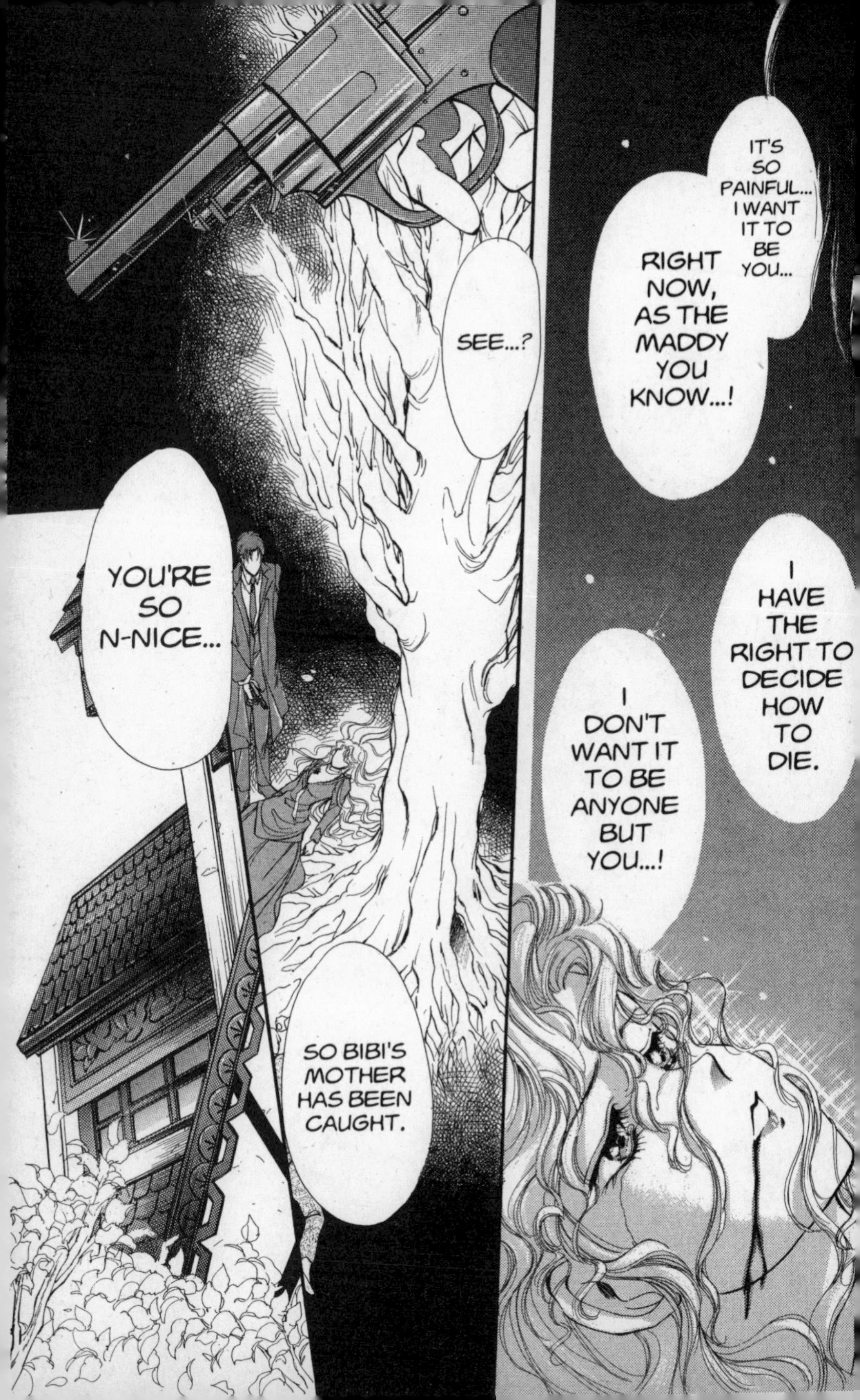
IT'S SO PAINFUL... I WANT IT TO BE YOU...
RIGHT NOW, AS THE MADDY YOU KNOW...!
I HAVE THE RIGHT TO DECIDE HOW TO DIE.
I DON'T WANT IT TO BE ANYONE BUT YOU...!
SEE...?
YOU'RE SO N-NICE...
SO BIBI'S MOTHER HAS BEEN CAUGHT.

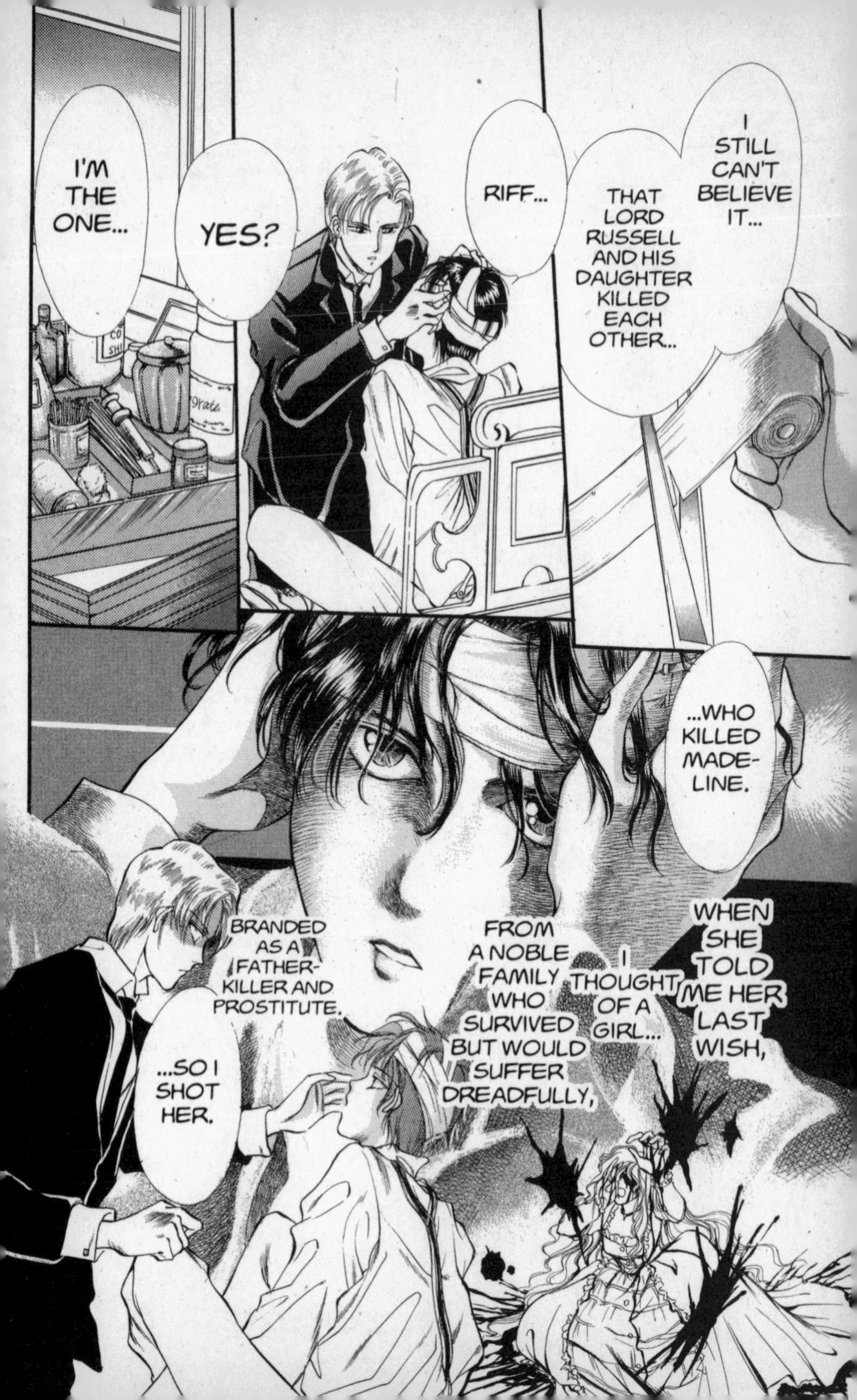
I STILL CAN'T BELIEVE IT...
THAT LORD RUSSELL AND HIS DAUGHTER KILLED EACH OTHER...
RIFF...
YES?
I'M THE ONE...
...WHO KILLED MADE-LINE.
WHEN SHE TOLD ME HER LAST WISH,
I THOUGHT OF A GIRL...
FROM A NOBLE FAMILY WHO SURVIVED BUT WOULD SUFFER DREADFULLY,
BRANDED AS A FATHER-KILLER AND PROSTITUTE.
...SO I SHOT HER.

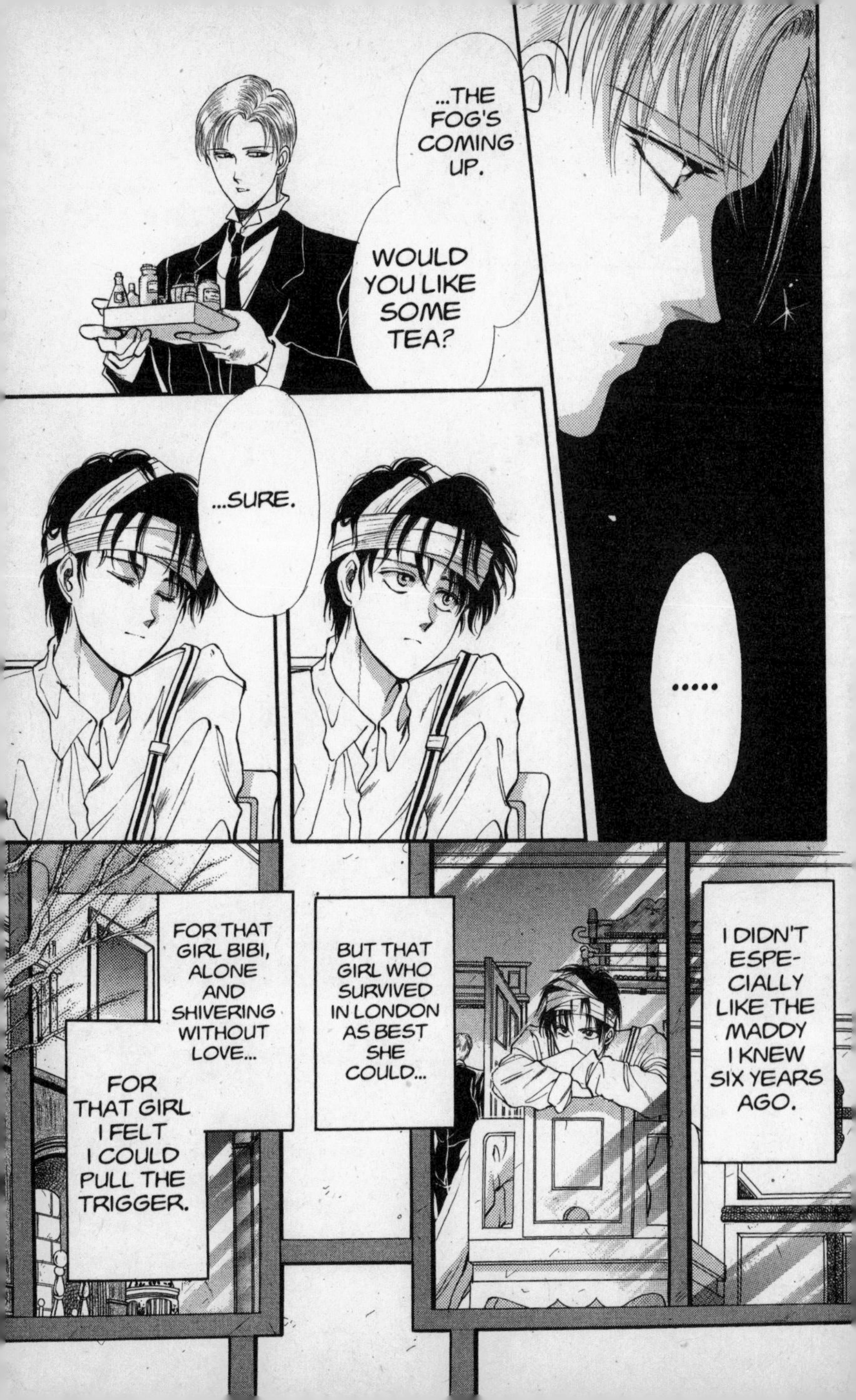
.....
...THE FOG'S COMING UP.
WOULD YOU LIKE SOME TEA?
...SURE.
I DIDN'T ESPE-CIALLY LIKE THE MADDY I KNEW SIX YEARS AGO.
BUT THAT GIRL WHO SURVIVED IN LONDON AS BEST SHE COULD...
FOR THAT GIRL BIBI, ALONE AND SHIVERING WITHOUT LOVE...
FOR THAT GIRL I FELT I COULD PULL THE TRIGGER.

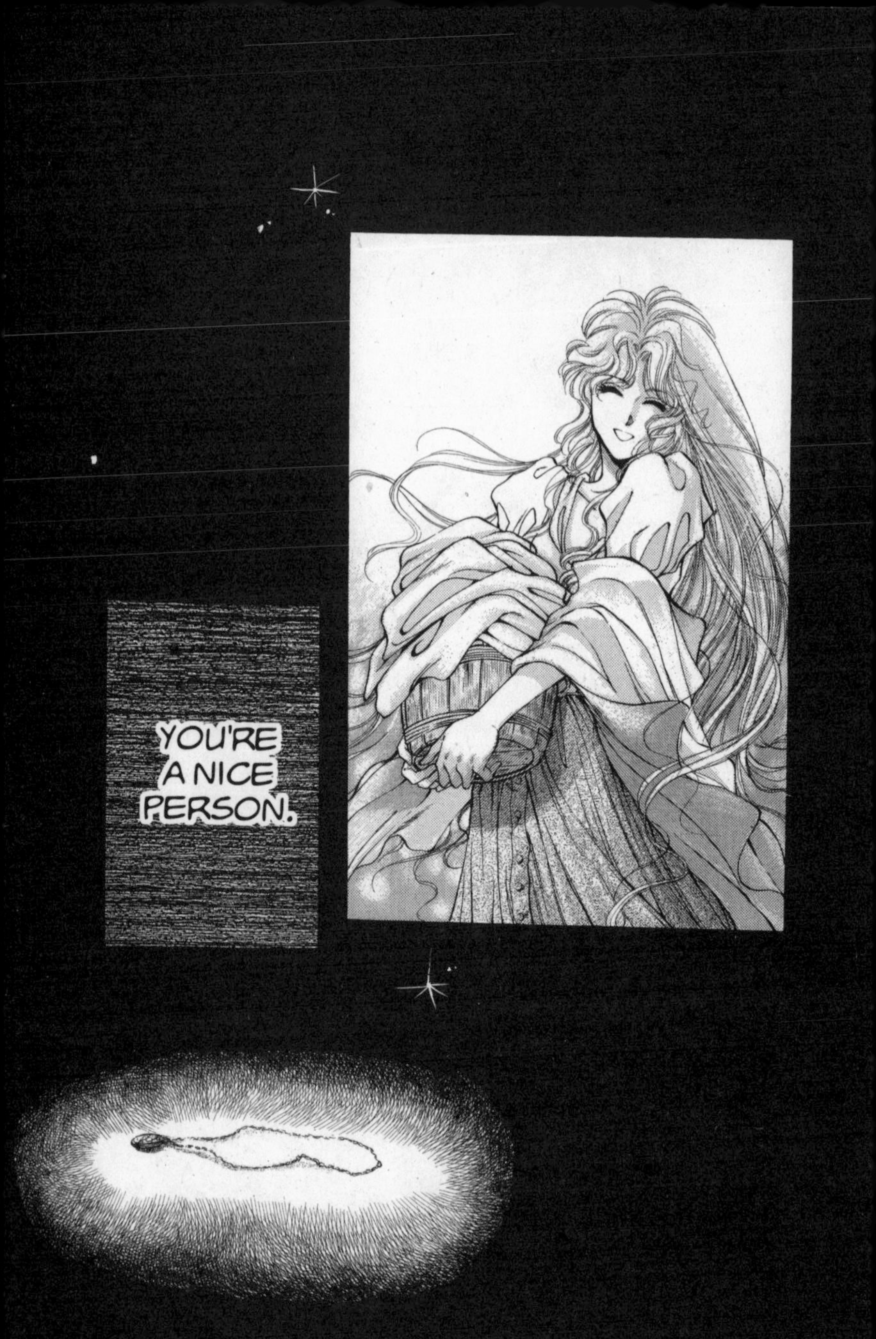
YOU'RE A NICE PERSON.

Branded Bibi/The End

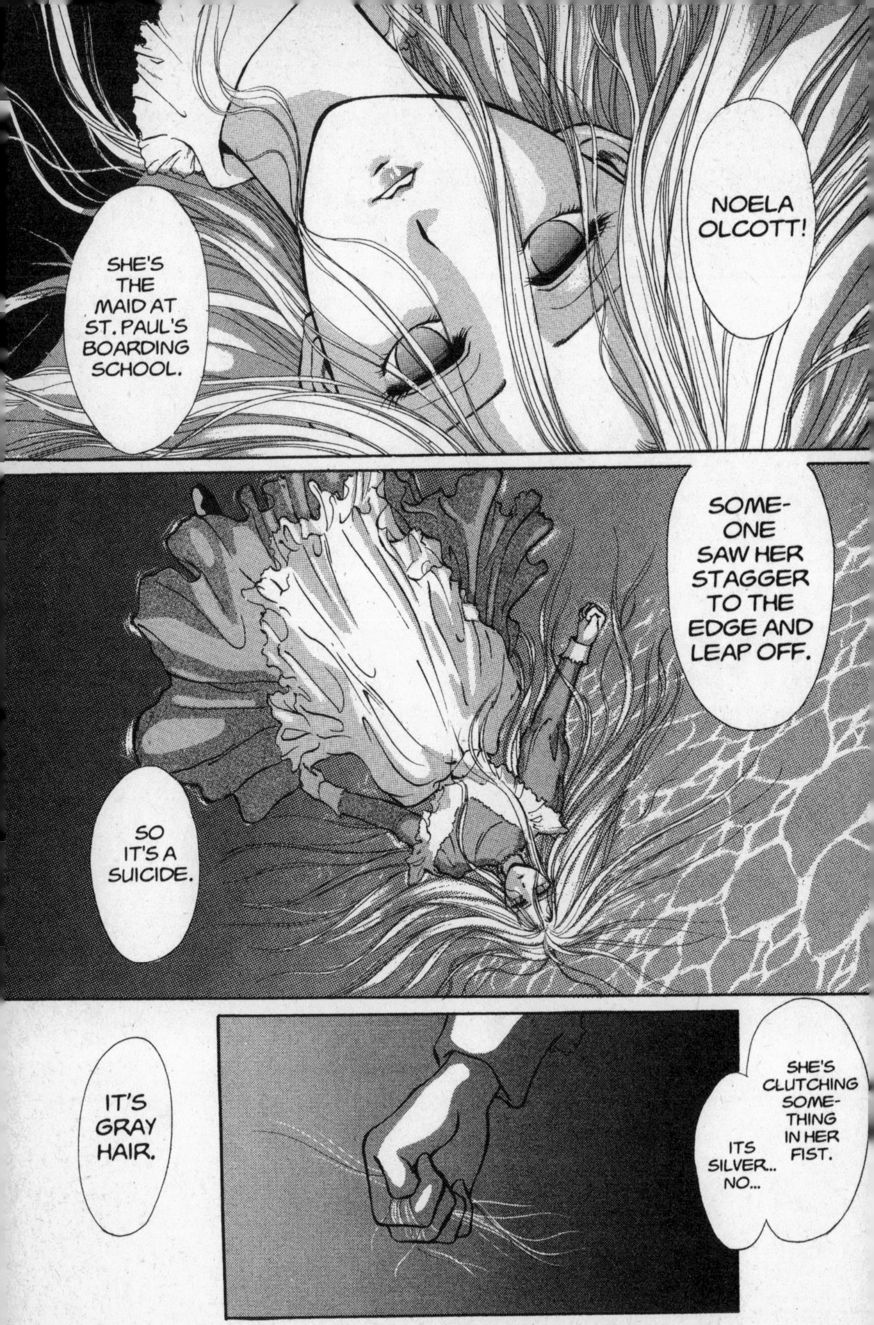
NOELA OLCOTT!
SHE'S THE MAID AT ST. PAUL'S BOARDING SCHOOL.
SOME-ONE SAW HER STAGGER TO THE EDGE AND LEAP OFF.
SO IT'S A SUICIDE.
SHE'S CLUTCHING SOME-THING IN HER FIST.
ITS SILVER... NO...
IT'S GRAY HAIR.

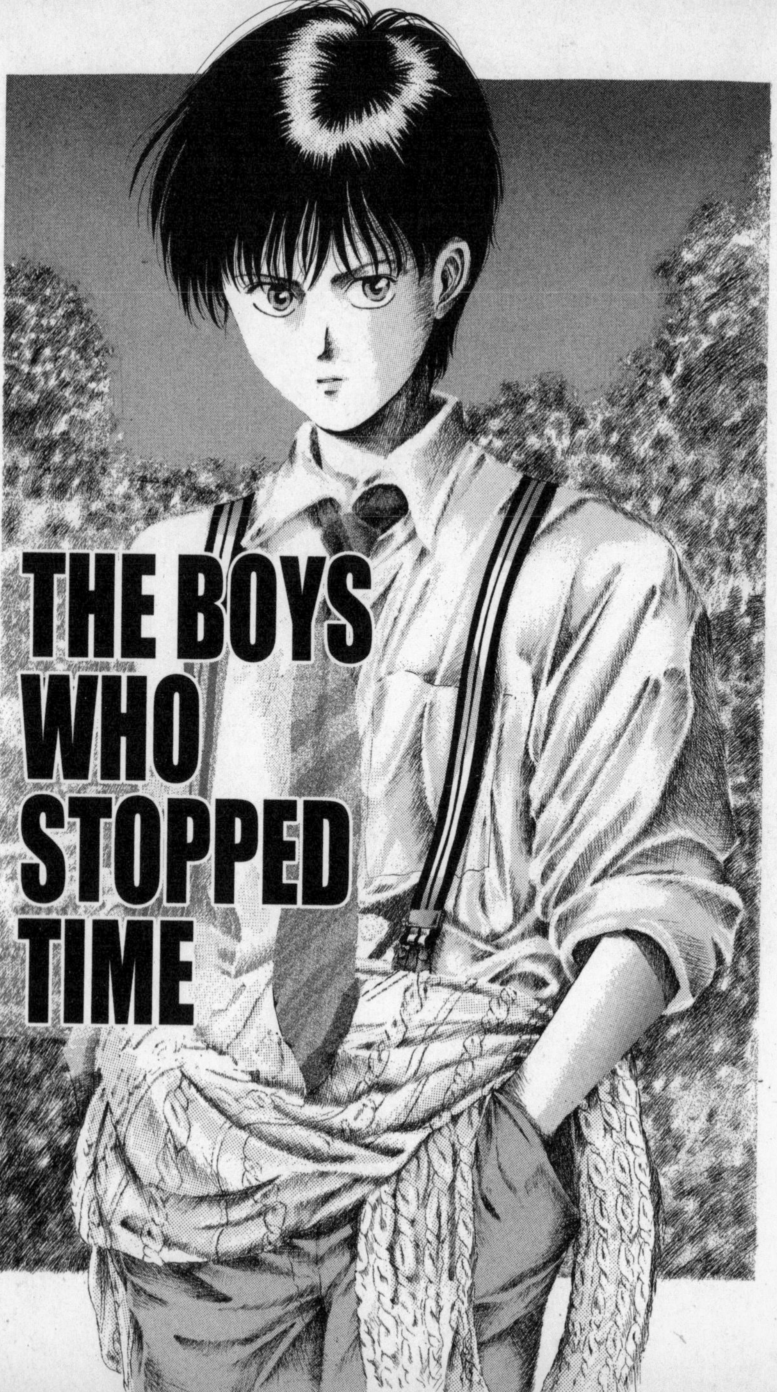
THE BOYS WHO STOPPED TIME

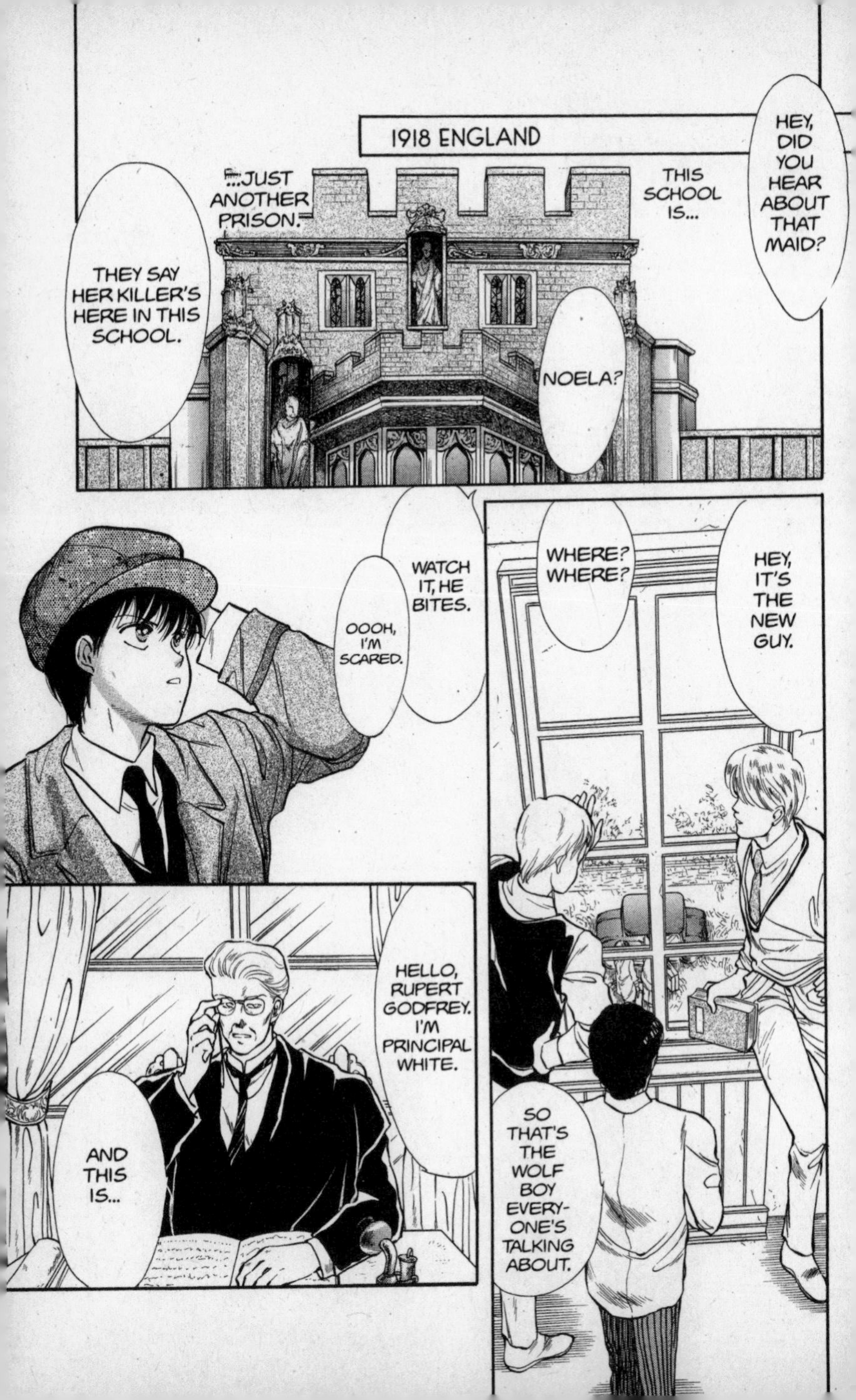
1918 ENGLAND
HEY, DID YOU HEAR ABOUT THAT MAID?
THIS SCHOOL IS...
...JUST ANOTHER PRISON.
NOELA?
THEY SAY HER KILLER'S HERE IN THIS SCHOOL.
HEY, IT'S THE NEW GUY.
WHERE? WHERE?
SO THAT'S THE WOLF BOY EVERYONE'S TALKING ABOUT.
WATCH IT, HE BITES.
OOOH, I'M SCARED.
HELLO, RUPERT GODFREY. I'M PRINCIPAL WHITE.
AND THIS IS...

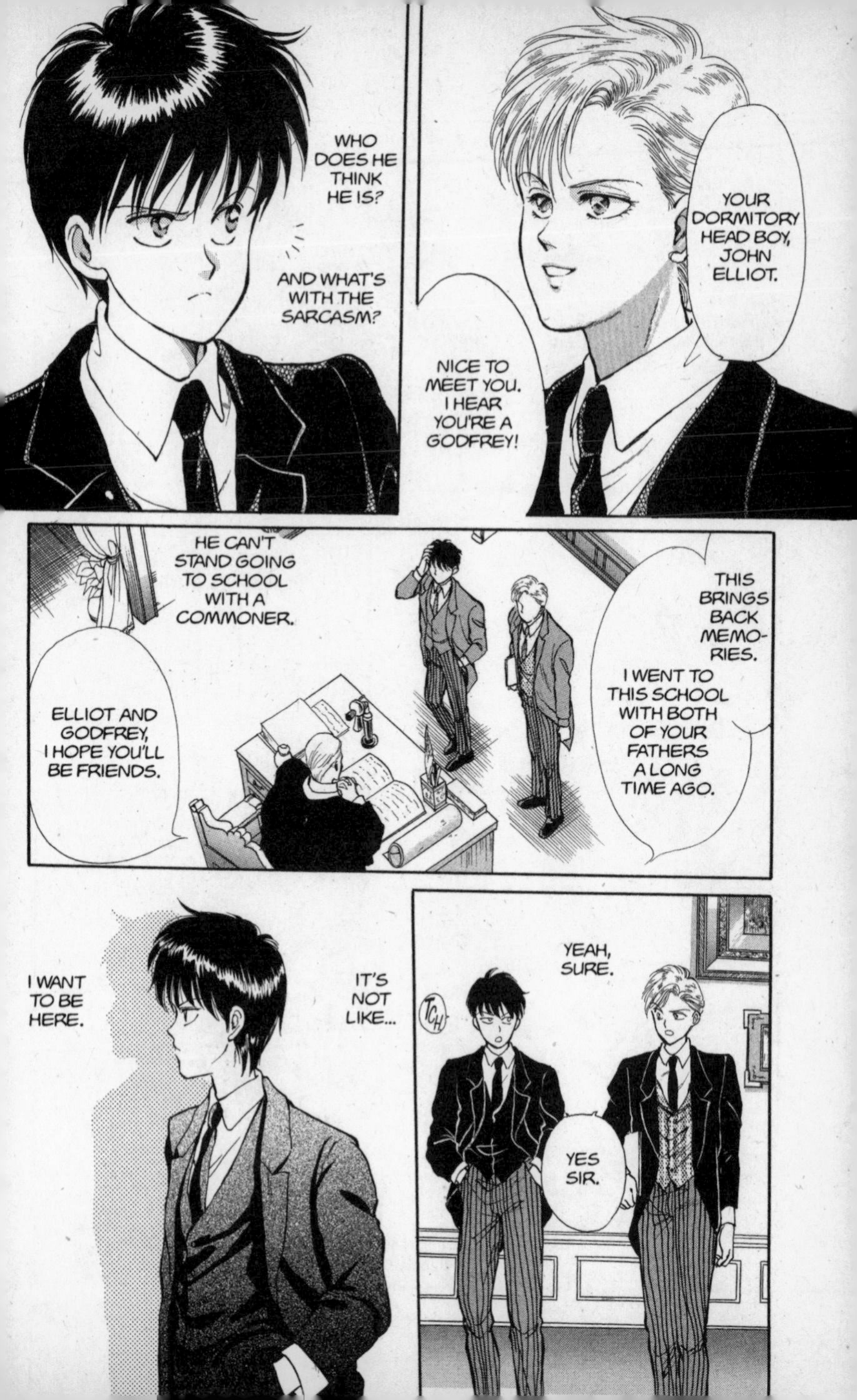
YOUR DORMITORY HEAD BOY, JOHN ELLIOT.
NICE TO MEET YOU. I HEAR YOU'RE A GODFREY!
WHO DOES HE THINK HE IS?
AND WHAT'S WITH THE SARCASM?
THIS BRINGS BACK MEMO-RIES.
I WENT TO THIS SCHOOL WITH BOTH OF YOUR FATHERS A LONG TIME AGO.
HE CAN'T STAND GOING TO SCHOOL WITH A COMMONER.
ELLIOT AND GODFREY, I HOPE YOU'LL BE FRIENDS.
YEAH, SURE.
TCH
YES SIR.
IT'S NOT LIKE...
I WANT TO BE HERE.

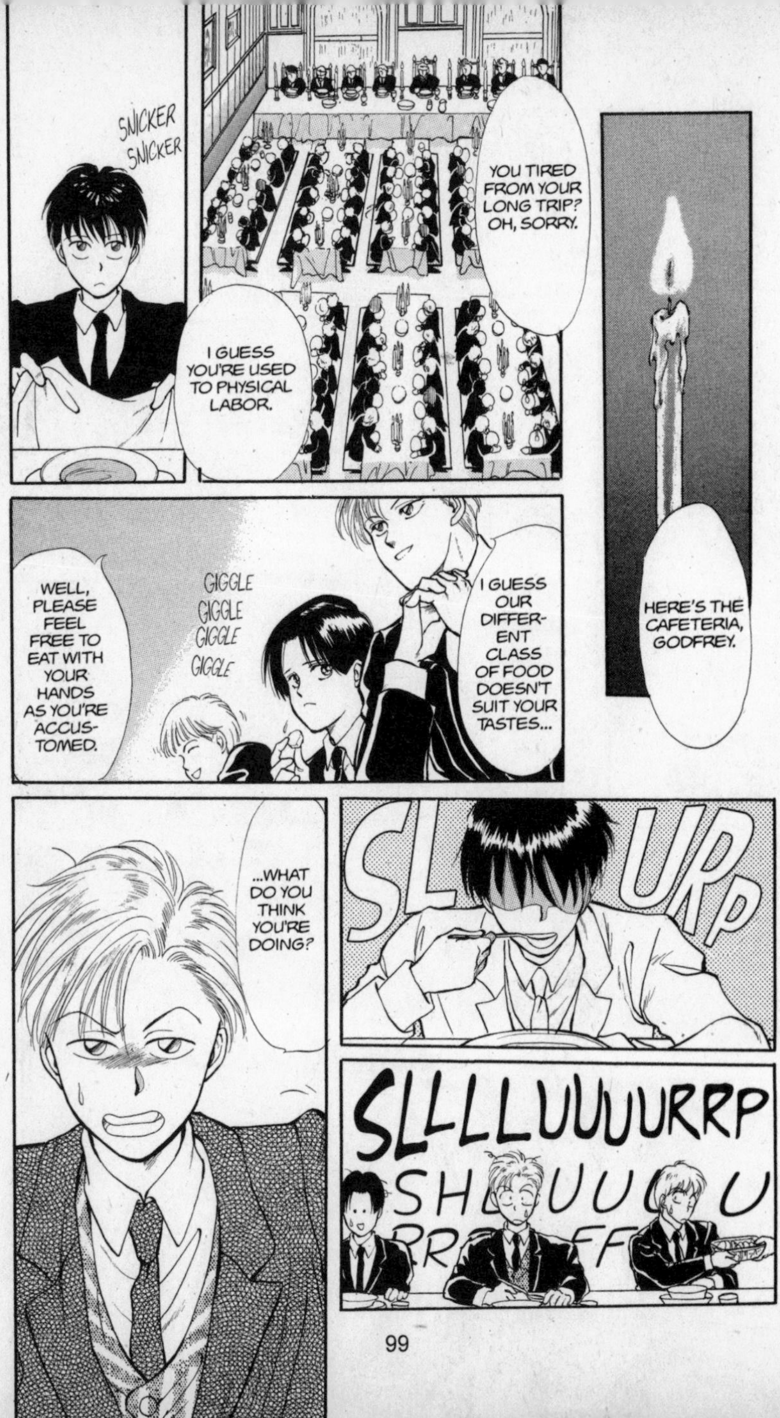
HERE'S THE CAFETERIA, GODFREY.
YOU TIRED FROM YOUR LONG TRIP? OH, SORRY.
I GUESS YOU'RE USED TO PHYSICAL LABOR.
SNICKER SNICKER
I GUESS OUR DIFFER-ENT CLASS OF FOOD DOESN'T SUIT YOUR TASTES...
GIGGLE GIGGLE GIGGLE GIGGLE
WELL, PLEASE FEEL FREE TO EAT WITH YOUR HANDS AS YOU'RE ACCUS-TOMED.
SLURP
SLLLUUUURRP
...WHAT DO YOU THINK YOU'RE DOING?

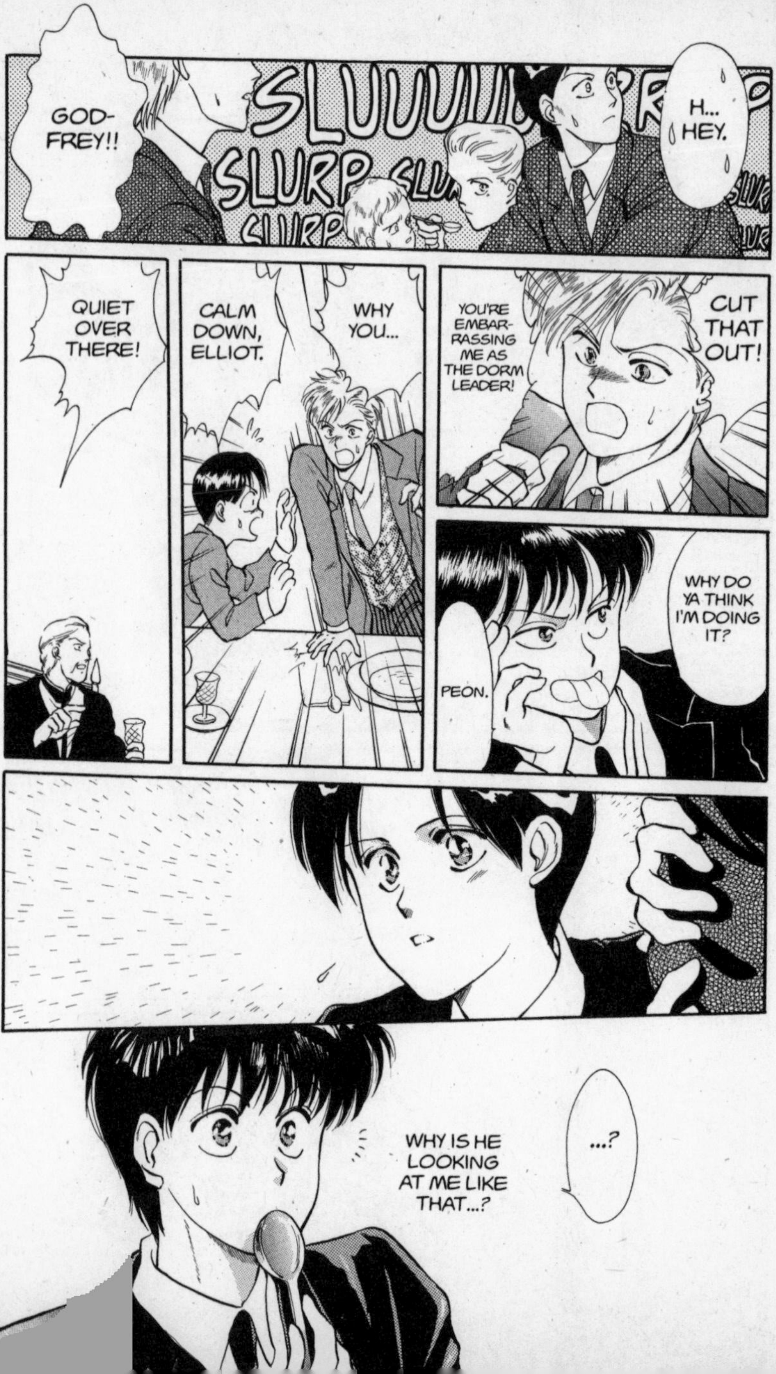
H... HEY.
SLURP
GOD-FREY!!
CUT THAT OUT!
YOU'RE EMBARRASSING ME AS THE DORM LEADER!
WHY DO YA THINK I'M DOING IT?
PEON.
WHY YOU...
CALM DOWN, ELLIOT.
QUIET OVER THERE!
...?
WHY IS HE LOOKING AT ME LIKE THAT...?

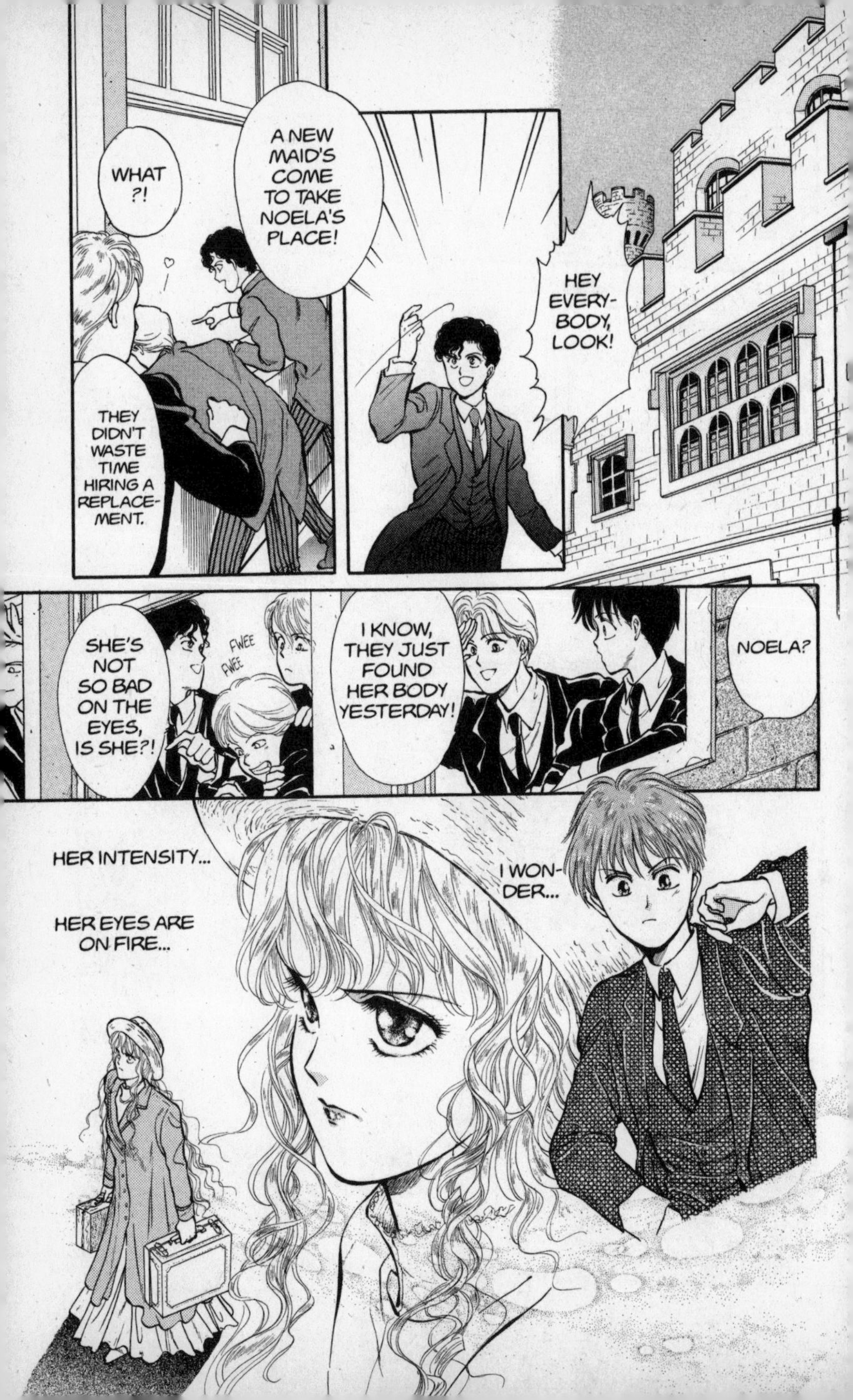
HEY EVERY-BODY, LOOK!
A NEW MAID'S COME TO TAKE NOELA'S PLACE!
WHAT ?!
THEY DIDN'T WASTE TIME HIRING A REPLACE-MENT.
NOELA?
I KNOW, THEY JUST FOUND HER BODY YESTERDAY!
SHE'S NOT SO BAD ON THE EYES, IS SHE?!
FWEE
FWEE
I WON-DER...
HER INTENSITY...
HER EYES ARE ON FIRE...

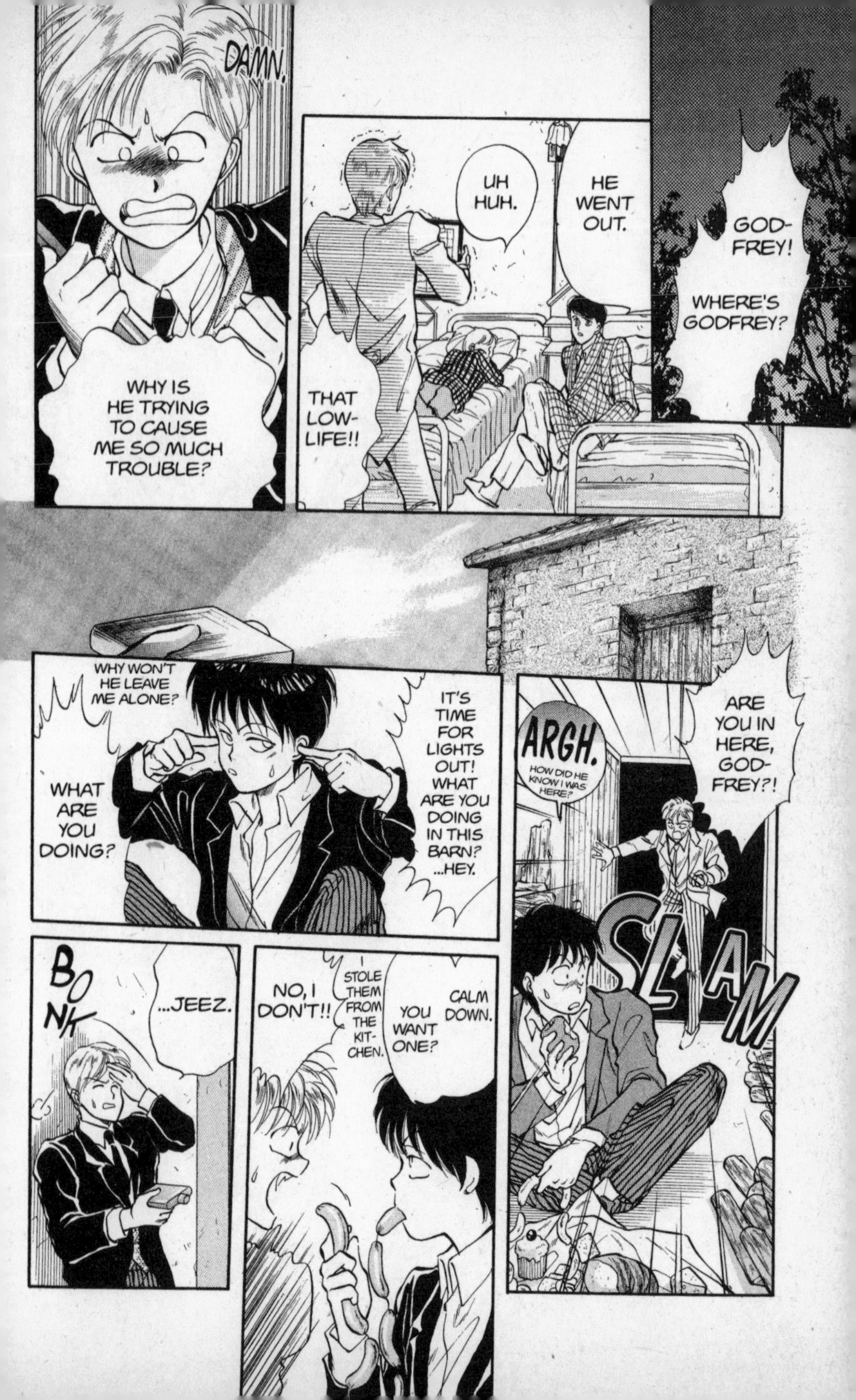
GOD-FREY!
WHERE'S GODFREY?
HE WENT OUT.
UH HUH.
THAT LOW-LIFE!!
DAMN.
WHY IS HE TRYING TO CAUSE ME SO MUCH TROUBLE?
ARE YOU IN HERE, GOD-FREY?!
ARGH.
HOW DID HE KNOW I WAS HERE?
SLAM
IT'S TIME FOR LIGHTS OUT! WHAT ARE YOU DOING IN THIS BARN? ...HEY.
WHY WON'T HE LEAVE ME ALONE?
WHAT ARE YOU DOING?
CALM DOWN.
YOU WANT ONE?
I STOLE THEM FROM THE KIT-CHEN.
NO, I DON'T!!
BONK
...JEEZ.

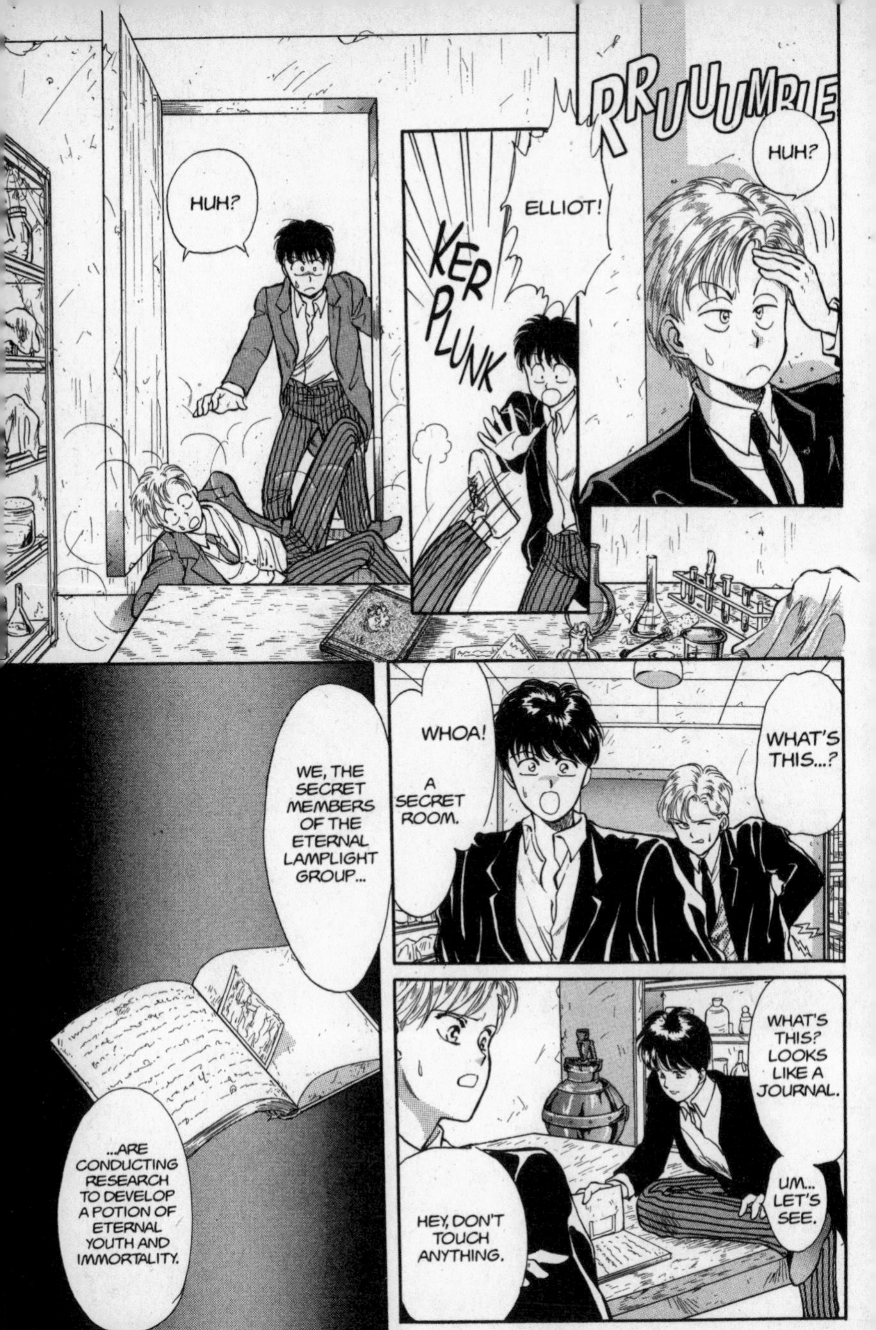
RRUUUMBLE
HUH?
ELLIOT!
KER PLUNK
HUH?
WHAT'S THIS...?
WHOA!
A SECRET ROOM.
WHAT'S THIS? LOOKS LIKE A JOURNAL.
UM... LET'S SEE.
HEY, DON'T TOUCH ANYTHING.
WE, THE SECRET MEMBERS OF THE ETERNAL LAMPLIGHT GROUP...
...ARE CONDUCTING RESEARCH TO DEVELOP A POTION OF ETERNAL YOUTH AND IMMORTALITY.

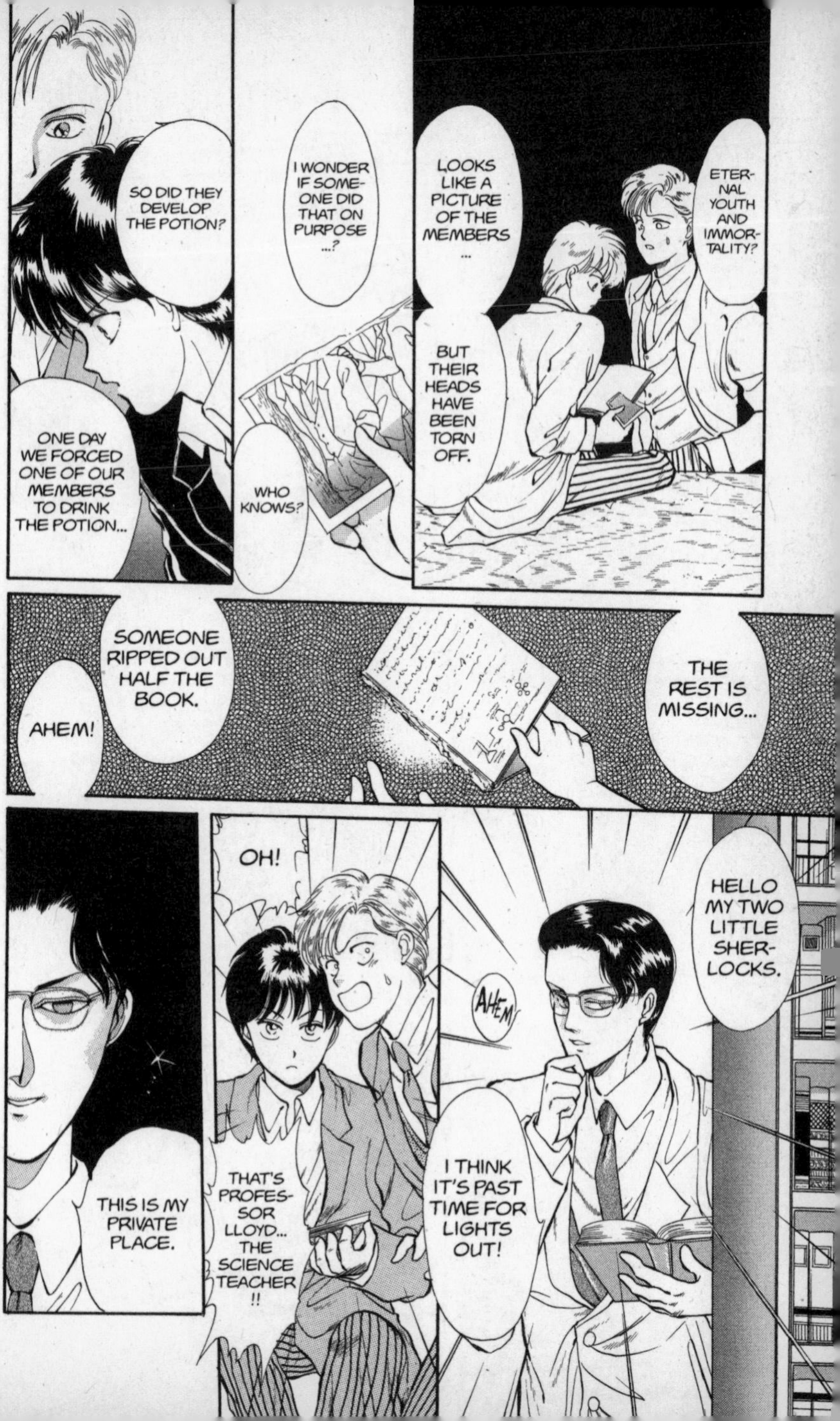
ETERNAL YOUTH AND IMMORTALITY?
LOOKS LIKE A PICTURE OF THE MEMBERS...
BUT THEIR HEADS HAVE BEEN TORN OFF.
I WONDER IF SOMEONE DID THAT ON PURPOSE...?
WHO KNOWS?
SO DID THEY DEVELOP THE POTION?
ONE DAY WE FORCED ONE OF OUR MEMBERS TO DRINK THE POTION...
THE REST IS MISSING...
SOMEONE RIPPED OUT HALF THE BOOK.
AHEM!
HELLO MY TWO LITTLE SHERLOCKS.
AHEM
I THINK IT'S PAST TIME FOR LIGHTS OUT!
OH!
THAT'S PROFESSOR LLOYD... THE SCIENCE TEACHER!!
THIS IS MY PRIVATE PLACE.

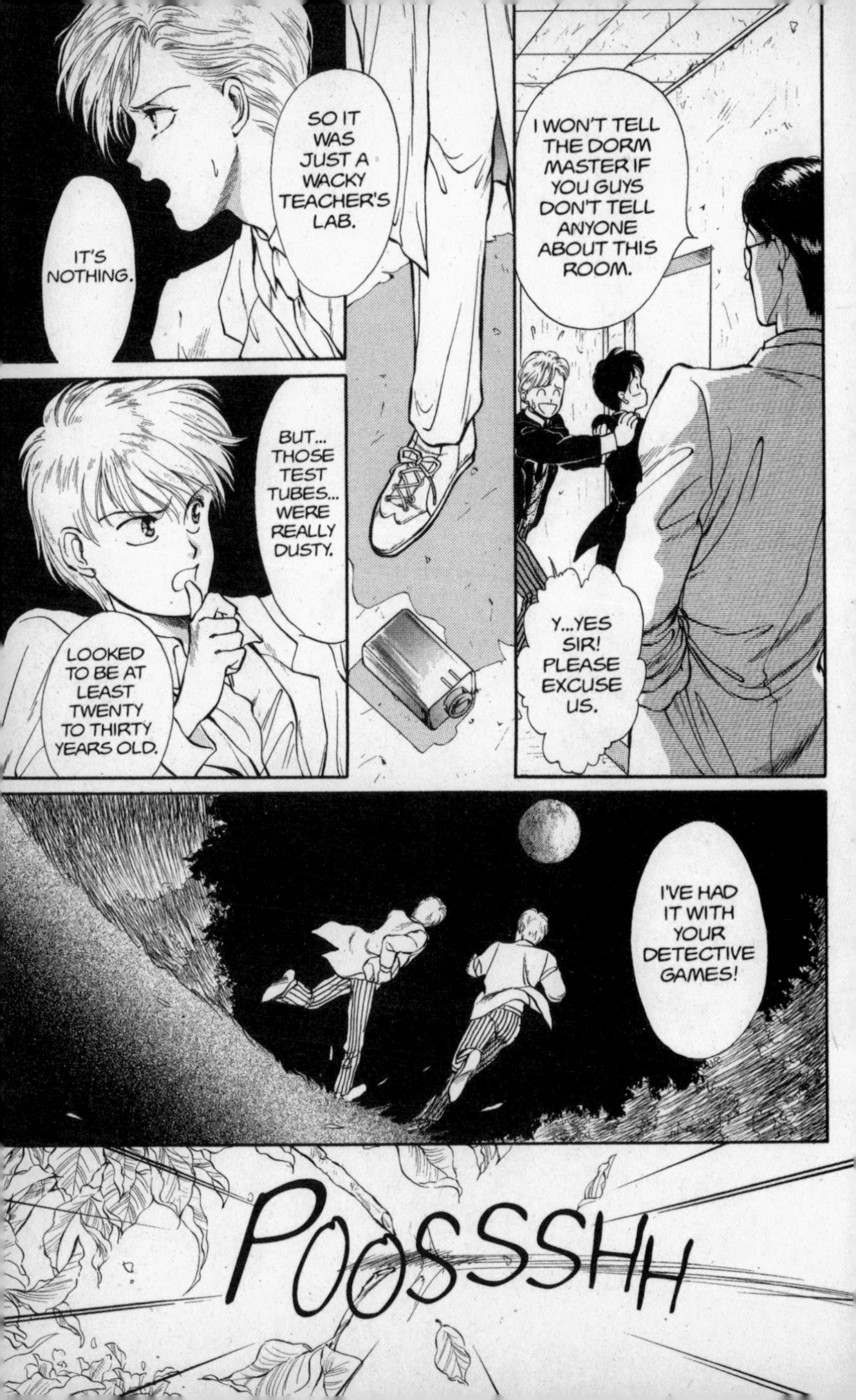
I WON'T TELL THE DORM MASTER IF YOU GUYS DON'T TELL ANYONE ABOUT THIS ROOM.
Y...YES SIR! PLEASE EXCUSE US.
SO IT WAS JUST A WACKY TEACHER'S LAB.
IT'S NOTHING.
BUT... THOSE TEST TUBES... WERE REALLY DUSTY.
LOOKED TO BE AT LEAST TWENTY TO THIRTY YEARS OLD.
I'VE HAD IT WITH YOUR DETECTIVE GAMES!
POOSSSHH

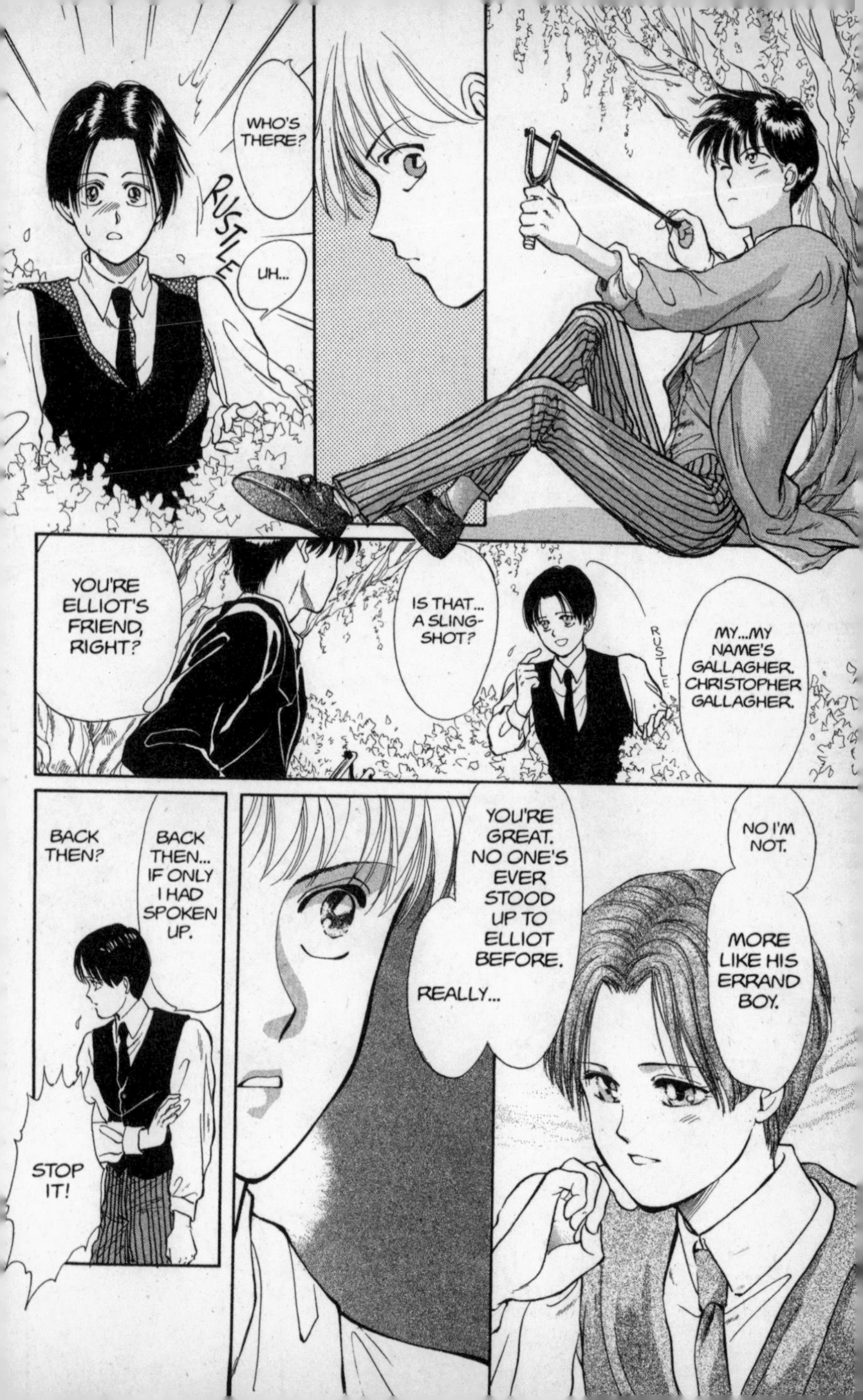
WHO'S THERE?
UH...
RUSTLE
MY...MY NAME'S GALLAGHER. CHRISTOPHER GALLAGHER.
RUSTLE
IS THAT... A SLING-SHOT?
YOU'RE ELLIOT'S FRIEND, RIGHT?
YOU'RE GREAT. NO ONE'S EVER STOOD UP TO ELLIOT BEFORE.
NO I'M NOT.
MORE LIKE HIS ERRAND BOY.
REALLY...
BACK THEN... IF ONLY I HAD SPOKEN UP.
BACK THEN?
STOP IT!

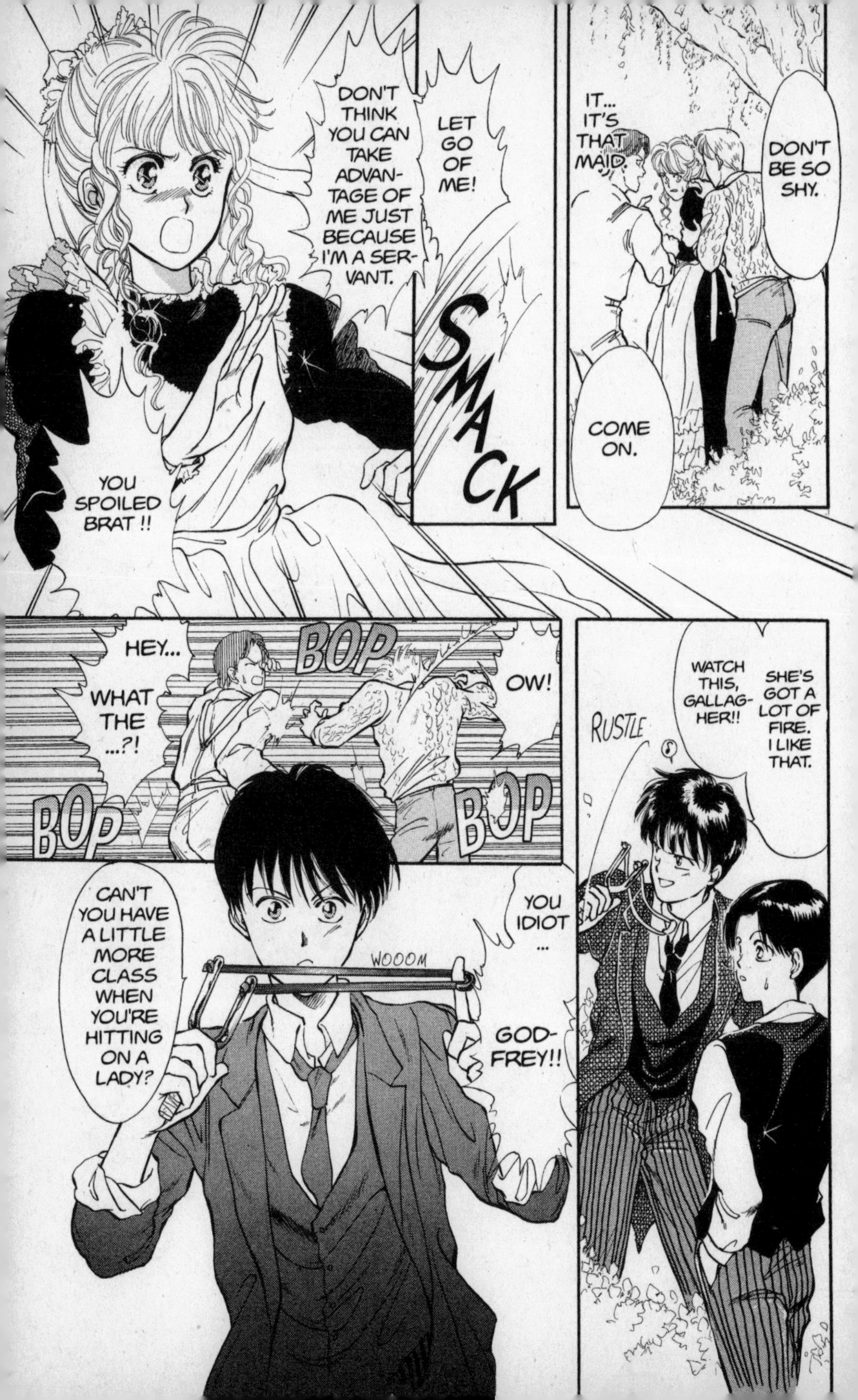
DON'T BE SO SHY.
IT... IT'S THAT MAID.
COME ON.
SMACK
LET GO OF ME!
DON'T THINK YOU CAN TAKE ADVANTAGE OF ME JUST BECAUSE I'M A SERVANT.
YOU SPOILED BRAT !!
SHE'S GOT A LOT OF FIRE. I LIKE THAT.
WATCH THIS, GALLAGHER!!
RUSTLE
OW!
BOP
HEY...
WHAT THE ...?!
BOP
BOP
YOU IDIOT ...
GODFREY!!
WOOOM
CAN'T YOU HAVE A LITTLE MORE CLASS WHEN YOU'RE HITTING ON A LADY?

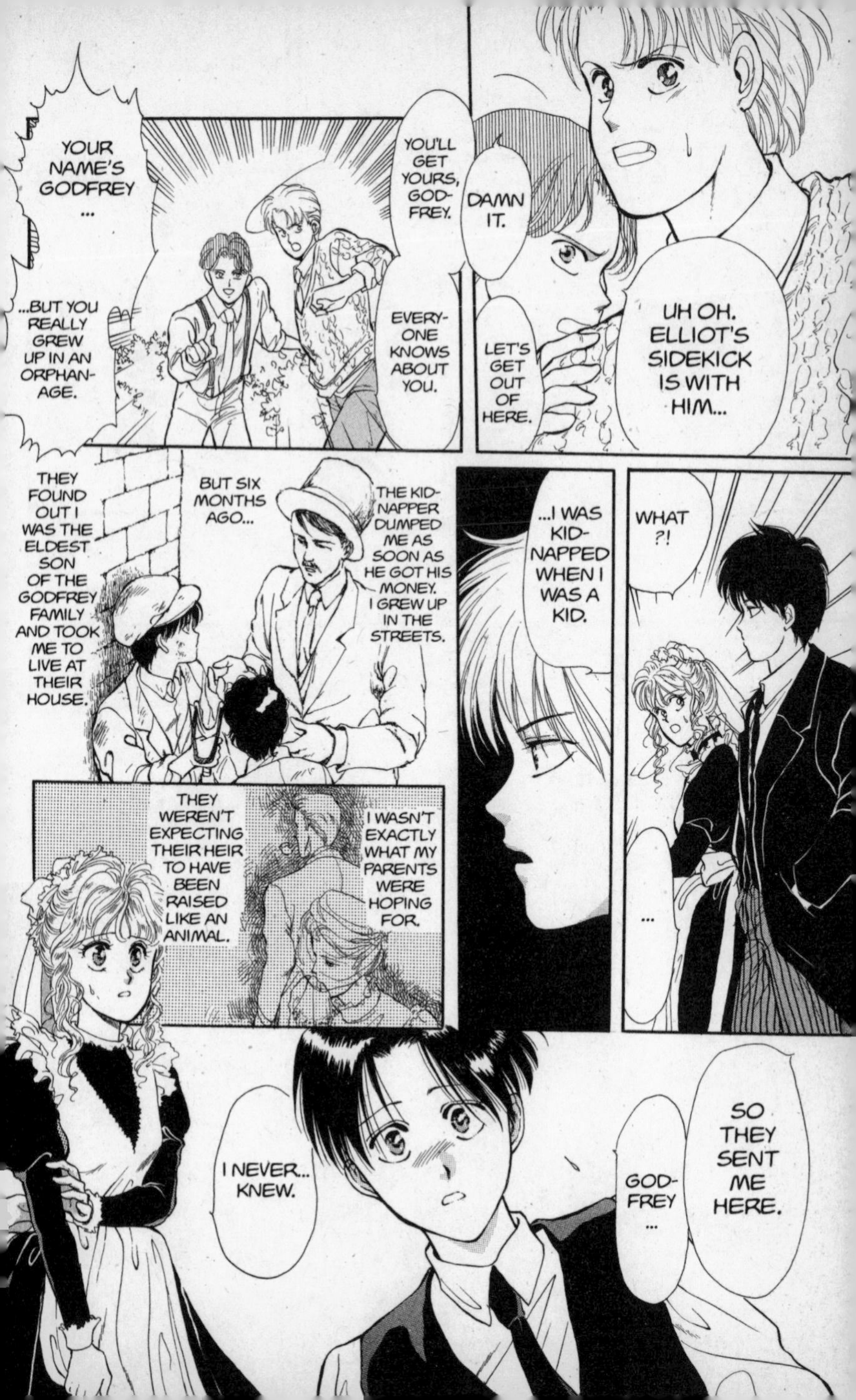
DAMN IT.
UH OH. ELLIOT'S SIDEKICK IS WITH HIM...
LET'S GET OUT OF HERE.
YOU'LL GET YOURS, GOD-FREY.
EVERY-ONE KNOWS ABOUT YOU.
YOUR NAME'S GODFREY ...
...BUT YOU REALLY GREW UP IN AN ORPHAN-AGE.
WHAT ?!
...
...I WAS KID-NAPPED WHEN I WAS A KID.
THE KID-NAPPER DUMPED ME AS SOON AS HE GOT HIS MONEY. I GREW UP IN THE STREETS.
BUT SIX MONTHS AGO...
THEY FOUND OUT I WAS THE ELDEST SON OF THE GODFREY FAMILY AND TOOK ME TO LIVE AT THEIR HOUSE.
I WASN'T EXACTLY WHAT MY PARENTS WERE HOPING FOR.
THEY WEREN'T EXPECTING THEIR HEIR TO HAVE BEEN RAISED LIKE AN ANIMAL.
SO THEY SENT ME HERE.
GOD-FREY ...
I NEVER... KNEW.

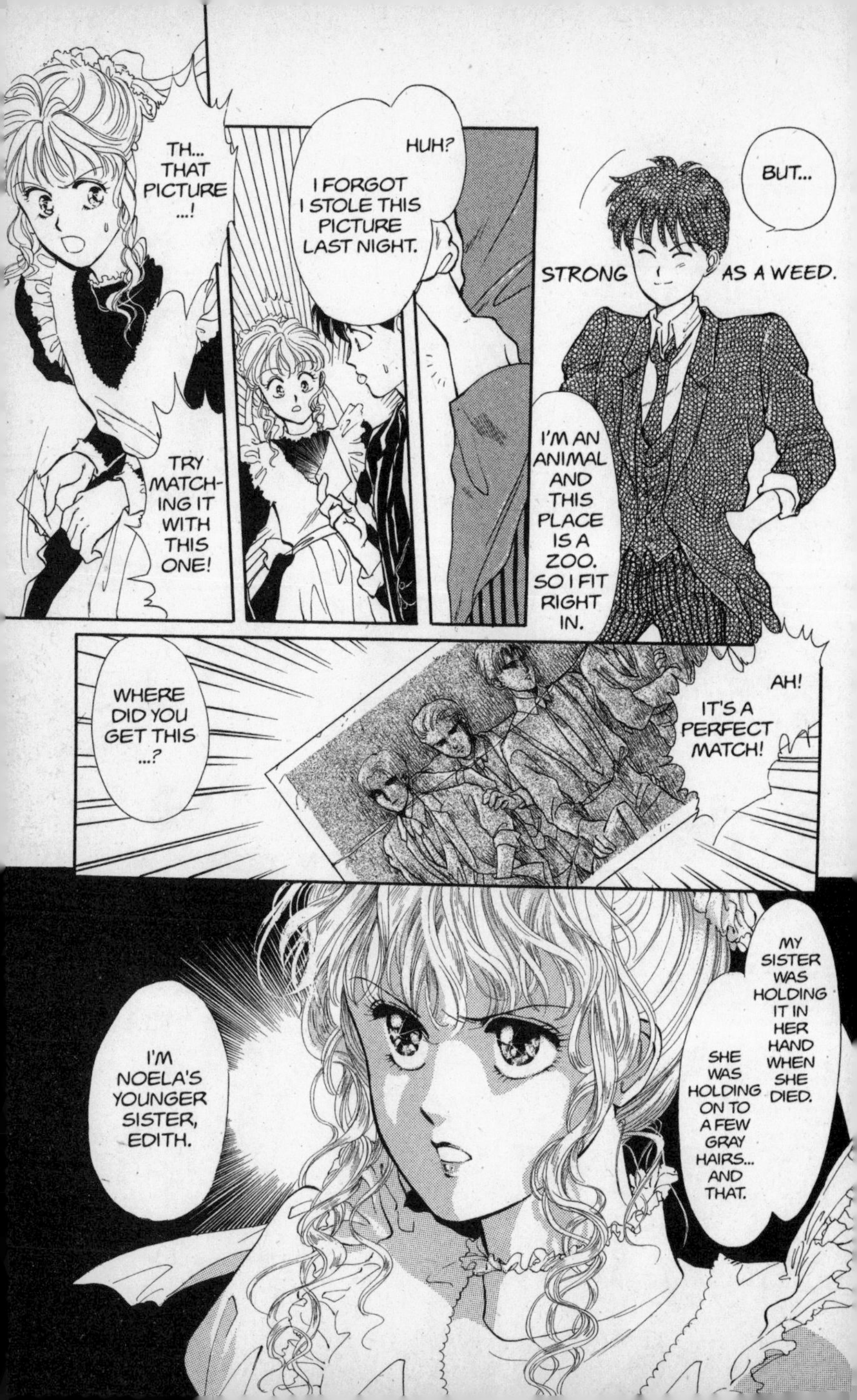
BUT...
STRONG AS A WEED.
I'M AN ANIMAL AND THIS PLACE IS A ZOO. SO I FIT RIGHT IN.
HUH?
I FORGOT I STOLE THIS PICTURE LAST NIGHT.
TH... THAT PICTURE ...!
TRY MATCHING IT WITH THIS ONE!
AH!
IT'S A PERFECT MATCH!
WHERE DID YOU GET THIS ...?
MY SISTER WAS HOLDING IT IN HER HAND WHEN SHE DIED.
SHE WAS HOLDING ON TO A FEW GRAY HAIRS... AND THAT.
I'M NOELA'S YOUNGER SISTER, EDITH.

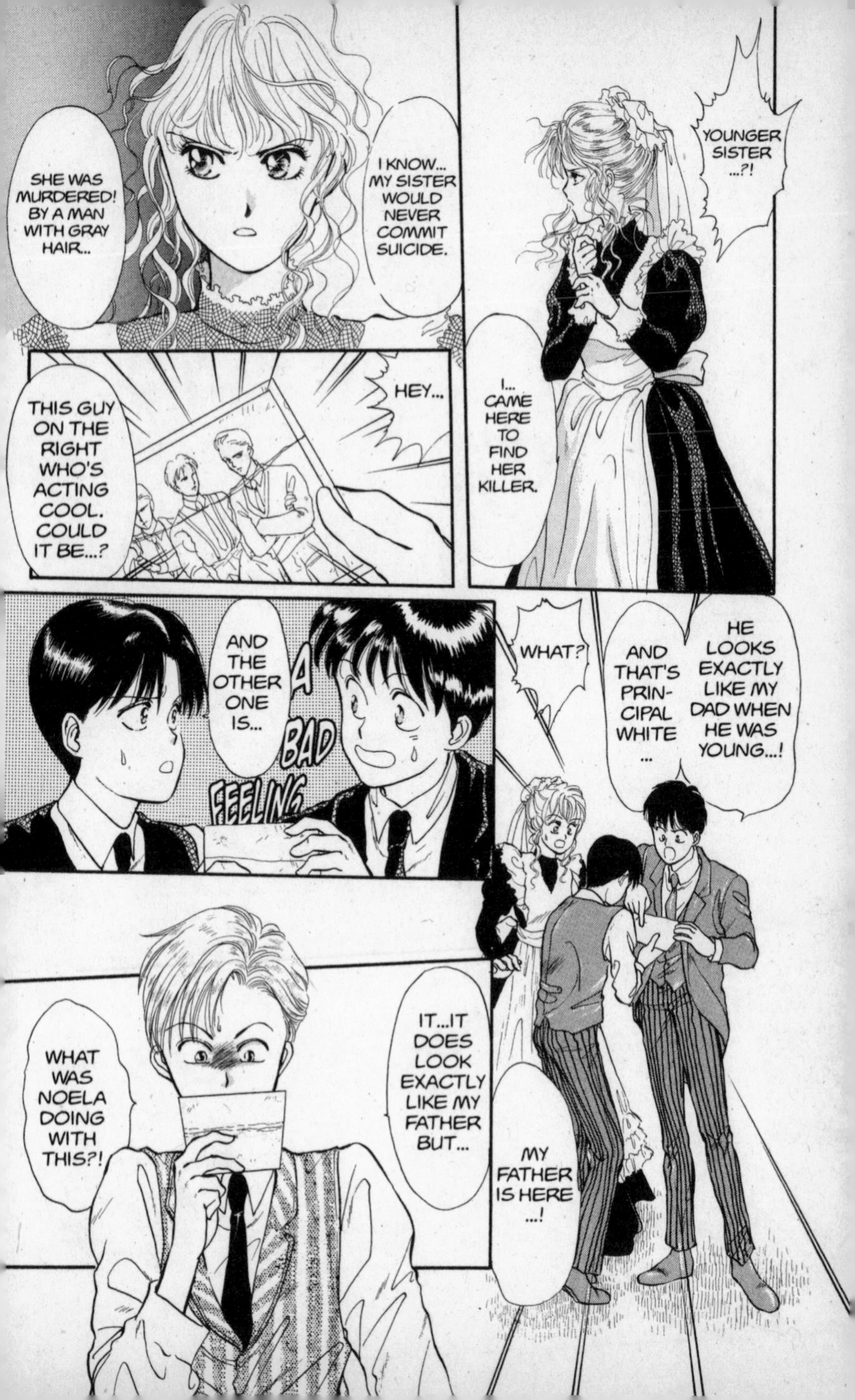
YOUNGER SISTER ...?!
I... CAME HERE TO FIND HER KILLER.
I KNOW... MY SISTER WOULD NEVER COMMIT SUICIDE.
SHE WAS MURDERED! BY A MAN WITH GRAY HAIR...
HEY...
THIS GUY ON THE RIGHT WHO'S ACTING COOL. COULD IT BE...?
HE LOOKS EXACTLY LIKE MY DAD WHEN HE WAS YOUNG...!
AND THAT'S PRIN-CIPAL WHITE ...
WHAT?
MY FATHER IS HERE ...!
AND THE OTHER ONE IS...
BAD FEELING
IT...IT DOES LOOK EXACTLY LIKE MY FATHER BUT...
WHAT WAS NOELA DOING WITH THIS?!

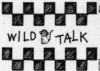

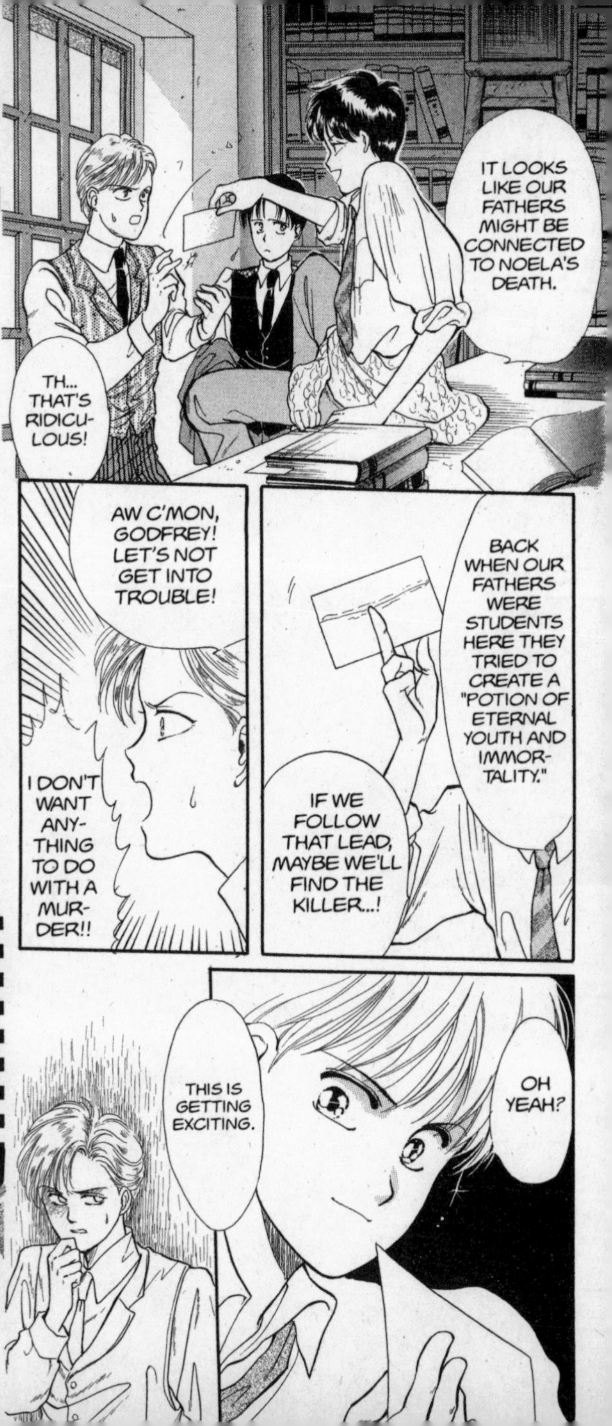
IT LOOKS LIKE OUR FATHERS MIGHT BE CONNECTED TO NOELA'S DEATH.
TH... THAT'S RIDICULOUS!
BACK WHEN OUR FATHERS WERE STUDENTS HERE THEY TRIED TO CREATE A "POTION OF ETERNAL YOUTH AND IMMORTALITY."
IF WE FOLLOW THAT LEAD, MAYBE WE'LL FIND THE KILLER...!
AW C'MON, GODFREY! LET'S NOT GET INTO TROUBLE!
I DON'T WANT ANYTHING TO DO WITH A MURDER!!
OH YEAH?
THIS IS GETTING EXCITING.

WILD TALK

THIS IS A REMAKE OF A STORY I THOUGHT UP LONG AGO. I'M FINALLY FEELING GOOD ABOUT WRITING A MURDER MYSTERY. HEH HEH HEH. IT'S MOSTLY INFLUENCED BY THE MOVIE, ***YOUNG SHERLOCK HOLMES***, BUT I'D LIKE TO ALSO TALK A LITTLE BIT ABOUT ***DEAD POETS SOCIETY***, WHICH I JUST LOVED. ON THE SURFACE IT SEEMS LIKE AN ORDINARY MOVIE ABOUT A SCHOOL, BUT THERE'S A LOT OF CLASSICAL CONTENT THAT CLICKED WITH ME. I REALLY LIKED THE RAMBUNCTIOUS CHARLIE, BUT I WAS DISAPPOINTED WHEN HE WAS LEFT OUT OF THE FINAL SCENE. TOO BAD! HE WAS ABOUT 30 IN REAL LIFE WHEN HE MADE THAT MOVIE. ROBIN WILLIAMS IS GREAT AS THE TEACHER TOO. I'M SURE THAT I'M NOT THE ONLY PERSON WHO WAS MOVED TO TEARS BY THAT PAINFUL AND BEAUTIFUL FINAL SCENE! MAKE SURE YOU WATCH IT IN A PEACEFUL STATE OF MIND: IT'S A GREAT MOVIE SO TRY TO RENT IT!

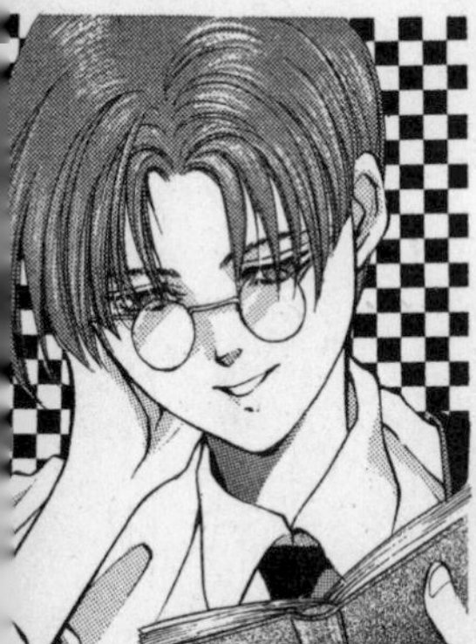

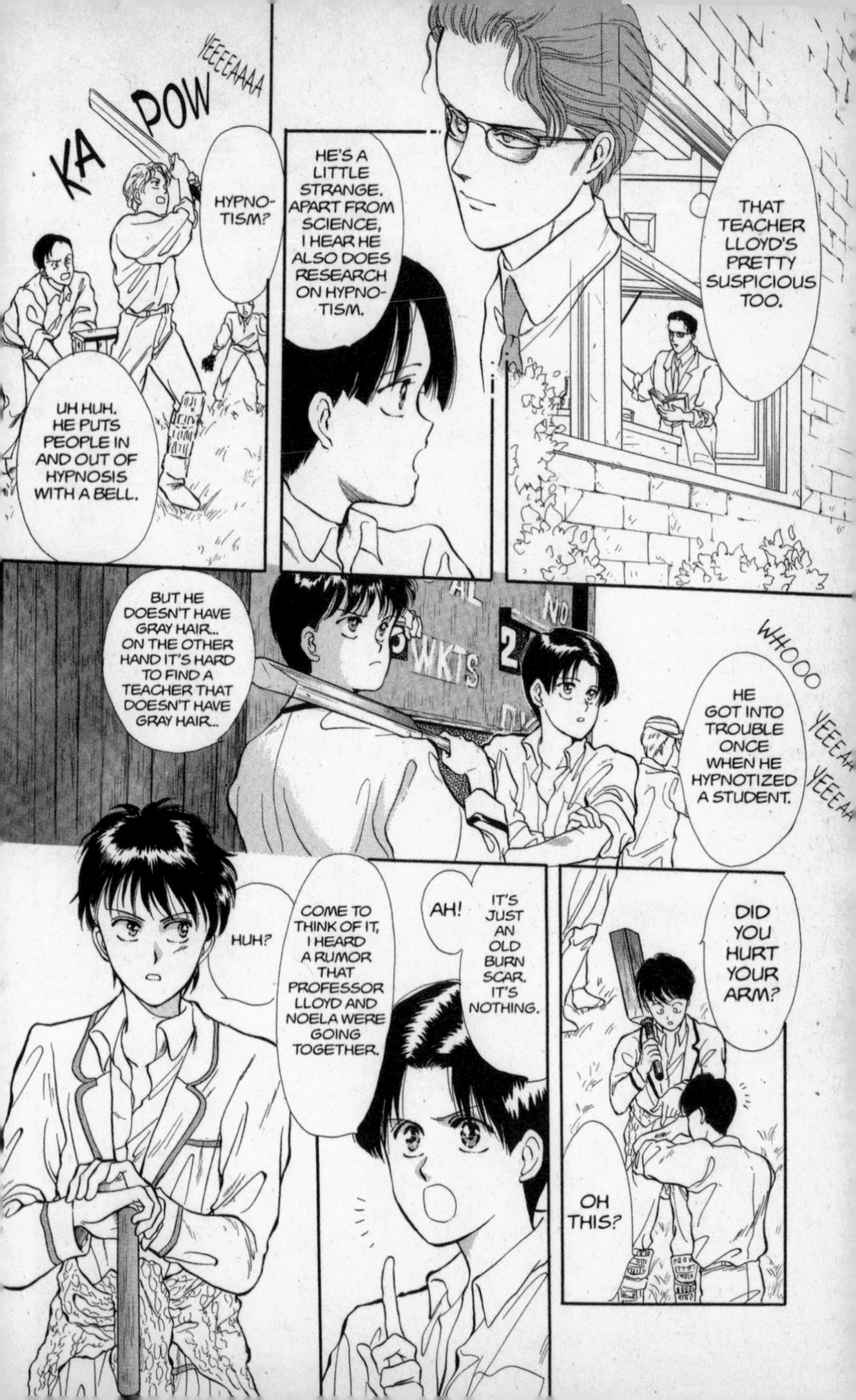
THAT TEACHER LLOYD'S PRETTY SUSPICIOUS TOO.
HE'S A LITTLE STRANGE. APART FROM SCIENCE, I HEAR HE ALSO DOES RESEARCH ON HYPNOTISM.
YEEEAAAA
KA POW
HYPNOTISM?
UH HUH. HE PUTS PEOPLE IN AND OUT OF HYPNOSIS WITH A BELL.
WHOOO
YEEEAA
YEEEAA
HE GOT INTO TROUBLE ONCE WHEN HE HYPNOTIZED A STUDENT.
BUT HE DOESN'T HAVE GRAY HAIR... ON THE OTHER HAND IT'S HARD TO FIND A TEACHER THAT DOESN'T HAVE GRAY HAIR...
DID YOU HURT YOUR ARM?
OH THIS?
IT'S JUST AN OLD BURN SCAR. IT'S NOTHING.
AH!
COME TO THINK OF IT, I HEARD A RUMOR THAT PROFESSOR LLOYD AND NOELA WERE GOING TOGETHER.
HUH?

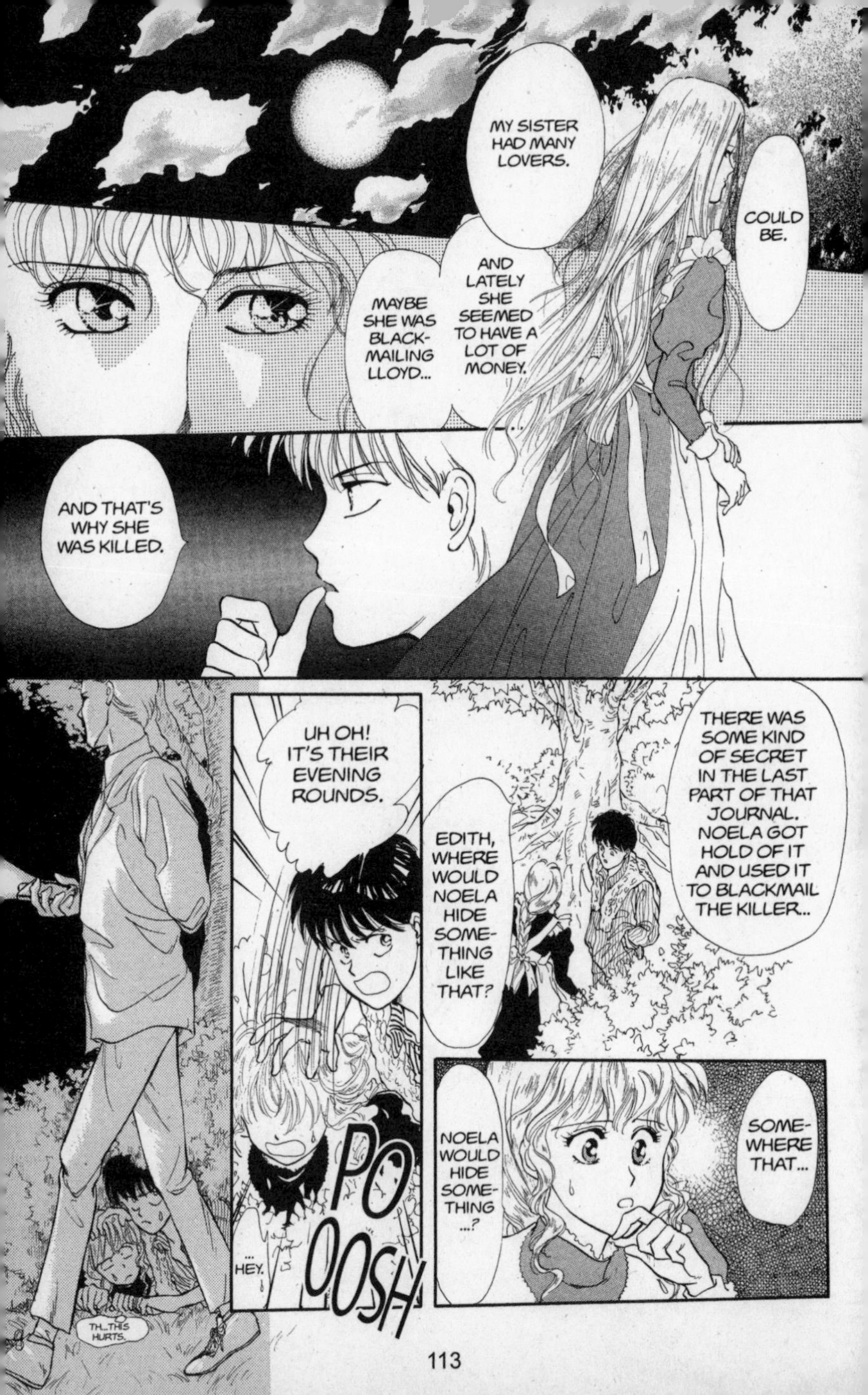
MY SISTER HAD MANY LOVERS.
AND LATELY SHE SEEMED TO HAVE A LOT OF MONEY.
MAYBE SHE WAS BLACK-MAILING LLOYD...
COULD BE.
AND THAT'S WHY SHE WAS KILLED.
THERE WAS SOME KIND OF SECRET IN THE LAST PART OF THAT JOURNAL. NOELA GOT HOLD OF IT AND USED IT TO BLACKMAIL THE KILLER...
EDITH, WHERE WOULD NOELA HIDE SOME-THING LIKE THAT?
SOME-WHERE THAT...
NOELA WOULD HIDE SOME-THING ...?
UH OH! IT'S THEIR EVENING ROUNDS.
... HEY.
POOOSH
TH...THIS HURTS.

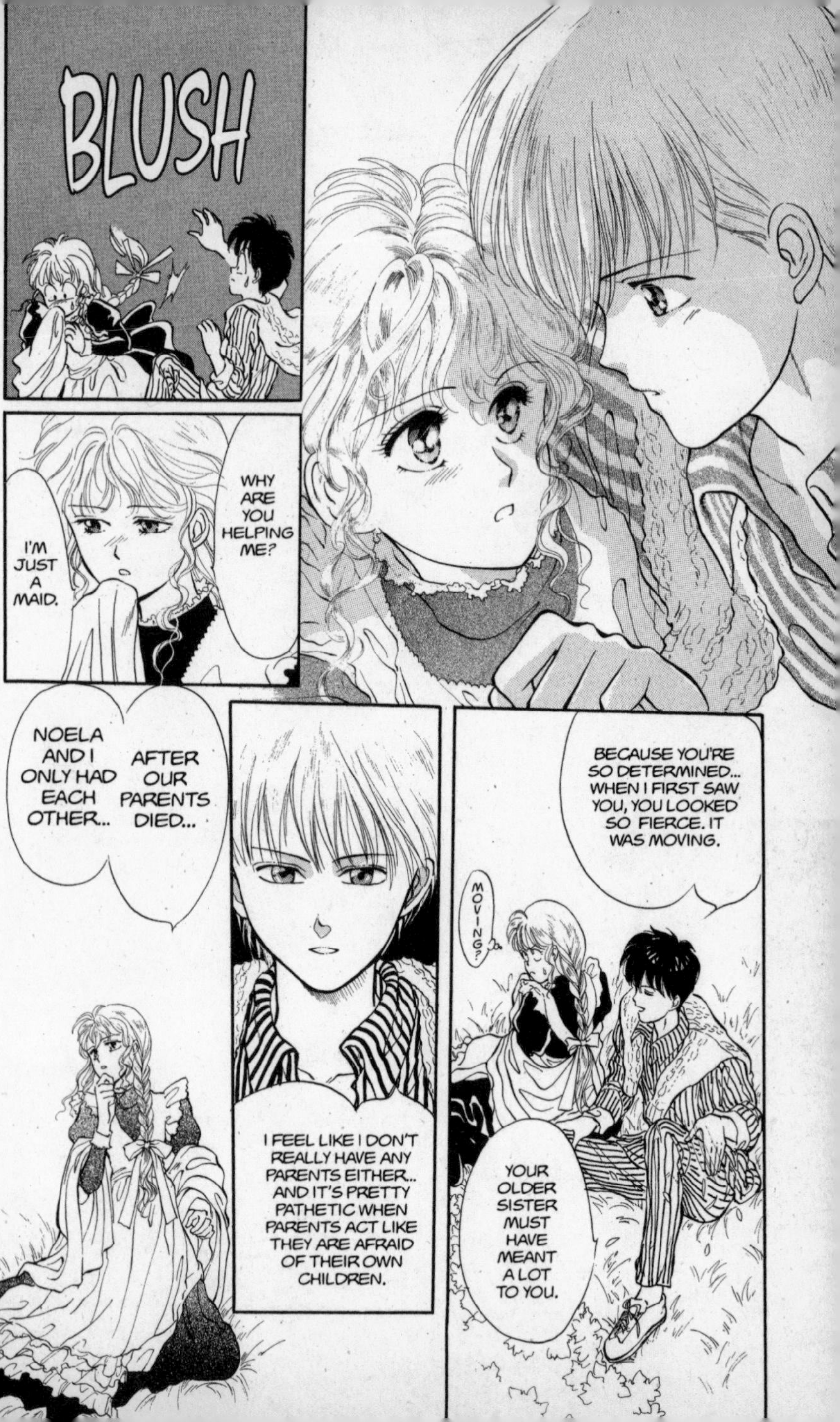
BLUSH
WHY ARE YOU HELPING ME?
I'M JUST A MAID.
BECAUSE YOU'RE SO DETERMINED... WHEN I FIRST SAW YOU, YOU LOOKED SO FIERCE. IT WAS MOVING.
MOVING?
YOUR OLDER SISTER MUST HAVE MEANT A LOT TO YOU.
I FEEL LIKE I DON'T REALLY HAVE ANY PARENTS EITHER... AND IT'S PRETTY PATHETIC WHEN PARENTS ACT LIKE THEY ARE AFRAID OF THEIR OWN CHILDREN.
NOELA AND I ONLY HAD EACH OTHER... AFTER OUR PARENTS DIED...

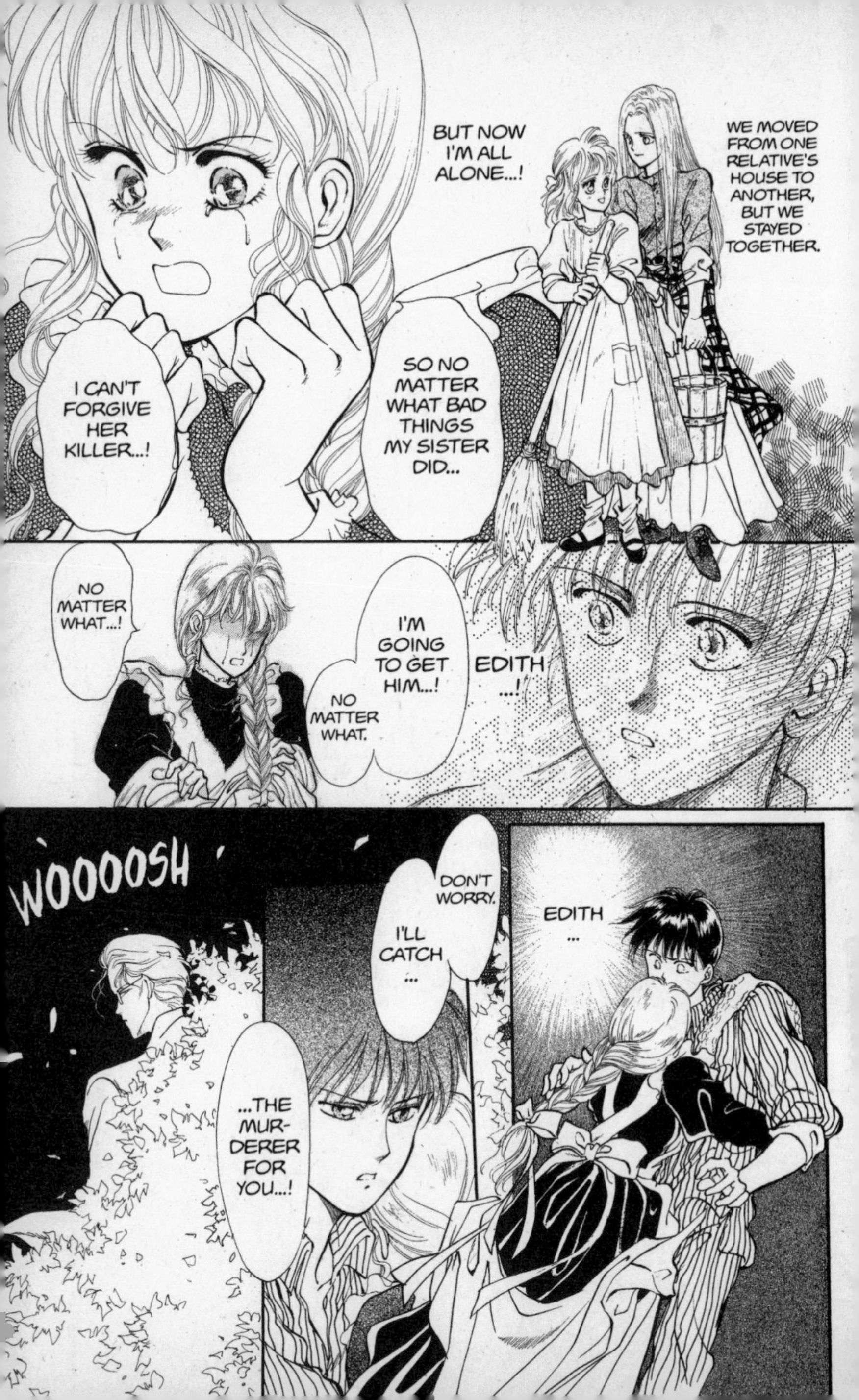
WE MOVED FROM ONE RELATIVE'S HOUSE TO ANOTHER, BUT WE STAYED TOGETHER.
BUT NOW I'M ALL ALONE...!
SO NO MATTER WHAT BAD THINGS MY SISTER DID...
I CAN'T FORGIVE HER KILLER...!
EDITH ...!
I'M GOING TO GET HIM...!
NO MATTER WHAT.
NO MATTER WHAT...!
EDITH ...
DON'T WORRY.
I'LL CATCH ...
...THE MURDERER FOR YOU...!
WOOOOSH

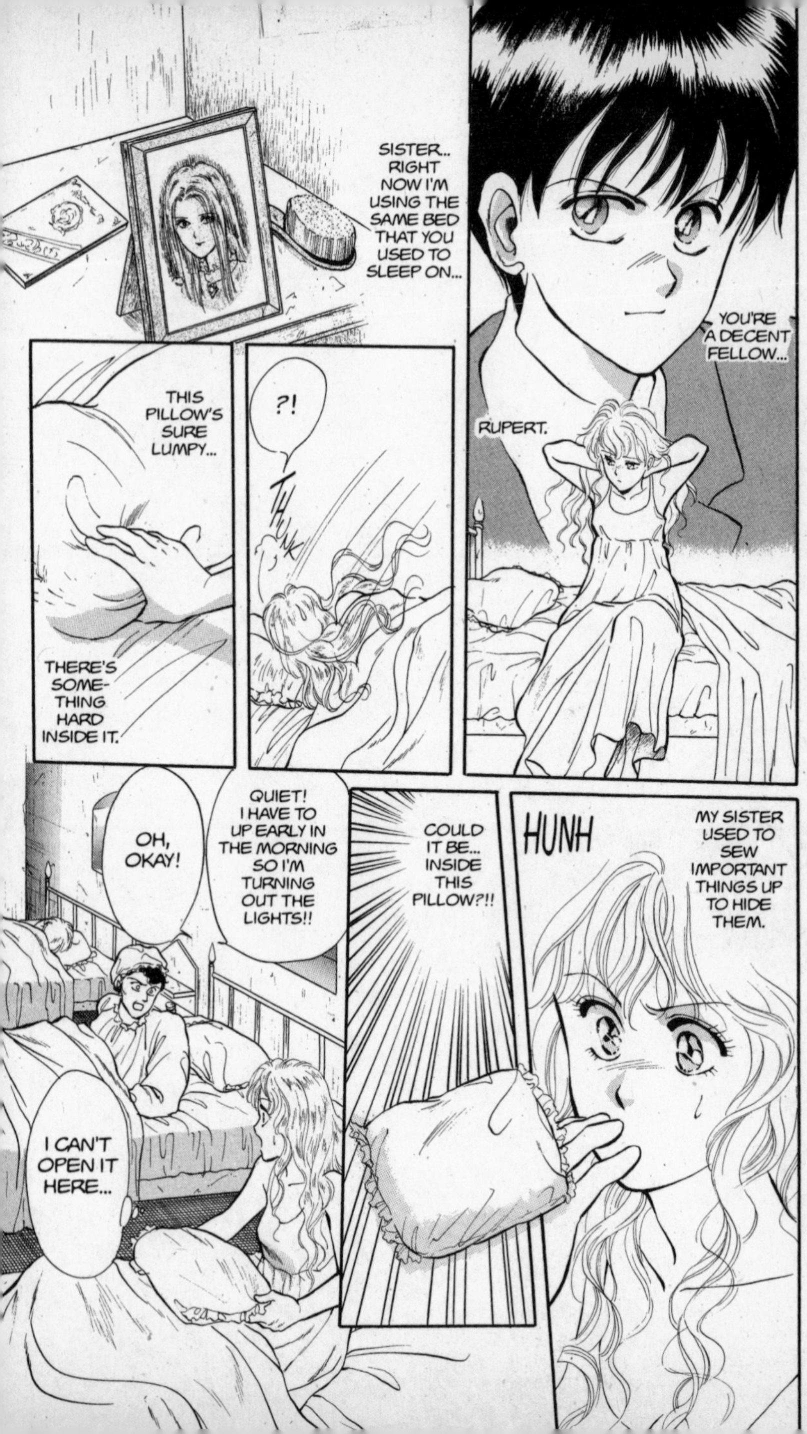
YOU'RE A DECENT FELLOW...
RUPERT.
SISTER.. RIGHT NOW I'M USING THE SAME BED THAT YOU USED TO SLEEP ON...
?!
THUNK
THIS PILLOW'S SURE LUMPY...
THERE'S SOME-THING HARD INSIDE IT.
HUNH
MY SISTER USED TO SEW IMPORTANT THINGS UP TO HIDE THEM.
COULD IT BE... INSIDE THIS PILLOW?!!
QUIET! I HAVE TO UP EARLY IN THE MORNING SO I'M TURNING OUT THE LIGHTS!!
OH, OKAY!
I CAN'T OPEN IT HERE...

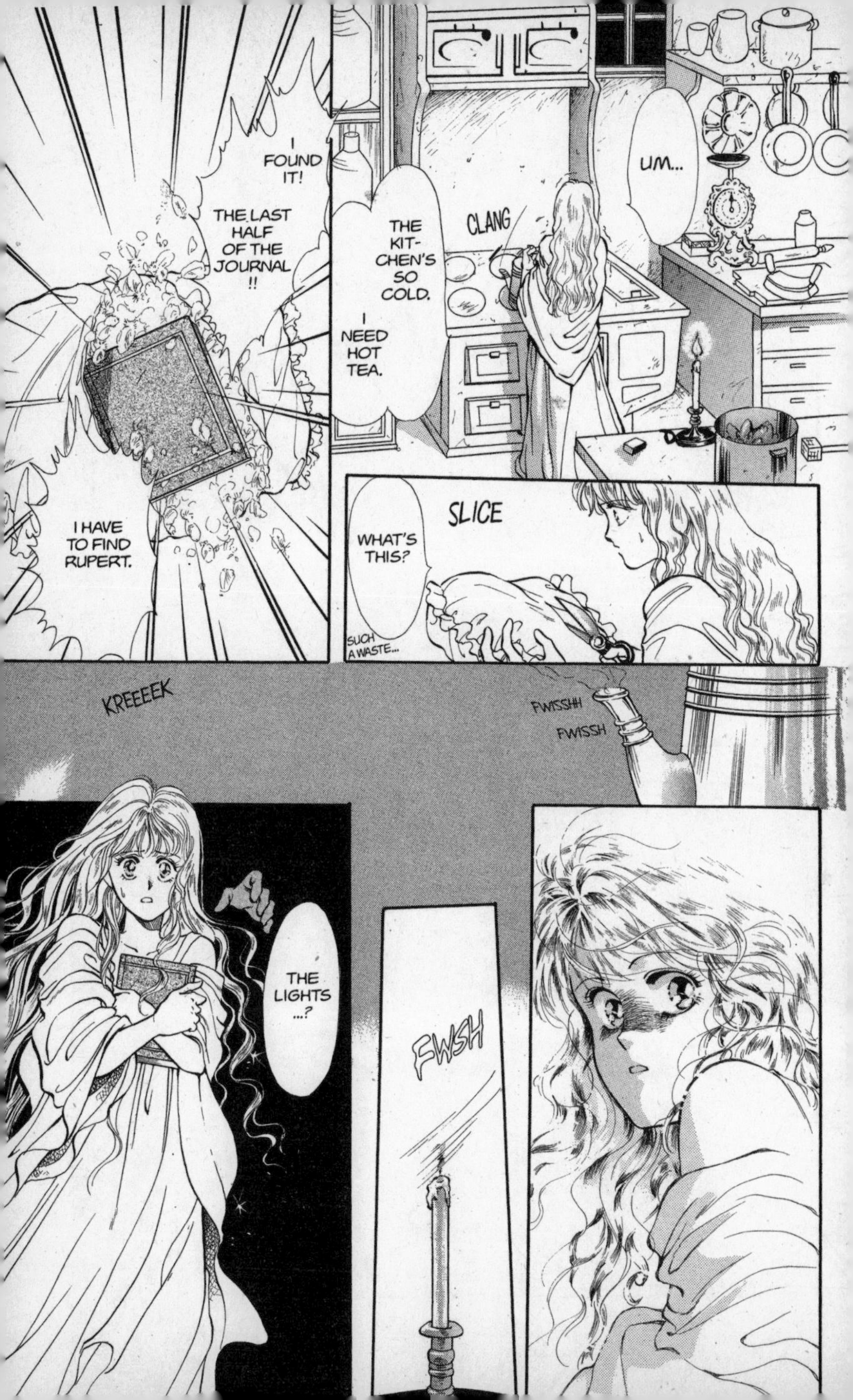
UM...
CLANG
THE KIT-CHEN'S SO COLD.
I NEED HOT TEA.
SLICE
WHAT'S THIS?
SUCH A WASTE...
I FOUND IT!
THE LAST HALF OF THE JOURNAL !!
I HAVE TO FIND RUPERT.
FWISSHH
FWISSH
KREEEEK
FWSH
THE LIGHTS ...?

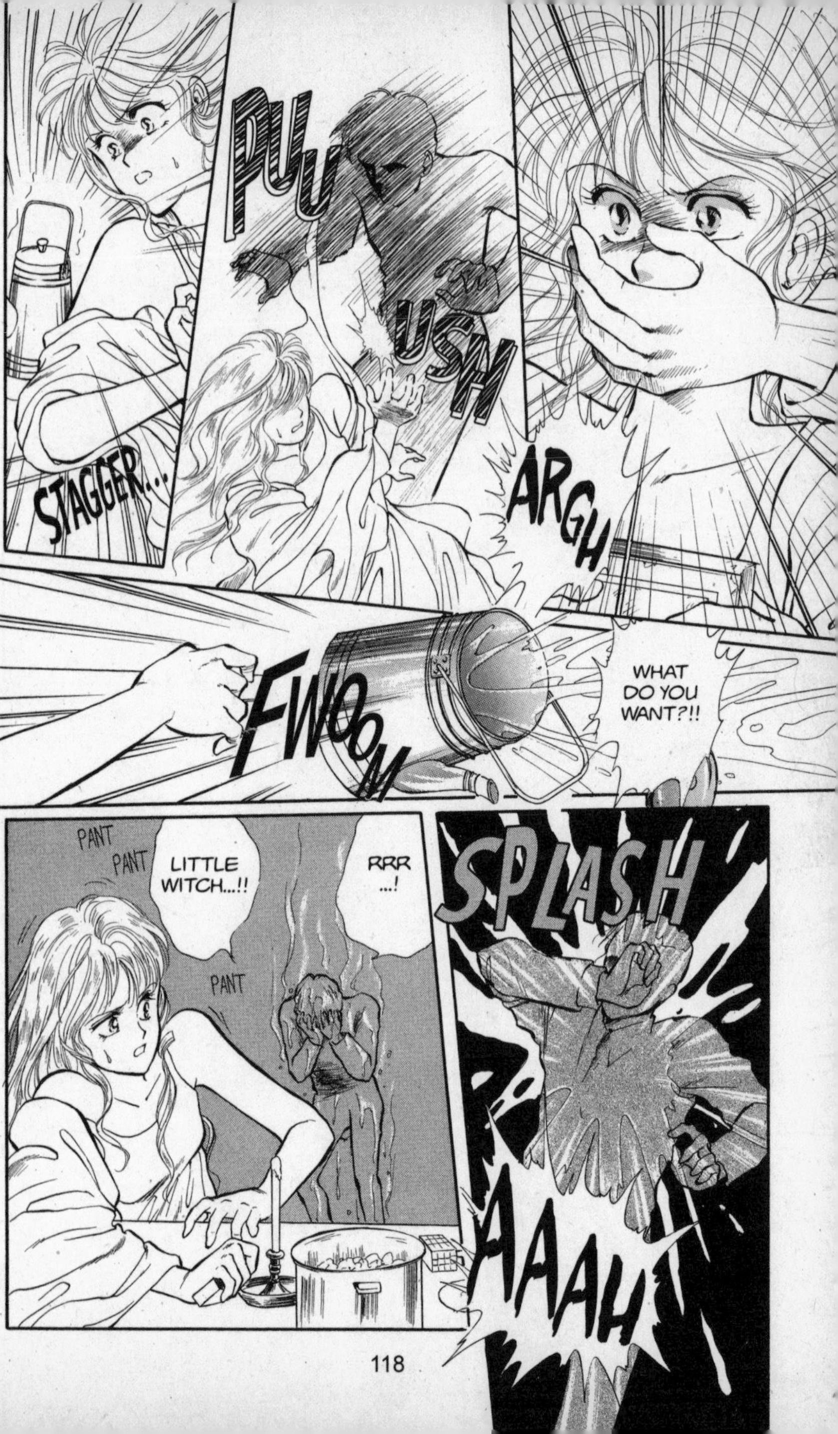
ARGH
PUUSH
STAGGER...
WHAT DO YOU WANT?!!
FWOOM
SPLASH
AAAAH
RRR ...!
LITTLE WITCH...!!
PANT PANT
PANT

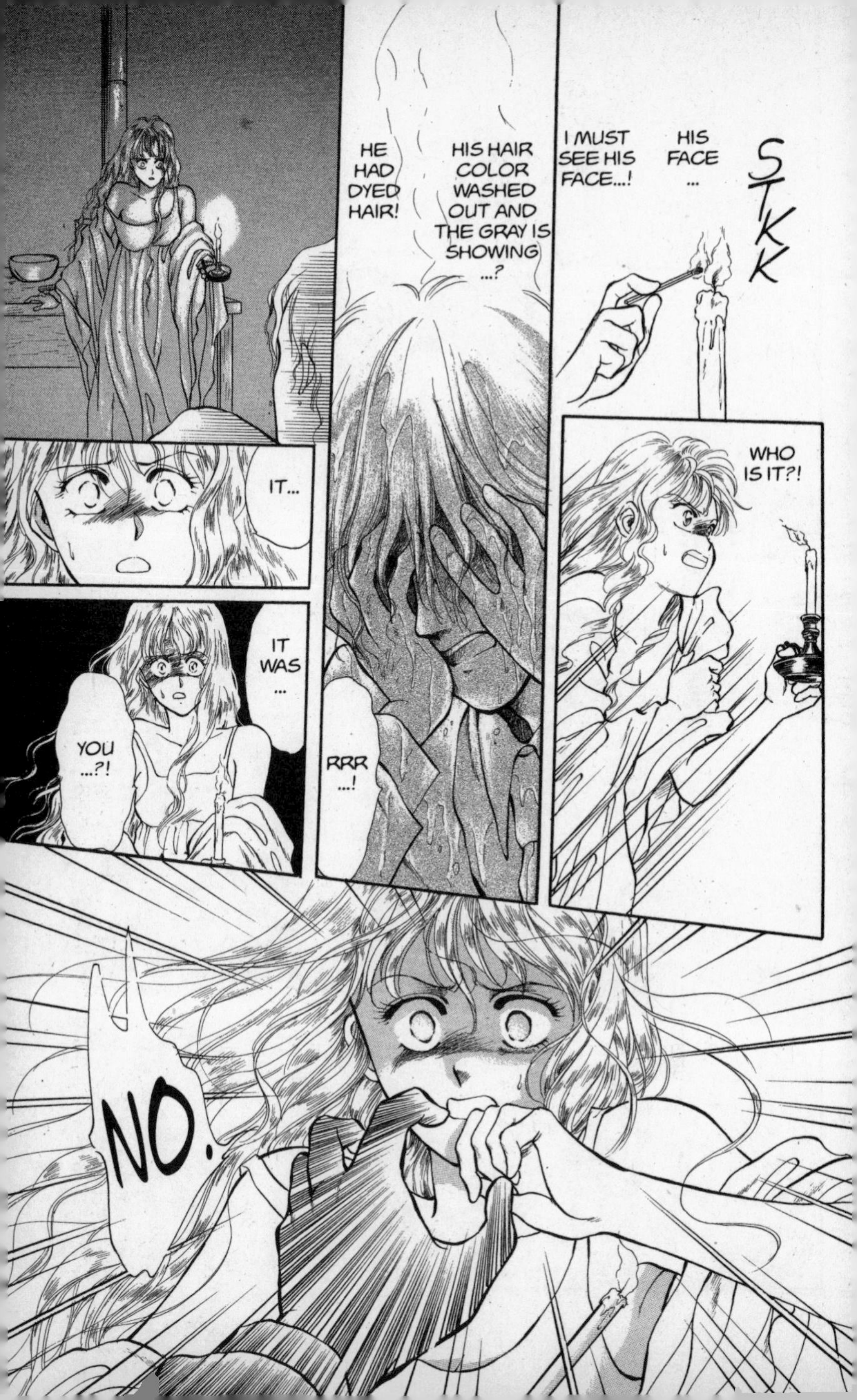
STKK
HIS FACE ...
I MUST SEE HIS FACE...!
WHO IS IT?!
HIS HAIR COLOR WASHED OUT AND THE GRAY IS SHOWING ...?
HE HAD DYED HAIR!
RRR ...!
IT...
IT WAS ...
YOU ...?!
NO.

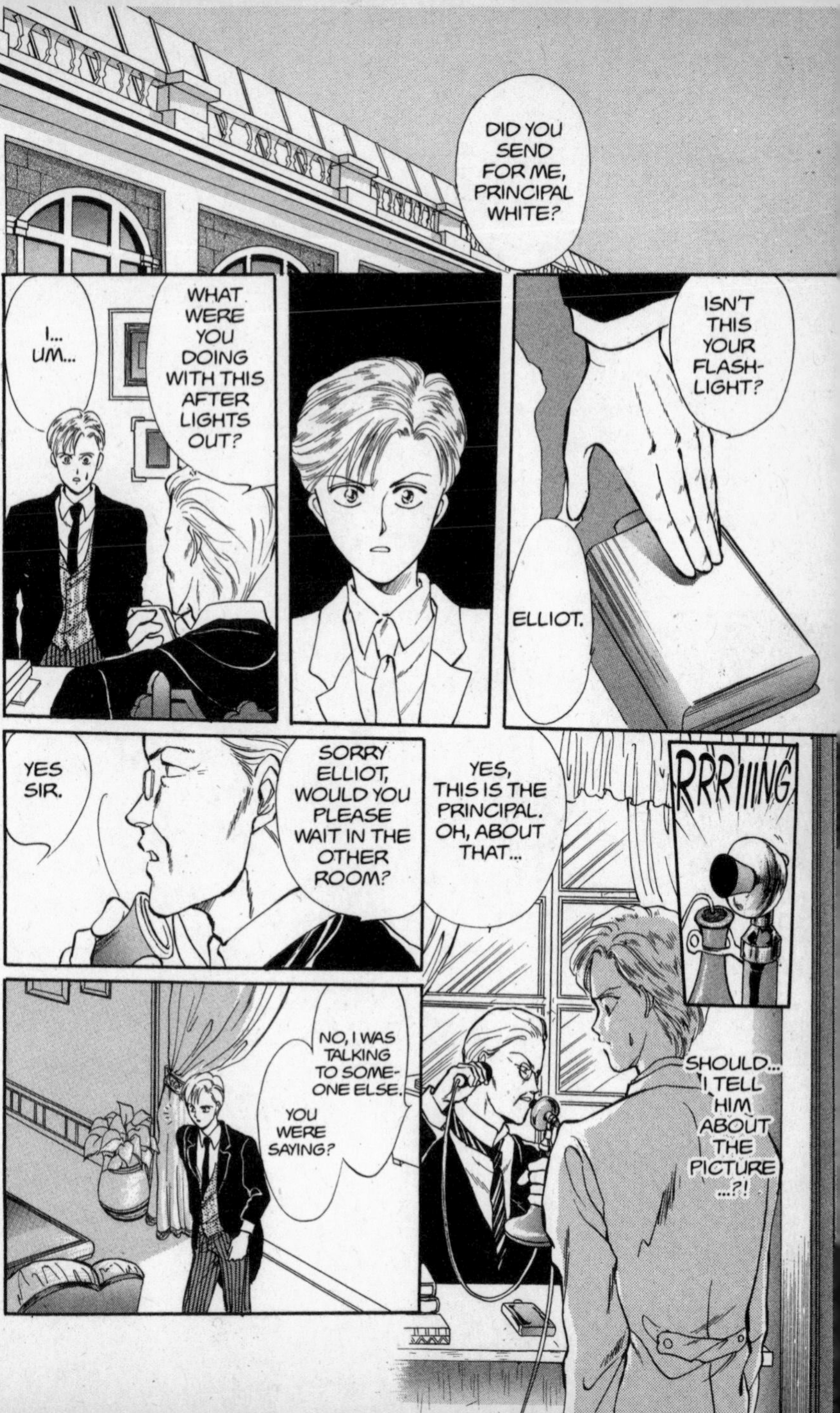
DID YOU SEND FOR ME, PRINCIPAL WHITE?
ISN'T THIS YOUR FLASHLIGHT?
ELLIOT.
WHAT WERE YOU DOING WITH THIS AFTER LIGHTS OUT?
I... UM...
RRRIIING
YES, THIS IS THE PRINCIPAL. OH, ABOUT THAT...
SORRY ELLIOT, WOULD YOU PLEASE WAIT IN THE OTHER ROOM?
YES SIR.
SHOULD... I TELL HIM ABOUT THE PICTURE ...?!
NO, I WAS TALKING TO SOMEONE ELSE.
YOU WERE SAYING?

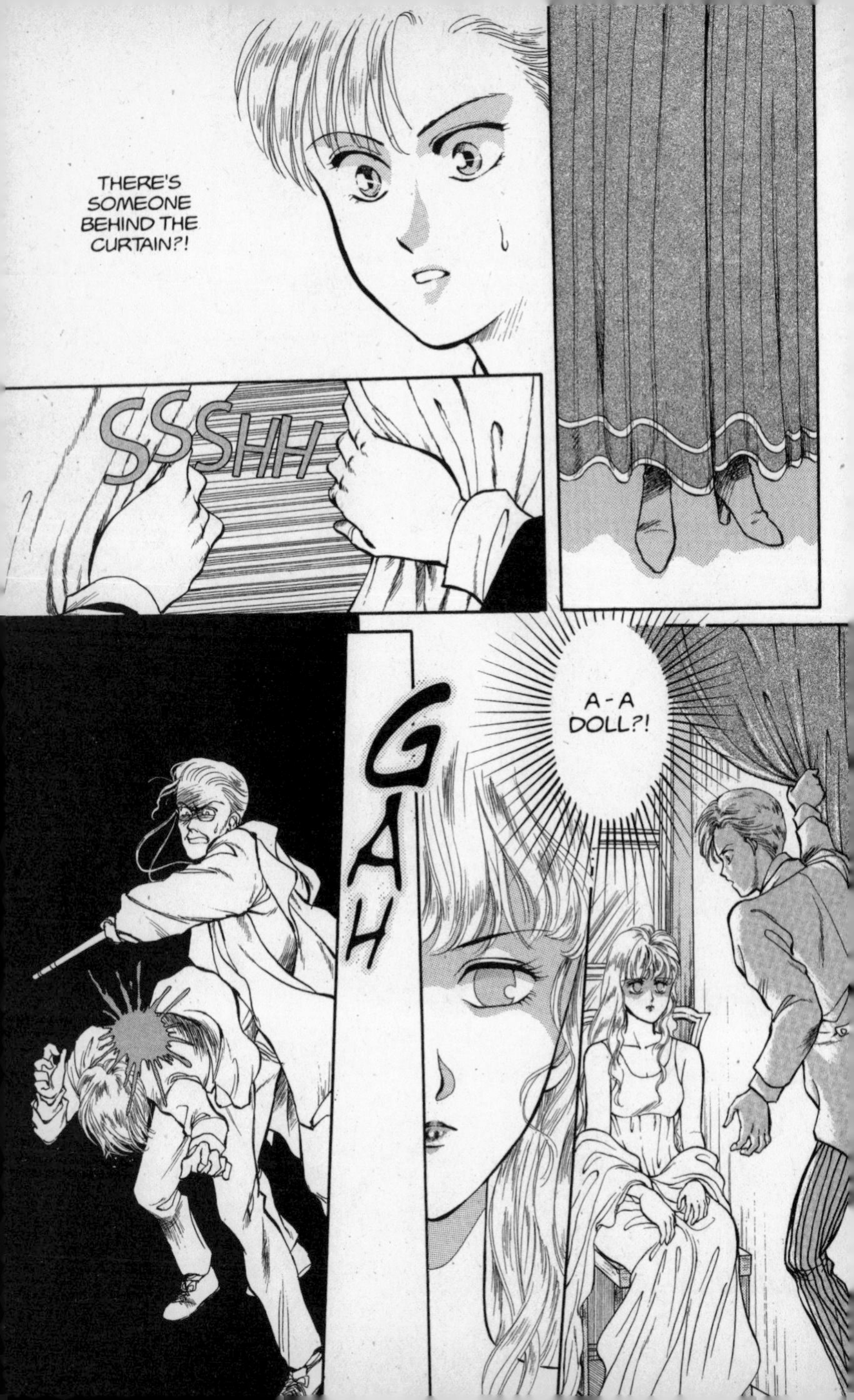
THERE'S SOMEONE BEHIND THE CURTAIN?!
SSSHH
A-A DOLL?!
GAH

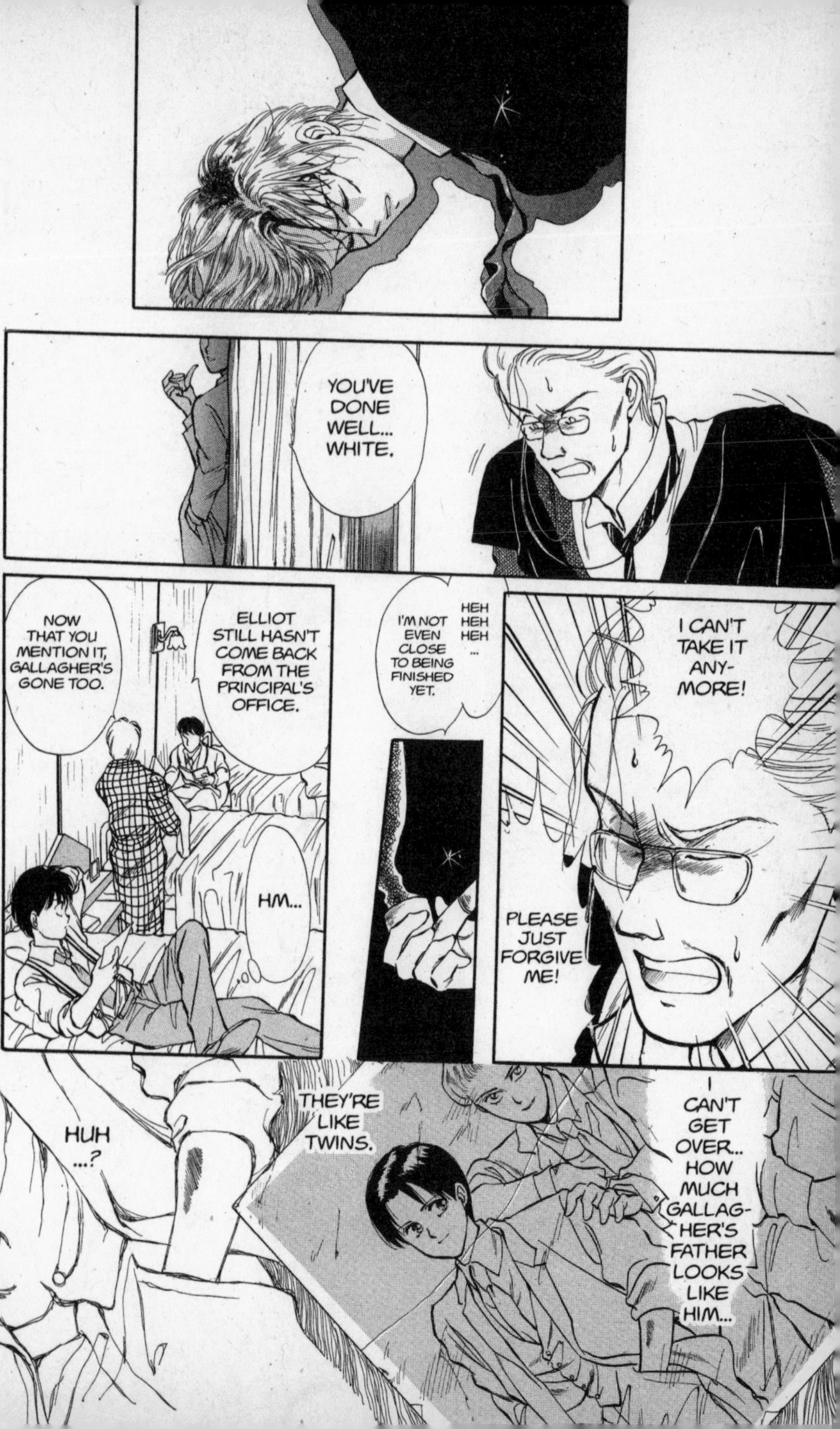
YOU'VE DONE WELL... WHITE.
I CAN'T TAKE IT ANY-MORE!
PLEASE JUST FORGIVE ME!
HEH HEH HEH ...
I'M NOT EVEN CLOSE TO BEING FINISHED YET.
ELLIOT STILL HASN'T COME BACK FROM THE PRINCIPAL'S OFFICE.
NOW THAT YOU MENTION IT, GALLAGHER'S GONE TOO.
HM...
I CAN'T GET OVER... HOW MUCH GALLAGHER'S FATHER LOOKS LIKE HIM...
THEY'RE LIKE TWINS.
HUH ...?

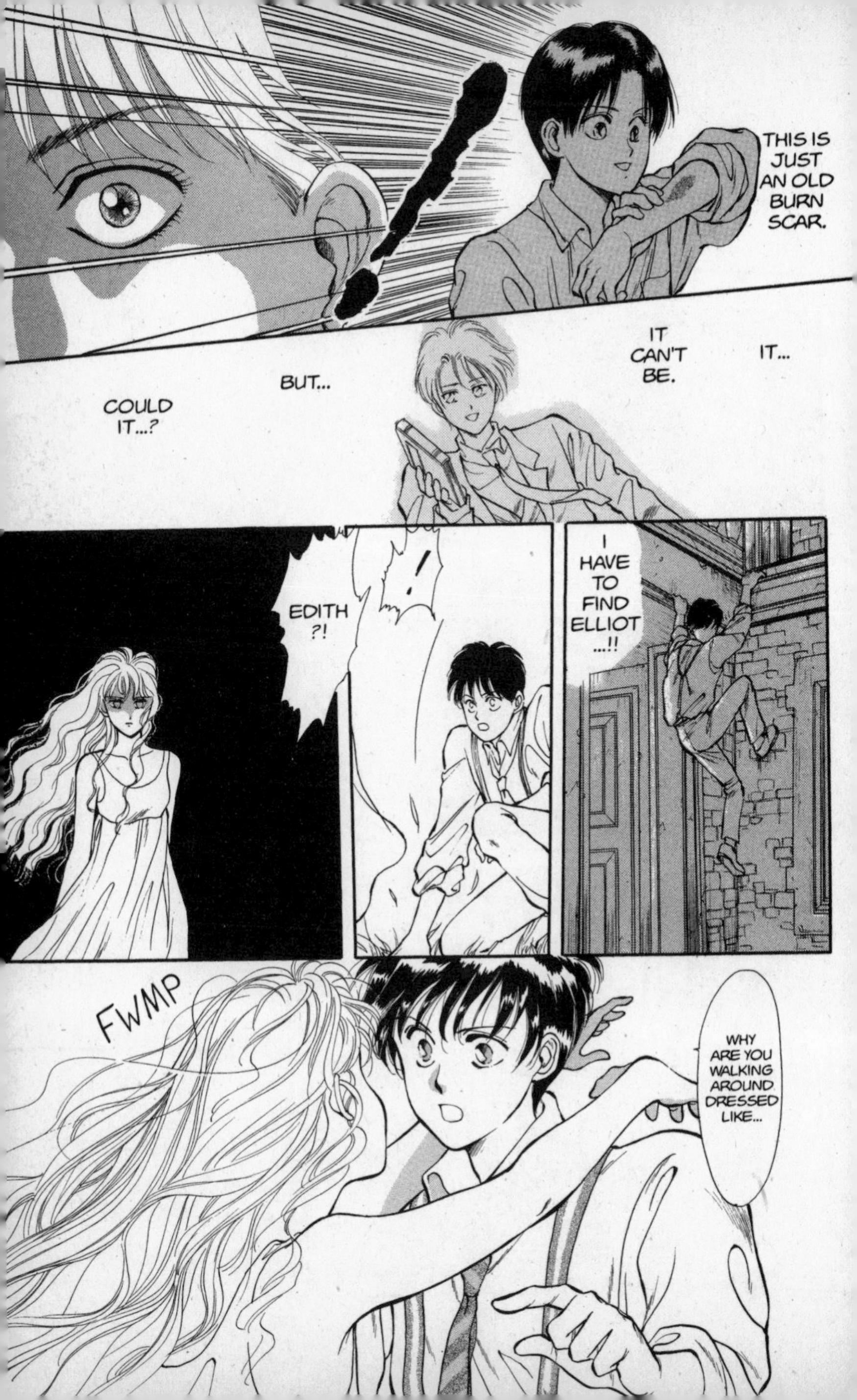
THIS IS JUST AN OLD BURN SCAR.
IT...
IT CAN'T BE.
BUT...
COULD IT...?
I HAVE TO FIND ELLIOT ...!!
!
EDITH ?!
WHY ARE YOU WALKING AROUND DRESSED LIKE...
FWMP

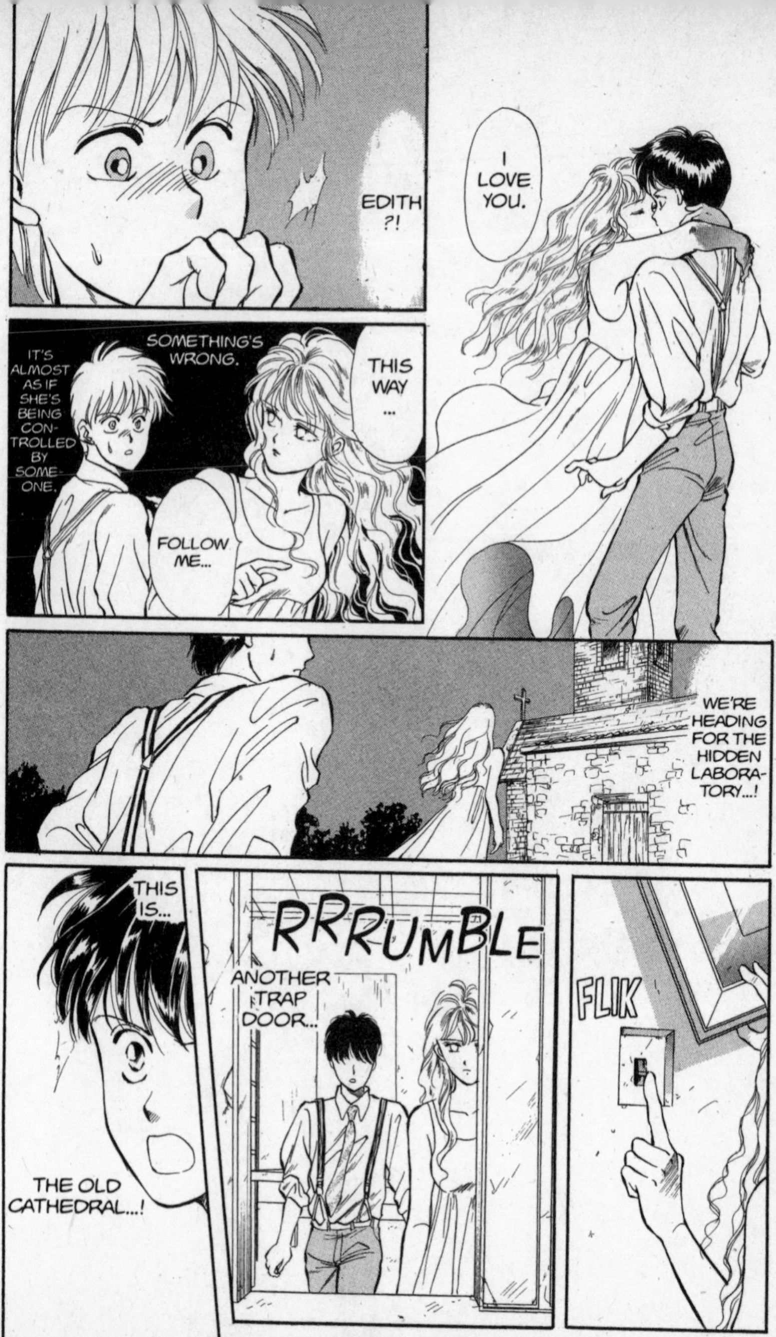
I LOVE YOU.
EDITH ?!
THIS WAY ...
SOMETHING'S WRONG.
IT'S ALMOST AS IF SHE'S BEING CON-TROLLED BY SOME-ONE.
FOLLOW ME...
WE'RE HEADING FOR THE HIDDEN LABORA-TORY...!
FLIK
RRRUMBLE
ANOTHER TRAP DOOR...
THIS IS...
THE OLD CATHEDRAL...!

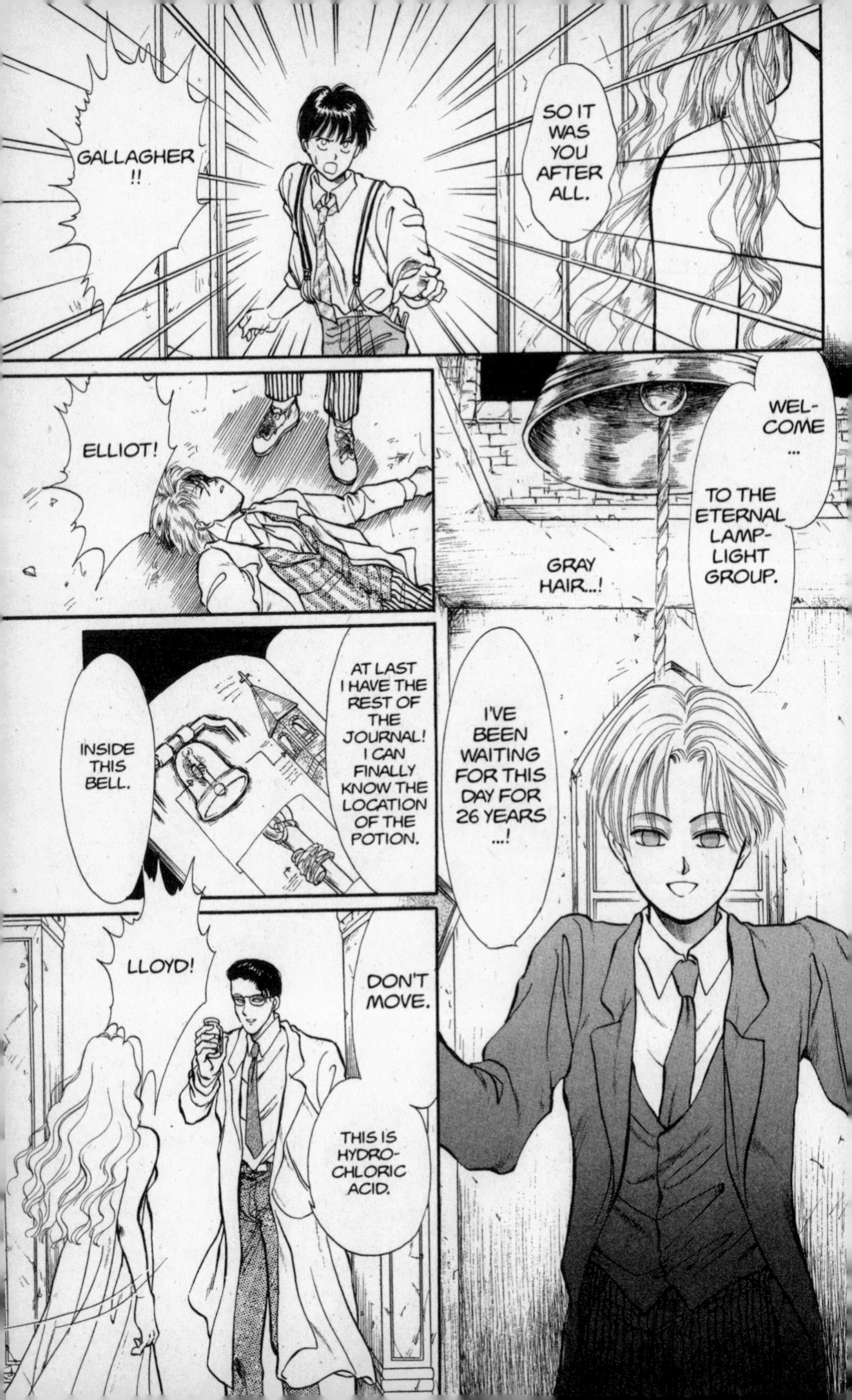
SO IT WAS YOU AFTER ALL.
GALLAGHER !!
WEL-COME ...
TO THE ETERNAL LAMP-LIGHT GROUP.
GRAY HAIR...!
I'VE BEEN WAITING FOR THIS DAY FOR 26 YEARS ...!
ELLIOT!
AT LAST I HAVE THE REST OF THE JOURNAL! I CAN FINALLY KNOW THE LOCATION OF THE POTION.
INSIDE THIS BELL.
DON'T MOVE.
THIS IS HYDRO-CHLORIC ACID.
LLOYD!

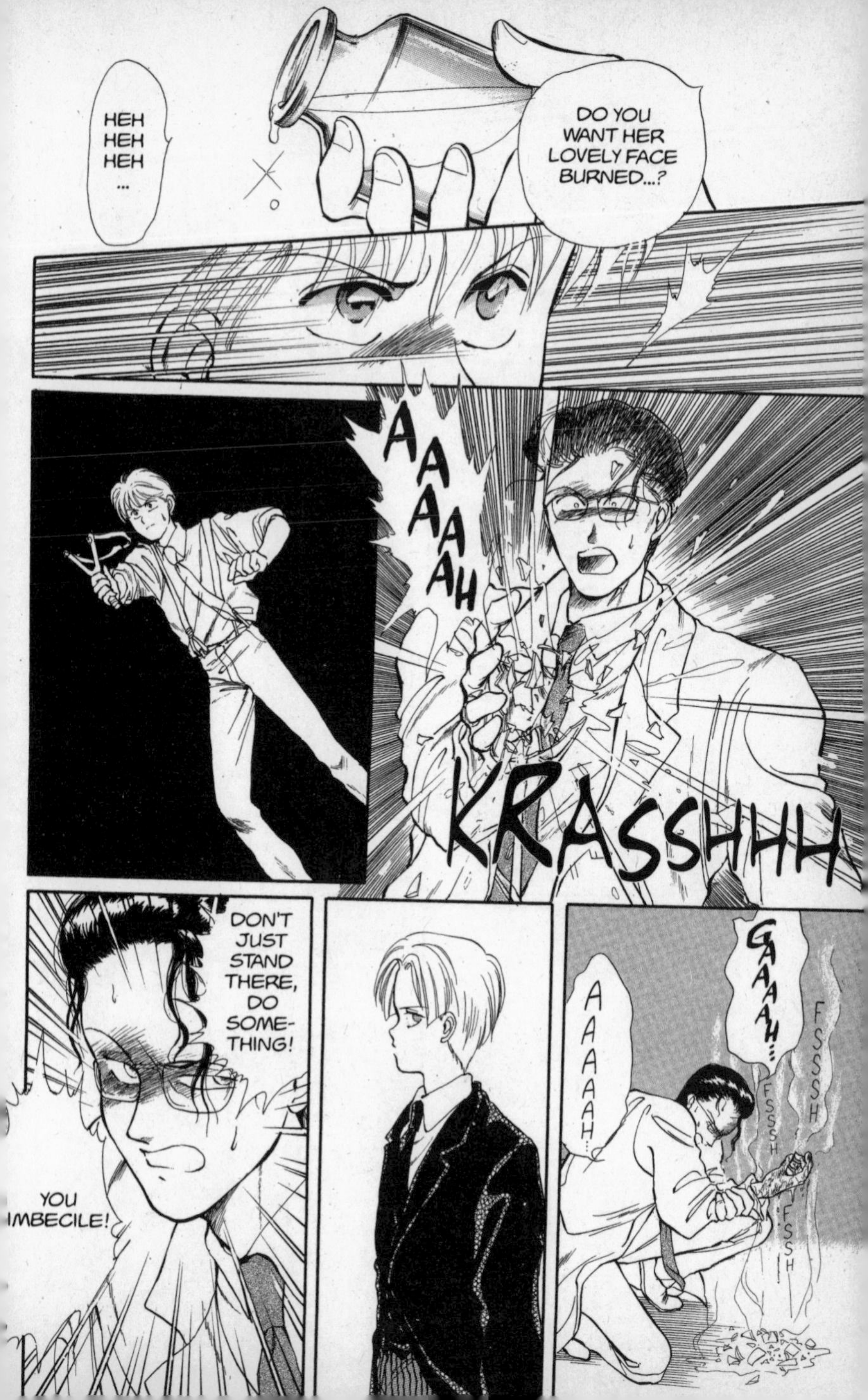
DO YOU WANT HER LOVELY FACE BURNED...?
HEH HEH HEH ...
AAAAAH
KRASSHHH
GAAAAH...
FSSSH
AAAAAAH...
FSSSH
FSSH
DON'T JUST STAND THERE, DO SOME-THING!
YOU IMBECILE!

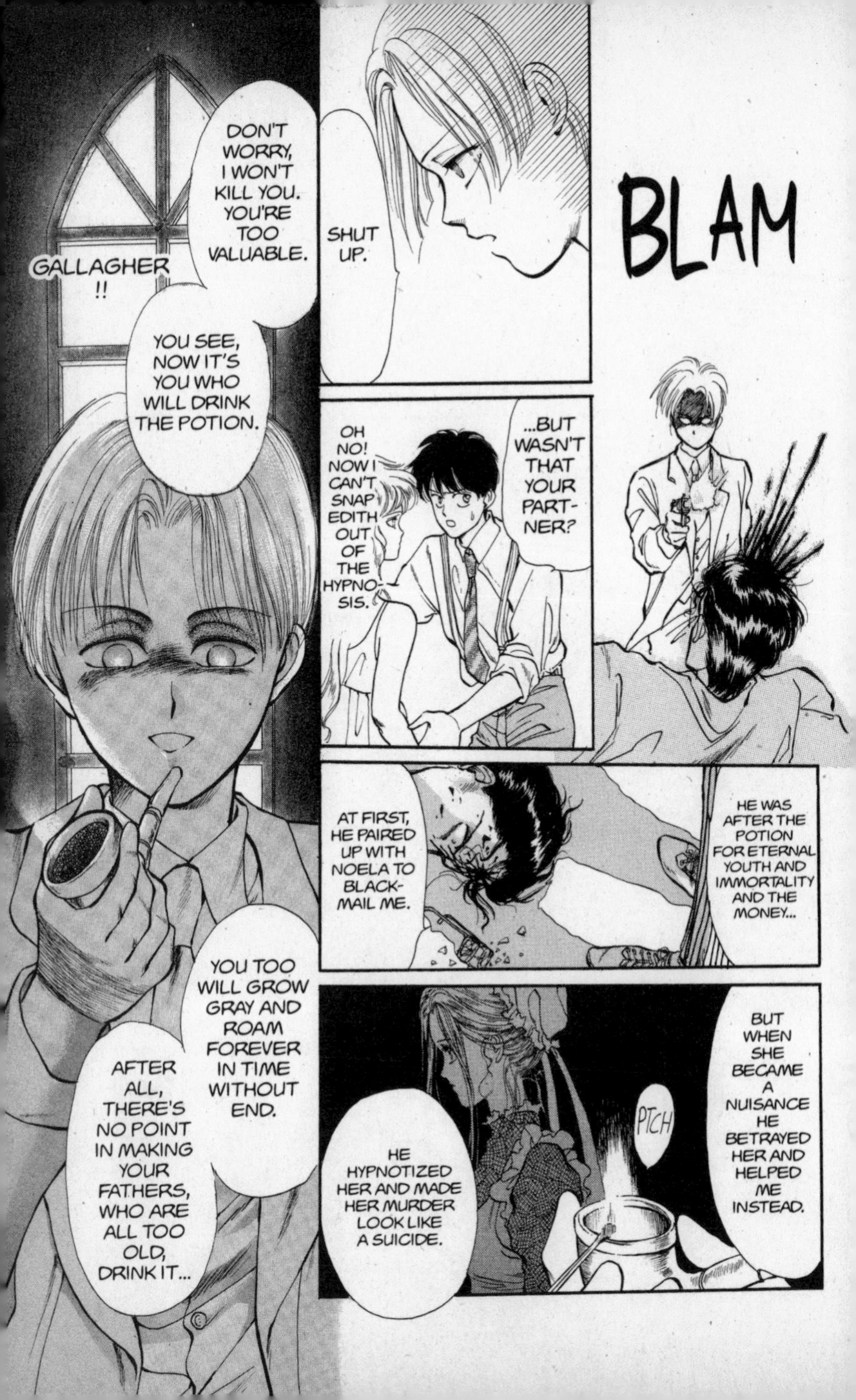
BLAM
SHUT UP.
...BUT WASN'T THAT YOUR PARTNER?
OH NO! NOW I CAN'T SNAP EDITH OUT OF THE HYPNOSIS.
HE WAS AFTER THE POTION FOR ETERNAL YOUTH AND IMMORTALITY AND THE MONEY...
AT FIRST, HE PAIRED UP WITH NOELA TO BLACKMAIL ME.
BUT WHEN SHE BECAME A NUISANCE HE BETRAYED HER AND HELPED ME INSTEAD.
PTCH
HE HYPNOTIZED HER AND MADE HER MURDER LOOK LIKE A SUICIDE.
GALLAGHER !!
DON'T WORRY, I WON'T KILL YOU. YOU'RE TOO VALUABLE.
YOU SEE, NOW IT'S YOU WHO WILL DRINK THE POTION.
YOU TOO WILL GROW GRAY AND ROAM FOREVER IN TIME WITHOUT END.
AFTER ALL, THERE'S NO POINT IN MAKING YOUR FATHERS, WHO ARE ALL TOO OLD, DRINK IT...

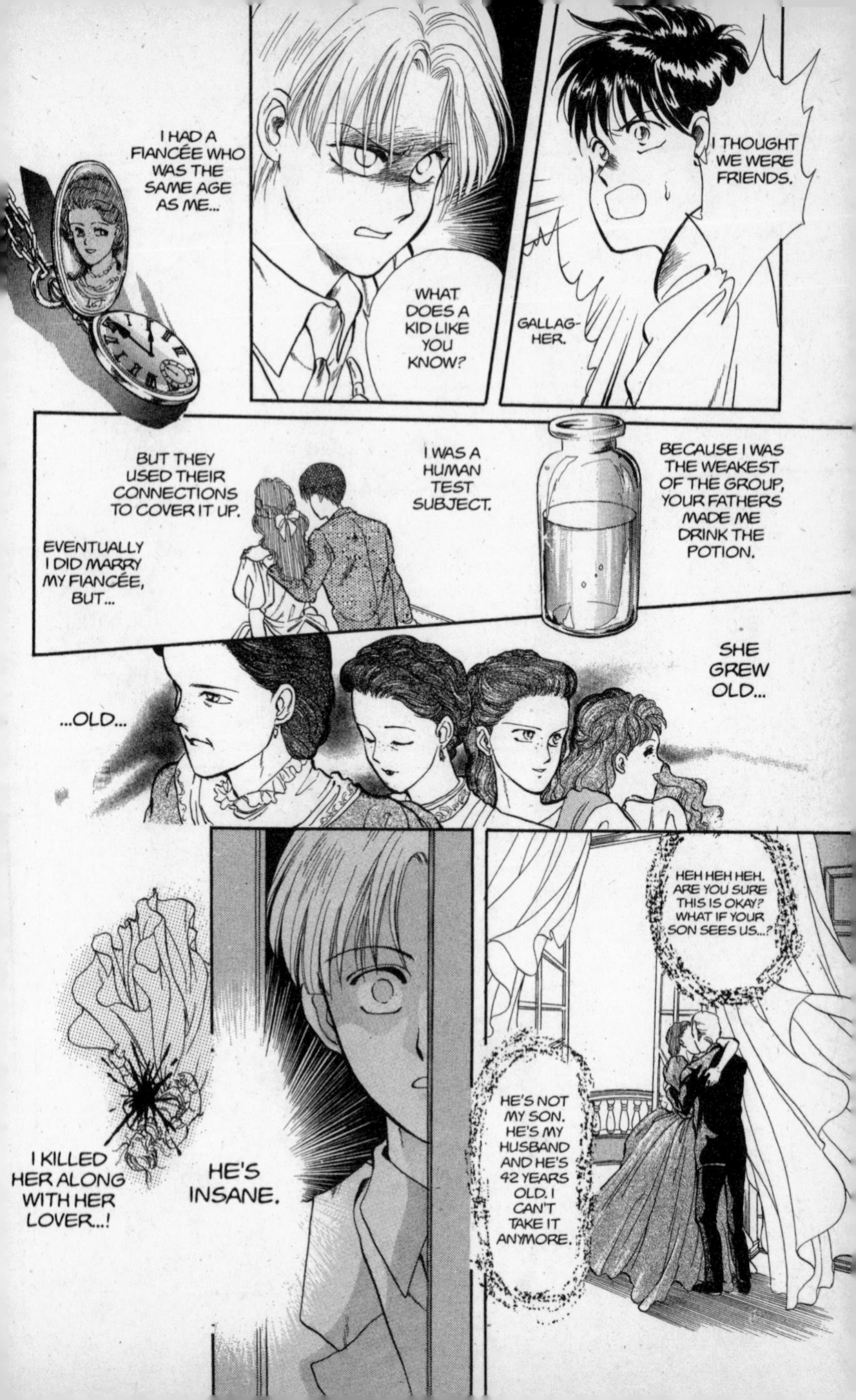
I THOUGHT WE WERE FRIENDS.
GALLAG-HER.
WHAT DOES A KID LIKE YOU KNOW?
I HAD A FIANCÉE WHO WAS THE SAME AGE AS ME...
BECAUSE I WAS THE WEAKEST OF THE GROUP, YOUR FATHERS MADE ME DRINK THE POTION.
I WAS A HUMAN TEST SUBJECT.
BUT THEY USED THEIR CONNECTIONS TO COVER IT UP.
EVENTUALLY I DID MARRY MY FIANCÉE, BUT...
SHE GREW OLD...
...OLD...
HEH HEH HEH. ARE YOU SURE THIS IS OKAY? WHAT IF YOUR SON SEES US...?
HE'S NOT MY SON. HE'S MY HUSBAND AND HE'S 42 YEARS OLD. I CAN'T TAKE IT ANYMORE.
HE'S INSANE.
I KILLED HER ALONG WITH HER LOVER...!

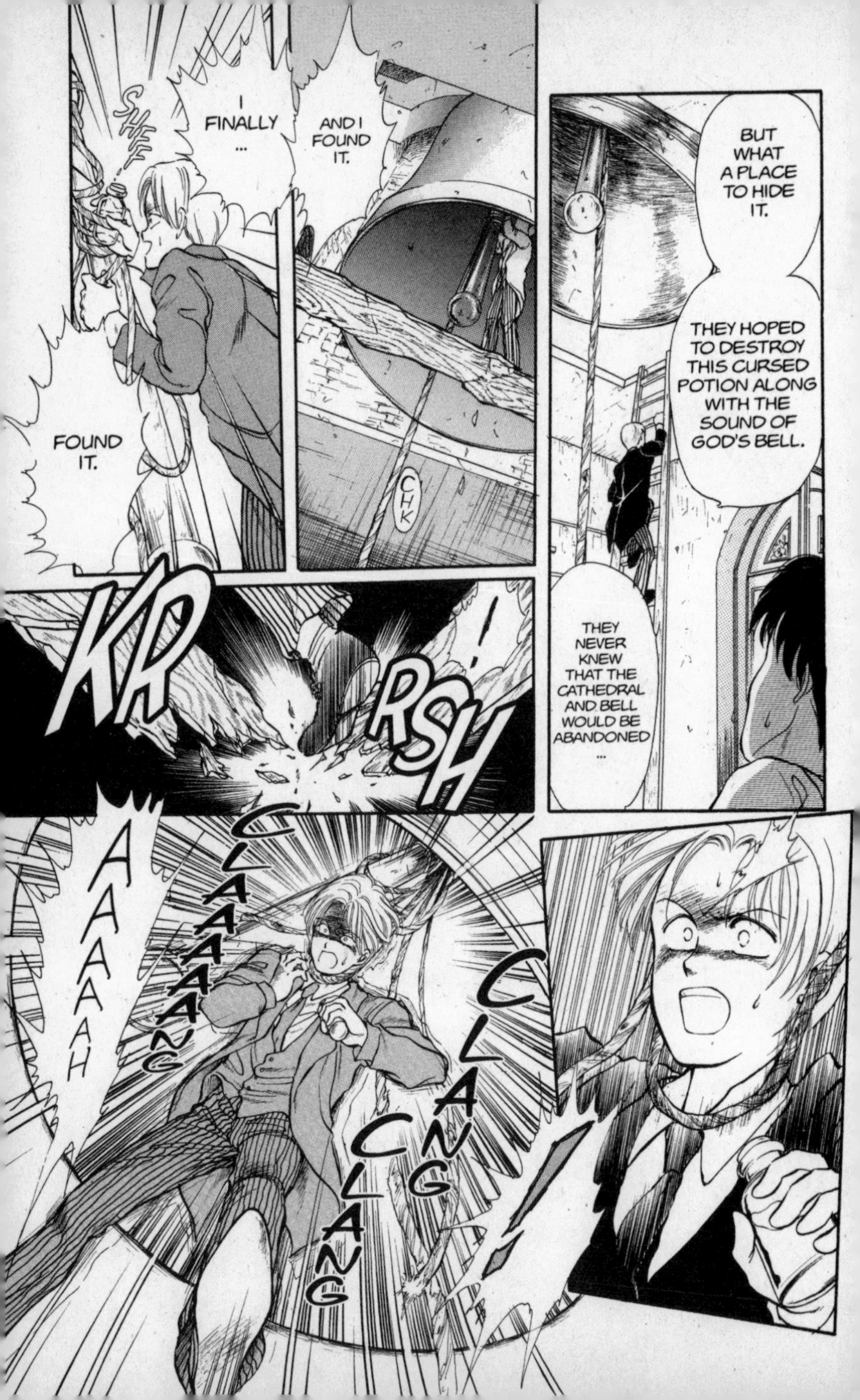
BUT WHAT A PLACE TO HIDE IT.
THEY HOPED TO DESTROY THIS CURSED POTION ALONG WITH THE SOUND OF GOD'S BELL.
THEY NEVER KNEW THAT THE CATHEDRAL AND BELL WOULD BE ABANDONED ...
AND I FOUND IT.
CHK
I FINALLY ...
SHFF
FOUND IT.
!
KRRSH
CLANG
CLANG
AAAAAH
CLAAAAANG

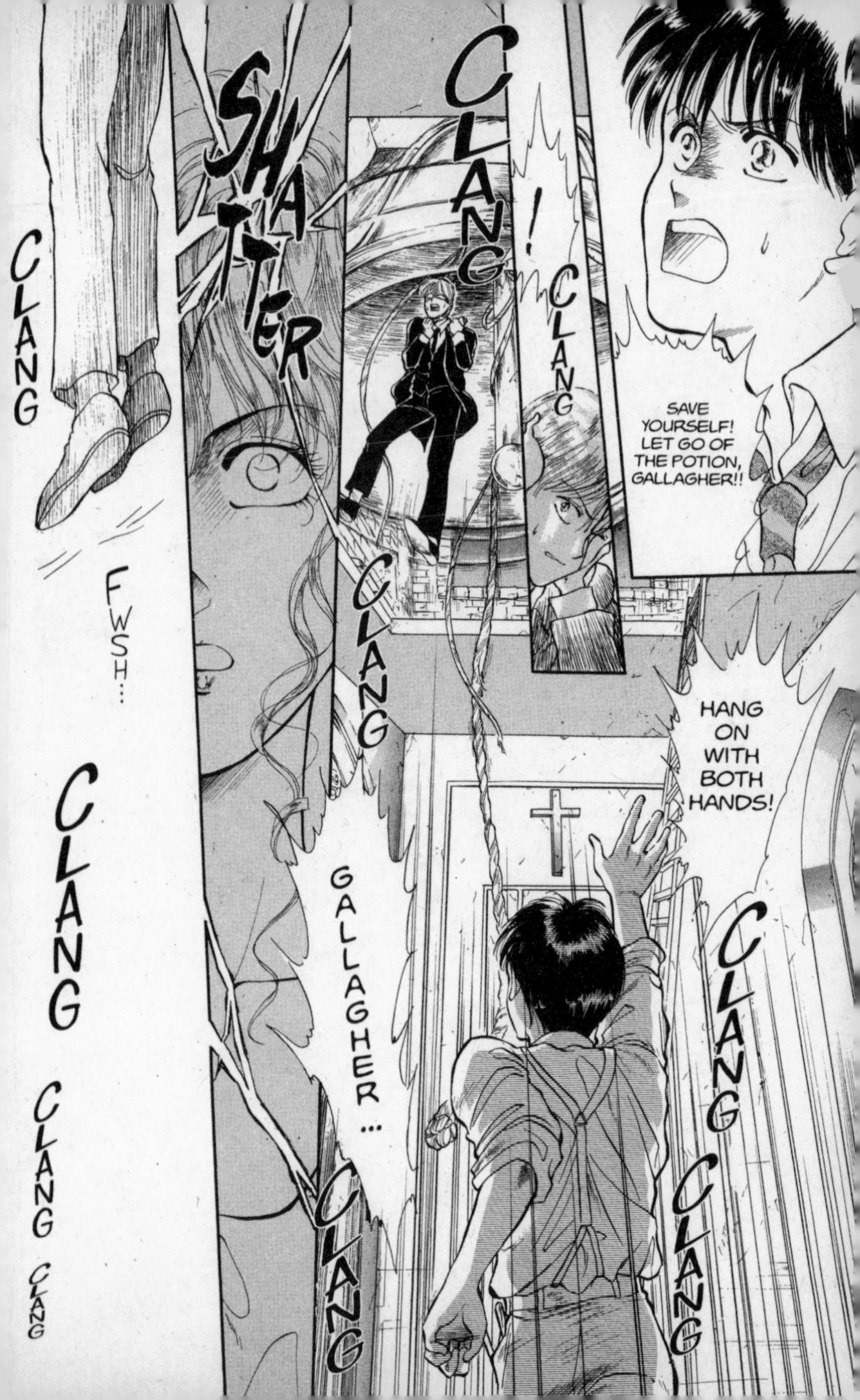
SAVE YOURSELF! LET GO OF THE POTION, GALLAGHER!!
CLANG
CLANG!
CLANG
SHATTER
CLANG
HANG ON WITH BOTH HANDS!
CLANG
CLANG
CLANG
GALLAGHER...
FWSH...
CLANG
CLANG
CLANG
CLANG

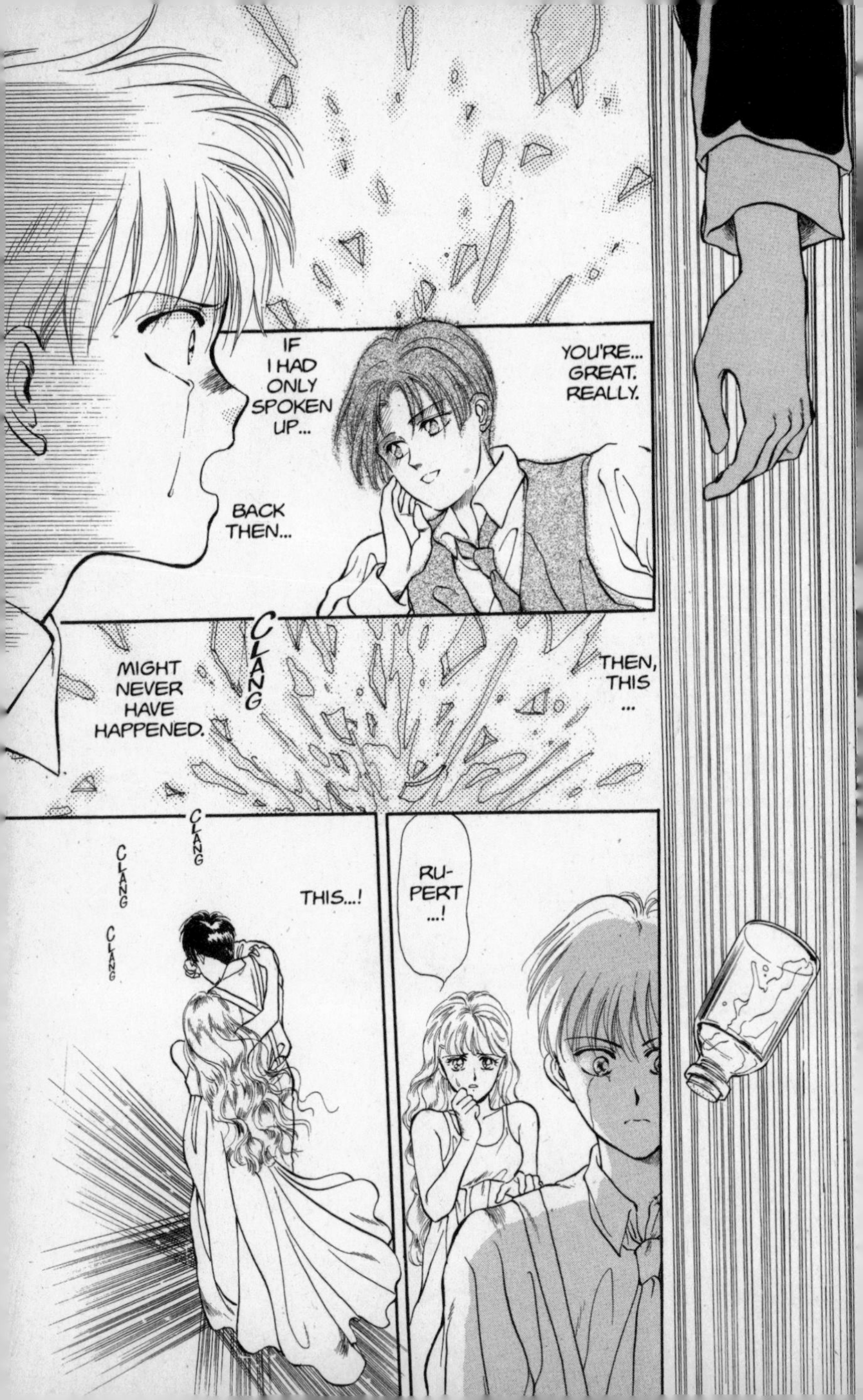
YOU'RE... GREAT. REALLY.
IF I HAD ONLY SPOKEN UP...
BACK THEN...
THEN, THIS ...
CLANG
MIGHT NEVER HAVE HAPPENED.
RU-PERT ...!
THIS...!
CLANG
CLANG
CLANG

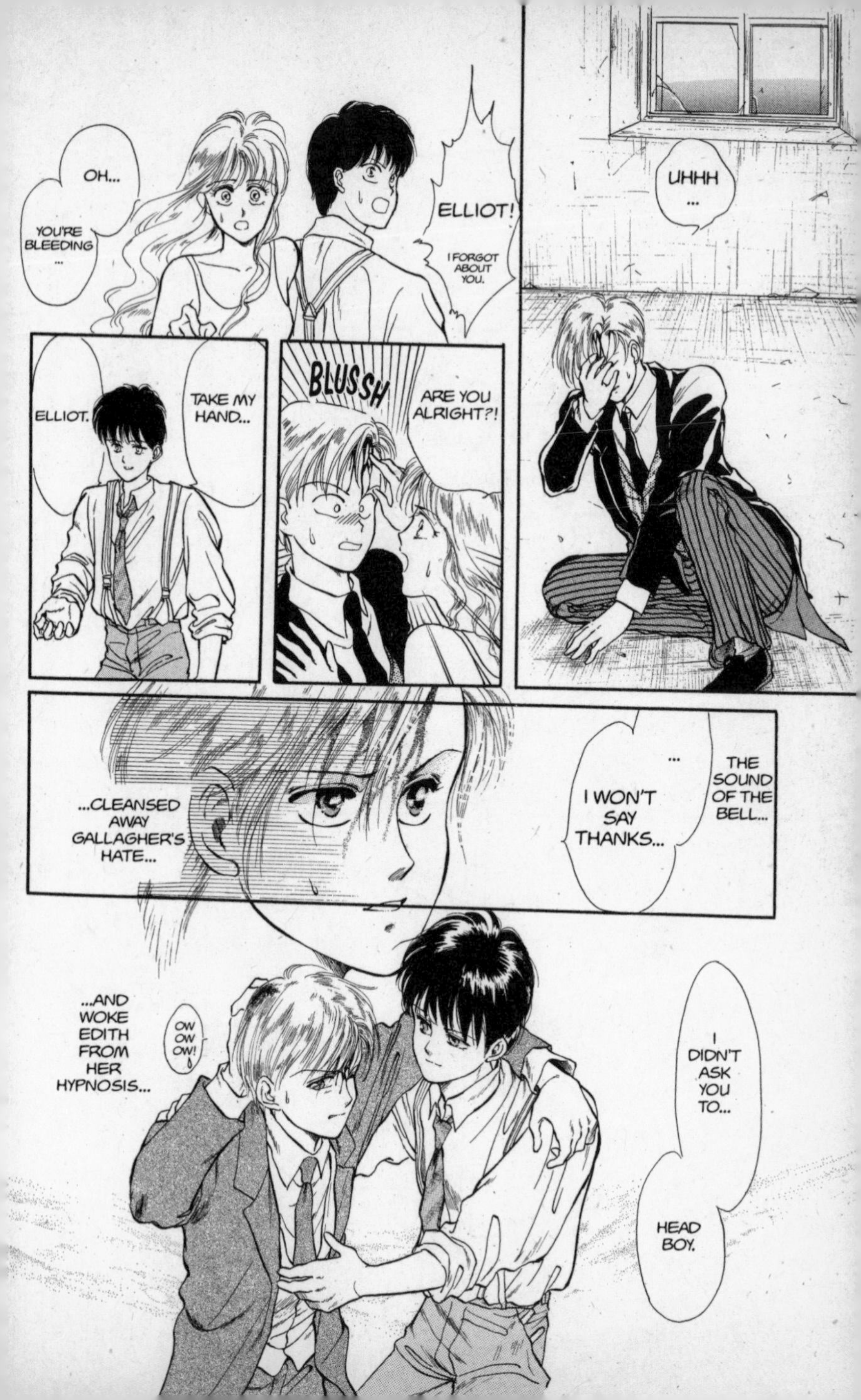
UHHH ...
ELLIOT!
I FORGOT ABOUT YOU.
OH...
YOU'RE BLEEDING ...
BLUSSH
ARE YOU ALRIGHT?!
TAKE MY HAND...
ELLIOT.
THE SOUND OF THE BELL...
... I WON'T SAY THANKS...
...CLEANSED AWAY GALLAGHER'S HATE...
I DIDN'T ASK YOU TO...
HEAD BOY.
OW OW OW!
...AND WOKE EDITH FROM HER HYPNOSIS...

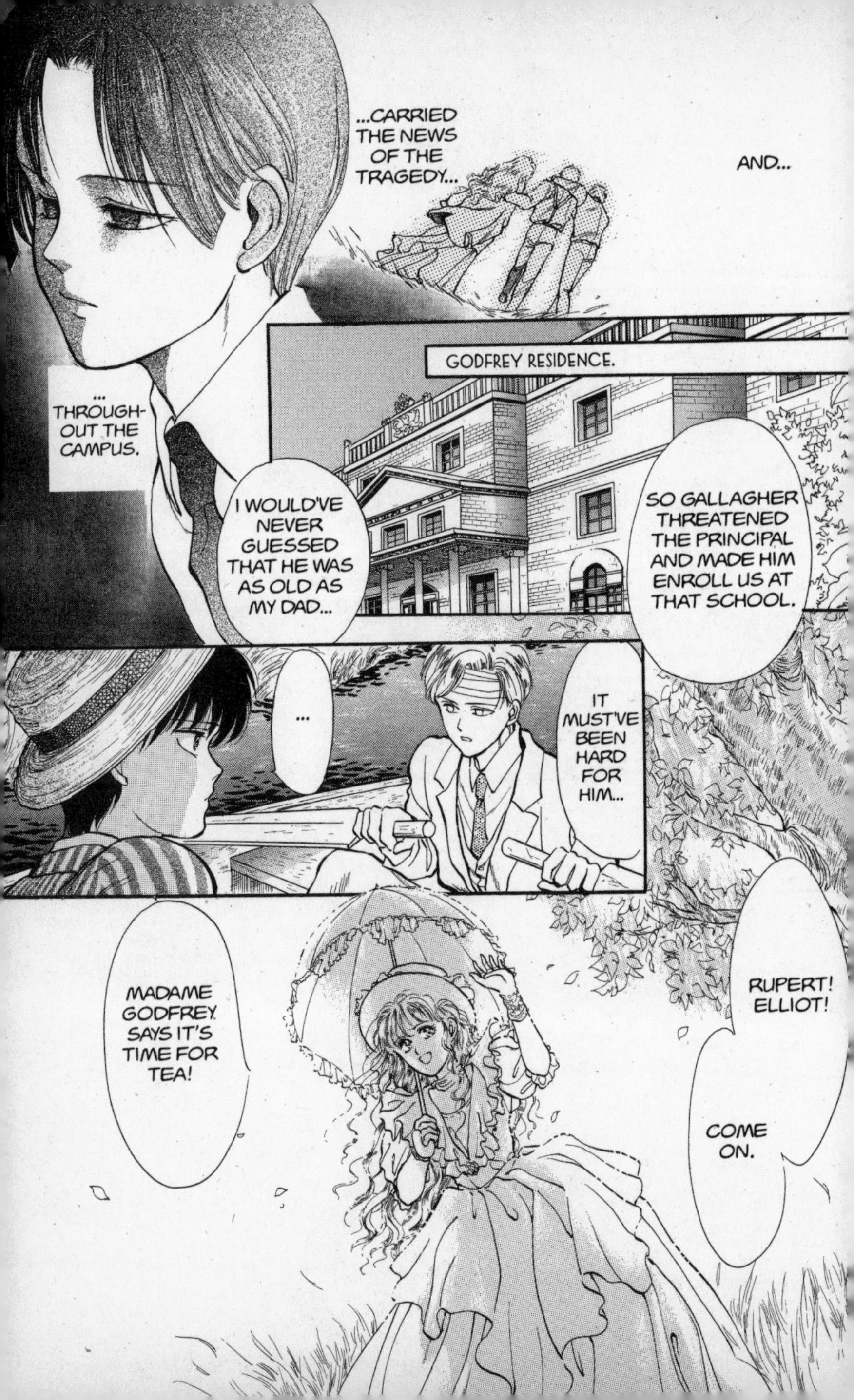
AND...
...CARRIED THE NEWS OF THE TRAGEDY...
... THROUGH-OUT THE CAMPUS.
GODFREY RESIDENCE.
SO GALLAGHER THREATENED THE PRINCIPAL AND MADE HIM ENROLL US AT THAT SCHOOL.
I WOULD'VE NEVER GUESSED THAT HE WAS AS OLD AS MY DAD...
IT MUST'VE BEEN HARD FOR HIM...
...
RUPERT! ELLIOT!
COME ON.
MADAME GODFREY. SAYS IT'S TIME FOR TEA!

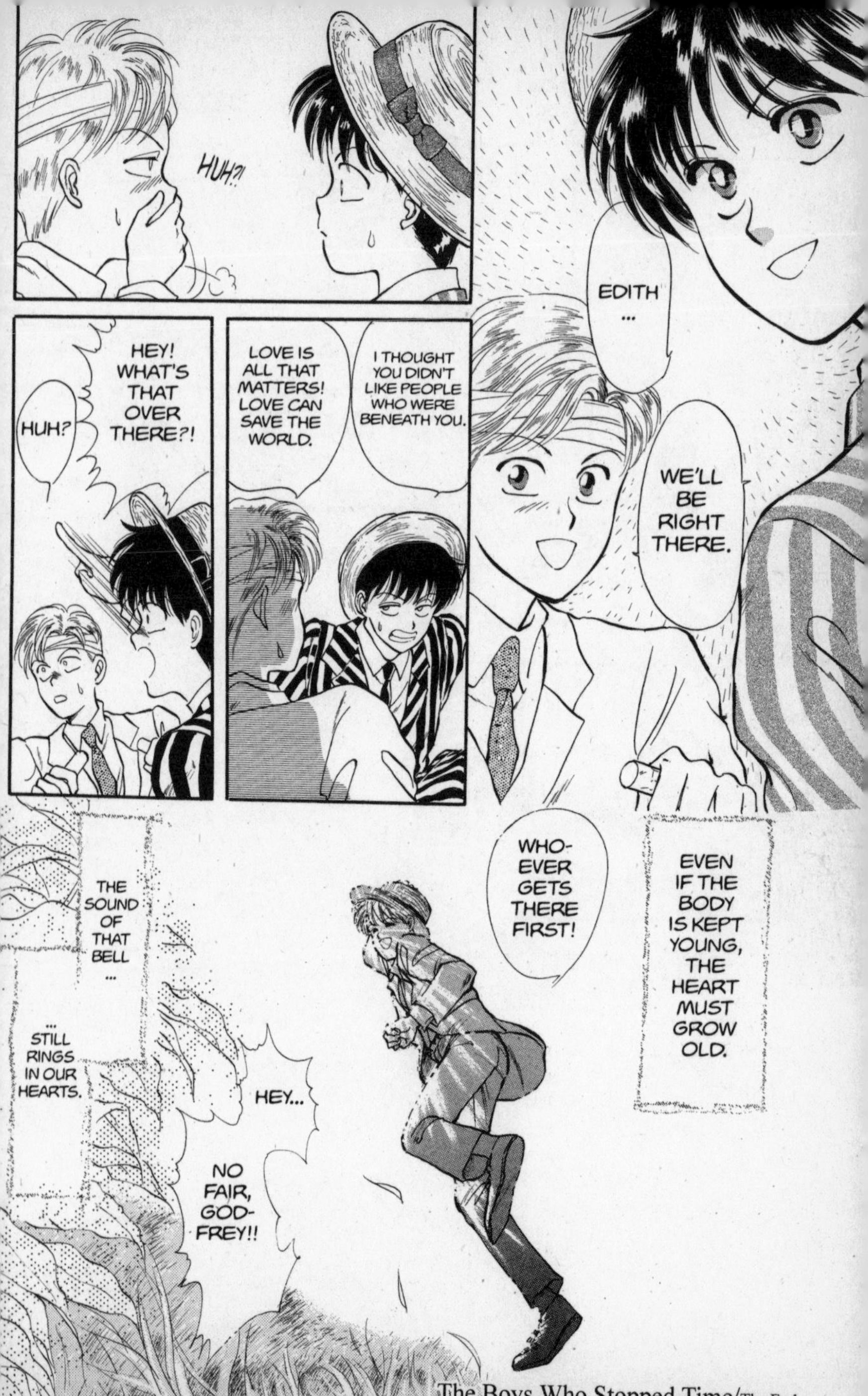

EDITH ...
WE'LL BE RIGHT THERE.
HUH?!
I THOUGHT YOU DIDN'T LIKE PEOPLE WHO WERE BENEATH YOU.
LOVE IS ALL THAT MATTERS! LOVE CAN SAVE THE WORLD.
HEY! WHAT'S THAT OVER THERE?!
HUH?
EVEN IF THE BODY IS KEPT YOUNG, THE HEART MUST GROW OLD.
WHO-EVER GETS THERE FIRST!
HEY...
NO FAIR, GOD-FREY!!
THE SOUND OF THAT BELL ...
... STILL RINGS IN OUR HEARTS.

The Boys Who Stopped Time/The End

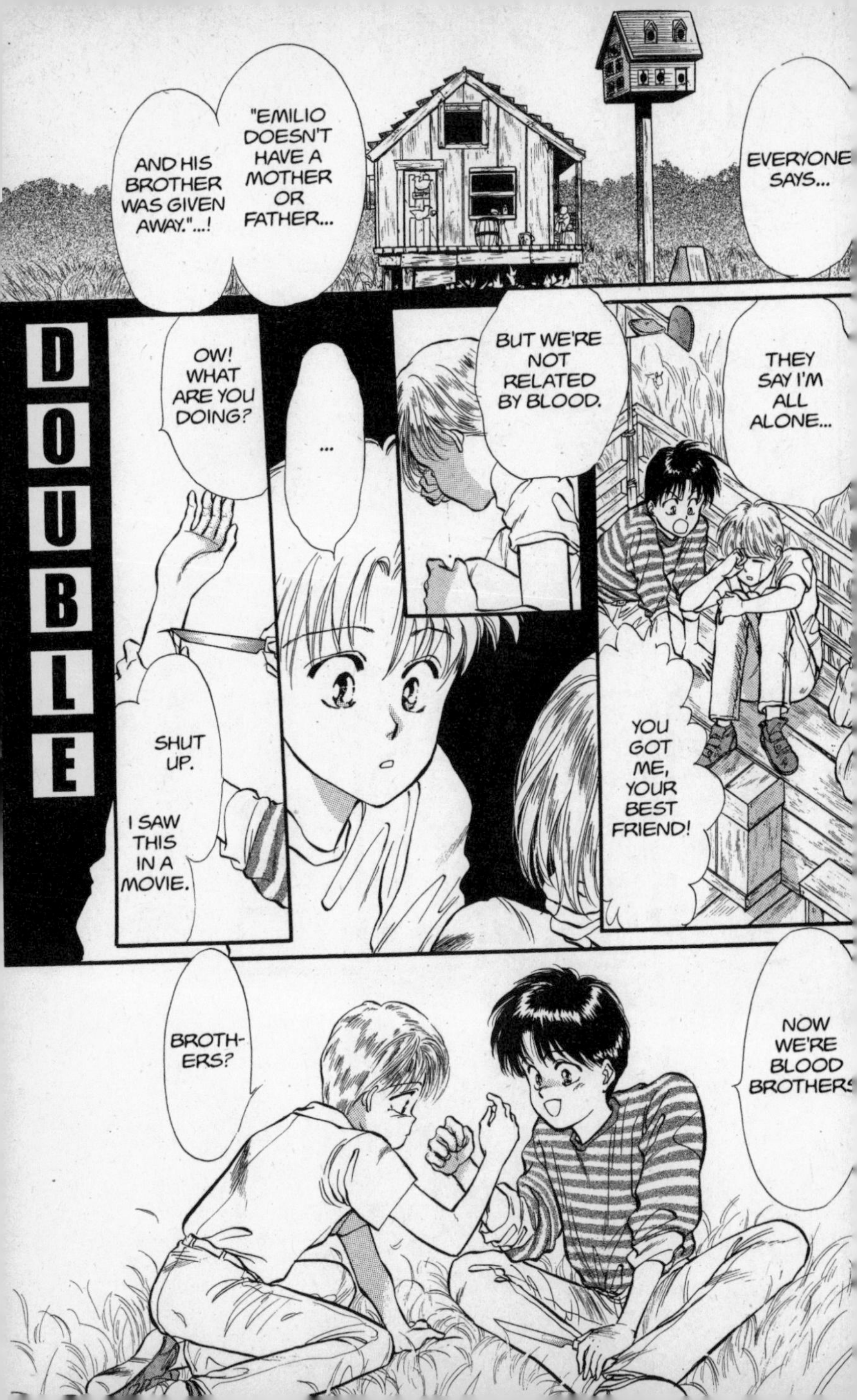
EVERYONE SAYS...
"EMILIO DOESN'T HAVE A MOTHER OR FATHER...
AND HIS BROTHER WAS GIVEN AWAY."...!
THEY SAY I'M ALL ALONE...
YOU GOT ME, YOUR BEST FRIEND!
BUT WE'RE NOT RELATED BY BLOOD.
...
OW! WHAT ARE YOU DOING?
SHUT UP.
I SAW THIS IN A MOVIE.
DOUBLE
NOW WE'RE BLOOD BROTHERS
BROTH-ERS?

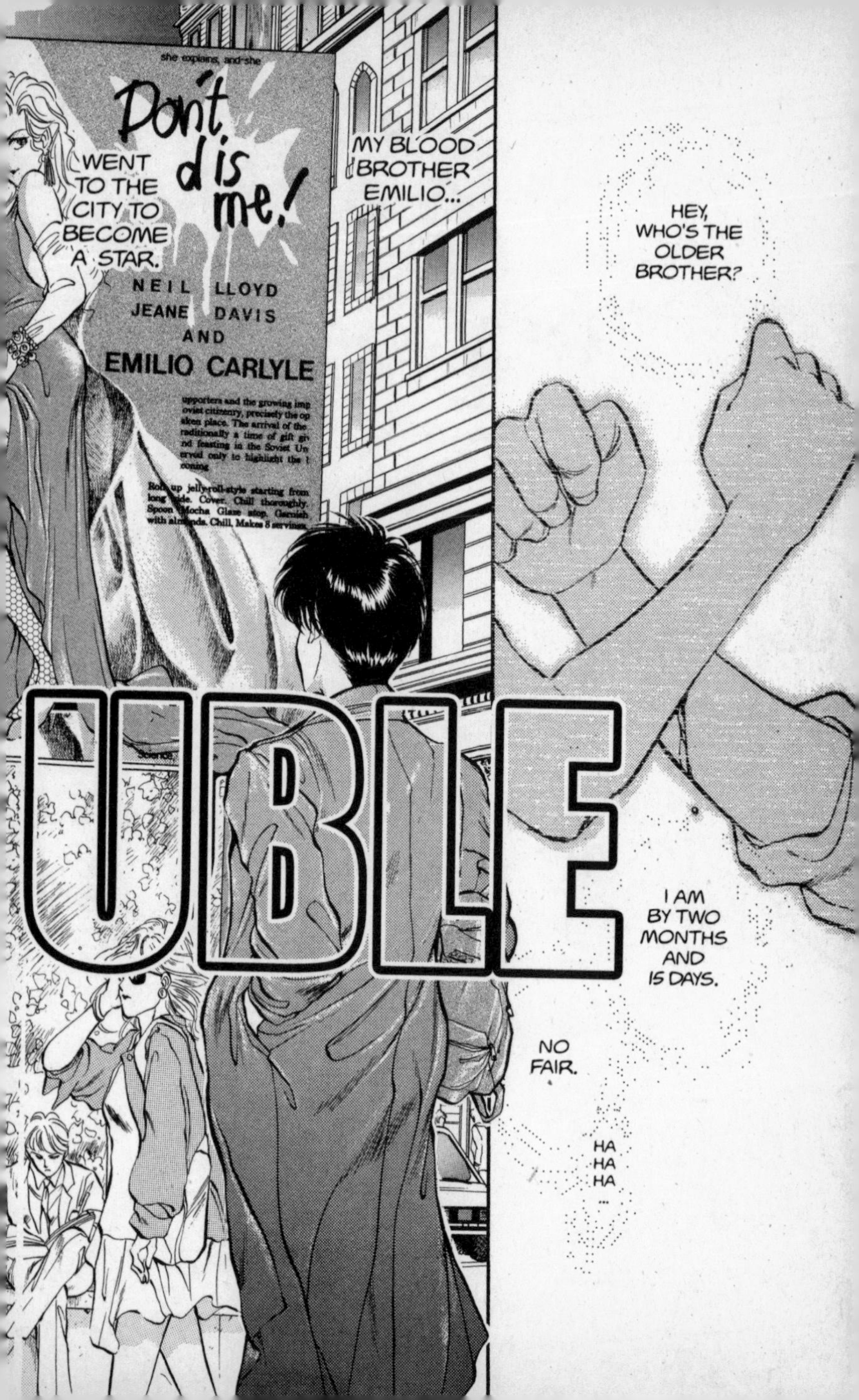
HEY, WHO'S THE OLDER BROTHER?
I AM BY TWO MONTHS AND 15 DAYS.
NO FAIR.
HA HA HA ...
MY BLOOD BROTHER EMILIO...
WENT TO THE CITY TO BECOME A STAR.
Don't d is me!
NEIL LLOYD
JEANE DAVIS
AND
EMILIO CARLYLE
UBLE

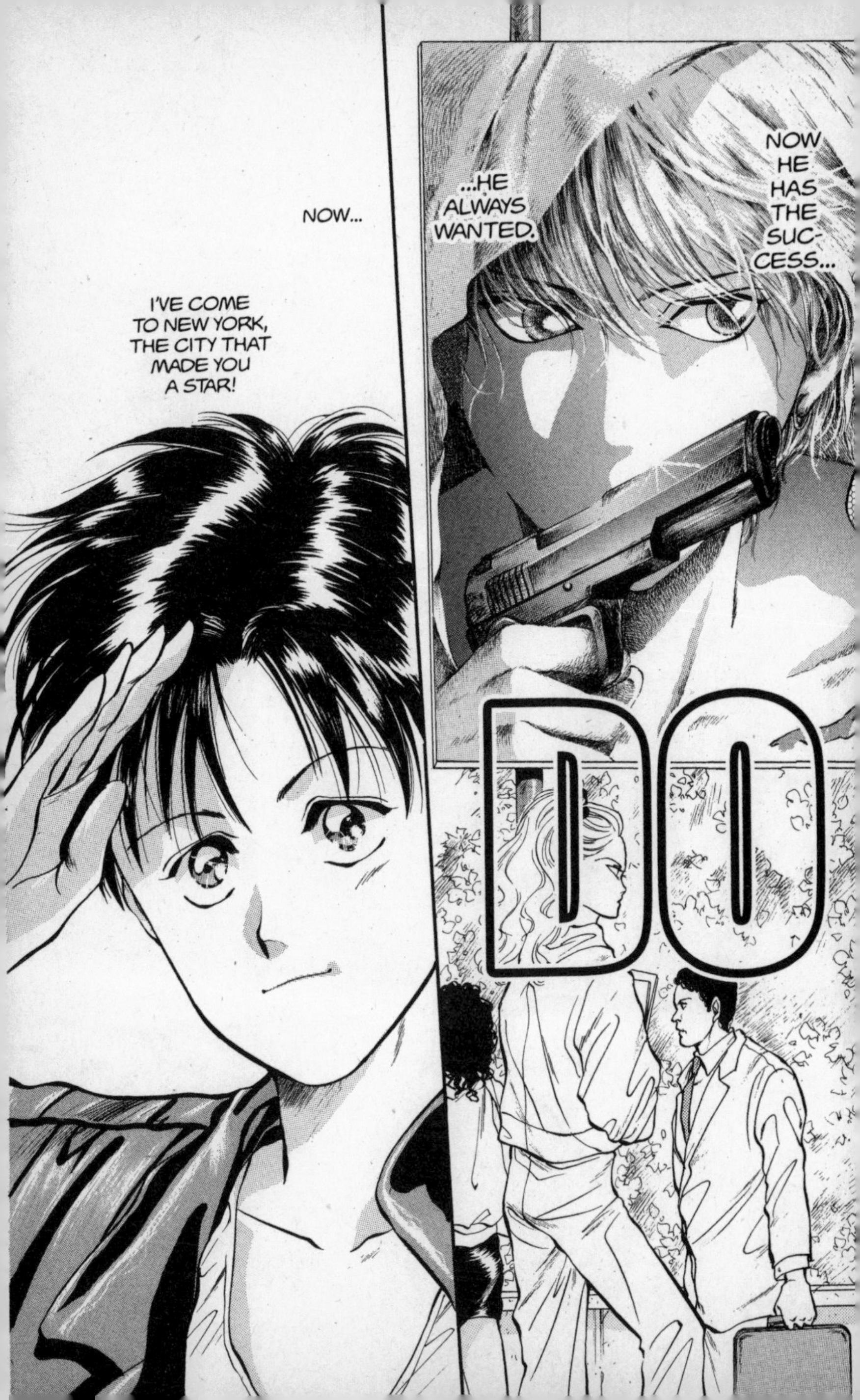
NOW HE HAS THE SUC-CESS...
...HE ALWAYS WANTED.
DO
NOW...
I'VE COME TO NEW YORK, THE CITY THAT MADE YOU A STAR!

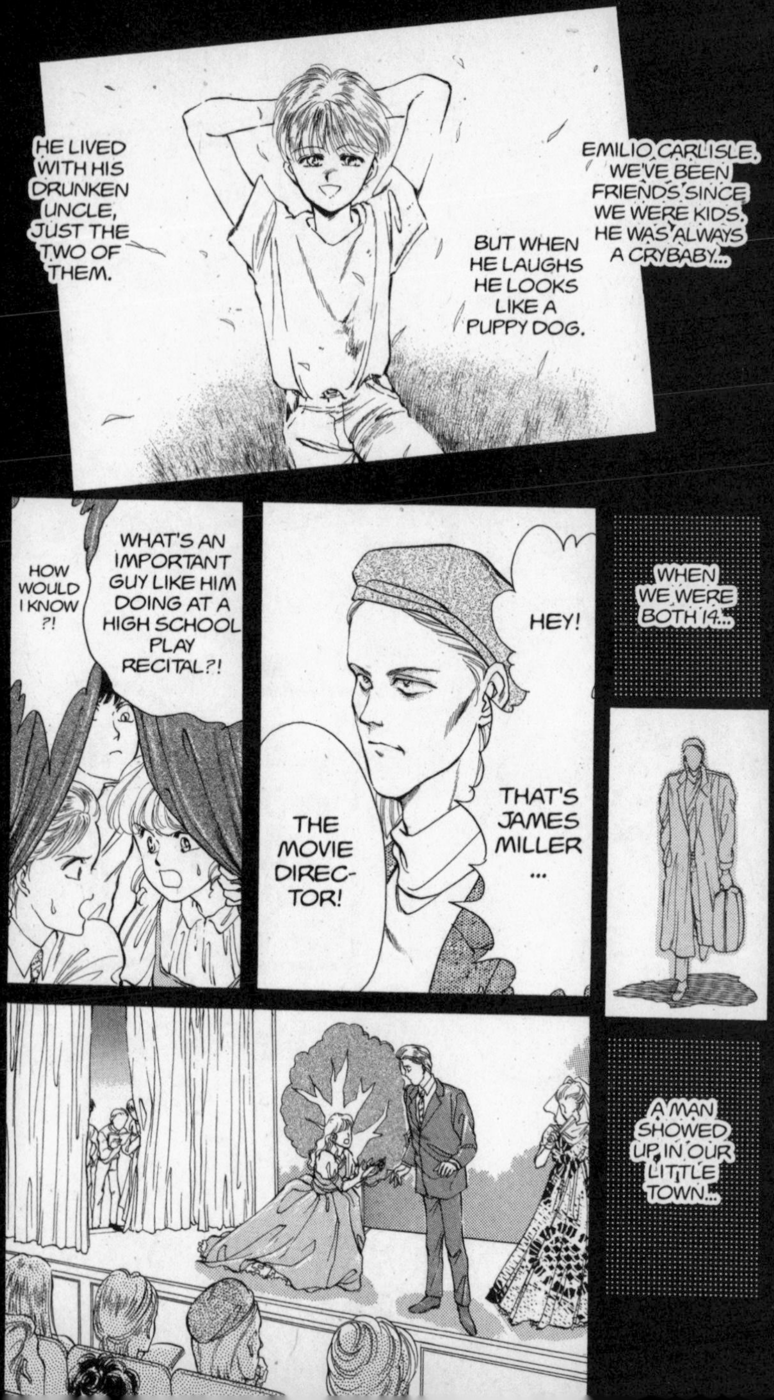
EMILIO CARLISLE. WE'VE BEEN FRIENDS SINCE WE WERE KIDS. HE WAS ALWAYS A CRYBABY...
BUT WHEN HE LAUGHS HE LOOKS LIKE A PUPPY DOG.
HE LIVED WITH HIS DRUNKEN UNCLE, JUST THE TWO OF THEM.
WHEN WE WERE BOTH 14...
A MAN SHOWED UP IN OUR LITTLE TOWN...
HEY!
THAT'S JAMES MILLER ...
THE MOVIE DIRECTOR!
WHAT'S AN IMPORTANT GUY LIKE HIM DOING AT A HIGH SCHOOL PLAY RECITAL?!
HOW WOULD I KNOW ?!

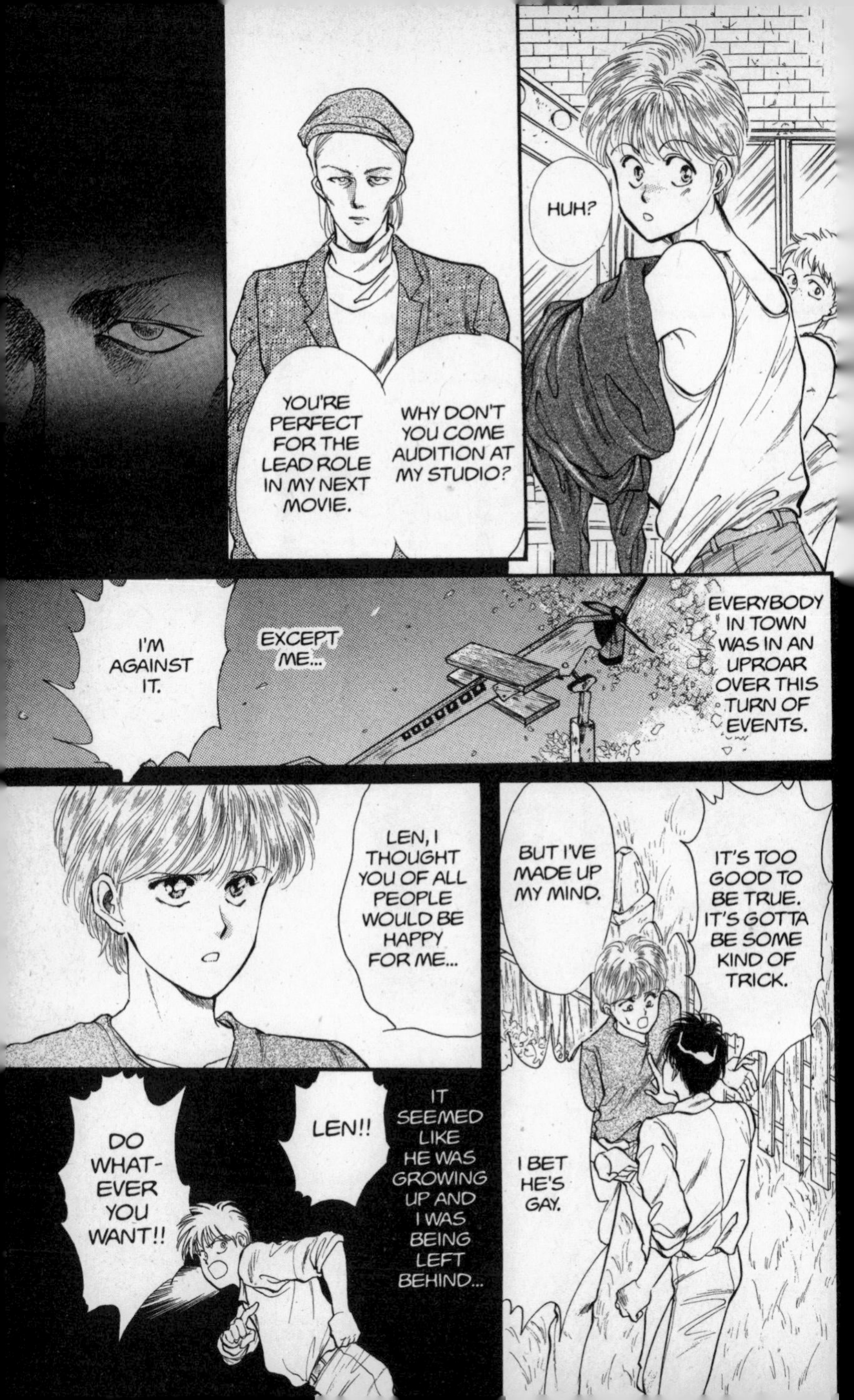

HUH?
WHY DON'T YOU COME AUDITION AT MY STUDIO?
YOU'RE PERFECT FOR THE LEAD ROLE IN MY NEXT MOVIE.
EVERYBODY IN TOWN WAS IN AN UPROAR OVER THIS TURN OF EVENTS.
EXCEPT ME...
I'M AGAINST IT.
IT'S TOO GOOD TO BE TRUE. IT'S GOTTA BE SOME KIND OF TRICK.
BUT I'VE MADE UP MY MIND.
I BET HE'S GAY.
LEN, I THOUGHT YOU OF ALL PEOPLE WOULD BE HAPPY FOR ME...
IT SEEMED LIKE HE WAS GROWING UP AND I WAS BEING LEFT BEHIND...
LEN!!
DO WHAT-EVER YOU WANT!!

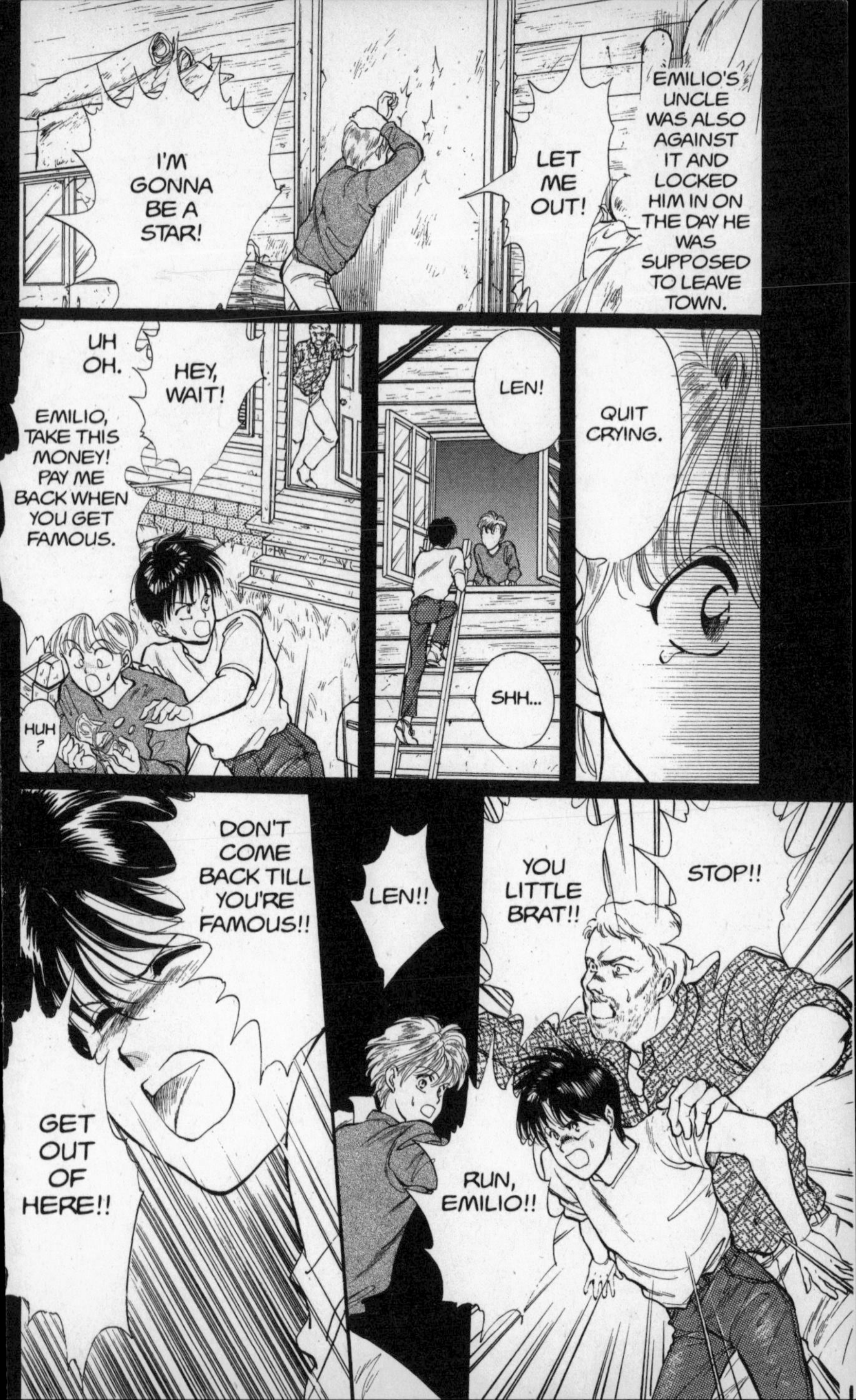
EMILIO'S UNCLE WAS ALSO AGAINST IT AND LOCKED HIM IN ON THE DAY HE WAS SUPPOSED TO LEAVE TOWN.
LET ME OUT!
I'M GONNA BE A STAR!
QUIT CRYING.
LEN!
SHH...
HEY, WAIT!
UH OH.
EMILIO, TAKE THIS MONEY! PAY ME BACK WHEN YOU GET FAMOUS.
HUH?
STOP!!
YOU LITTLE BRAT!!
RUN, EMILIO!!
LEN!!
DON'T COME BACK TILL YOU'RE FAMOUS!!
GET OUT OF HERE!!

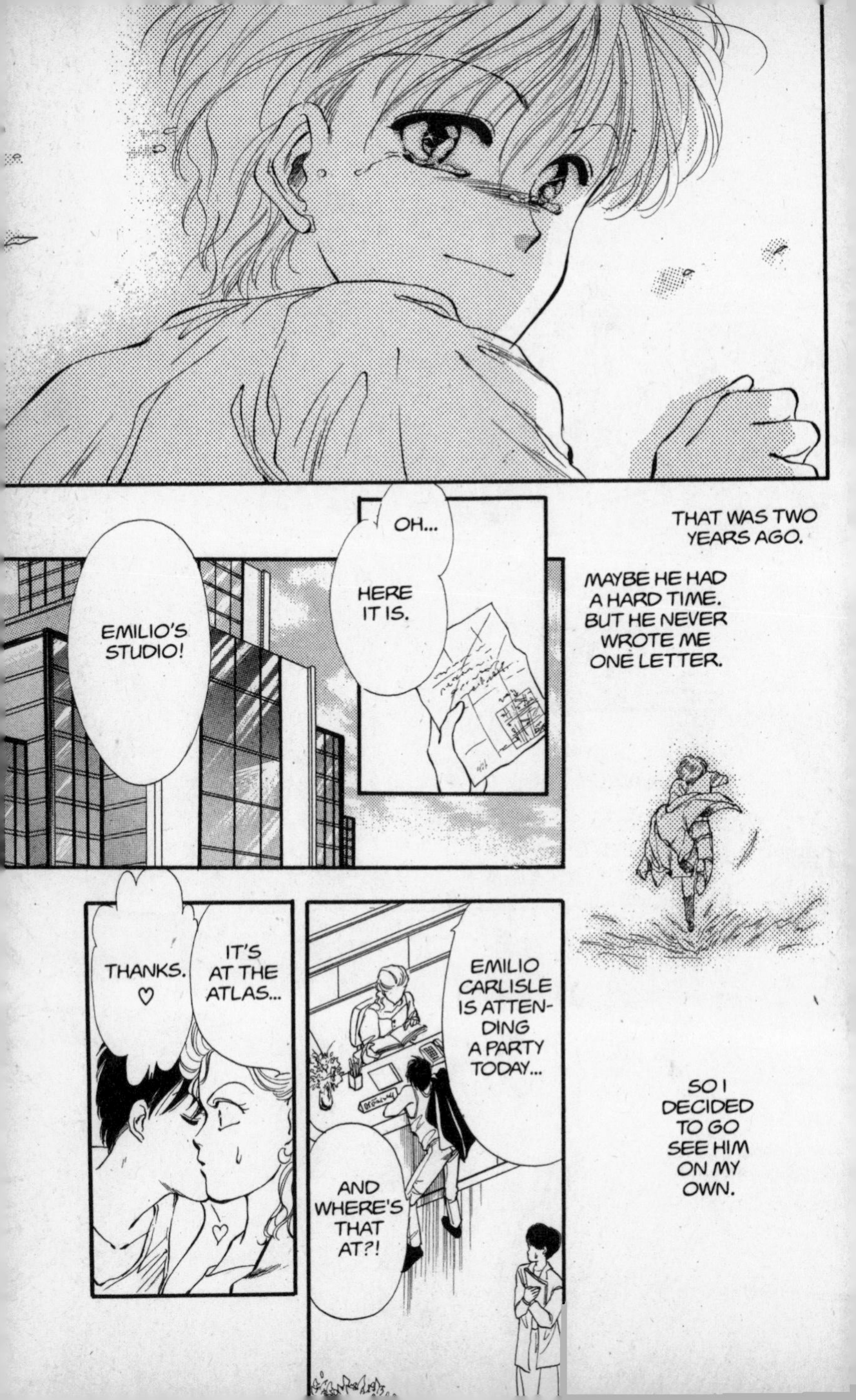
THAT WAS TWO YEARS AGO.
MAYBE HE HAD A HARD TIME. BUT HE NEVER WROTE ME ONE LETTER.
SO I DECIDED TO GO SEE HIM ON MY OWN.
OH...
HERE IT IS.
EMILIO'S STUDIO!
EMILIO CARLISLE IS ATTEN-DING A PARTY TODAY...
AND WHERE'S THAT AT?!
IT'S AT THE ATLAS...
THANKS. ♡

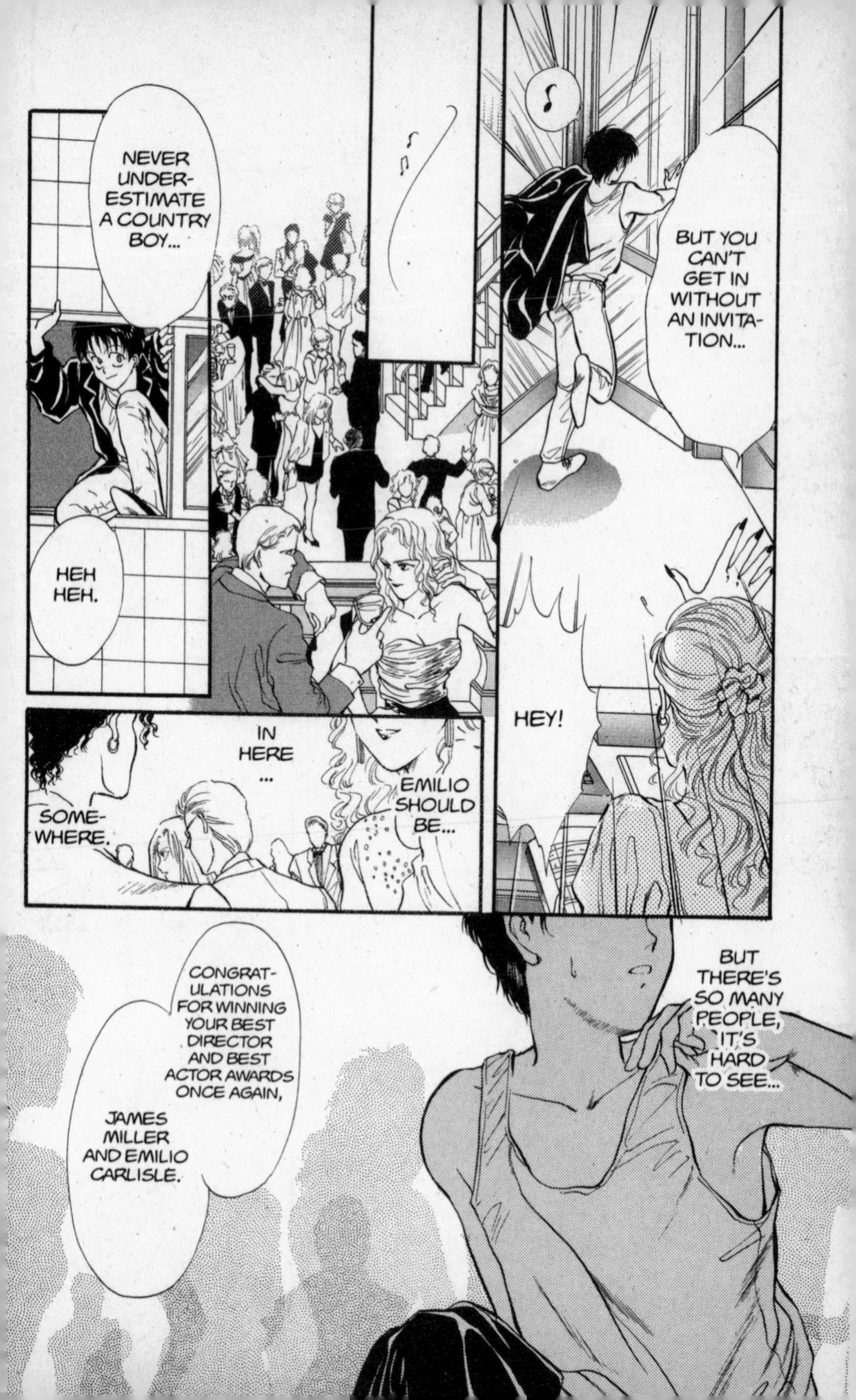
BUT YOU CAN'T GET IN WITHOUT AN INVITATION...
NEVER UNDER-ESTIMATE A COUNTRY BOY...
HEH HEH.
HEY!
EMILIO SHOULD BE...
IN HERE ...
SOME-WHERE.
BUT THERE'S SO MANY PEOPLE, IT'S HARD TO SEE...
CONGRATULATIONS FOR WINNING YOUR BEST DIRECTOR AND BEST ACTOR AWARDS ONCE AGAIN,
JAMES MILLER AND EMILIO CARLISLE.

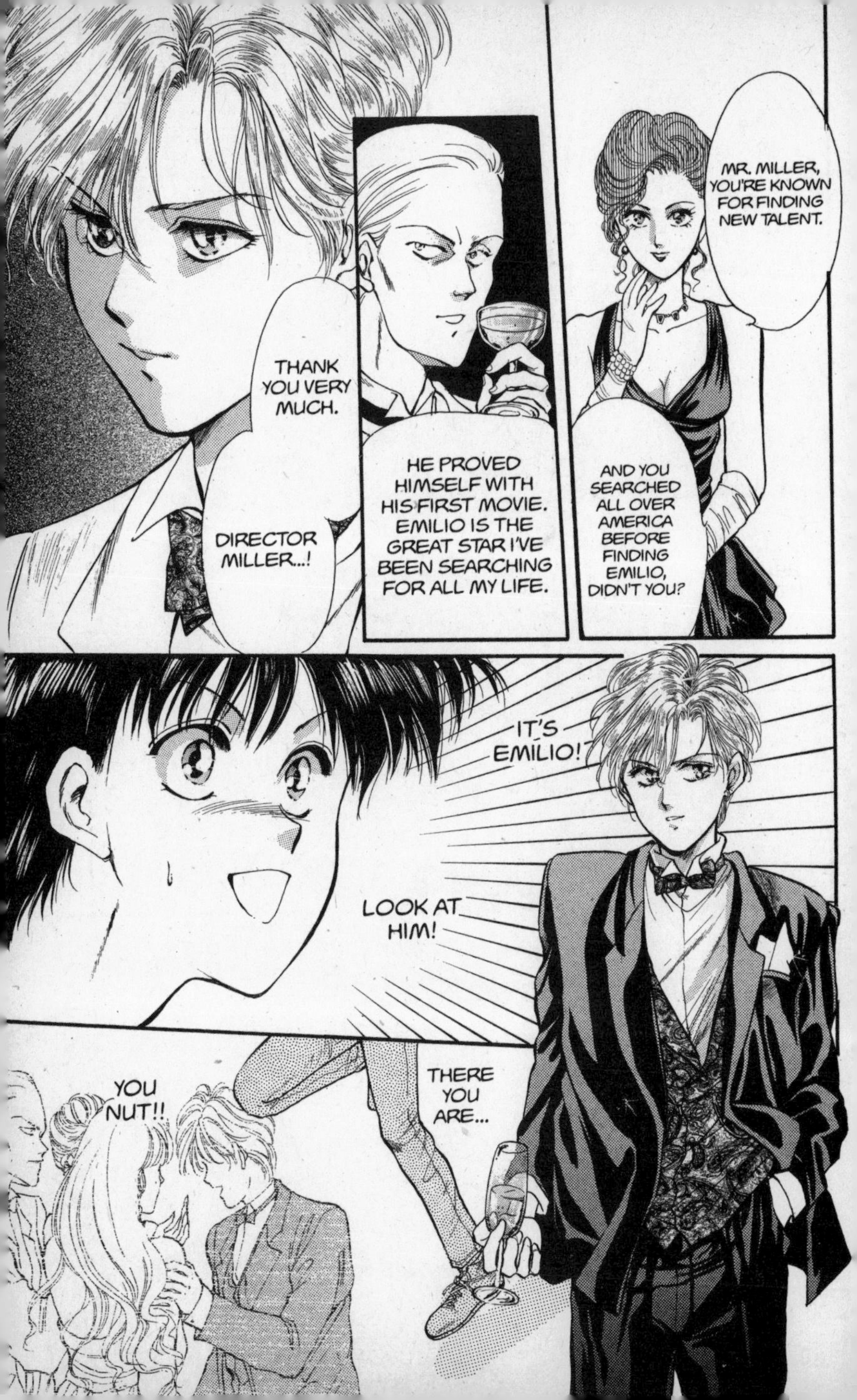
MR. MILLER, YOU'RE KNOWN FOR FINDING NEW TALENT.
AND YOU SEARCHED ALL OVER AMERICA BEFORE FINDING EMILIO, DIDN'T YOU?
HE PROVED HIMSELF WITH HIS FIRST MOVIE. EMILIO IS THE GREAT STAR I'VE BEEN SEARCHING FOR ALL MY LIFE.
THANK YOU VERY MUCH.
DIRECTOR MILLER...!
IT'S EMILIO!
LOOK AT HIM!
THERE YOU ARE...
YOU NUT!!

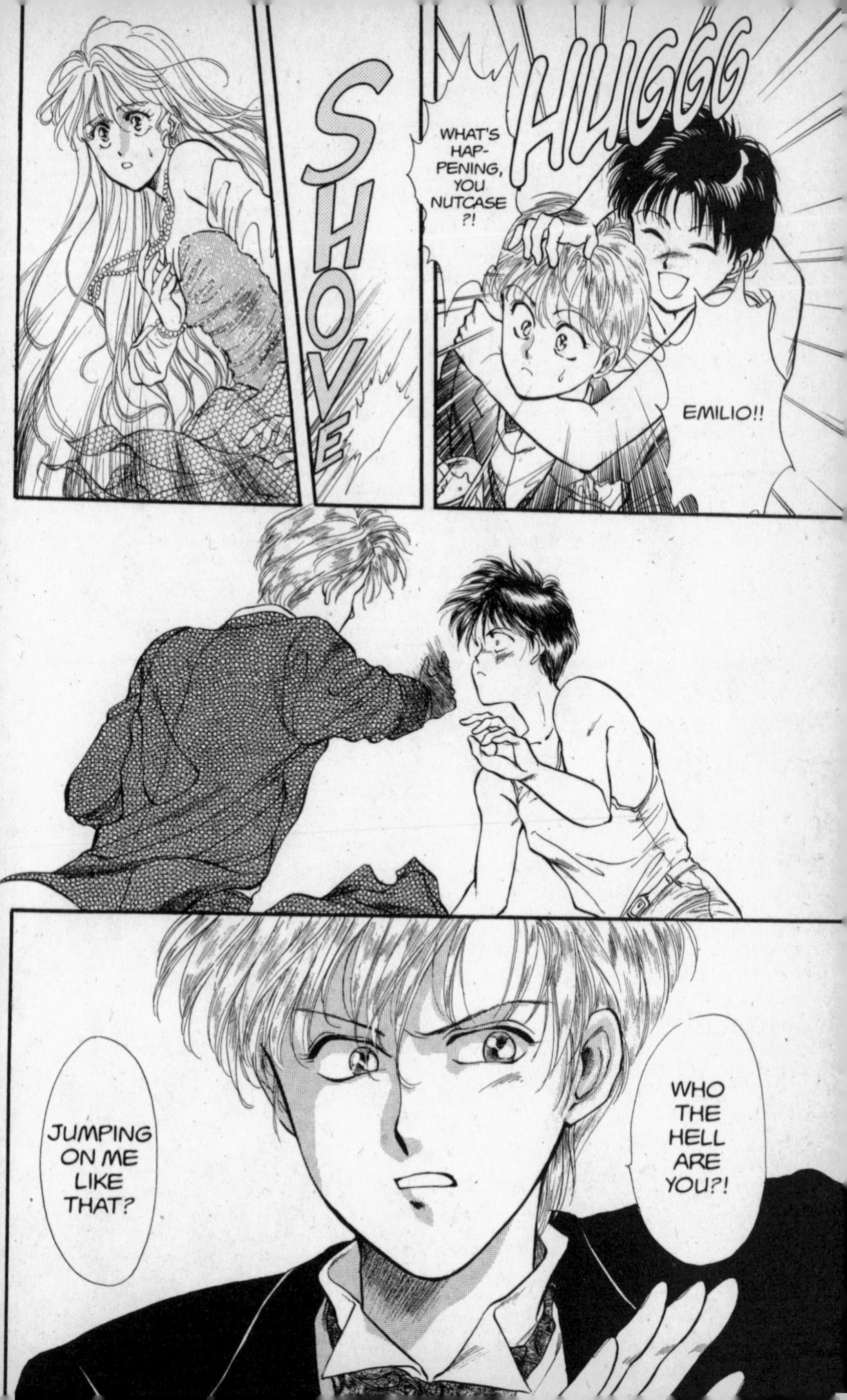
HUGGG
EMILIO!!
WHAT'S HAP-PENING, YOU NUTCASE?!
SHOVE
WHO THE HELL ARE YOU?!
JUMPING ON ME LIKE THAT?

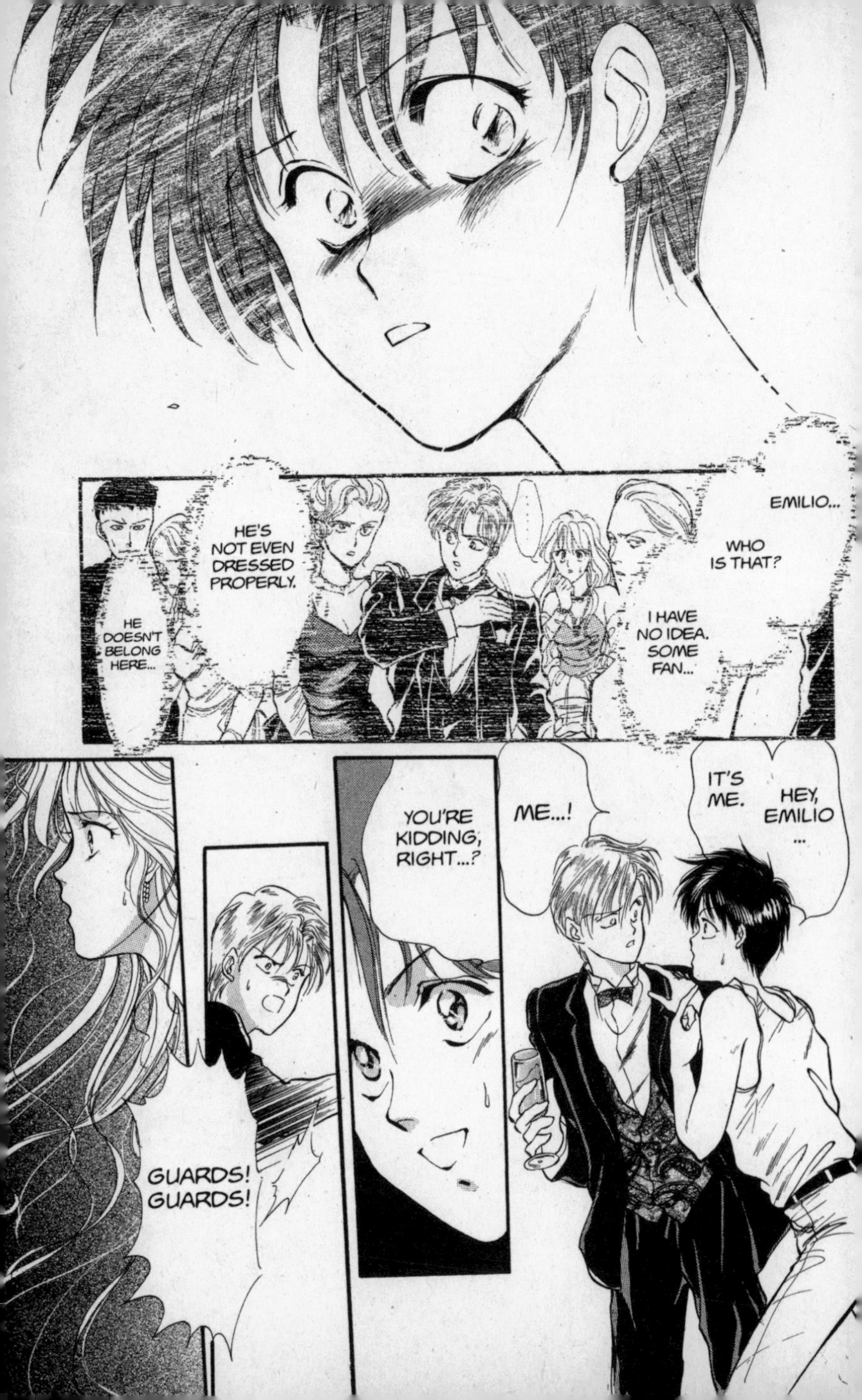
EMILIO...
WHO IS THAT?
I HAVE NO IDEA. SOME FAN...
HE'S NOT EVEN DRESSED PROPERLY.
HE DOESN'T BELONG HERE...
HEY, EMILIO ...
IT'S ME.
ME...!
YOU'RE KIDDING, RIGHT...?
GUARDS! GUARDS!

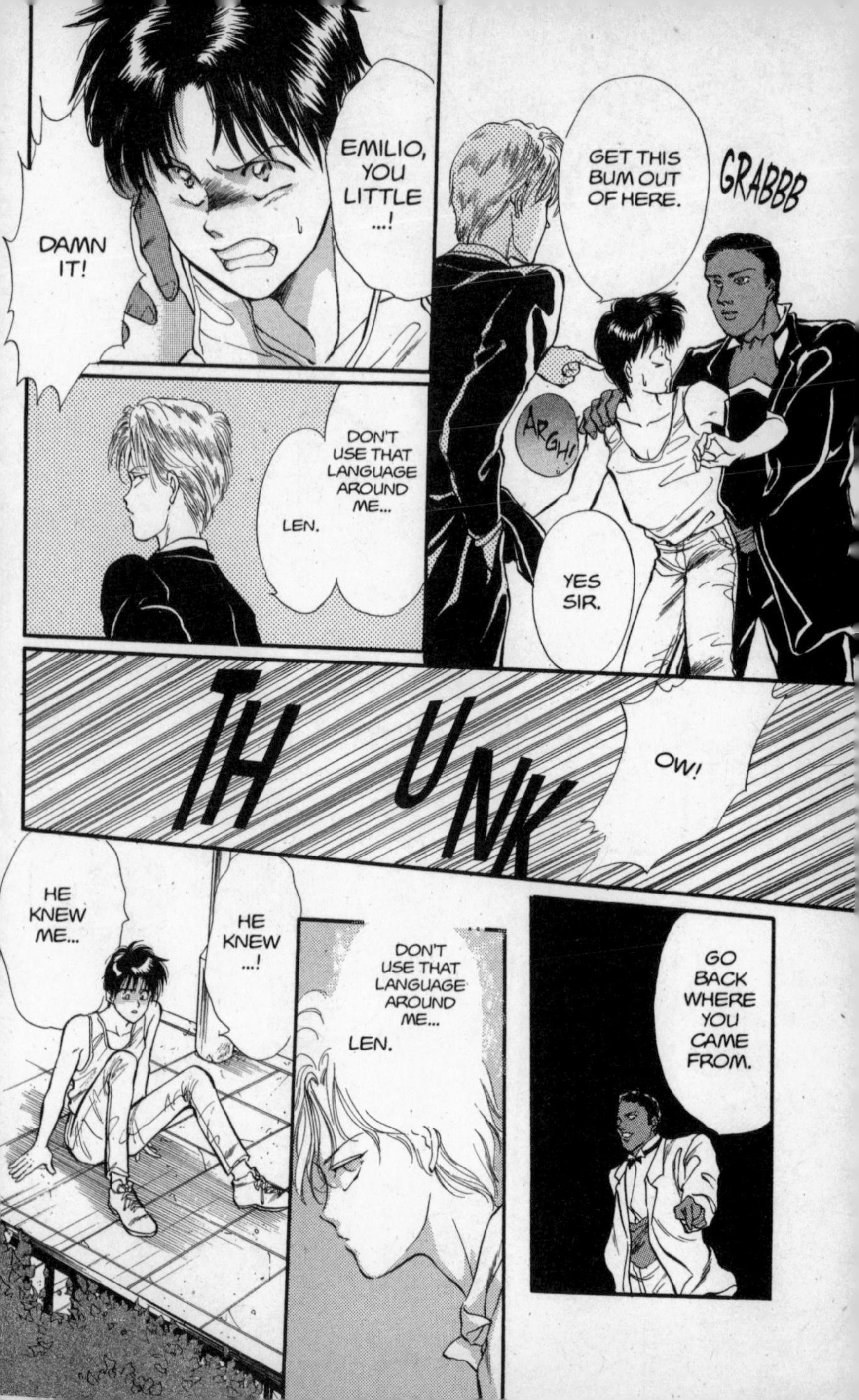
GET THIS BUM OUT OF HERE.
GRABBB
ARGH!
YES SIR.
EMILIO, YOU LITTLE ...!
DAMN IT!
DON'T USE THAT LANGUAGE AROUND ME...
LEN.
OW!
THUNK
GO BACK WHERE YOU CAME FROM.
DON'T USE THAT LANGUAGE AROUND ME...
LEN.
HE KNEW ...!
HE KNEW ME...

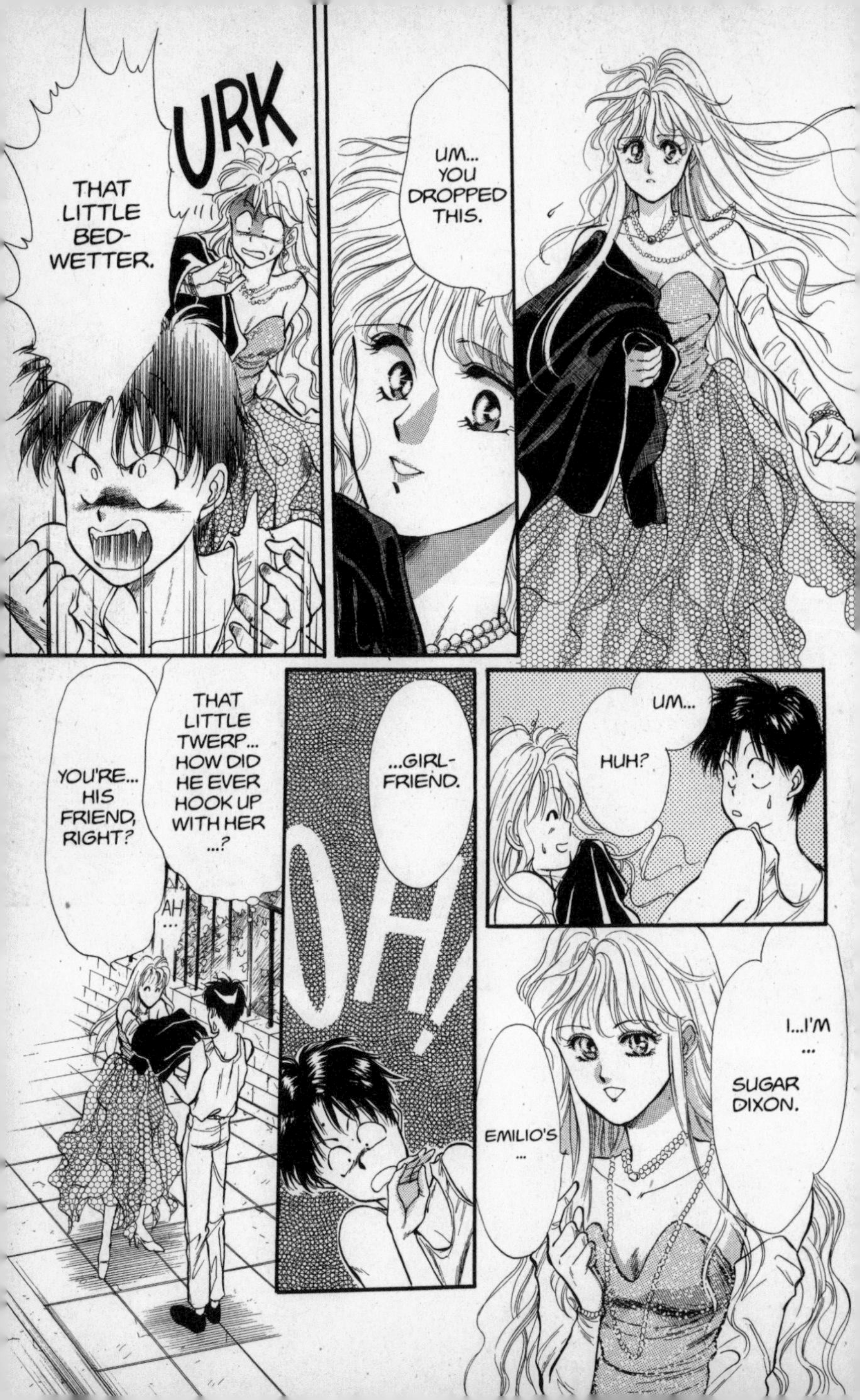
UM... YOU DROPPED THIS.
URK
THAT LITTLE BED-WETTER.
UM...
HUH?
I...I'M ... SUGAR DIXON.
EMILIO'S ...
...GIRL-FRIEND.
OH!
THAT LITTLE TWERP... HOW DID HE EVER HOOK UP WITH HER ...?
YOU'RE... HIS FRIEND, RIGHT?
AH ...

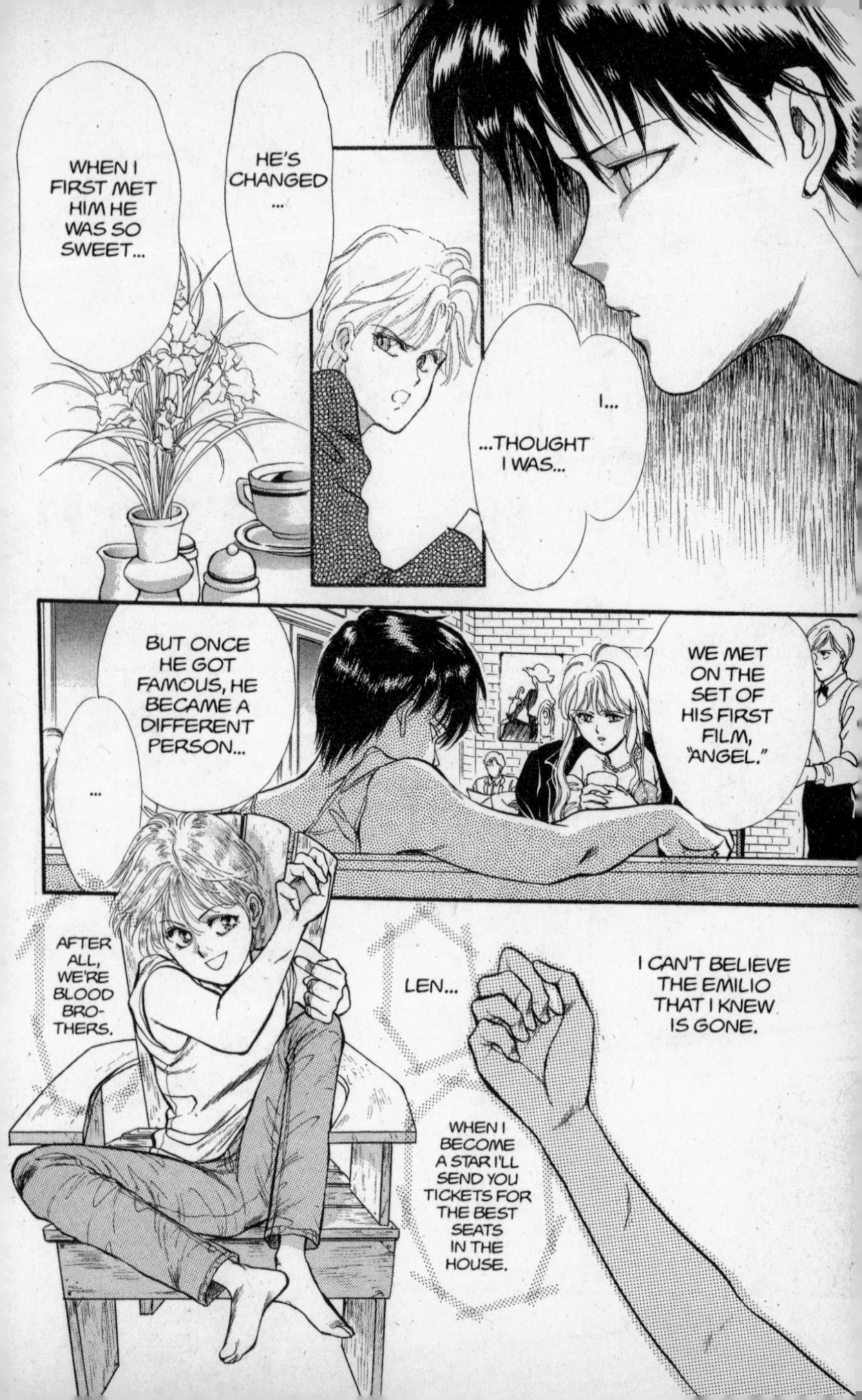

I...
...THOUGHT I WAS...
HE'S CHANGED ...
WHEN I FIRST MET HIM HE WAS SO SWEET...
WE MET ON THE SET OF HIS FIRST FILM, "ANGEL."
BUT ONCE HE GOT FAMOUS, HE BECAME A DIFFERENT PERSON...
...
I CAN'T BELIEVE THE EMILIO THAT I KNEW IS GONE.
LEN...
WHEN I BECOME A STAR I'LL SEND YOU TICKETS FOR THE BEST SEATS IN THE HOUSE.
AFTER ALL, WE'RE BLOOD BRO-THERS.

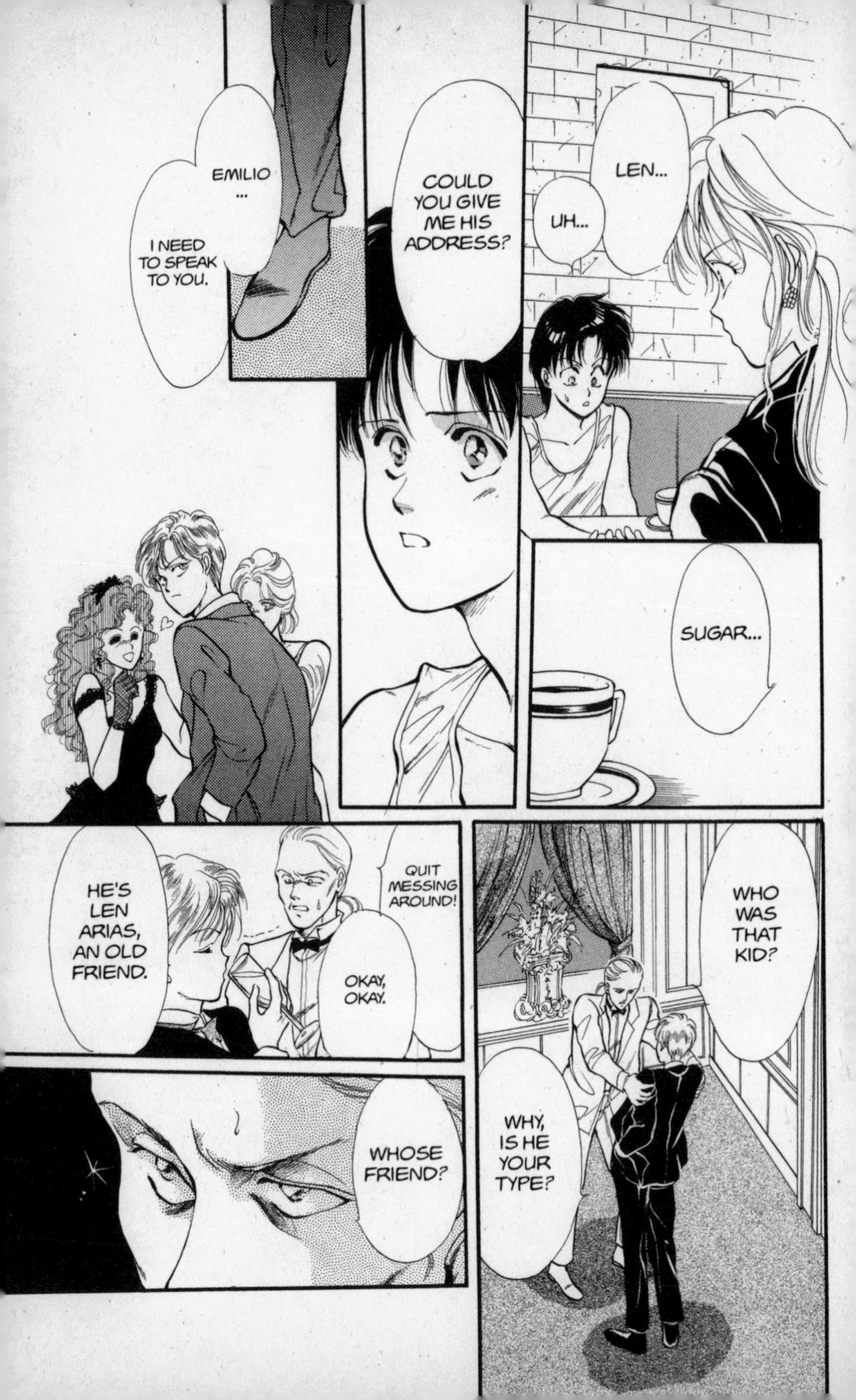
LEN...
UH...
SUGAR...
COULD YOU GIVE ME HIS ADDRESS?
EMILIO ...
I NEED TO SPEAK TO YOU.
WHO WAS THAT KID?
WHY, IS HE YOUR TYPE?
QUIT MESSING AROUND!
OKAY, OKAY.
HE'S LEN ARIAS, AN OLD FRIEND.
WHOSE FRIEND?

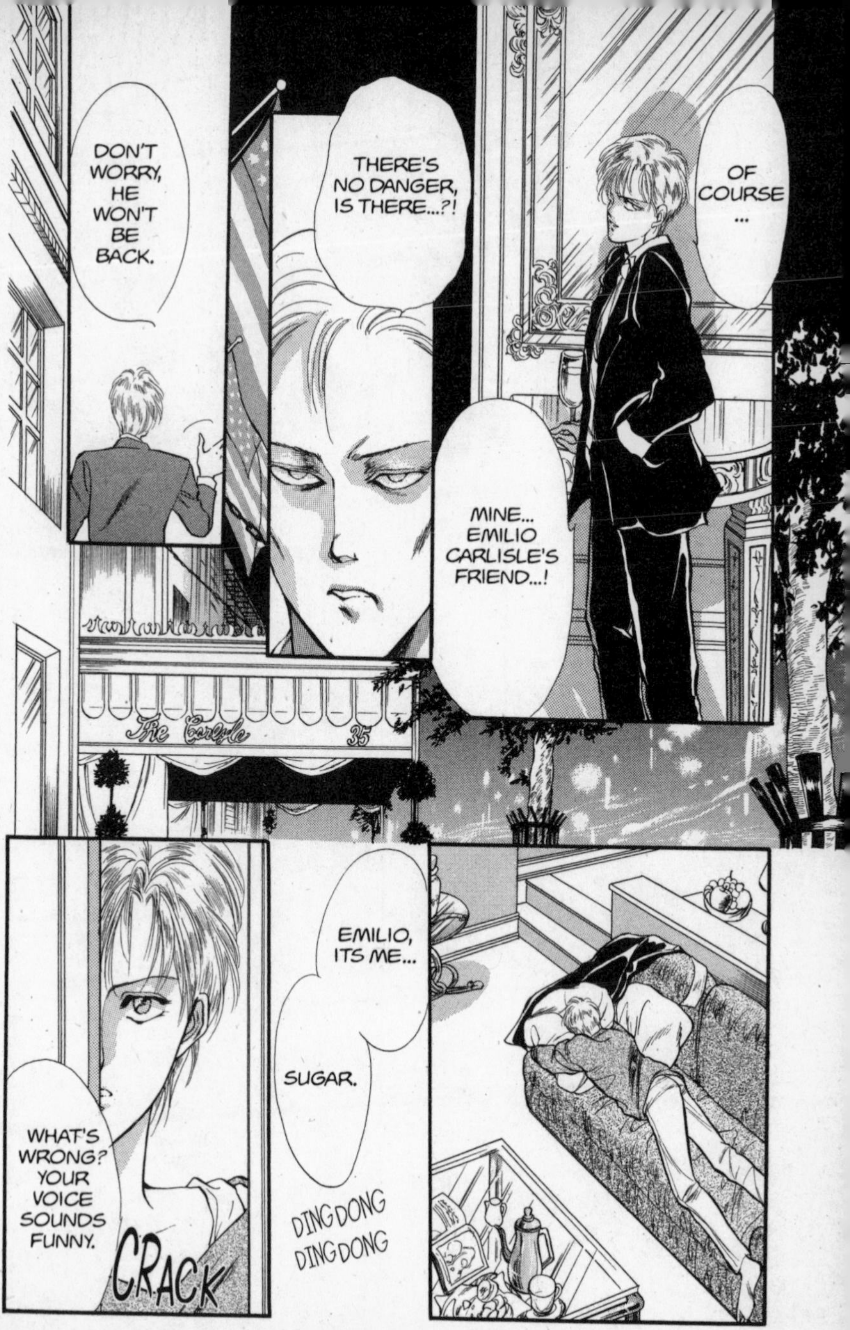
OF COURSE...
MINE... EMILIO CARLISLE'S FRIEND...!
THERE'S NO DANGER, IS THERE...?!
DON'T WORRY, HE WON'T BE BACK.
EMILIO, ITS ME...
SUGAR.
DING DONG DING DONG
WHAT'S WRONG? YOUR VOICE SOUNDS FUNNY.
CRACK

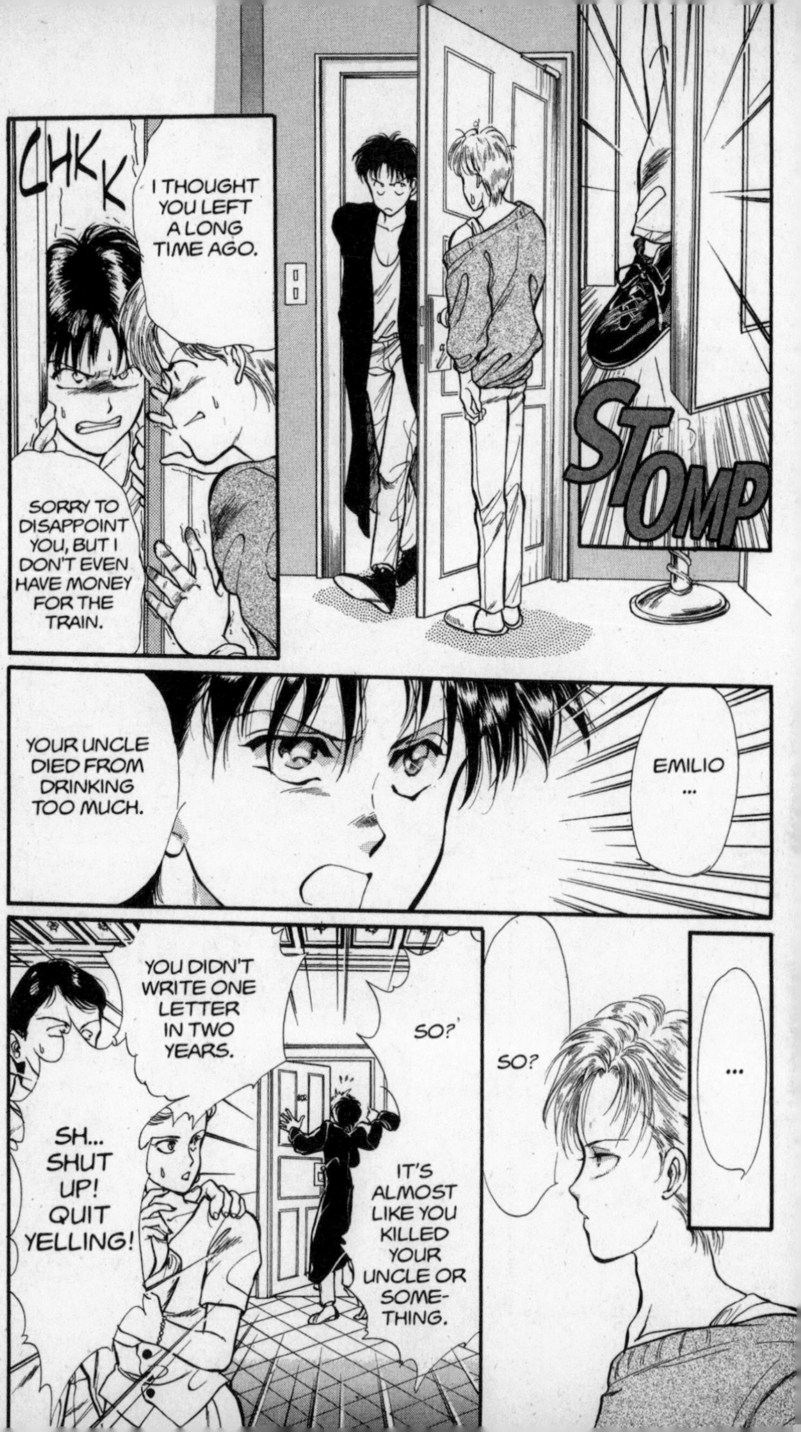
STOMP
CHKK
I THOUGHT YOU LEFT A LONG TIME AGO.
SORRY TO DISAPPOINT YOU, BUT I DON'T EVEN HAVE MONEY FOR THE TRAIN.
EMILIO ...
YOUR UNCLE DIED FROM DRINKING TOO MUCH.
...
SO?
SO?'
YOU DIDN'T WRITE ONE LETTER IN TWO YEARS.
IT'S ALMOST LIKE YOU KILLED YOUR UNCLE OR SOME-THING.
SH... SHUT UP! QUIT YELLING!

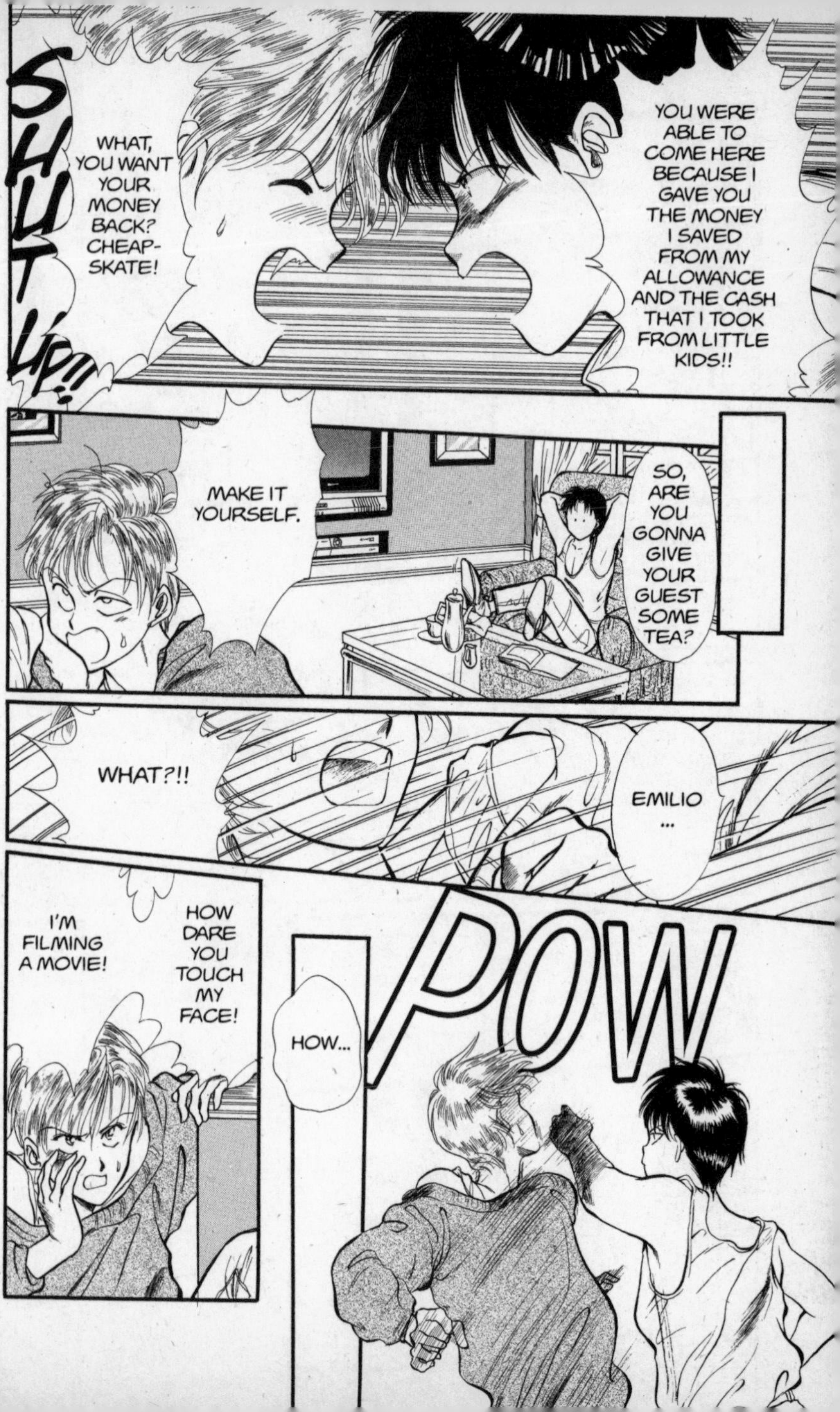
YOU WERE ABLE TO COME HERE BECAUSE I GAVE YOU THE MONEY I SAVED FROM MY ALLOWANCE AND THE CASH THAT I TOOK FROM LITTLE KIDS!!
WHAT, YOU WANT YOUR MONEY BACK? CHEAP-SKATE!
SHUT UP!!
SO, ARE YOU GONNA GIVE YOUR GUEST SOME TEA?
MAKE IT YOURSELF.
EMILIO ...
WHAT?!!
POW
HOW...
HOW DARE YOU TOUCH MY FACE!
I'M FILMING A MOVIE!

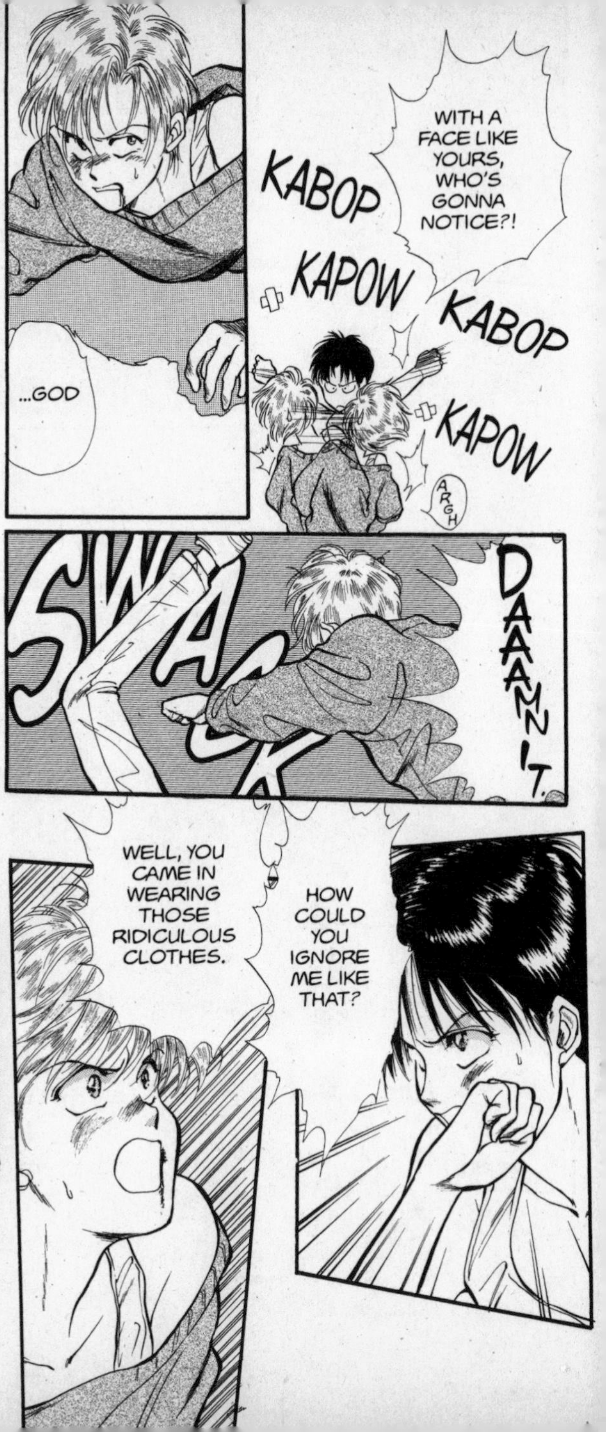
WITH A FACE LIKE YOURS, WHO'S GONNA NOTICE?!
KABOP
KAPOW
KABOP
KAPOW
ARGH
...GOD
DAAAMNIT.
SWACK
HOW COULD YOU IGNORE ME LIKE THAT?
WELL, YOU CAME IN WEARING THOSE RIDICULOUS CLOTHES.

WILD TALK

I'VE SAID THIS BEFORE BUT I THOUGHT UP THIS STORY AFTER WATCHING ***NEW CINEMA PARADISE***. I GOT EMILIO'S NAME FROM ONE OF MY FOUR DARLINGS, EMILIO ESTEVEZ. (BY THE WAY, THE OTHER THREE ARE GARY OLDMAN, RUPERT GRAVES, AND KYLE MCMULLEN.) AND I MODELED DIRECTOR MILLER AFTER DARIO ARGENTO... IT WAS REALLY RARE FOR ME TO WRITE THE STORY DIALOGUE SO QUICKLY! I FEEL AS THOUGH I REALLY BECAME ABSORBED IN THE WRITING. BUT BECAUSE IT'S A PIECE THAT I DID SO LONG AGO, MY DRAWING STYLE HAS CHANGED QUITE A BIT SINCE THEN. WHAT? NOT REALLY? I THINK I GOT LEN'S NAME FROM THE MAIN CHARACTER IN THE MOVIE ***FOOTLOOSE*** THAT KEVIN BACON STARRED IN. THIS IS MY FAVORITE STORY IN THIS VOLUME. IF I DRAW EMILIO NOW, HE LOOKS LIKE THIS.

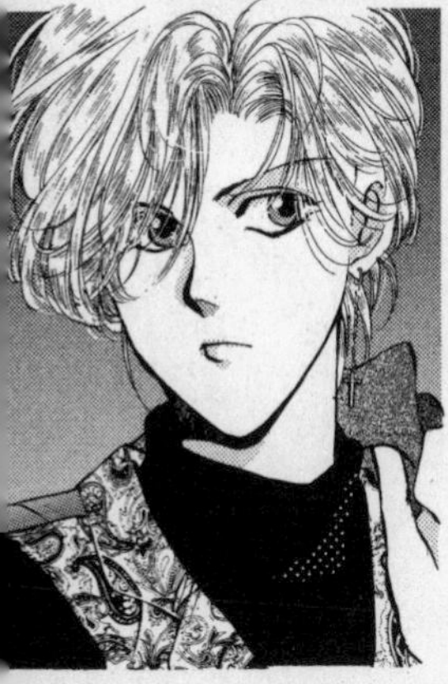

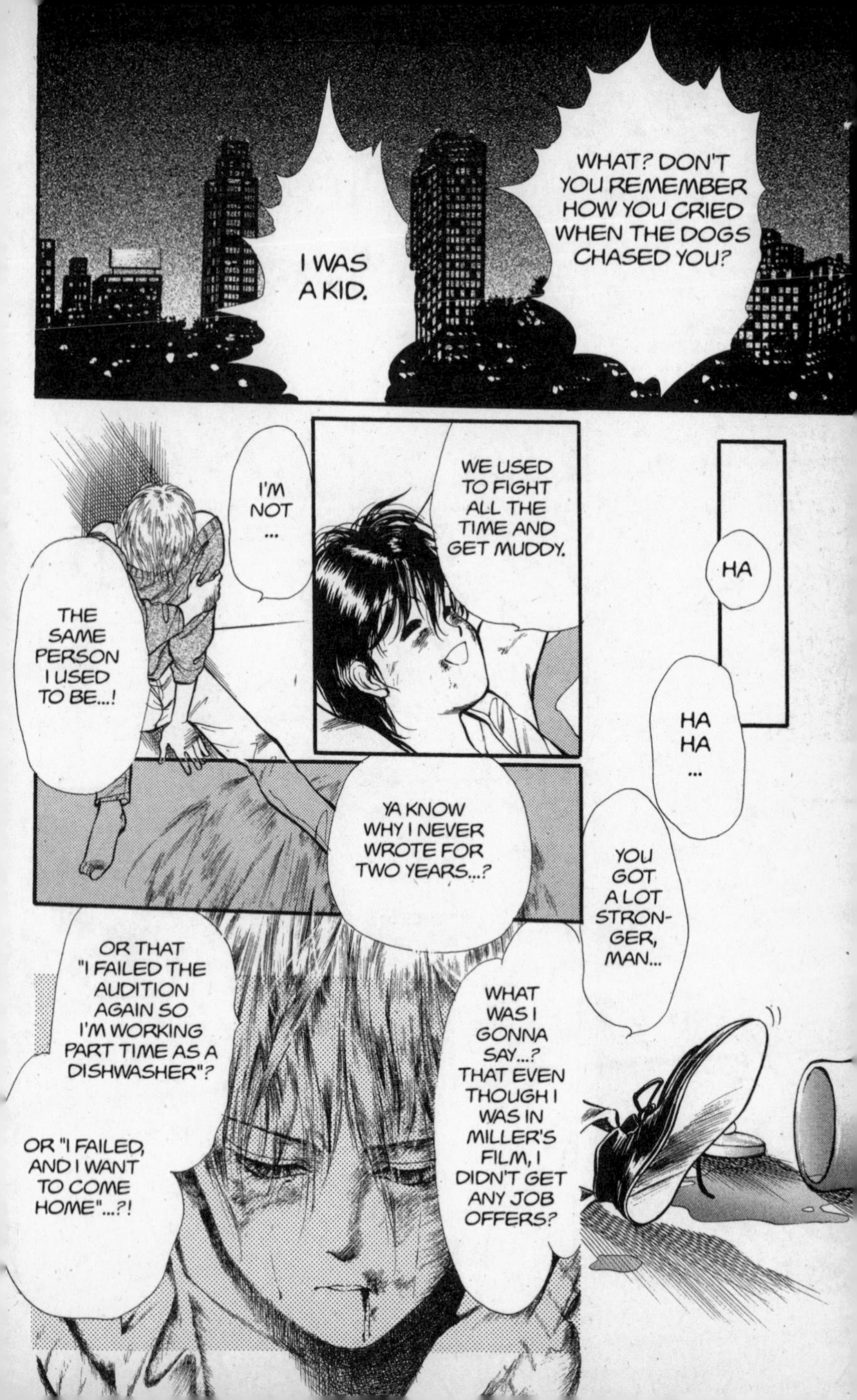
WHAT? DON'T YOU REMEMBER HOW YOU CRIED WHEN THE DOGS CHASED YOU?
I WAS A KID.
HA
HA HA ...
YOU GOT A LOT STRONGER, MAN...
WE USED TO FIGHT ALL THE TIME AND GET MUDDY.
I'M NOT ...
THE SAME PERSON I USED TO BE...!
YA KNOW WHY I NEVER WROTE FOR TWO YEARS...?
WHAT WAS I GONNA SAY...? THAT EVEN THOUGH I WAS IN MILLER'S FILM, I DIDN'T GET ANY JOB OFFERS?
OR THAT "I FAILED THE AUDITION AGAIN SO I'M WORKING PART TIME AS A DISHWASHER"?
OR "I FAILED, AND I WANT TO COME HOME"...?!

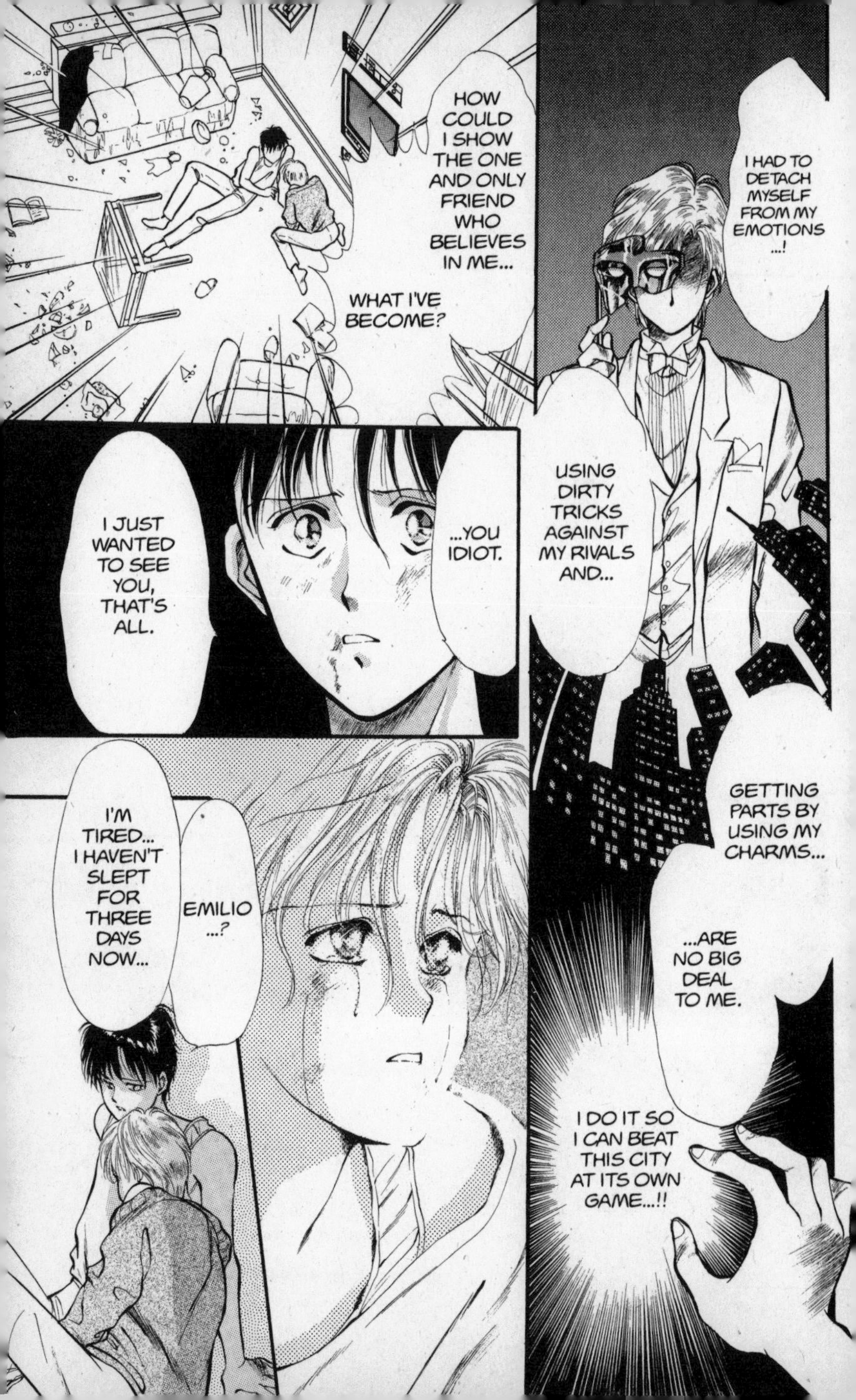
I HAD TO DETACH MYSELF FROM MY EMOTIONS ...!
USING DIRTY TRICKS AGAINST MY RIVALS AND...
GETTING PARTS BY USING MY CHARMS...
...ARE NO BIG DEAL TO ME.
I DO IT SO I CAN BEAT THIS CITY AT ITS OWN GAME...!!
HOW COULD I SHOW THE ONE AND ONLY FRIEND WHO BELIEVES IN ME...
WHAT I'VE BECOME?
...YOU IDIOT.
I JUST WANTED TO SEE YOU, THAT'S ALL.
EMILIO ...?
I'M TIRED... I HAVEN'T SLEPT FOR THREE DAYS NOW...

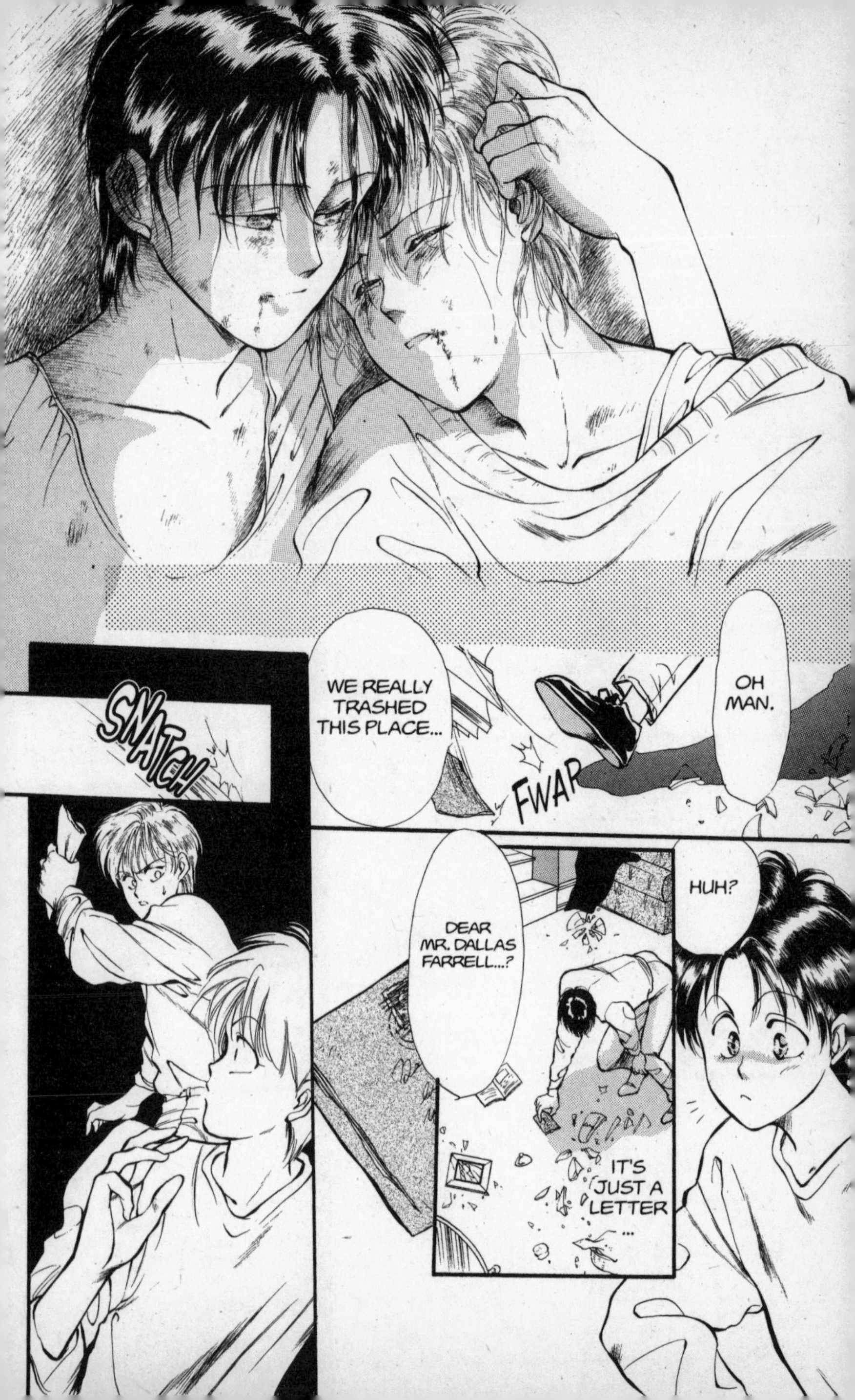
OH MAN.
WE REALLY TRASHED THIS PLACE...
FWAP
HUH?
DEAR MR. DALLAS FARRELL...?
IT'S JUST A LETTER ...
SNATCH

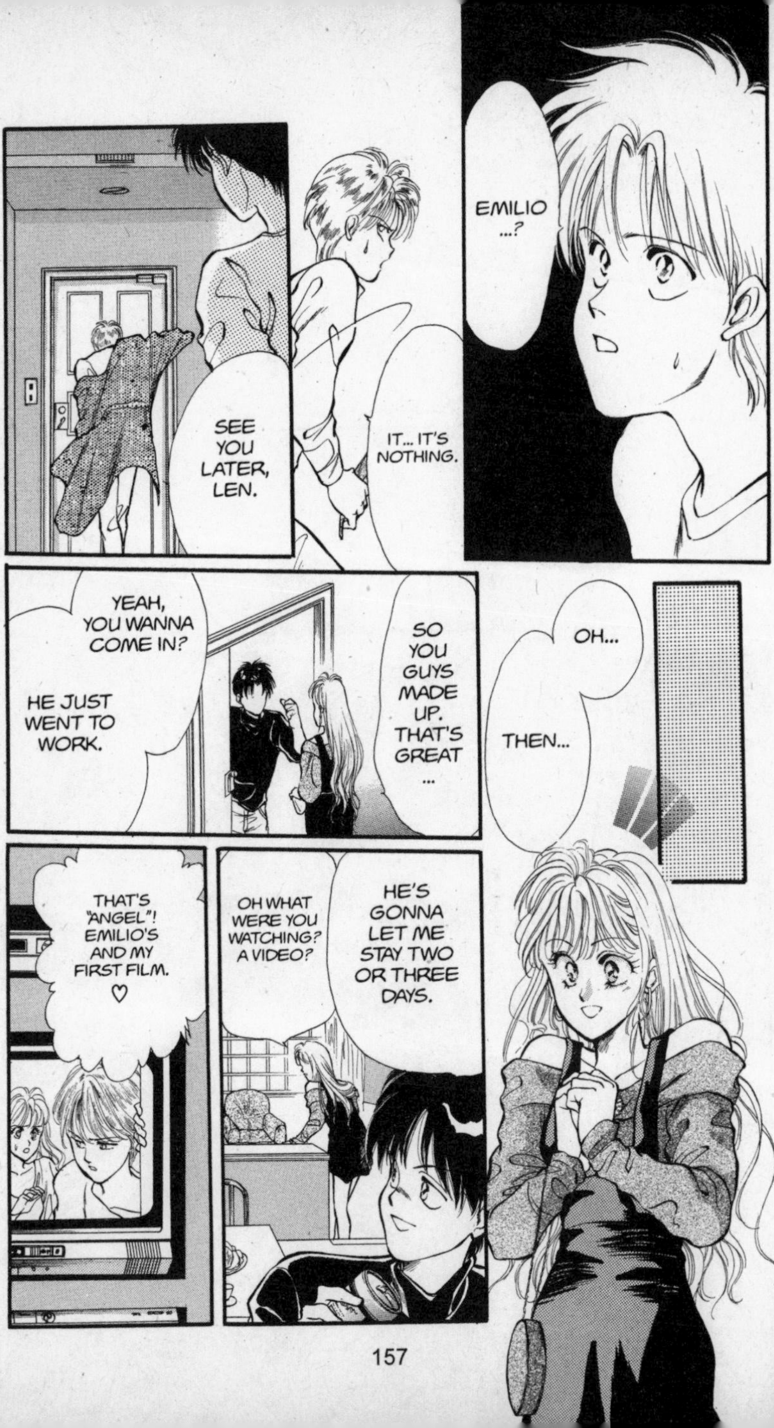
EMILIO ...?
IT... IT'S NOTHING.
SEE YOU LATER, LEN.
OH... THEN...
SO YOU GUYS MADE UP. THAT'S GREAT ...
YEAH, YOU WANNA COME IN?
HE JUST WENT TO WORK.
HE'S GONNA LET ME STAY TWO OR THREE DAYS.
OH WHAT WERE YOU WATCHING? A VIDEO?
THAT'S "ANGEL"! EMILIO'S AND MY FIRST FILM. ♡

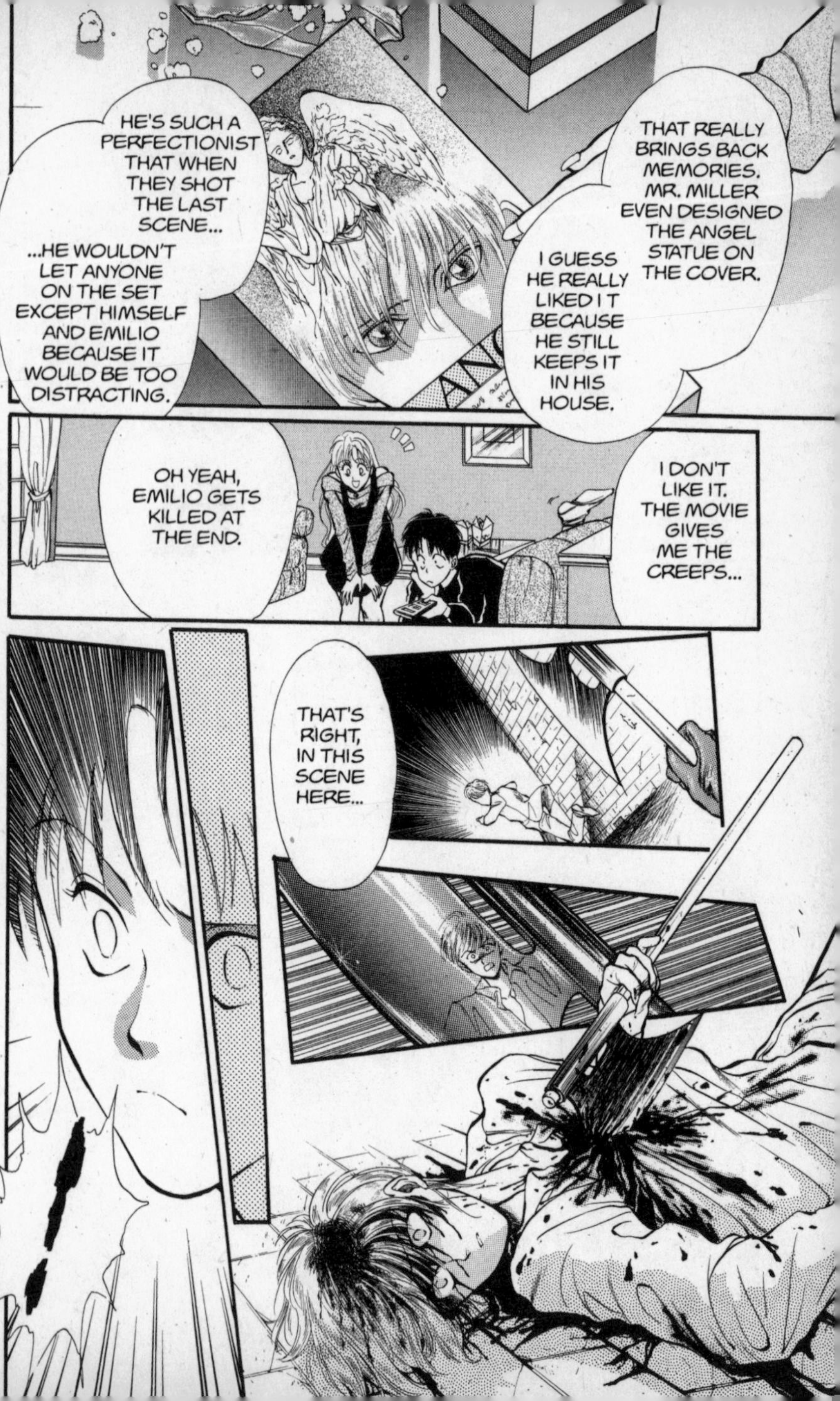
THAT REALLY BRINGS BACK MEMORIES. MR. MILLER EVEN DESIGNED THE ANGEL STATUE ON THE COVER.
I GUESS HE REALLY LIKED IT BECAUSE HE STILL KEEPS IT IN HIS HOUSE.
HE'S SUCH A PERFECTIONIST THAT WHEN THEY SHOT THE LAST SCENE...
...HE WOULDN'T LET ANYONE ON THE SET EXCEPT HIMSELF AND EMILIO BECAUSE IT WOULD BE TOO DISTRACTING.
I DON'T LIKE IT. THE MOVIE GIVES ME THE CREEPS...
OH YEAH, EMILIO GETS KILLED AT THE END.
THAT'S RIGHT, IN THIS SCENE HERE...

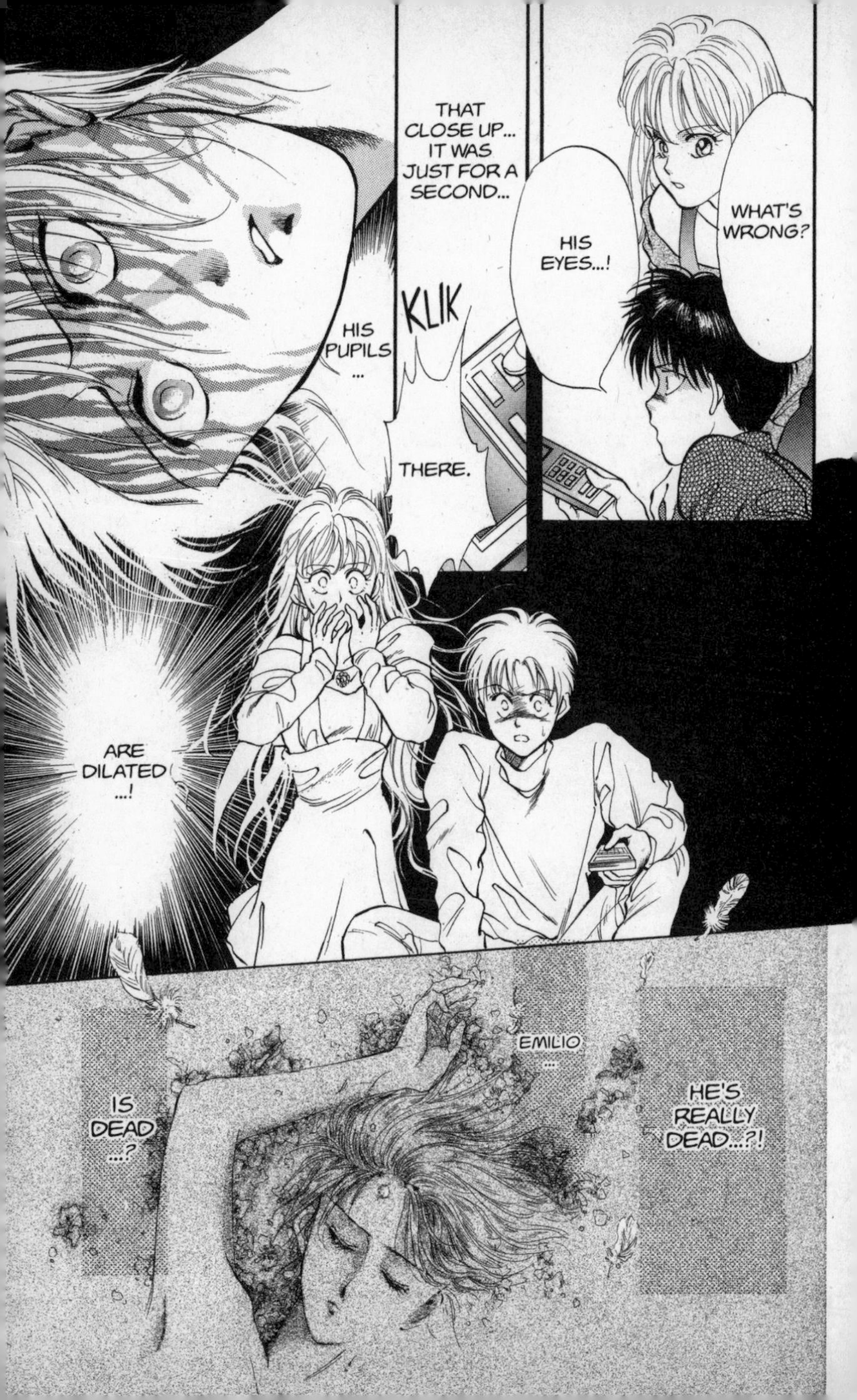
WHAT'S WRONG?
HIS EYES...!
THAT CLOSE UP... IT WAS JUST FOR A SECOND...
KLIK
THERE.
HIS PUPILS ...
ARE DILATED ...!
HE'S REALLY DEAD...?!
EMILIO ...
IS DEAD ...?

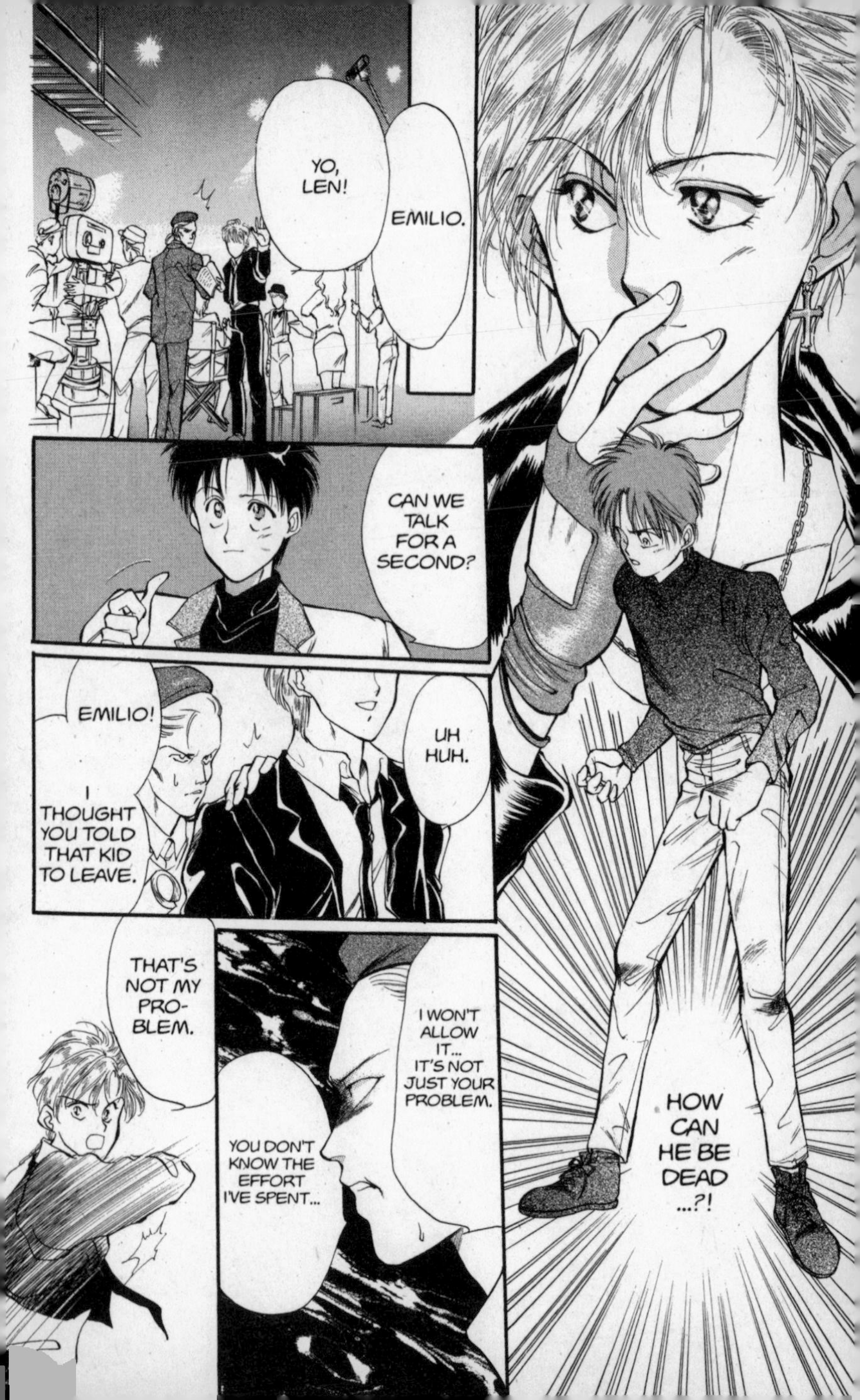
HOW CAN HE BE DEAD ...?!
YO, LEN!
EMILIO.
CAN WE TALK FOR A SECOND?
UH HUH.
EMILIO!
I THOUGHT YOU TOLD THAT KID TO LEAVE.
I WON'T ALLOW IT... IT'S NOT JUST YOUR PROBLEM.
YOU DON'T KNOW THE EFFORT I'VE SPENT...
THAT'S NOT MY PROBLEM.

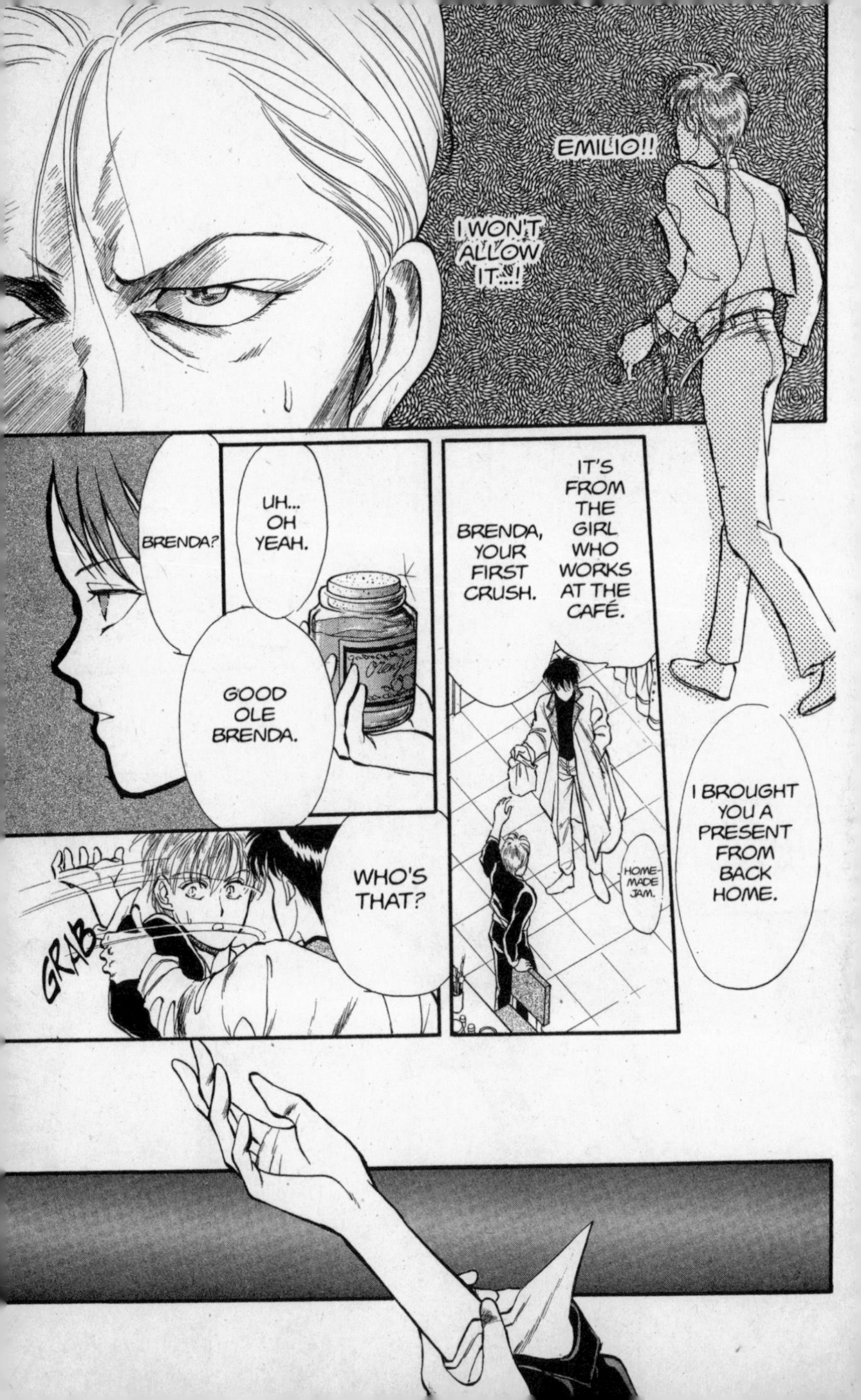
EMILIO!!
I WON'T ALLOW IT...!
I BROUGHT YOU A PRESENT FROM BACK HOME.
HOME-MADE JAM.
IT'S FROM THE GIRL WHO WORKS AT THE CAFÉ.
BRENDA, YOUR FIRST CRUSH.
UH... OH YEAH.
GOOD OLE BRENDA.
BRENDA?
WHO'S THAT?
GRAB

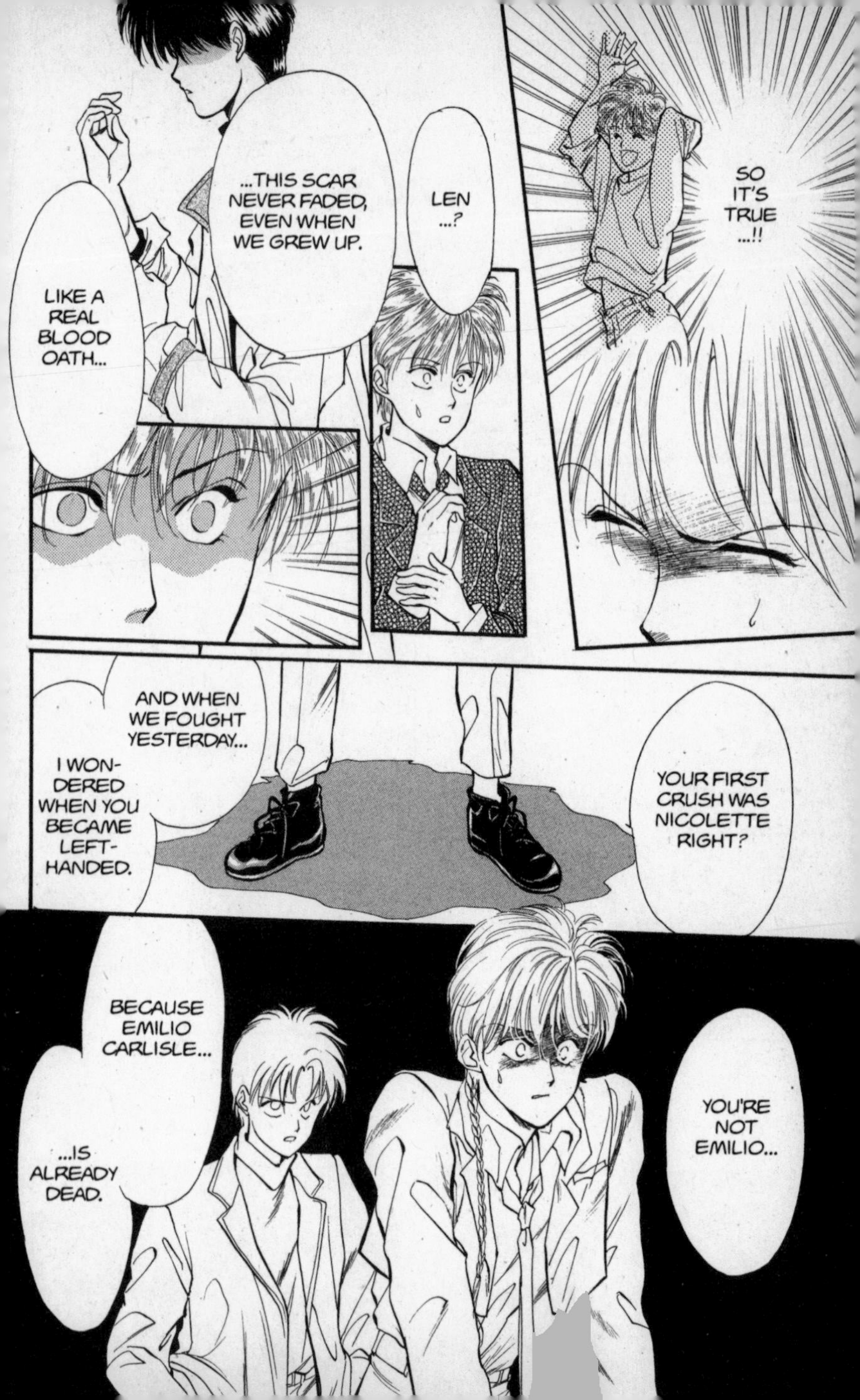
SO IT'S TRUE ...!!
...THIS SCAR NEVER FADED, EVEN WHEN WE GREW UP.
LIKE A REAL BLOOD OATH...
LEN ...?
YOUR FIRST CRUSH WAS NICOLETTE RIGHT?
AND WHEN WE FOUGHT YESTERDAY...
I WONDERED WHEN YOU BECAME LEFT-HANDED.
YOU'RE NOT EMILIO...
BECAUSE EMILIO CARLISLE...
...IS ALREADY DEAD.

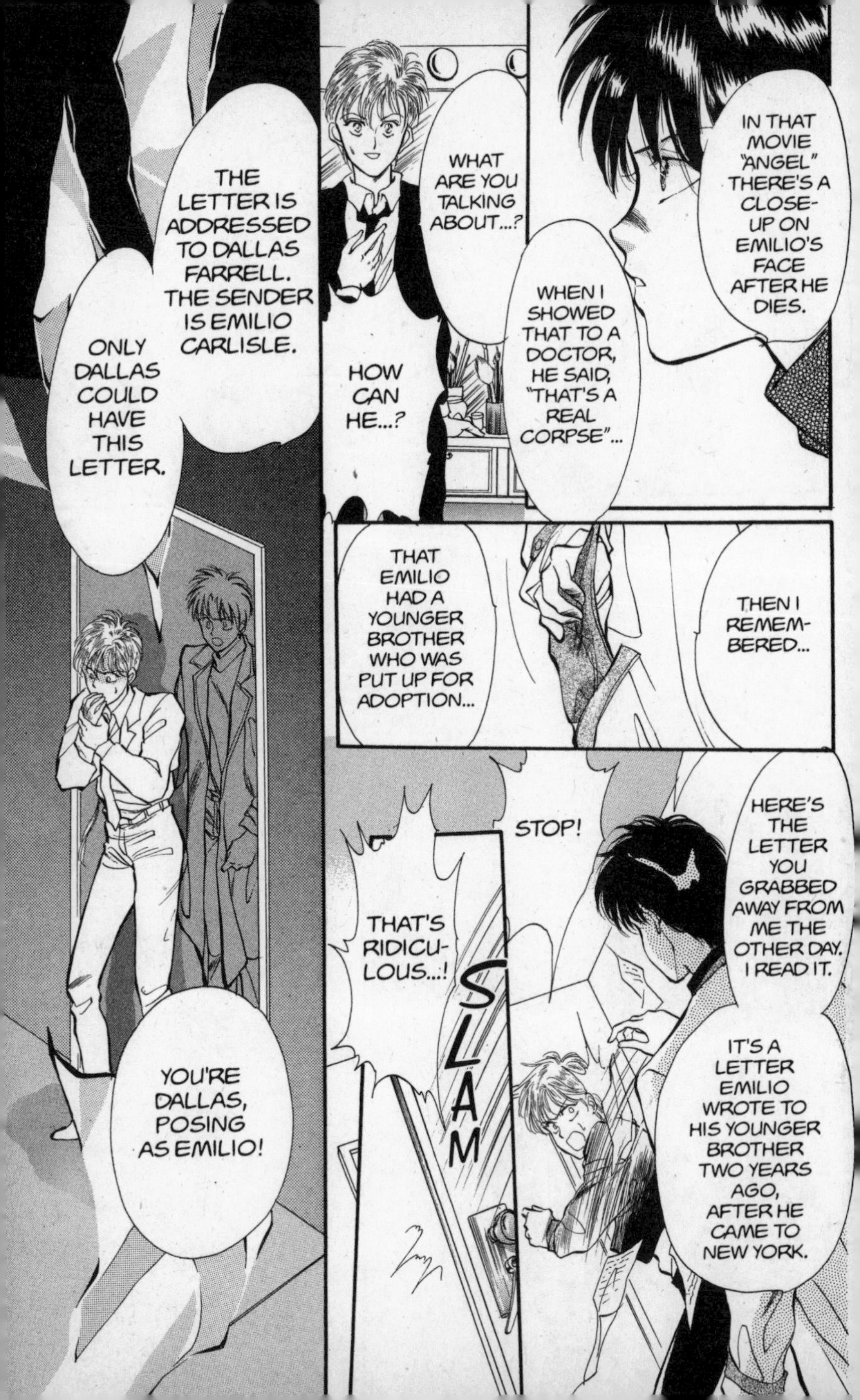
IN THAT MOVIE "ANGEL" THERE'S A CLOSE-UP ON EMILIO'S FACE AFTER HE DIES.
WHEN I SHOWED THAT TO A DOCTOR, HE SAID, "THAT'S A REAL CORPSE"...
WHAT ARE YOU TALKING ABOUT...?
HOW CAN HE...?
THEN I REMEM-BERED...
THAT EMILIO HAD A YOUNGER BROTHER WHO WAS PUT UP FOR ADOPTION...
HERE'S THE LETTER YOU GRABBED AWAY FROM ME THE OTHER DAY. I READ IT.
IT'S A LETTER EMILIO WROTE TO HIS YOUNGER BROTHER TWO YEARS AGO, AFTER HE CAME TO NEW YORK.
STOP!
THAT'S RIDICU-LOUS...!
SLAM
THE LETTER IS ADDRESSED TO DALLAS FARRELL. THE SENDER IS EMILIO CARLISLE.
ONLY DALLAS COULD HAVE THIS LETTER.
YOU'RE DALLAS, POSING AS EMILIO!

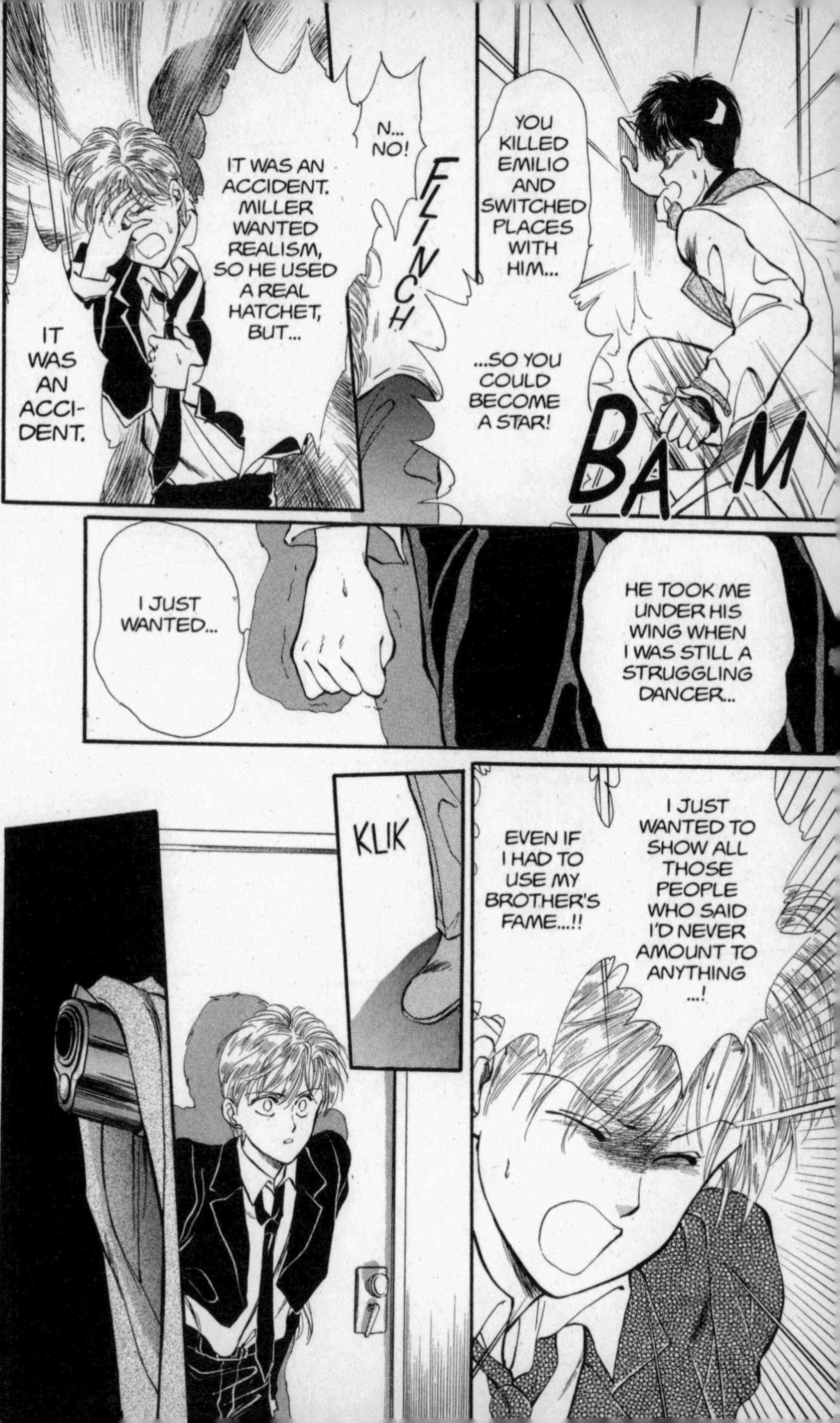
YOU KILLED EMILIO AND SWITCHED PLACES WITH HIM...
...SO YOU COULD BECOME A STAR!
BAM
N... NO!
FLINCH
IT WAS AN ACCIDENT. MILLER WANTED REALISM, SO HE USED A REAL HATCHET, BUT...
IT WAS AN ACCI-DENT.
HE TOOK ME UNDER HIS WING WHEN I WAS STILL A STRUGGLING DANCER...
I JUST WANTED...
I JUST WANTED TO SHOW ALL THOSE PEOPLE WHO SAID I'D NEVER AMOUNT TO ANYTHING ...!
EVEN IF I HAD TO USE MY BROTHER'S FAME...!!
KLIK

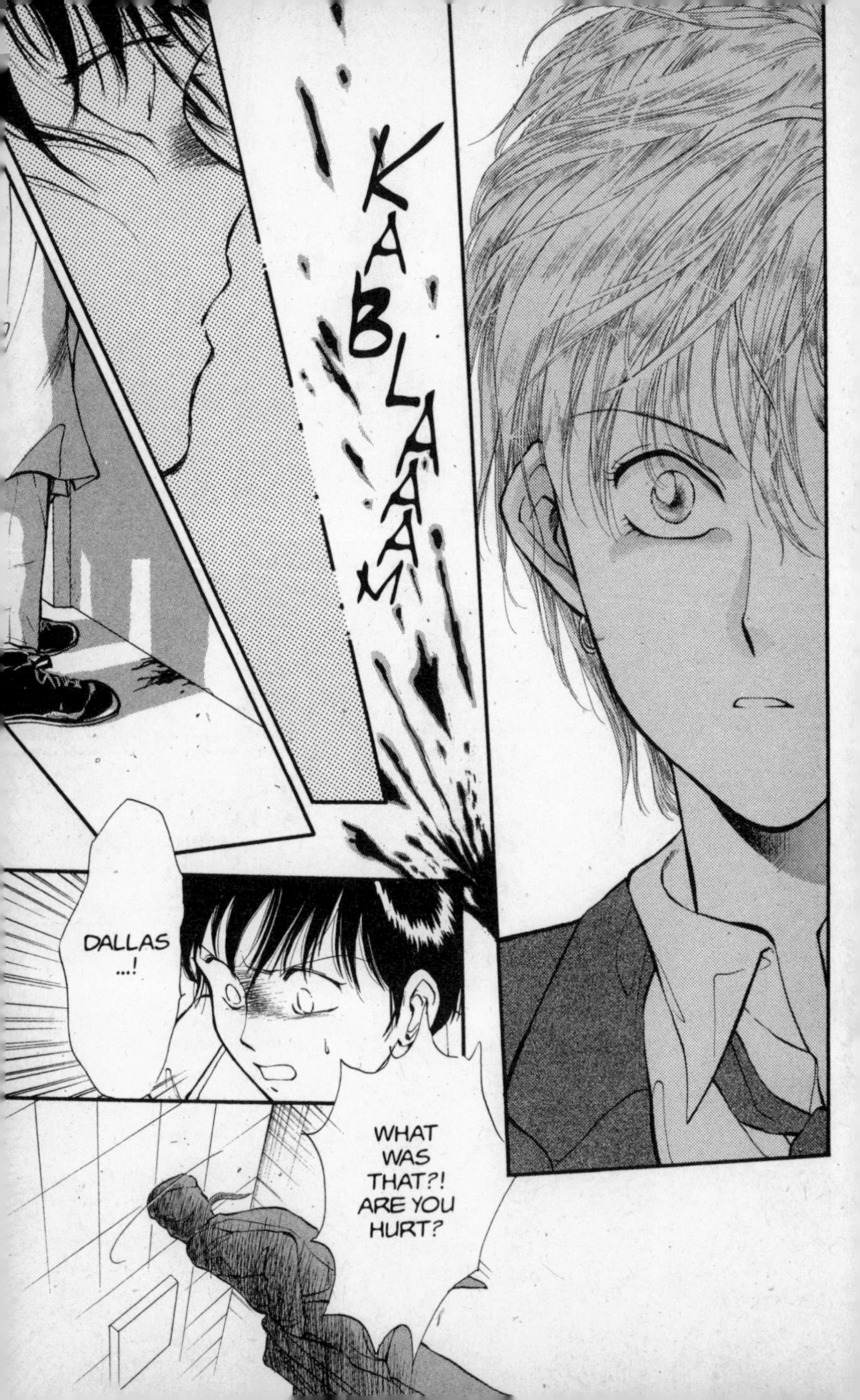
KABLAAAM
DALLAS ...!
WHAT WAS THAT?! ARE YOU HURT?

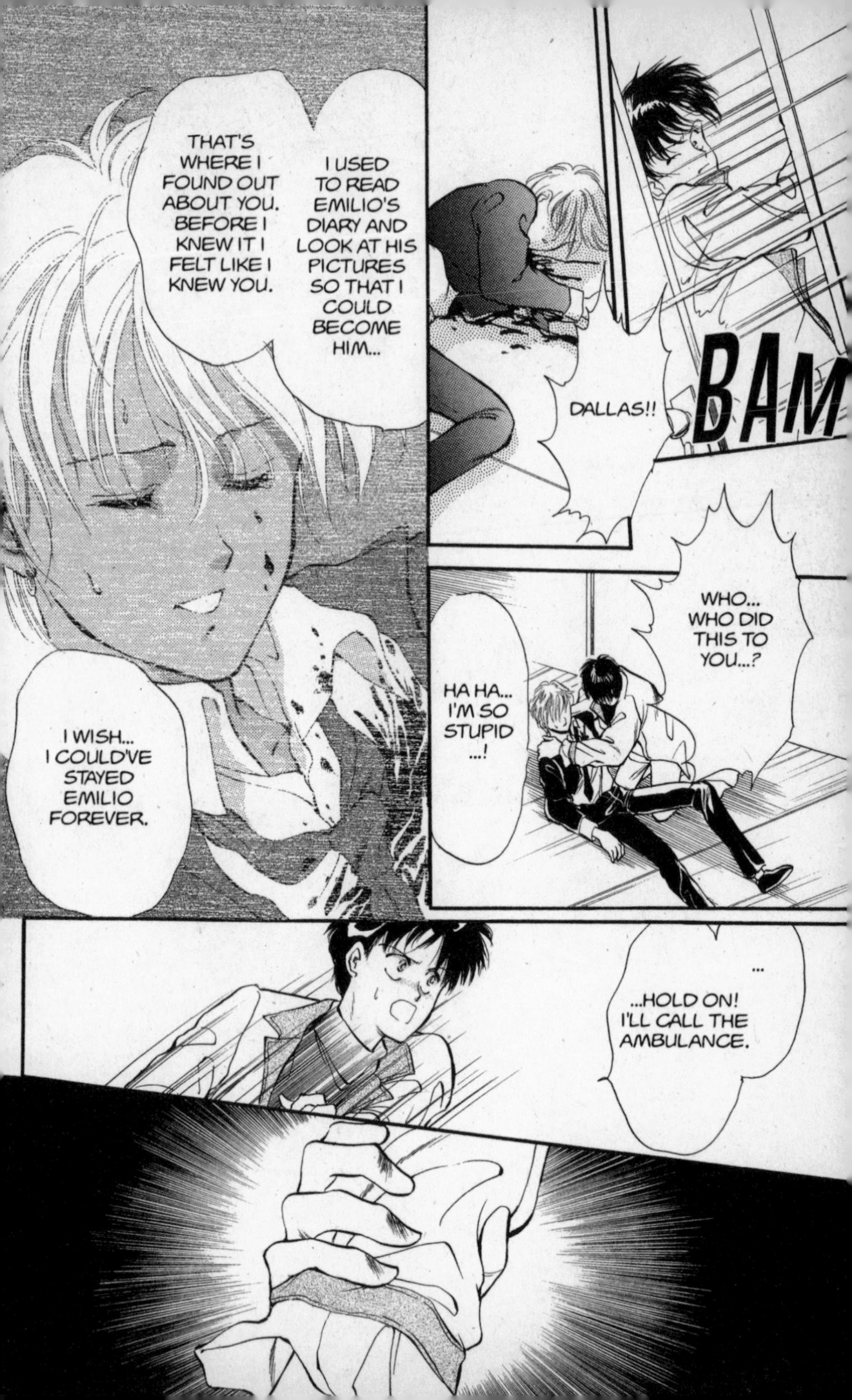
BAM
DALLAS!!
WHO... WHO DID THIS TO YOU...?
HA HA... I'M SO STUPID ...!
I USED TO READ EMILIO'S DIARY AND LOOK AT HIS PICTURES SO THAT I COULD BECOME HIM...
THAT'S WHERE I FOUND OUT ABOUT YOU. BEFORE I KNEW IT I FELT LIKE I KNEW YOU.
I WISH... I COULD'VE STAYED EMILIO FOREVER.
... ...HOLD ON! I'LL CALL THE AMBULANCE.

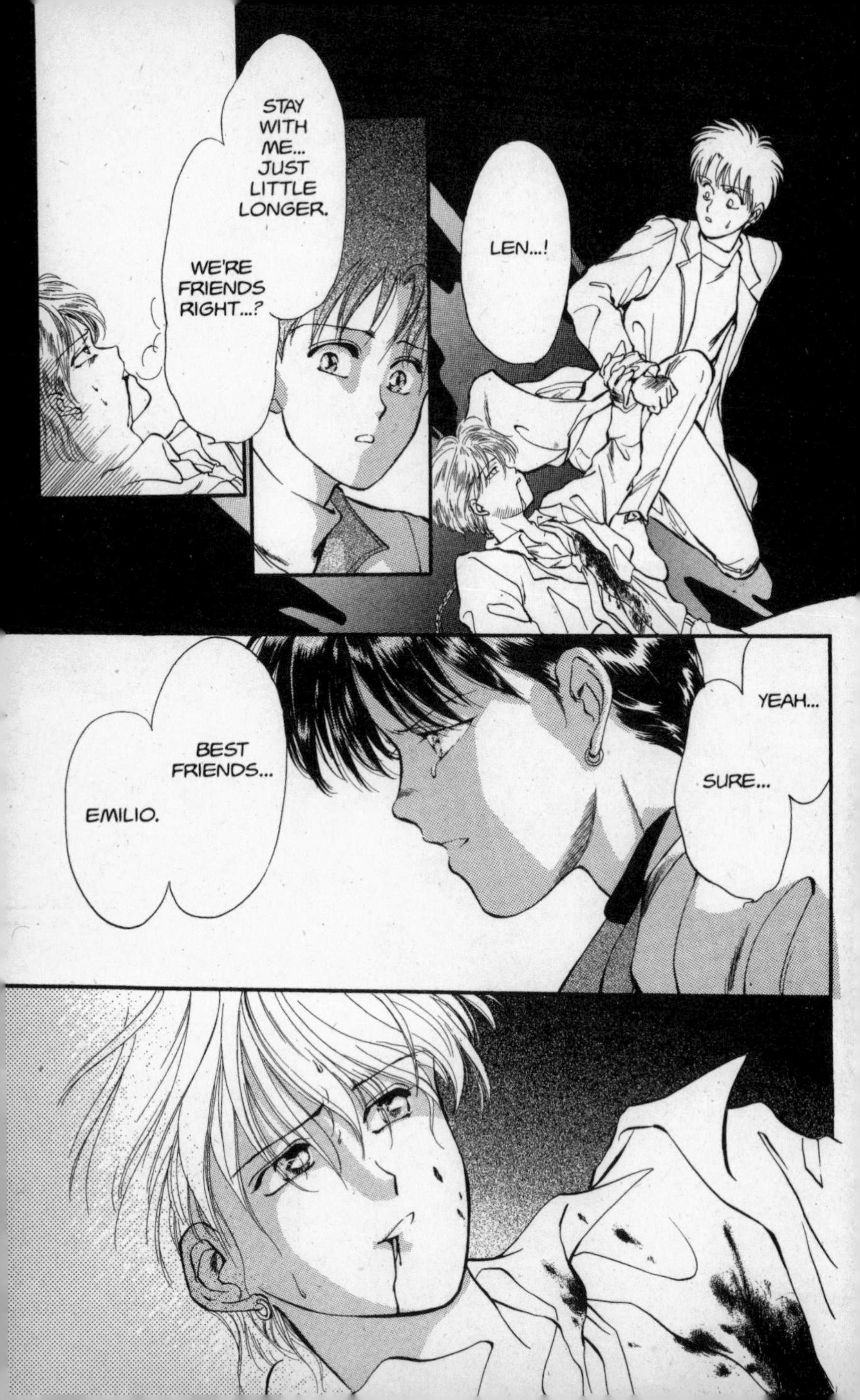
LEN...!
STAY WITH ME... JUST LITTLE LONGER.
WE'RE FRIENDS RIGHT...?
YEAH...
SURE...
BEST FRIENDS...
EMILIO.

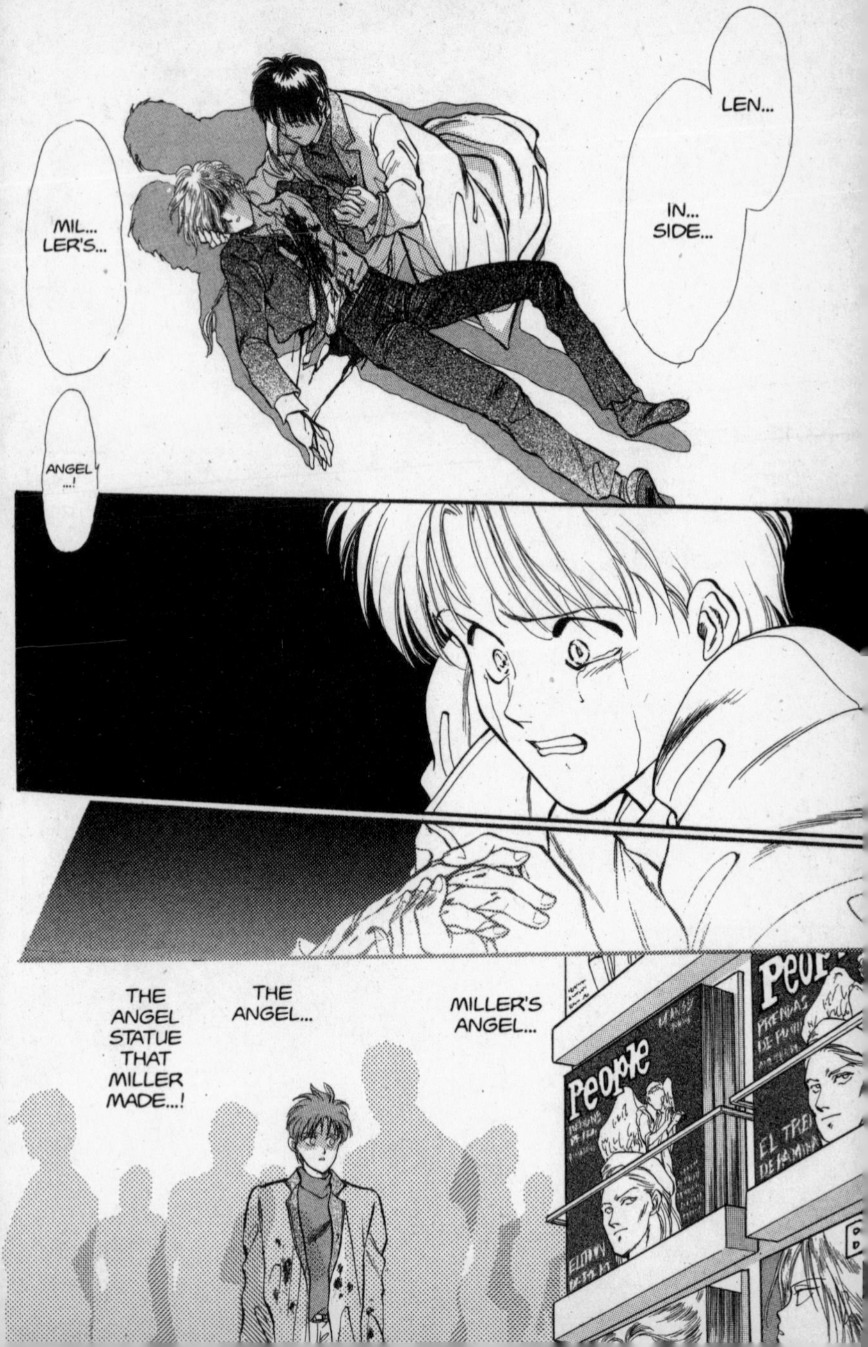
LEN...
IN... SIDE...
MIL... LER'S...
ANGEL ...!
MILLER'S ANGEL...
THE ANGEL...
THE ANGEL STATUE THAT MILLER MADE...!
People
People

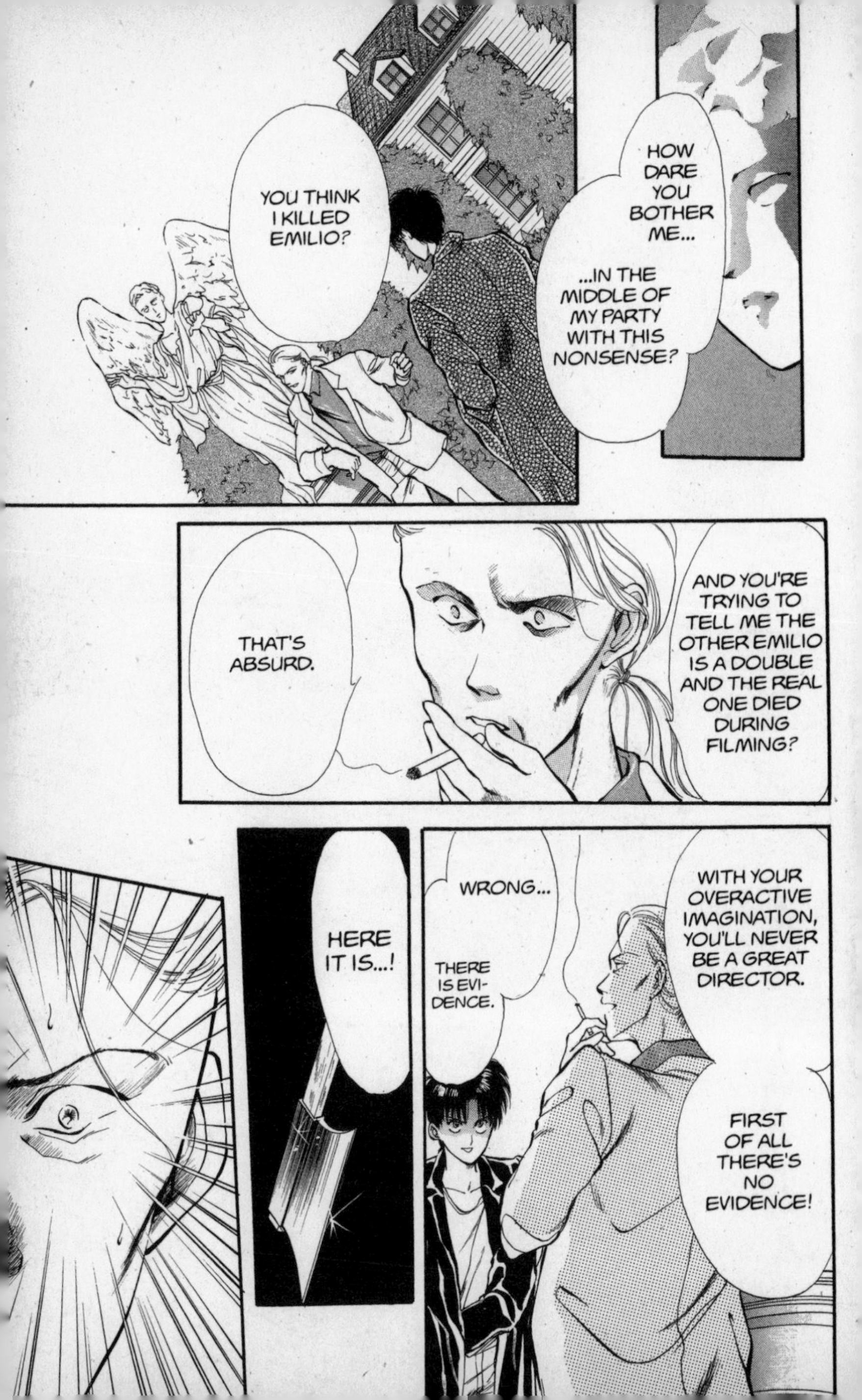
HOW DARE YOU BOTHER ME...
...IN THE MIDDLE OF MY PARTY WITH THIS NONSENSE?
YOU THINK I KILLED EMILIO?
AND YOU'RE TRYING TO TELL ME THE OTHER EMILIO IS A DOUBLE AND THE REAL ONE DIED DURING FILMING?
THAT'S ABSURD.
WITH YOUR OVERACTIVE IMAGINATION, YOU'LL NEVER BE A GREAT DIRECTOR.
FIRST OF ALL THERE'S NO EVIDENCE!
WRONG...
THERE IS EVI-DENCE.
HERE IT IS...!

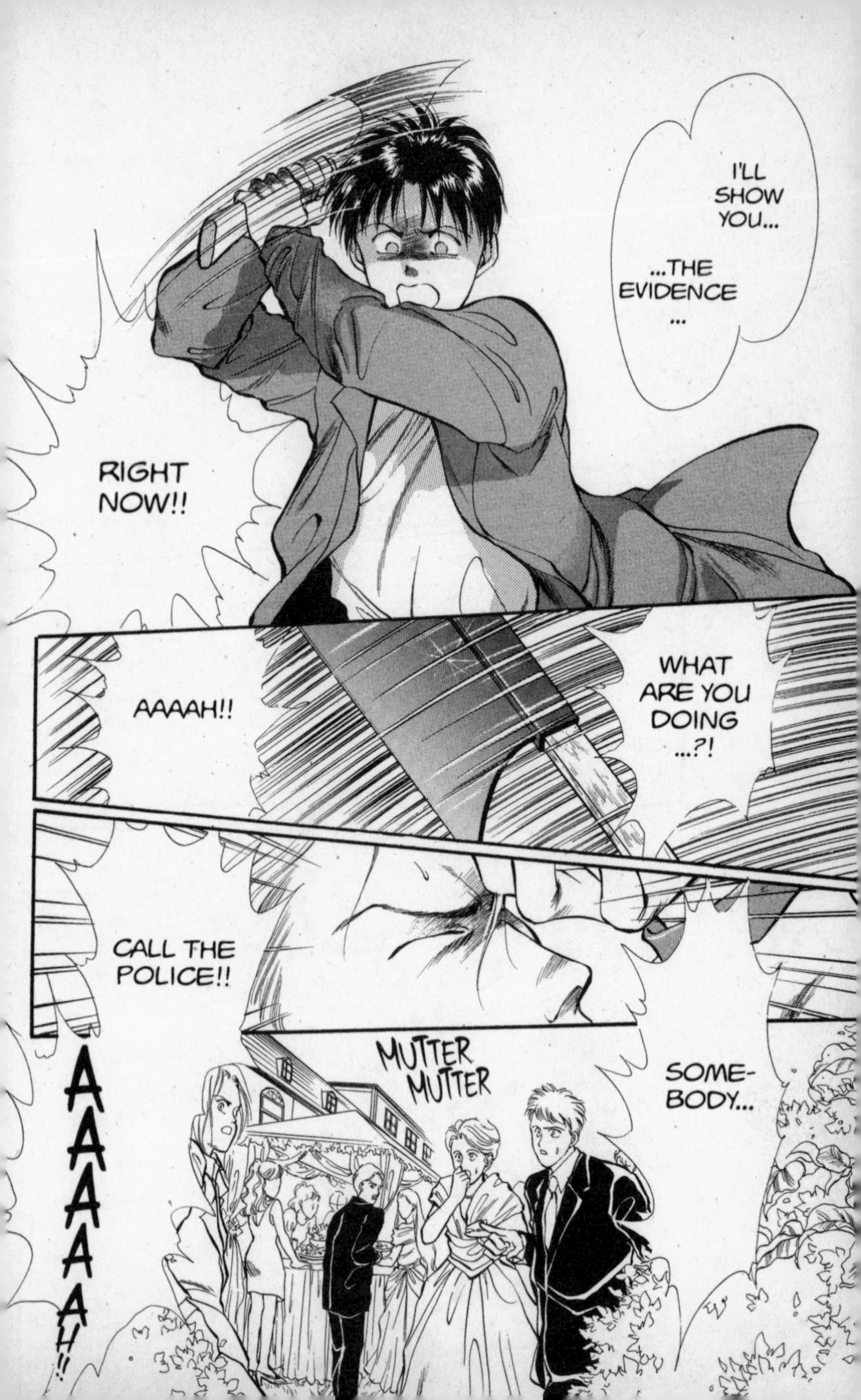
I'LL SHOW YOU...
...THE EVIDENCE ...
RIGHT NOW!!
WHAT ARE YOU DOING ...?!
AAAAH!!
CALL THE POLICE!!
SOME-BODY...
MUTTER MUTTER
AAAAAH!!

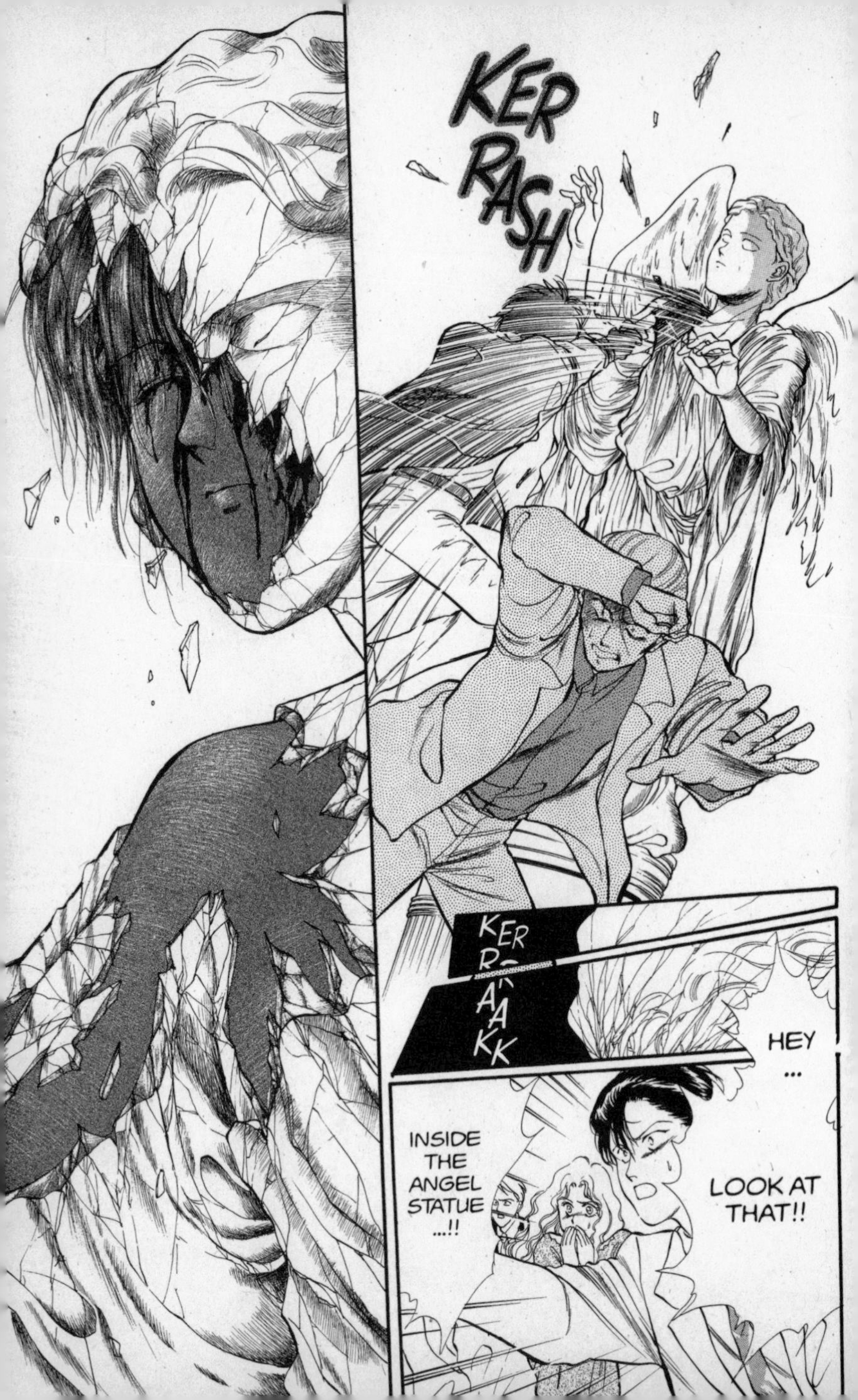
KER RASH
KER RAAKK
HEY ...
LOOK AT THAT!!
INSIDE THE ANGEL STATUE ...!!

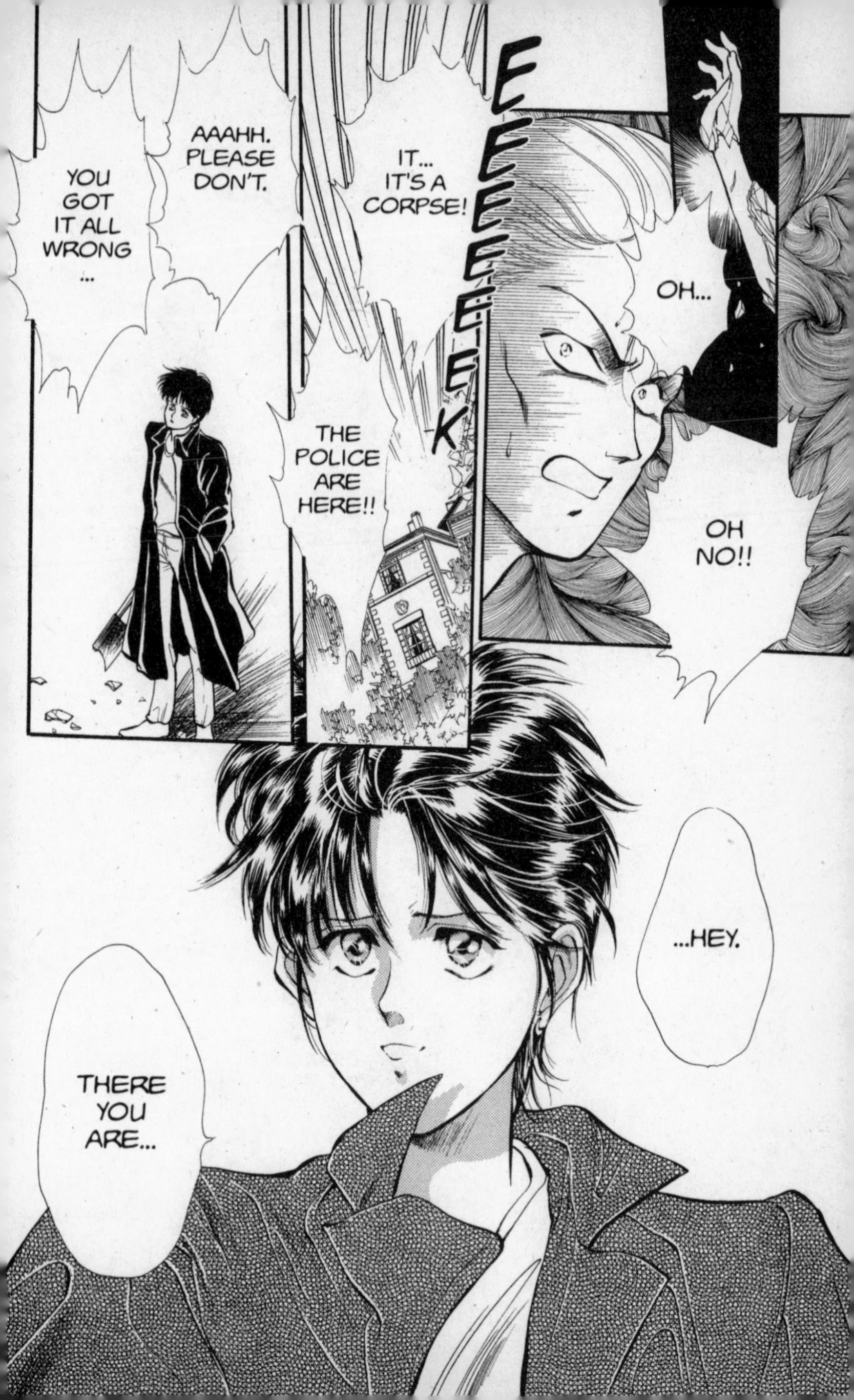
OH...
OH NO!!
EEEEEEEEEEK
IT... IT'S A CORPSE!
THE POLICE ARE HERE!!
AAAHH. PLEASE DON'T.
YOU GOT IT ALL WRONG...
...HEY.
THERE YOU ARE...

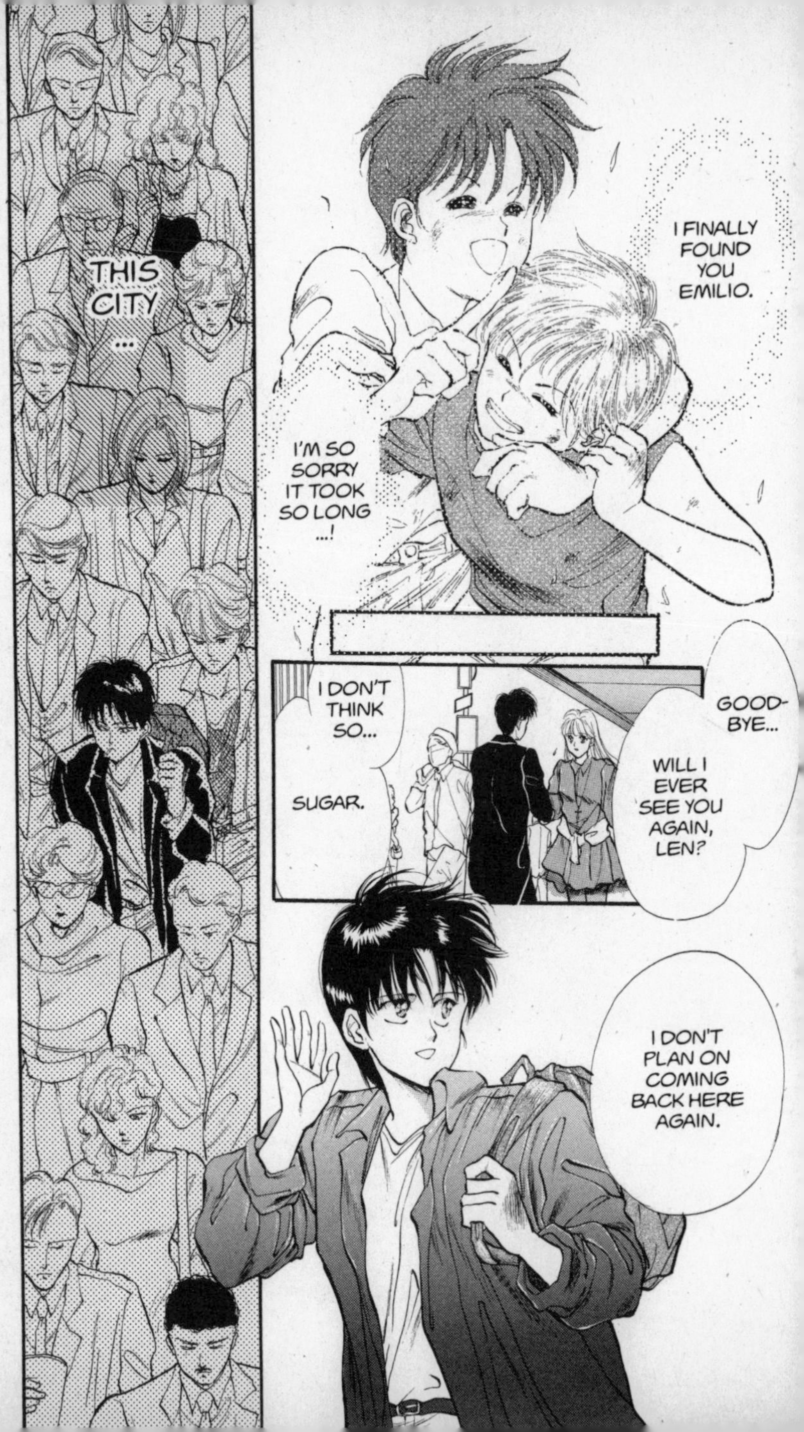
I FINALLY FOUND YOU EMILIO.
I'M SO SORRY IT TOOK SO LONG ...!
GOOD-BYE...
WILL I EVER SEE YOU AGAIN, LEN?
I DON'T THINK SO...
SUGAR.
I DON'T PLAN ON COMING BACK HERE AGAIN.
THIS CITY ...

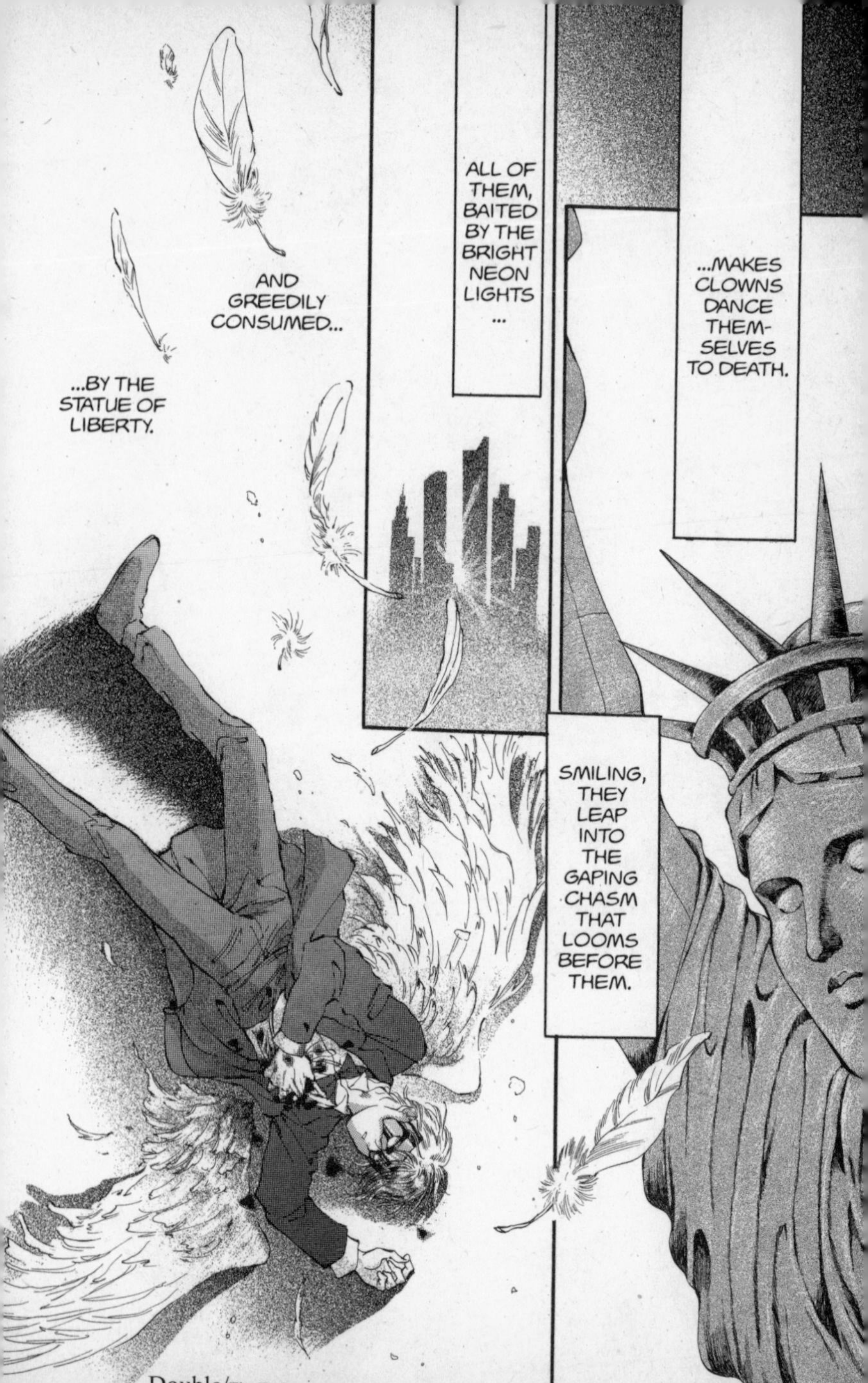
...MAKES CLOWNS DANCE THEM-SELVES TO DEATH.
SMILING, THEY LEAP INTO THE GAPING CHASM THAT LOOMS BEFORE THEM.
ALL OF THEM, BAITED BY THE BRIGHT NEON LIGHTS ...
AND GREEDILY CONSUMED...
...BY THE STATUE OF LIBERTY.

Double/The End

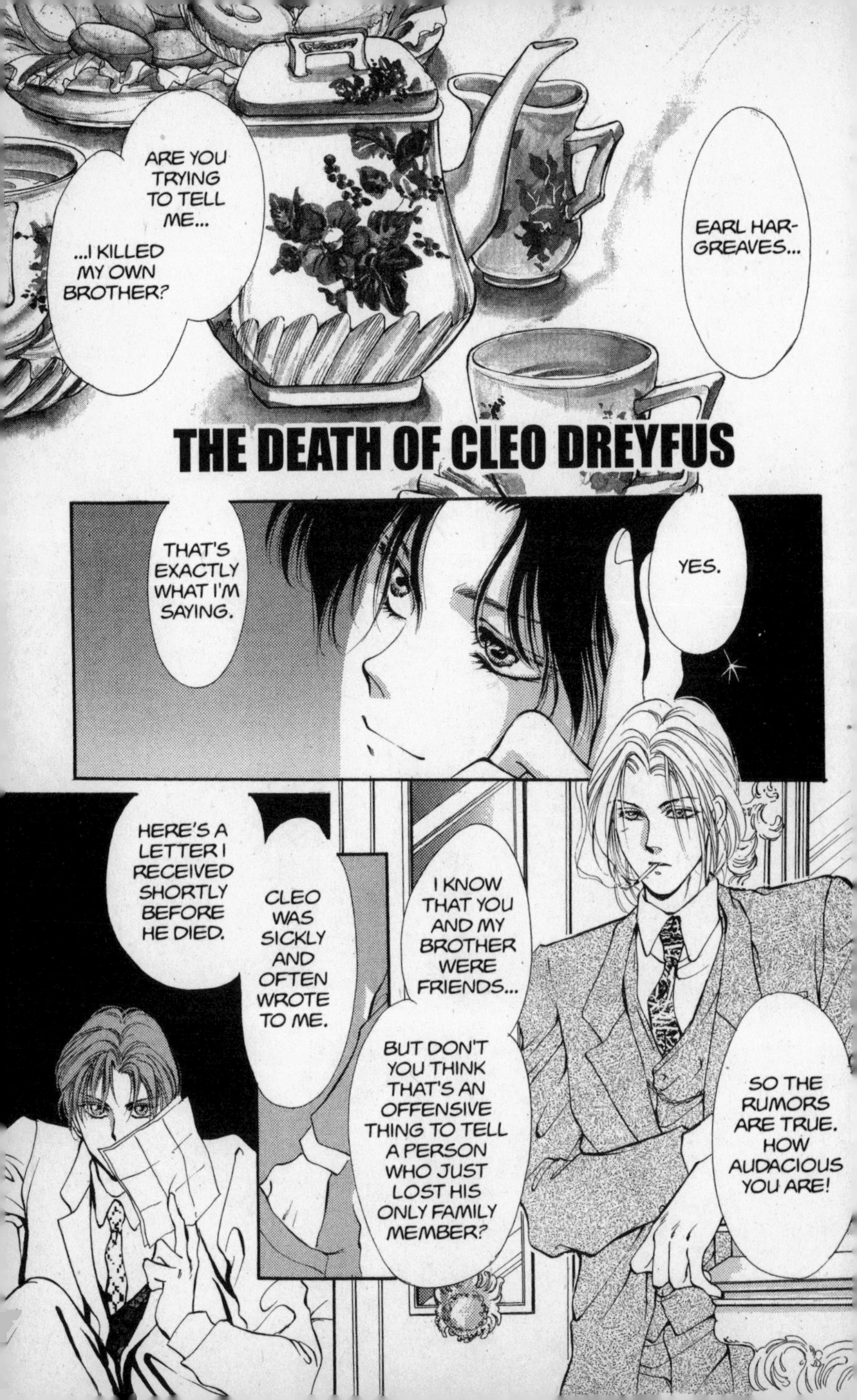
EARL HAR-GREAVES...
ARE YOU TRYING TO TELL ME...
...I KILLED MY OWN BROTHER?
THE DEATH OF CLEO DREYFUS
YES.
THAT'S EXACTLY WHAT I'M SAYING.
SO THE RUMORS ARE TRUE. HOW AUDACIOUS YOU ARE!
I KNOW THAT YOU AND MY BROTHER WERE FRIENDS...
BUT DON'T YOU THINK THAT'S AN OFFENSIVE THING TO TELL A PERSON WHO JUST LOST HIS ONLY FAMILY MEMBER?
CLEO WAS SICKLY AND OFTEN WROTE TO ME.
HERE'S A LETTER I RECEIVED SHORTLY BEFORE HE DIED.

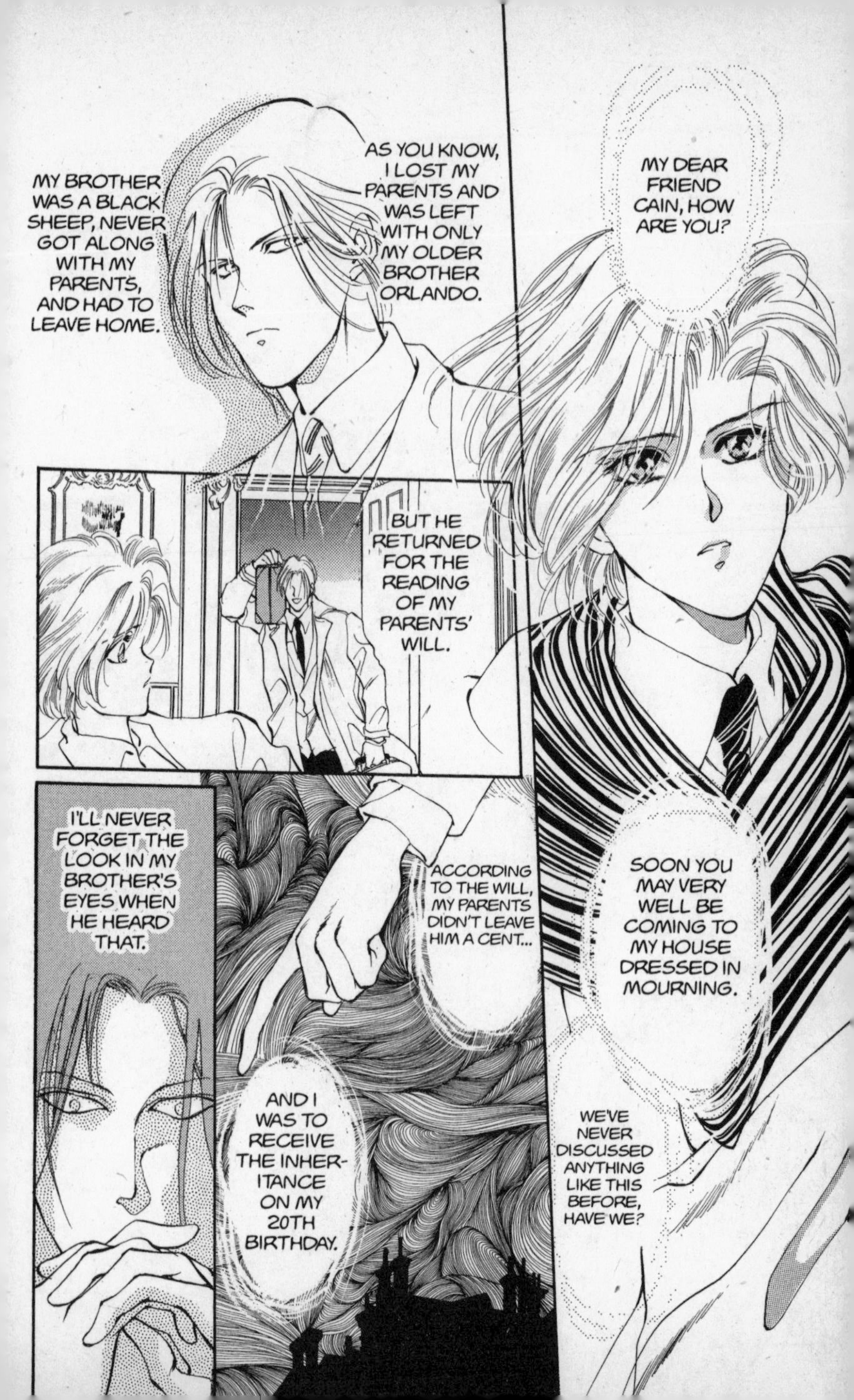
MY DEAR FRIEND CAIN, HOW ARE YOU?
SOON YOU MAY VERY WELL BE COMING TO MY HOUSE DRESSED IN MOURNING.
WE'VE NEVER DISCUSSED ANYTHING LIKE THIS BEFORE, HAVE WE?
AS YOU KNOW, I LOST MY PARENTS AND WAS LEFT WITH ONLY MY OLDER BROTHER ORLANDO.
MY BROTHER WAS A BLACK SHEEP, NEVER GOT ALONG WITH MY PARENTS, AND HAD TO LEAVE HOME.
BUT HE RETURNED FOR THE READING OF MY PARENTS' WILL.
ACCORDING TO THE WILL, MY PARENTS DIDN'T LEAVE HIM A CENT...
AND I WAS TO RECEIVE THE INHER-ITANCE ON MY 20TH BIRTHDAY.
I'LL NEVER FORGET THE LOOK IN MY BROTHER'S EYES WHEN HE HEARD THAT.

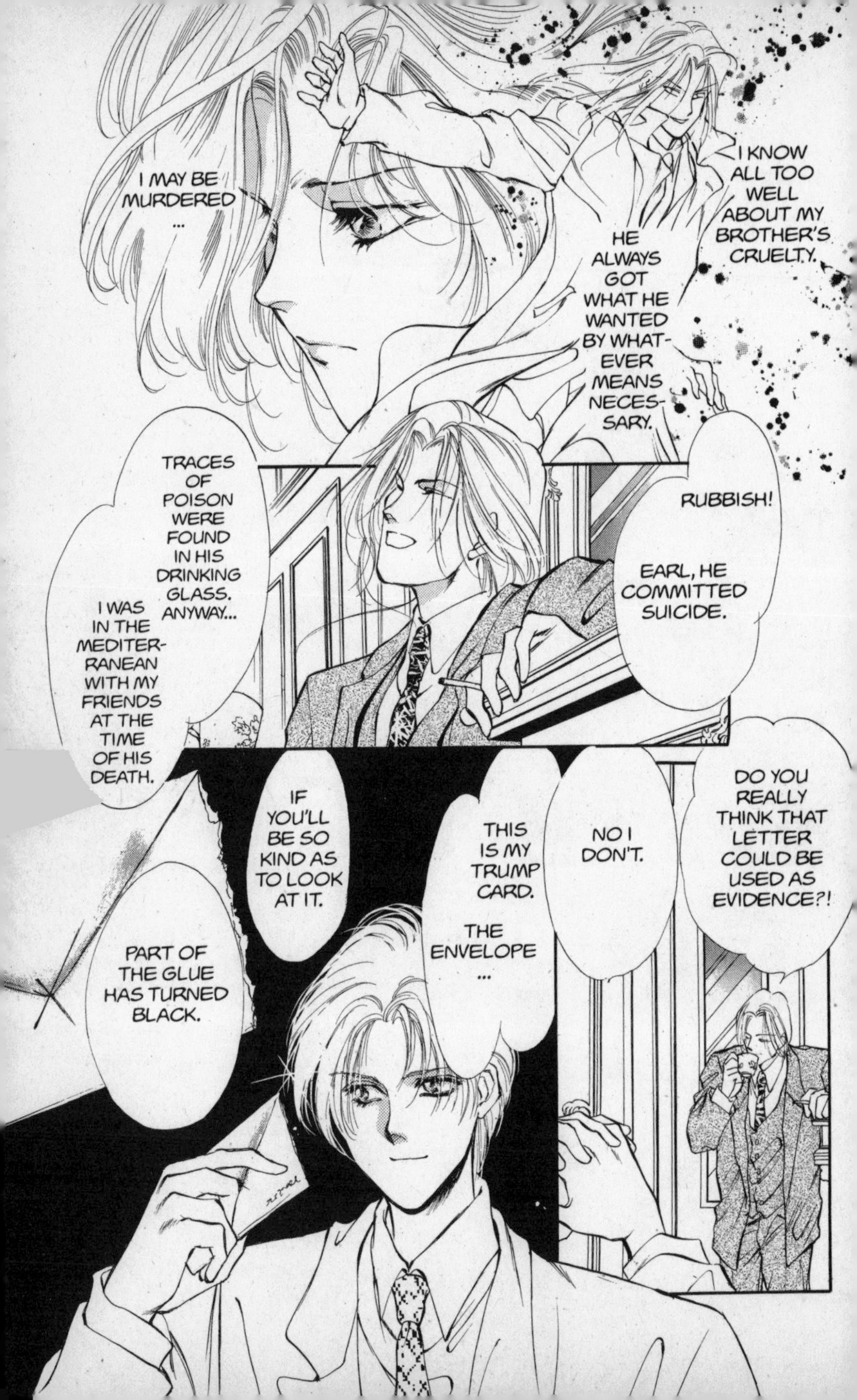
I KNOW ALL TOO WELL ABOUT MY BROTHER'S CRUELTY.
HE ALWAYS GOT WHAT HE WANTED BY WHAT-EVER MEANS NECES-SARY.
I MAY BE MURDERED ...
RUBBISH!
EARL, HE COMMITTED SUICIDE.
TRACES OF POISON WERE FOUND IN HIS DRINKING GLASS. ANYWAY...
I WAS IN THE MEDITER-RANEAN WITH MY FRIENDS AT THE TIME OF HIS DEATH.
DO YOU REALLY THINK THAT LETTER COULD BE USED AS EVIDENCE?!
NO I DON'T.
THIS IS MY TRUMP CARD.
THE ENVELOPE ...
IF YOU'LL BE SO KIND AS TO LOOK AT IT.
PART OF THE GLUE HAS TURNED BLACK.

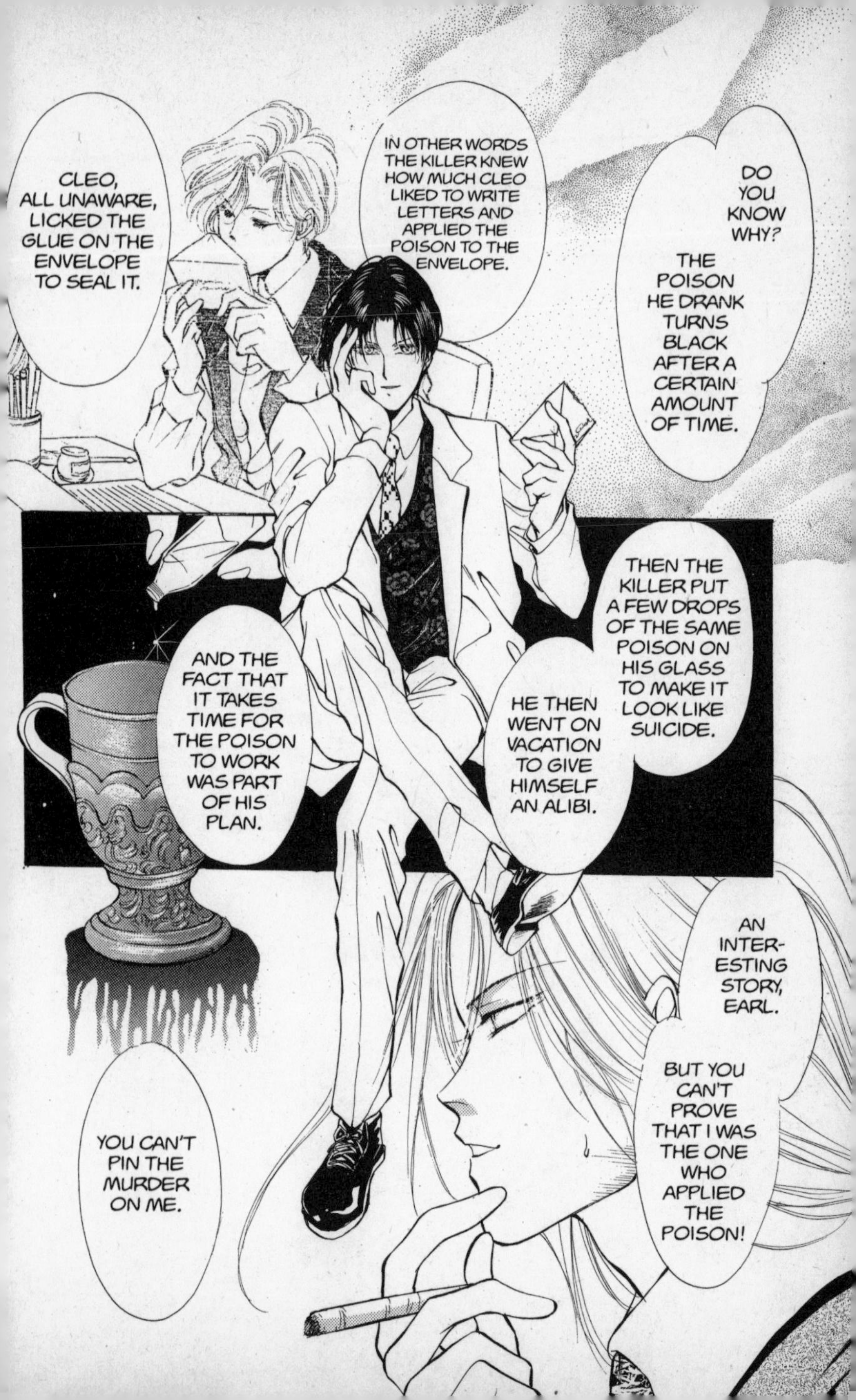
DO YOU KNOW WHY?
THE POISON HE DRANK TURNS BLACK AFTER A CERTAIN AMOUNT OF TIME.
IN OTHER WORDS THE KILLER KNEW HOW MUCH CLEO LIKED TO WRITE LETTERS AND APPLIED THE POISON TO THE ENVELOPE.
CLEO, ALL UNAWARE, LICKED THE GLUE ON THE ENVELOPE TO SEAL IT.
THEN THE KILLER PUT A FEW DROPS OF THE SAME POISON ON HIS GLASS TO MAKE IT LOOK LIKE SUICIDE.
HE THEN WENT ON VACATION TO GIVE HIMSELF AN ALIBI.
AND THE FACT THAT IT TAKES TIME FOR THE POISON TO WORK WAS PART OF HIS PLAN.
AN INTER-ESTING STORY, EARL.
BUT YOU CAN'T PROVE THAT I WAS THE ONE WHO APPLIED THE POISON!
YOU CAN'T PIN THE MURDER ON ME.

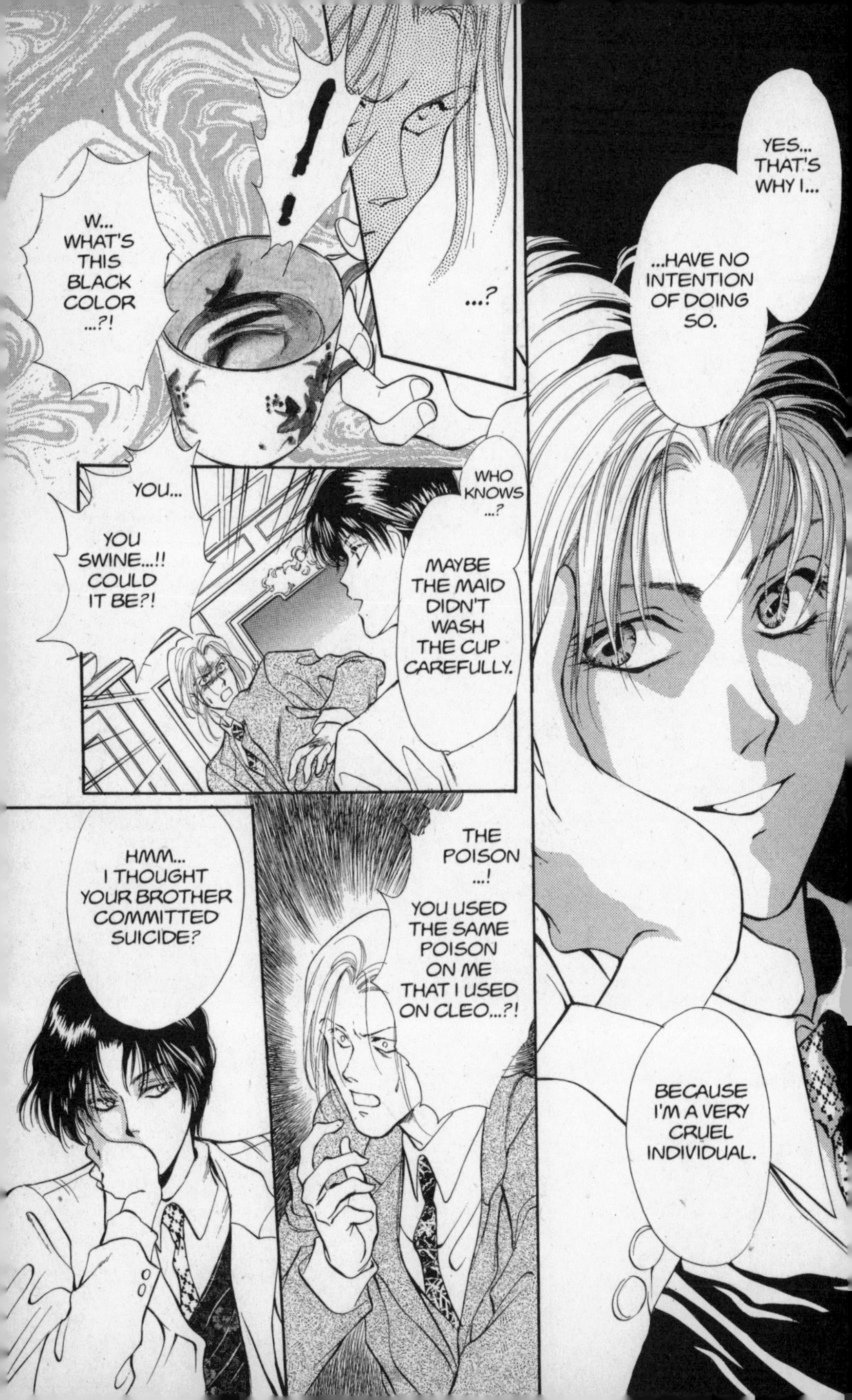
YES... THAT'S WHY I...
...HAVE NO INTENTION OF DOING SO.
BECAUSE I'M A VERY CRUEL INDIVIDUAL.
!
...?
W... WHAT'S THIS BLACK COLOR ...?!
WHO KNOWS ...?
MAYBE THE MAID DIDN'T WASH THE CUP CAREFULLY.
YOU...
YOU SWINE...!! COULD IT BE?!
THE POISON ...!
YOU USED THE SAME POISON ON ME THAT I USED ON CLEO...?!
HMM... I THOUGHT YOUR BROTHER COMMITTED SUICIDE?

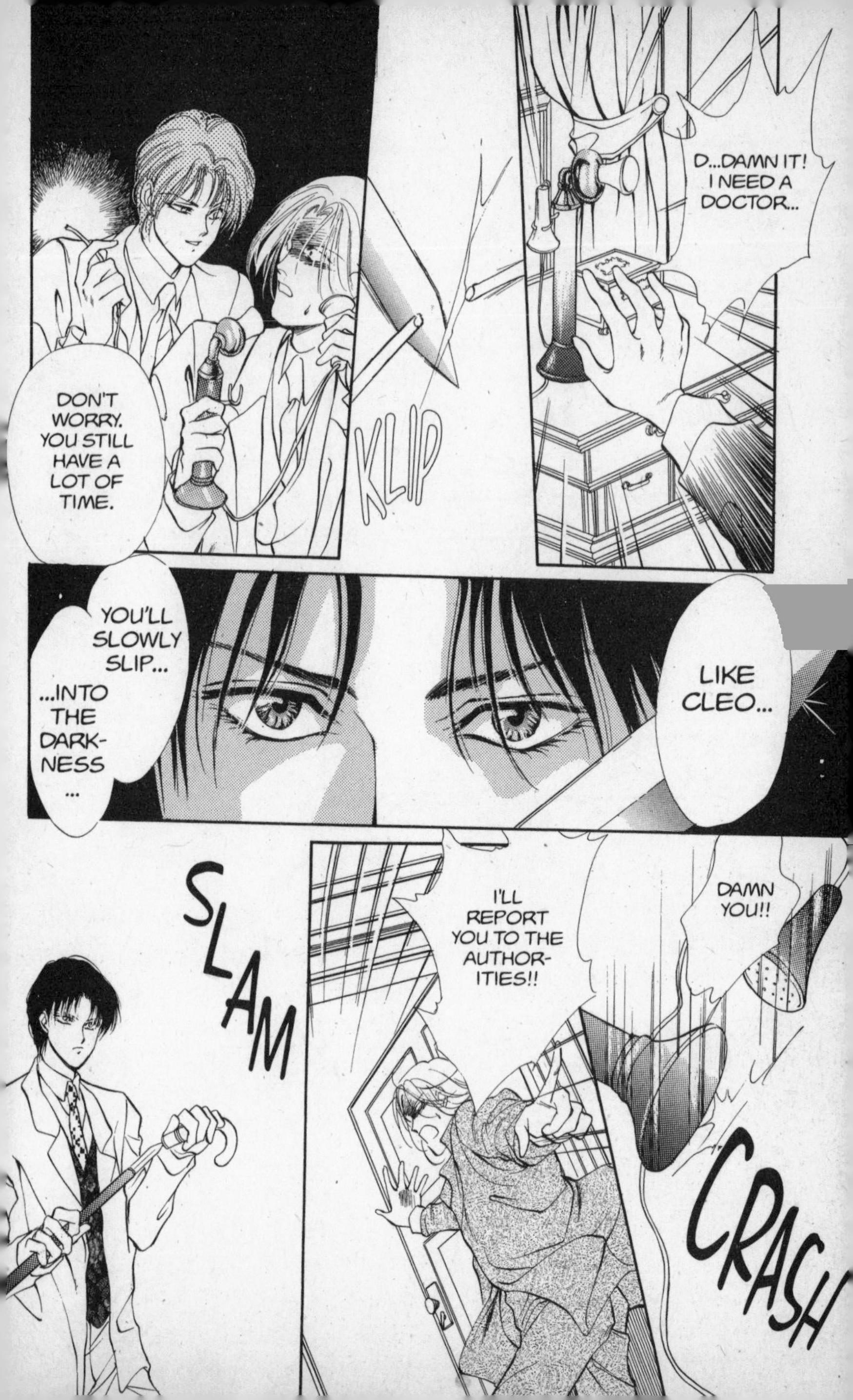
D...DAMN IT! I NEED A DOCTOR...
KLIP
DON'T WORRY. YOU STILL HAVE A LOT OF TIME.
LIKE CLEO...
YOU'LL SLOWLY SLIP...
...INTO THE DARKNESS...
DAMN YOU!!
CRASH
I'LL REPORT YOU TO THE AUTHORITIES!!
SLAM

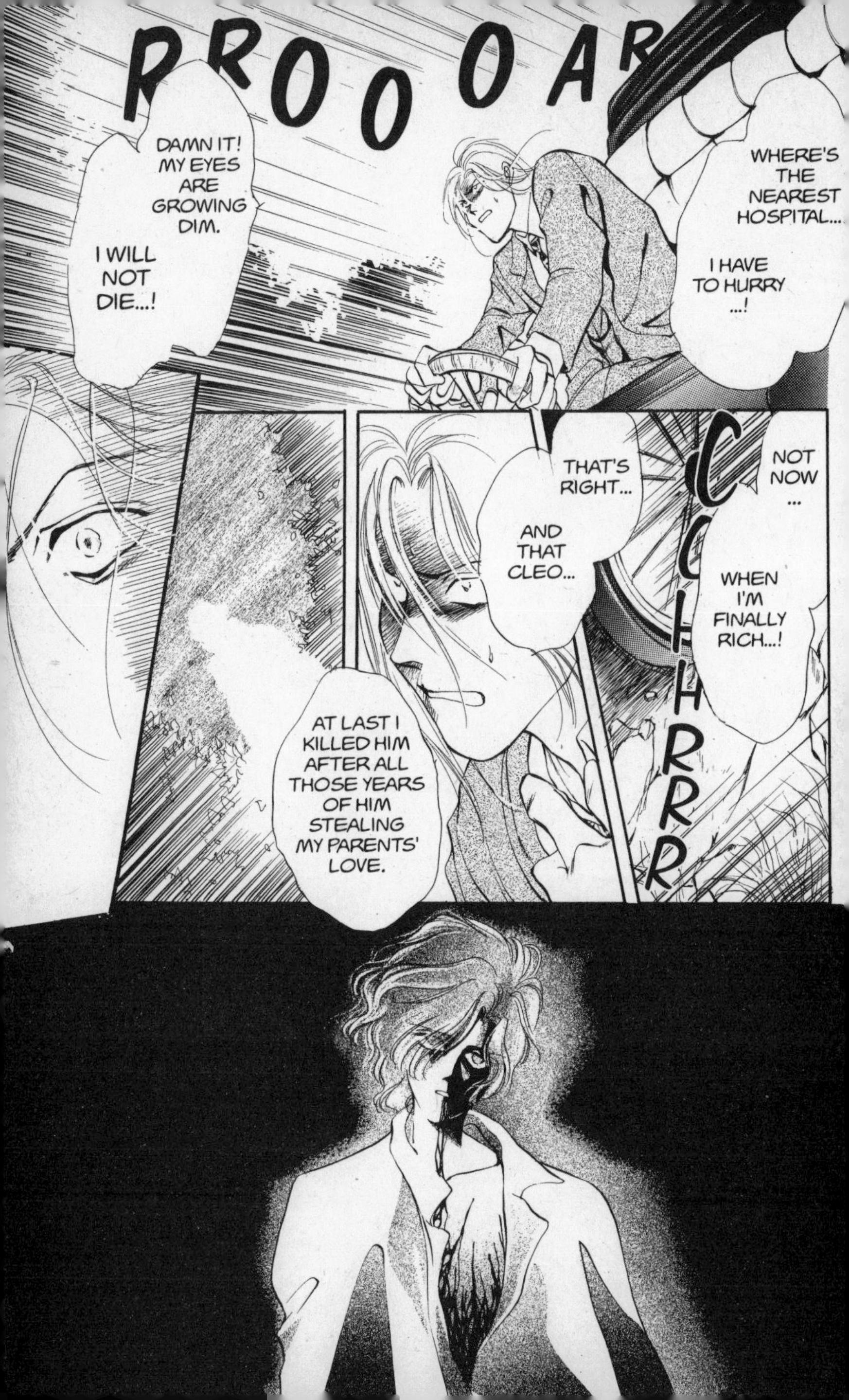
PROOOAR
WHERE'S THE NEAREST HOSPITAL...
I HAVE TO HURRY ...!
DAMN IT! MY EYES ARE GROWING DIM.
I WILL NOT DIE...!
NOT NOW ...
WHEN I'M FINALLY RICH...!
CCHHRRR
THAT'S RIGHT...
AND THAT CLEO...
AT LAST I KILLED HIM AFTER ALL THOSE YEARS OF HIM STEALING MY PARENTS' LOVE.

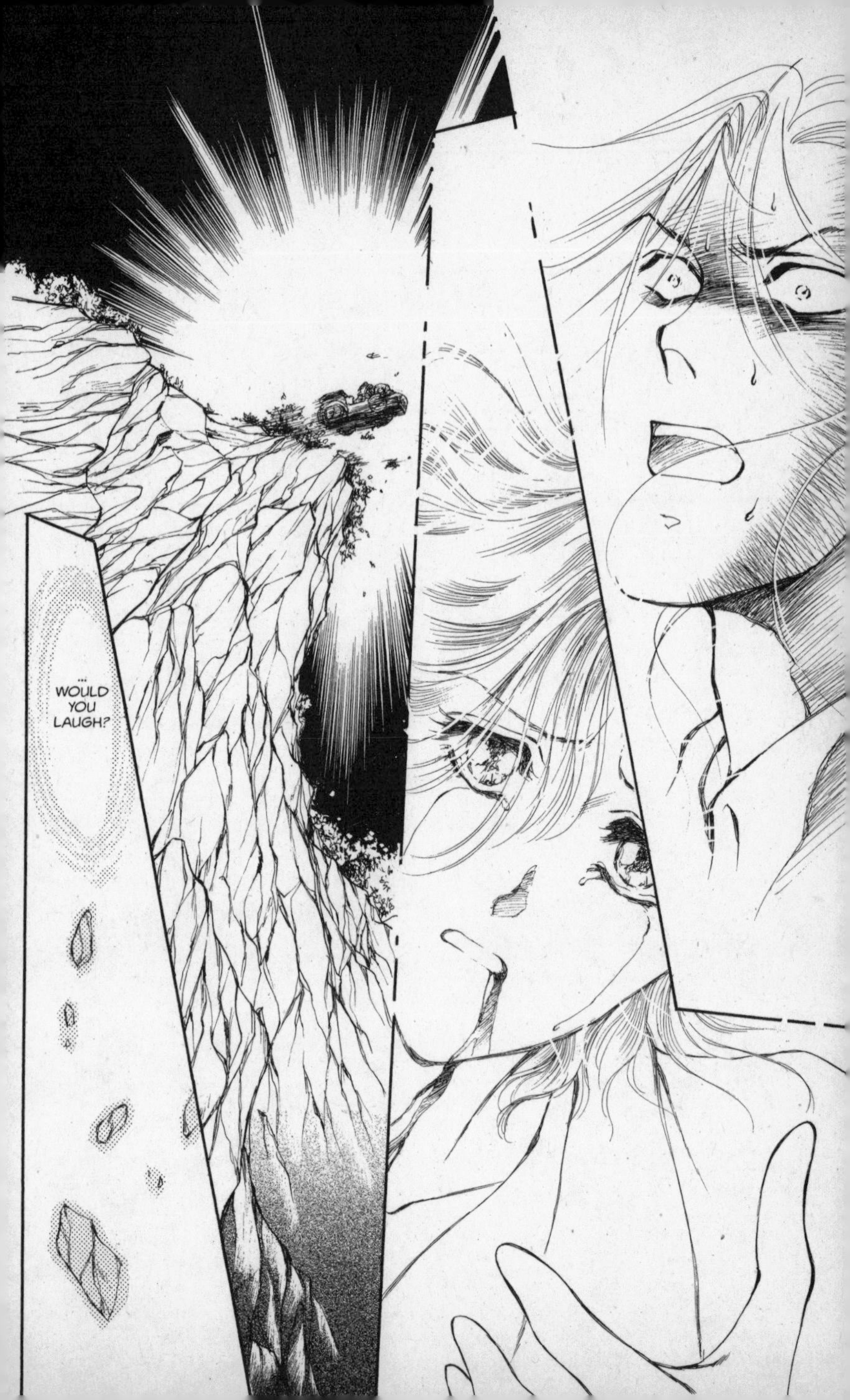
...WOULD YOU LAUGH?

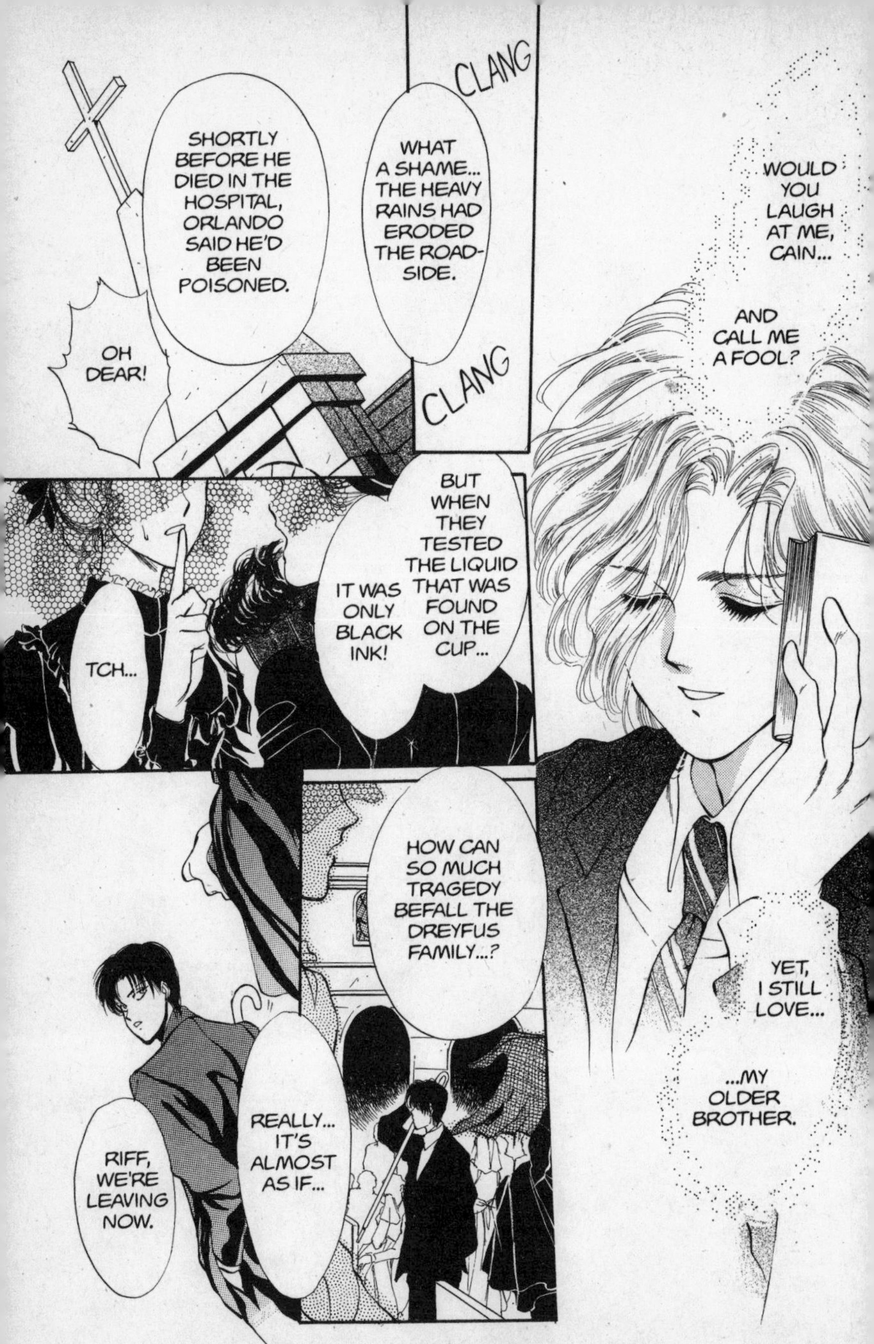
WOULD YOU LAUGH AT ME, CAIN...
AND CALL ME A FOOL?
YET, I STILL LOVE...
...MY OLDER BROTHER.
CLANG
CLANG
WHAT A SHAME... THE HEAVY RAINS HAD ERODED THE ROAD-SIDE.
SHORTLY BEFORE HE DIED IN THE HOSPITAL, ORLANDO SAID HE'D BEEN POISONED.
OH DEAR!
BUT WHEN THEY TESTED THE LIQUID THAT WAS FOUND ON THE CUP...
IT WAS ONLY BLACK INK!
TCH...
HOW CAN SO MUCH TRAGEDY BEFALL THE DREYFUS FAMILY...?
REALLY... IT'S ALMOST AS IF...
RIFF, WE'RE LEAVING NOW.

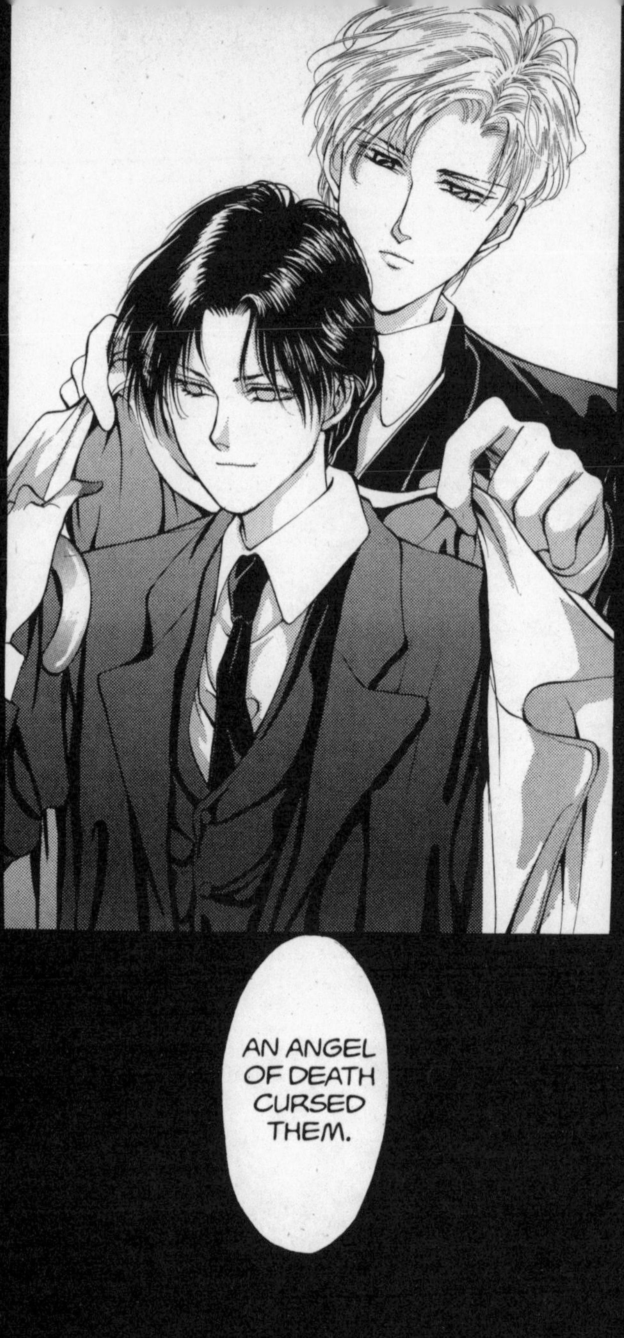
AN ANGEL OF DEATH CURSED THEM.

The Death of Cleo Dreyfus/The End

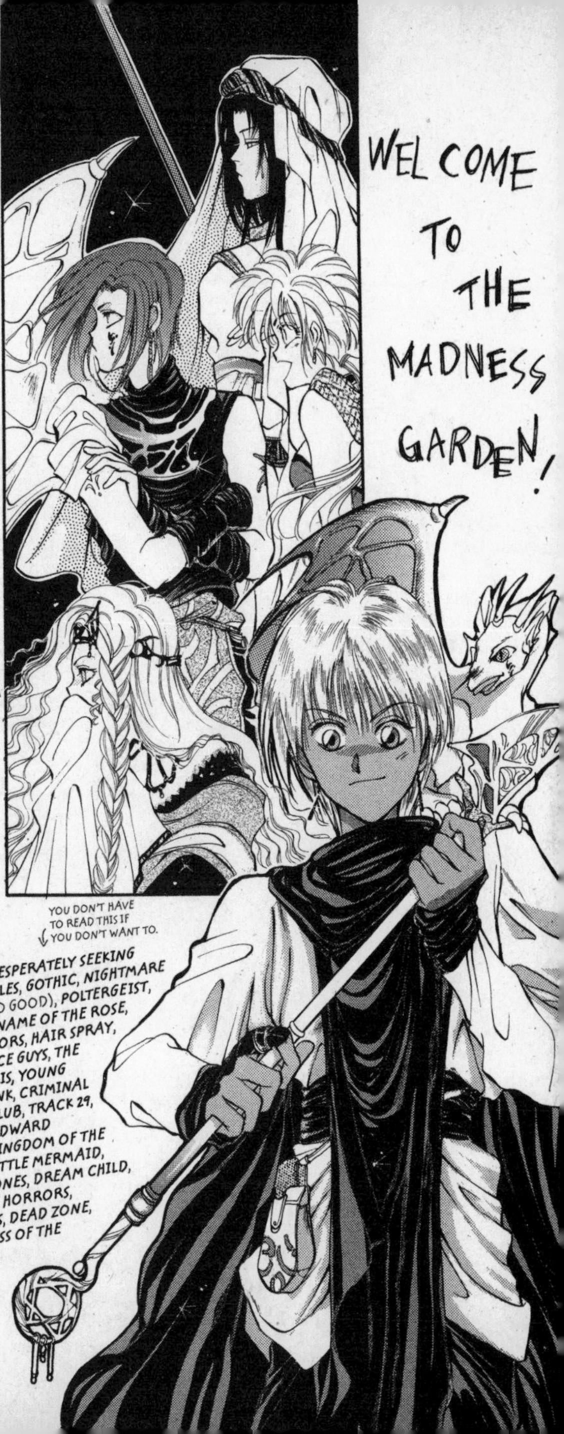
WELCOME TO THE MADNESS GARDEN!

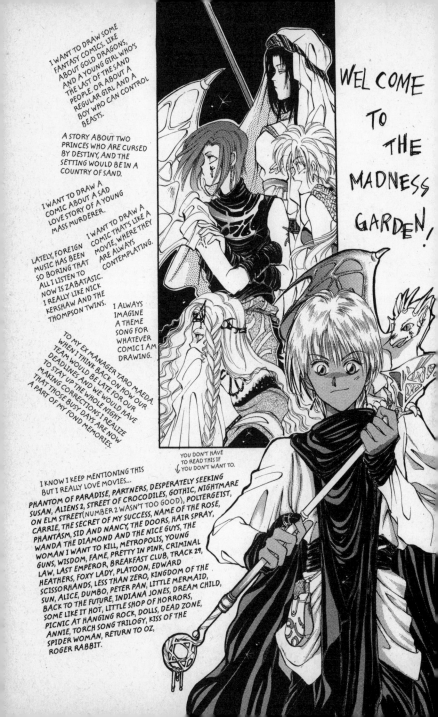

I WANT TO DRAW SOME FANTASY COMICS. LIKE ABOUT GOLD DRAGONS, AND A YOUNG GIRL WHO'S THE LAST OF THE SAND PEOPLE. OR ABOUT A REGULAR GIRL AND A BOY WHO CAN CONTROL BEASTS.

A STORY ABOUT TWO PRINCES WHO ARE CURSED BY DESTINY, AND THE SETTING WOULD BE IN A COUNTRY OF SAND.

I WANT TO DRAW A COMIC ABOUT A SAD LOVE STORY OF A YOUNG MASS MURDERER.

I WANT TO DRAW A COMIC THAT'S LIKE A MOVIE, WHERE THEY ARE ALWAYS CONTEMPLATING.

LATELY, FOREIGN MUSIC HAS BEEN SO BORING THAT ALL I LISTEN TO NOW IS ZABATASIC. I REALLY LIKE NICK KERSHAW AND THE THOMPSON TWINS.

I ALWAYS IMAGINE A THEME SONG FOR WHATEVER COMIC I AM DRAWING.

TO MY EX MANAGER TARO MAEDA. WHEN I THINK BACK ON HOW OUR TEAM WOULD BE LATE FOR OUR DEADLINES AND WE WOULD HAVE TO STAY UP THE WHOLE NIGHT MAKING CORRECTIONS I REALIZE THAT THOSE BUSY DAYS ARE NOW A PART OF MY FOND MEMORIES.

YOU DON'T HAVE TO READ THIS IF YOU DON'T WANT TO.

I KNOW I KEEP MENTIONING THIS BUT I REALLY LOVE MOVIES...

PHANTOM OF PARADISE, PARTNERS, DESPERATELY SEEKING SUSAN, ALIENS 2, STREET OF CROCODILES, GOTHIC, NIGHTMARE ON ELM STREET (NUMBER 2 WASN'T TOO GOOD), POLTERGEIST, CARRIE, THE SECRET OF MY SUCCESS, NAME OF THE ROSE, PHANTASM, SID AND NANCY, THE DOORS, HAIR SPRAY, WANDA THE DIAMOND AND THE NICE GUYS, THE WOMAN I WANT TO KILL, METROPOLIS, YOUNG GUNS, WISDOM, FAME, PRETTY IN PINK, CRIMINAL LAW, LAST EMPEROR, BREAKFAST CLUB, TRACK 29, HEATHERS, FOXY LADY, PLATOON, EDWARD SCISSORHANDS, LESS THAN ZERO, KINGDOM OF THE SUN, ALICE, DUMBO, PETER PAN, LITTLE MERMAID, BACK TO THE FUTURE, INDIANA JONES, DREAM CHILD, SOME LIKE IT HOT, LITTLE SHOP OF HORRORS, PICNIC AT HANGING ROCK, DOLLS, DEAD ZONE, ANNIE, TORCH SONG TRILOGY, KISS OF THE SPIDER WOMAN, RETURN TO OZ, ROGER RABBIT.

◆ CRUELTY FAIRY TALE ◆

BECAUSE OF THIS BOOK, ANOTHER ONE OF MY DREAMS HAS COME TRUE.
THIS IS THANKS TO EVERYONE RIGHT NOW WHO IS READING THIS BOOK. ♥
I'VE LEFT THIS FOR THE VERY END BUT I WOULD LIKE TO DEDICATE
THIS SAYING TO MY BELOVED CAT MIRU.

"LOVE AND HATE ARE TWO SIDES OF THE SAME COIN."
WELL THEN,

THE ⬤ END.

Creator: Kaori Yuki

Date of Birth: December 18

Blood Type: B

Major Works: *Angel Sanctuary*
and *Godchild*

Kaori Yuki was born in Tokyo and started drawing at a very early age. Following her debut work *Natsufuku no Erie* (Erie in Summer Uniform) in the Japanese magazine *Bessatsu Hana to Yume* (1987), she wrote a compelling series of short stories: *Zankoku na Douwatachi* (Cruel Fairy Tales), *Neji* (Screw), and *Sareki Ôkoku* (Gravel Kingdom).

As proven by her best-selling series *Angel Sanctuary* and *Godchild*, her celebrated body of work has etched an indelible mark on the gothic comics genre. She likes mysteries and British films, and is a fan of the movie *Dead Poets Society* and the show *Twin Peaks*.

THE CAIN SAGA, vol. 1
The Shojo Beat Manga Edition

STORY & ART BY **KAORI YUKI**

Translation/Akira Watanabe
Touch-up Art & Lettering/James Gaubatz & Andy Ristaino
Design/Izumi Evers
Editor/Joel Enos

Managing Editor/Megan Bates
Editorial Director/Elizabeth Kawasaki
VP & Editor in Chief/Yumi Hoashi
Sr. Director of Acquisitions/Rika Inouye
Sr. VP of Marketing/Liza Coppola
Exec. VP of Sales & Marketing/John Easum
Publisher/Hyoe Narita

Printed in Canada

Published by VIZ Media, LLC
P.O. Box 77010
San Francisco, CA 94107

Shojo Beat Manga Edition
10 9 8 7 6 5 4 3 2 1
First printing, October 2006

PARENTAL ADVISORY
THE CAIN SAGA is rated M for Mature and is recommended for mature readers. Contains graphic violence and adult themes.

store.viz.com

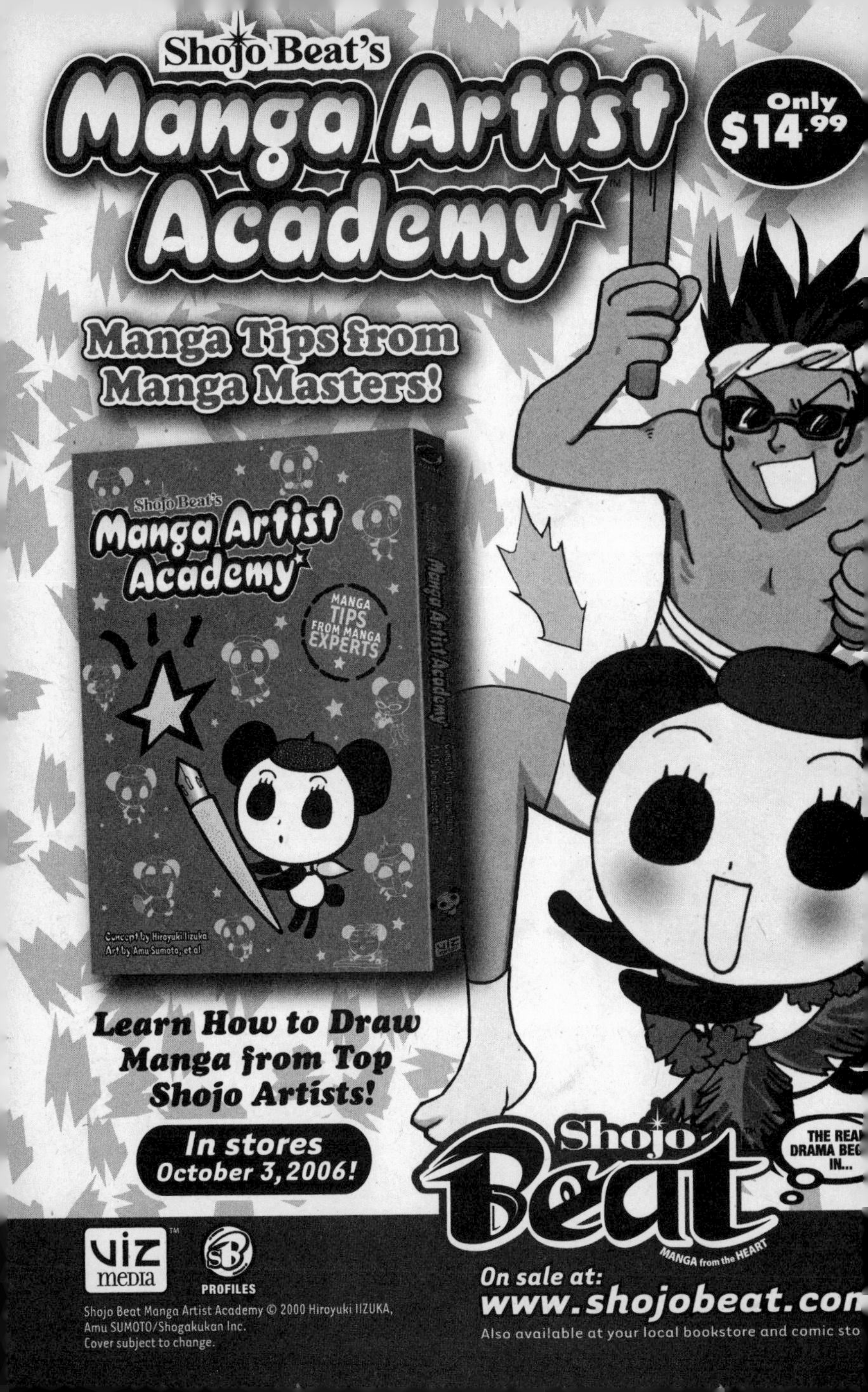
Shojo Beat's
Manga Artist Academy™
Only $14.99
Manga Tips from Manga Masters!
Shojo Beat's
Manga Artist Academy
MANGA TIPS FROM MANGA EXPERTS
Concept by Hiroyuki Iizuka
Art by Amu Sumoto, et al
Manga Artist Academy
Learn How to Draw Manga from Top Shojo Artists!
In stores October 3, 2006!
Shojo Beat™
MANGA from the HEART
THE REAL DRAMA BEG IN...
VIZ media
PROFILES
On sale at:
www.shojobeat.com
Also available at your local bookstore and comic sto
Shojo Beat Manga Artist Academy © 2000 Hiroyuki IIZUKA, Amu SUMOTO/Shogakukan Inc.
Cover subject to change.